THE A~Z OF
VEGETABLE GARDENING
IN SOUTH AFRICA

THE **A-Z** OF

JACK HADFIELD

VEGETABLE GARDENING IN SOUTH AFRICA

STRUIKHOF PUBLISHERS

Struikhof Publishers (Pty) Ltd
An operating division of
The Struik Group (Pty) Ltd
Struik House, Oswald Pirow Street
Foreshore, Cape Town 8001

Registration number 71/09721/07

First published by Purnell and Sons (S.A.) (Pty) Ltd as *Vegetable Gardening
in South Africa*
Completely revised and enlarged edition first published by C. Struik (Pty) Ltd
in 1985 (hard cover)
Second impression 1987 (soft cover)
This edition first published 1989

House editor: Douglas van der Horst
Illustrations by Nicci Page
Index compiled by Ethleen Lastovica

Typeset by McManus Bros (Pty) Ltd, Cape Town
Colour reproduction by Unifoto (Pty) Ltd, Cape Town
Printed and bound by National Book Printers, Goodwood

ISBN 0 947458 09 3

CONTENTS

Purple-Leaved Basil

White Grubs

Nicandra physaloides

AUTHOR'S ACKNOWLEDGEMENT

I would like to thank my typist, Miss Christine Finlay, for coping so patiently with my difficult handwriting.

PHOTOGRAPHIC ACKNOWLEDGEMENTS

The following individuals and companies generously supplied transparencies free of charge, or helped the publishers in various ways to obtain appropriate photographs: André Badenhorst of Buitenverwachting; Rob McGregor of Rennie's Farms; Bill and Pat Nimmo; Mr. A.E. Ohlhoff of Sonnenstrahl; Plant Chem (Pty) Ltd (Mr. C.M.W. Dane); Rohm and Haas (S.A.) (Pty) Ltd (Mr. D. Aligianis); Starke-Ayres Cape (Pty) Ltd (Messrs B. Cassingham, J. de Clercq and R. Tyson); Starke-Ayres Natal (Pty) Ltd (Mr. W.E. Kerr); Straathof's Seed and Bulb Co. (Pty) Ltd (Mr. C.A. Straathof).

The copyright in the photographs is held by the photographers and companies listed below. (Page numbers are printed in roman type, photograph numbers in *italic* type.)

R. Böck: 7 (bottom centre), 51/*1*, 55/*7*.
W.M. de Villiers: 58/*3*.
Doug Fitz-Gerald: 46/*1*, 46/*2*, 50/*3*, 51/*3*, 51/*4*, 55/*8*, 55/*10*, 58/*2*, 59/*7*, 77/*2*, 77/*4*, 77/*6*, 78/*1*, 78/*4*, 79/*6*, 80/*2*, 81/*4*, 83/*5*, 85/*6*, 85/*7*, 87/*6*, 89/*8*, 89/*9*, 89/*10*, 90/*1*.
Nancy Gardiner: 54/*3*, 58/*1*, 91/*1*, 91/*2*, 92/*1*, 92/*2*, 92/*6*.
Professor P.S. Knox-Davies: 46/*3*, 46/*4*, 46/*5*, 47/*7*, 47/*8*, 47/*9*, 47/*10*, 50/*1*, 50/*2*, 50/*4*, 51/*5*, 55/*9*.
Al Lastovica: 54/*2*.
Ethleen Lastovica: 7 (bottom right), 51/*2*, 54/*1*, 54/*6*, 59/*8*, 79/*7*, 79/*9*, 83/*9*, 91/*3*, 91/*4*, 92/*3*, 92/*7*.
Plant Chem (Pty) Ltd: 77/*1*, 77/*3*, 77/*5*, 78/*2*, 78/*3*, 78/*5*, 80/*1*.
Rohm and Haas (S.A.) (Pty) Ltd: 47/*6*.
Percy Sargeant: 50/*5*, 54/*4*, 54/*5*, 79/*8*, 80/*3*, 80/*4*.
A.S. Schoeman: 55/*11*, 55/*12*, 58/*4*, 59/*5*, 59/*6*.
Starke-Ayres Natal (Pty) Ltd: 82/*3*, 83/*6*.
Straathof's Seed and Bulb Co. (Pty) Ltd: 90/*4*.
Struikhof Publishers (Pty) Ltd: 86/*1*, 86/*2*, 88/*2*, 89/*6*, 89/*7*.
Struikhof Publishers (Pty) Ltd: (photographer Matthew Turnbull): front cover (both photographs, endpapers, title spread, 6 (all photographs), 10-11, 81/*1*, 81/*3*, 82/*1*, 82/*2*, 82/*4*, 83/*7*, 83/*8*, 84/*1*, 84/*2*, 84/*3*, 84/*4*, 84/*5*, 85/*8*, 85/*9*, 86/*3*, 86/*4*, 87/*5*, 87/*7*, 88/*1*, 88/*3*, 88/*4*, 89/*11*, 90/*2*, 90/*3*, 90/*5*.
L.A. Titchener: 81/*2*, 87/*8*, 88/*5*.
N.D. van der Horst: 7 (bottom left), 92/*4*, 92/*5*, 92/*8*, 92/*9*.

PART 1

- garden location and layout
- soils and nutrients
- garden planning and crop rotation
- tools and equipment
- watering, cultivating and weed control
- seed, sowing and transplanting
- pests and diseases
- container growing
- plastics in the vegetable garden

1 LOCATION AND LAYOUT OF THE VEGETABLE GARDEN

GARDEN LOCATION

The selection of a suitable site on which to establish the vegetable garden requires considerable thought, for an ill-chosen spot can be a great handicap from the beginning. Although the average home gardener has little choice, several points must be considered if the outlay on seed, fertilizer, manure and labour is to show profitable returns.

The ideal is level ground with good drainage, but a sloping site can also be used. If the ground is on a slight slope ensure that the gradient is even by filling in any depressions with soil taken from obvious high spots, or else some plants will receive excessive moisture while others, a metre away, will suffer from a lack of it. Germination is always patchy on uneven ground, making it difficult to obtain an even stand of seedlings. Examining the site after rain or a heavy watering will provide a useful guide to its trueness.

If the only ground available is on a moderate to steep slope it will be necessary to construct a number of terraces to conserve soil and moisture. The grade of the slope will determine the number of terraces necessary: moderate slopes may need two or three wide terraces, whereas steep slopes call for several narrower ones. On moderate slopes the terraces can be shaped with soil, but on steeper ones it is essential to build walls of concrete, brick or stone to prevent severe damage and soil loss during heavy storms. These terraces should preferably slope slightly back from the retaining bank or wall.

When constructing terraces, set the topsoil aside, level off the terraces with the subsoil, and then replace the topsoil in an even layer, especially if the subsoil is clayey. Failure to do this will result in terraces consisting of two clearly-defined soil types, and subsequent plantings will, for some time, be rather uneven despite generous treatment with compost or fertilizer. At all costs avoid creating low-lying spots, which are likely to become waterlogged after heavy rain.

Good drainage is essential in vegetable gardens, as no crops of consequence will tolerate 'wet feet' for very long. Too much soil moisture is detrimental to plant growth because the roots also need air to function properly. Roots and tubers developing in wet soil are susceptible to both internal and external disorders, which can result in severe losses and low storage quality. Saturated conditions also appreciably slow down the beneficial activities of soil organisms, which, like roots, must have air to flourish.

Where the drainage is in question, dig a hole 300 mm deep and of a similar diameter, soak the area well, and then fill the hole with water. If it drains away in 3-4 hours there should be no difficulty in raising satisfactory crops.

If drainage is a problem, raised beds, 900 mm to 1,2 m wide, can easily be constructed. First mark out the beds and pathways, and lay a garden line tightly along the edges of each intended bed. Then bring soil up from the paths on to the beds using a spade or African hoe. These beds should be constructed before any manures, compost or fertilizer are added.

If a large area is affected by poor drainage or if the soil is particularly heavy or clayey it may be necessary to lay one or more pipes to lead the water away to the lowest point. A 'soakaway' can be dug and filled with large stones if there is no drain or ditch to which the water can be led. The pipes should be placed at least 450 mm below the soil surface to be effective and to be out of the range of normal gardening operations. The pipes can be of any material, though perforated PVC and pitch-fibre pipes of 100 mm are easy to handle.

GARDEN LAYOUT

There are three principal methods of laying out the vegetable garden and each has advantages and drawbacks. One method, which we can call the 'open plan' method, is to dig over the whole area and sow or plant the different crops side by side in rows with

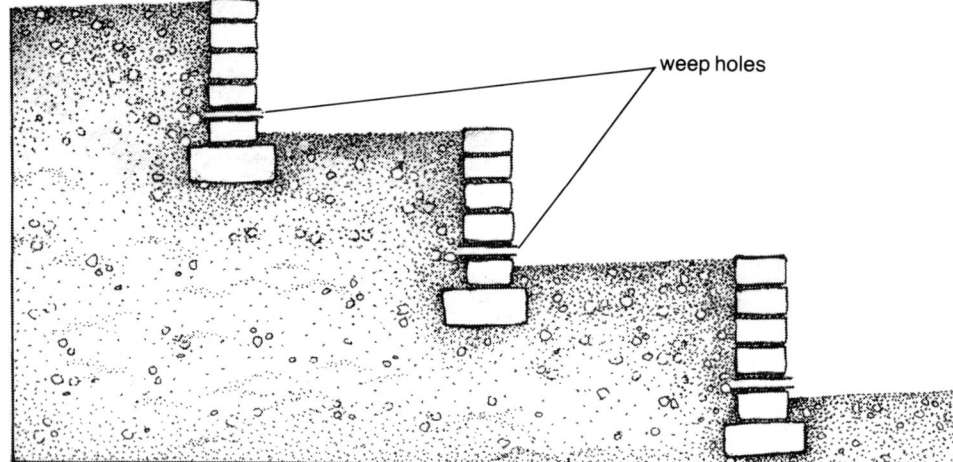

Permanent terraces on a steep slope.

weep holes

Terraced beds on a moderate slope.

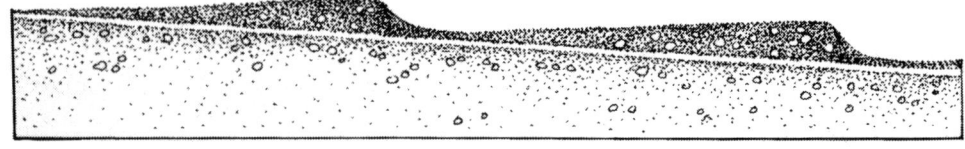

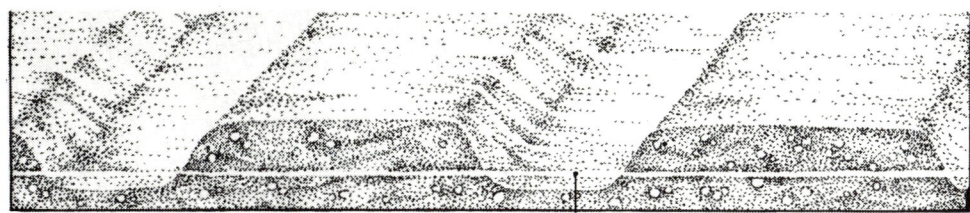

Raised beds to improve poor drainage.

normal soil level

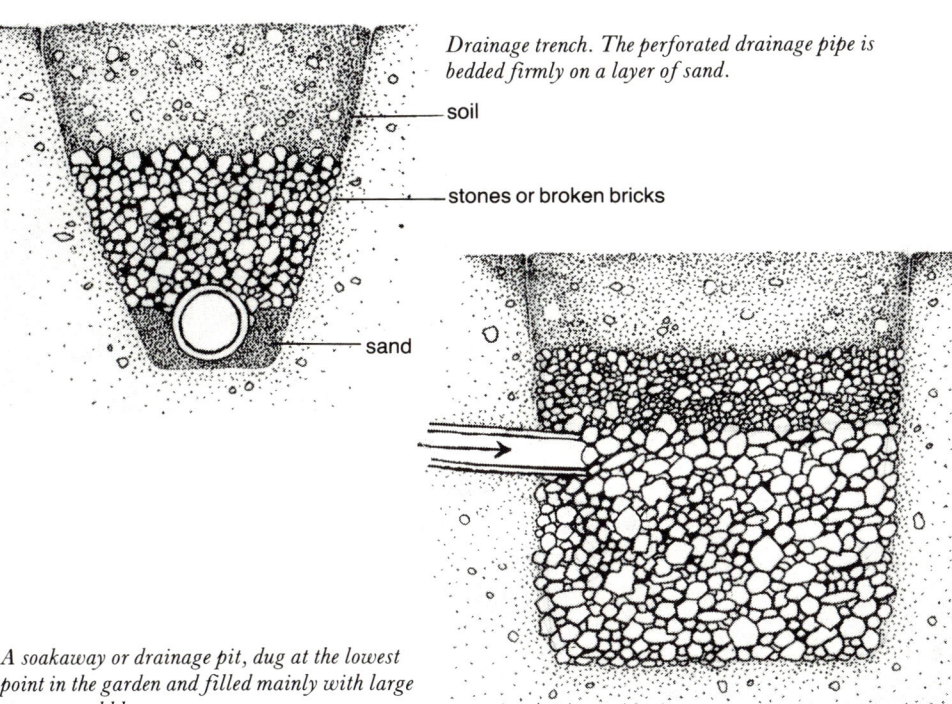

Drainage trench. The perforated drainage pipe is bedded firmly on a layer of sand.

soil

stones or broken bricks

sand

A soakaway or drainage pit, dug at the lowest point in the garden and filled mainly with large stones or rubble.

much more room to develop satisfactorily. Beds of this width still allow sowing, transplanting, thinning, weeding, cultivating and harvesting to be carried out comfortably from the paths, which can be 350-500 mm wide. This facility prevents too much treading and undesirable compaction of the soil.

In bed culture distinct rows can be avoided altogether and certain crops can instead be planted on the square or check planted. Square planting and check planting are methods of setting out transplants in order to get a high plant population and obtain the highest yields per square metre. This intensive planting will of course require a correspondingly high level of nutrients for the plants.

In square planting the plants are set out on a square grid (see illustration) and in check planting they are staggered. The optimum planting distances will depend on the vegetable being grown and also on the cultivar. In general it can be said that planting too closely will reduce the size of the vegetables owing to competition for nutrients, ground space and, where tomatoes are concerned, light.

One occasionally encounters suggestions that vegetables have a decorative value and can be advantageously planted amongst flowering annuals and perennials. There is very little merit in such a procedure because, apart from being unproductive, it exposes the vegetables to pests and diseases and thereby jeopardizes the organized growing of vegetables elsewhere in the garden.

SIZE OF THE GARDEN

Before deciding how big an area to devote to vegetables it is essential that the following points be considered: the size of the family to be supplied, the amount of water available during dry periods, the type of vegetables to be grown, and the amount of time the grower is prepared to spend on the project. A hundredth of a hectare intelligently planned and planted can provide an adequate quantity and variety of vegetables for a family of five. This is allowing for a few rows of 'new' potatoes and a few hills of pumpkins. If the full potato requirements of the family are to be met, considerably more ground is necessary. The grower with little ground available will get maximum satisfaction and benefit from his efforts by concentrating on closely-spaced crops such as carrots, beets, turnips, bush beans and lettuces, and by relying on outside sources for potatoes, pumpkins, cauliflowers and sweetcorn. It is far better to work 50 m² on profitable lines than to turn over ten times this area and use it in a slipshod fashion.

SHADE

'Shady' is a term often used to describe a desirable situation for certain garden plants,

no demarcated paths. This is the usual method where rain is experienced throughout the year and where little or no watering is required once the plants are established. It is a method particularly suited to level ground or ground with a slight slope.

An alternative method, often used in areas with a well-defined dry season, is to grow the vegetables in beds, each devoted to a single crop. In the dry season the beds can be level with the paths or slightly below path level, while in the wetter months they can be raised above the paths and raked flat or given a slight crown down the middle.

A third method, and one that appears to be rapidly gaining ground both overseas and in South Africa, is to have several permanent beds. These are usually situated within a framework of brick, concrete, asbestos off-cuts or timber. If timber is used it is essential that it be pressure treated with Creosote or Tanalith. This method is particularly suited to smaller gardens and gardens on difficult terrain, and is capable of producing the highest yields per square metre. It allows a high plant population within the bed area, discourages weeds because of the abundant crop growth, and facilitates all the cultural activities detailed later in this book.

A common mistake when using the bed method is to have paths that are too wide and beds that are too narrow. Beds can be of

any convenient length but must be at least 1,0-1,2 m wide if they are going to accommodate several rows of carrots, beets or beans, or 2-3 rows of vegetables such as cauliflowers or tomatoes, which require

Check (stagger) planting.

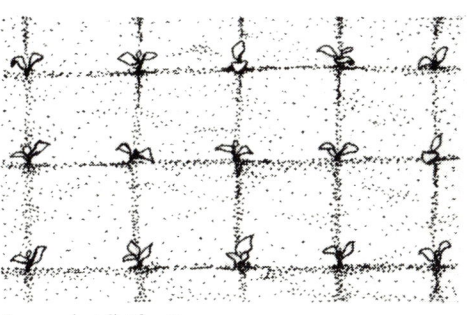

Square (grid) planting.

METHODS OF GARDEN LAYOUT (see page 12)

An 'open-plan' vegetable garden.

The bed method of garden layout.

The bed method, with permanently-enclosed beds.

but, without exception, these are never vegetables. No vegetables will produce satisfactorily if subjected to heavy shade for several hours a day, or to moderate shade throughout the day. Light is important for plant growth, being essential for chlorophyll formation and for the manufacture of carbon compounds by the leaves. Potatoes, particularly, are adversely affected by shade. This is because the tubers are simply storehouses for surplus starch produced by the leaves in conditions of high light intensity. When planted in shade of any degree the leaves barely manufacture sufficient starch for plant maintenance and growth, and tuber production is consequently depressed. No amount of fertilizer, manure or any other type of plant food can compensate for lack of adequate light.

If shade is unavoidable for a few hours daily in parts of the vegetable garden, try to plant these areas with cabbages, lettuce, Swiss chard or similar leaf crops, which appear to tolerate such conditions for short periods. But even these crops need several hours of full sunshine a day if they are to yield satisfactorily. Root vegetables will also tolerate some shade.

Shade from distant trees and buildings is not as damaging as shade thrown by the overhanging branches of mature fruit trees and ornamentals. These create heavy shade, and plants beneath them also suffer considerably from 'drip' during rainy periods – conditions that are conducive to the establishment and spread of serious fungal diseases. In addition, such trees rob growing crops of valuable moisture and plant food because of the extensive root systems they usually develop near the surface.

SHELTER

Shelter is different from shade and is often necessary in exposed situations and low-lying areas. A sheltered garden often allows the growing of tender plants, such as beans and tomatoes, to be continued during the colder months when unprotected plants would succumb. Shelter also protects staked tomatoes and other tall-growing crops from wind damage. Strong winds often cause considerable damage to pruned and staked tomatoes by whipping the plants and causing the immature green fruits to chafe against the support or against each other.

Permanent shelter can be provided by a building, a wall, a substantial wooden fence, a hedge or even a row of Napier grass or Cavendish bananas. A tall wooden fence, apart from acting as a windbreak, may also be useful as a support for runner beans, peas, lima beans or chayotes. If a hedge or other living shelter is used, care must be taken to ensure that its feeder roots do not compete for moisture or nutrients with the growing crop.

In areas where there is frost during the winter months, and in the absence of permanent shelter, considerable benefit can be derived from a temporary windbreak of Napier or other grass on a rough, light frame.

2 SOILS AND NUTRIENTS

SOILS

Most vegetable crops are heavy feeders, and to obtain satisfactory yields it is essential that the gardener has some knowledge of the capacity and limitations of his particular soil. Almost any soil can be modified to become a suitable medium for crop production if some of the practices described in this chapter are followed.

What is soil? It consists, principally, of mineral particles of various sizes and, in most soils, the blackish residues of plant and animal matter. These particles are graded according to size into four classes: coarse sand, fine sand, silt and clay. It is the relative proportions of these particle types in a soil that give it certain characteristics enabling it to be described as sandy loam, medium loam, sandy clay loam or clayey loam. An experienced gardener can usually judge the texture of a soil by rubbing a small quantity between finger and thumb, thus gauging the dominant particle size. This mineral portion of the soil is derived from parent rock of various types by chemical action and through the weathering effects of water, ice, wind and temperature over an extended period. Clayey soils are usually referred to as 'heavy' soils, and those containing a high percentage of sand are known as 'light' soils.

Particle size has a great influence on the moisture-holding capacity of a soil: the smaller the particles the more moisture they will hold. Clayey soils hold excessive quantities of water because they present a greater surface area per given volume of soil than any other class. They are probably the most difficult soils to work because during wet weather they become sticky and adhere tenaciously to boots and cultivating tools. On the other hand, during prolonged dry spells they become hard and compact and crack badly. Root, bulb and tuber plants, in particular, do not thrive in such extreme conditions, for even if satisfactory vegetative growth has been made, the crops are unable to swell and this invariably gives rise to badly-shaped produce of poor quality. Other vegetables, too, grow badly in heavy clay, as they are unable to develop extensive root systems because of the wet, hard conditions and the poor aeration.

Sandy soils hold relatively little water and are easy to work, even after considerable falls of rain, but they are often abused and damaged because of this very quality. To be productive, sandy soils must be supplied regularly with organic matter in some form, otherwise they will rapidly deteriorate and become infertile. A higher percentage of sand in a soil encourages root development, a property that gardeners often take advantage of when striking cuttings of herbaceous plants.

Sandy loams and medium loams have more balanced ratios of large and small particles and are the most suitable for vegetable growing. Ideal soil types are relatively rare, but by intelligent management almost any basic type can be modified and made productive.

Topsoil and subsoil

Topsoil is the upper or surface layer of soil, which, by the action of weathering agencies, the growth and decay of plant root systems, and the incorporation of organic matter, has become dark and loose. In most gardens the topsoil extends to a depth of 150-300 mm and it is in this region that annual plants, in particular, form most of their feeder roots and find most of their food.

A more compact layer of soil usually lies beneath the topsoil, and very often this is markedly different in colour and texture. This is the subsoil. It may contain certain plant foods, mostly in mineral form, but it is not an ideal medium for crop growth be-

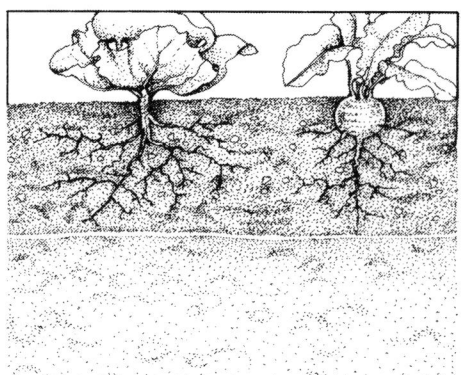

Topsoil and subsoil often differ greatly in colour and texture.

cause it invariably lacks humus and therefore has a poor structure. If the topsoil is shallow its depth can be improved by bringing up a little subsoil each year and mixing it thoroughly with the topsoil and with soil-improving materials.

The drainage of a garden depends upon the nature of the subsoil. If the subsoil is sandy or contains fine gravel it will allow excess moisture to drain away, but if it is clayey it forms an impervious layer and prevents, or slows down, this escape. As with topsoil, extremes in the sand and clay content create problems, excessive clay being, on the whole, the more serious.

ORGANIC MATTER

If a soil consisted only of 'rock meal' it would be infertile, for although the particles might contain considerable quantities of plant food, most of it would not be readily available to the plants. It is the humus or organic content of a soil that determines to a large extent the degree of fertility, and for centuries gardeners have recognized the important benefits of using organic materials even if the properties of these materials have not been fully understood.

Humus is perhaps best described as a product of the decomposition of plant and animal matter through the agency of micro-organisms. Although the soil chemist regards humus as being only the finely divided or colloidal residues, most gardeners use the term to describe any organic matter added to the soil. The regular addition of potential humus to the soil is the very foundation of fertility, especially in South Africa, where so many soils are notoriously deficient in this material.

Benefits of organic matter

The benefits of maintaining a high level of organic matter in the garden soil are legion, some being obvious to the average gardener while others are less easily understood. Firstly, a good and regular supply of organic matter increases the moisture-holding capacity of the soil, for it acts like a sponge, retaining many times its own weight of water. It does not hold only water, however, but also considerable quantities of plant food in solution that might otherwise be leached away.

A second property of organic matter is that it has a very beneficial effect on soil structure. Soil texture describes the size of the mineral particles in the soil, while soil structure describes the way in which these particles are aggregated together into 'crumbs' or granules. When organic matter is added to a soil containing a high percentage of sand, it binds the particles but still allows the necessary water and air to penetrate to the roots of growing plants.

On clayey soils, organic matter has the effect of opening up the compact layer, allowing air to penetrate more freely and, at the same time, facilitating the escape of excess soil water. When the organic matter in clayey soil is depleted the soil becomes more compact and, therefore, more unfavourable for the development of healthy root systems.

A third benefit of adding organic matter is that it stimulates the activities of the complex microscopic animal and vegetable populations in the soil by providing a ready supply of food and maintaining a more suitable environment, in terms of temperature and moisture content, for their multiplication. In mineral soils with a low organic content, microbiological activity is negligible and consequently fertility is often low. Fungi and bacteria are among the micro-organisms that abound in healthy fertile soils containing an abundance of organic matter, and even a single gram of soil may contain millions of these organisms.

Among the higher animal life in the soil, earthworms are by far the most important. The beneficial activities of these creatures are recognized by every gardener, although the green-keeper may find them rather tiresome. Unfortunately earthworms do not take kindly to the high temperatures and dry conditions that prevail in certain parts of South Africa for long periods. They are much more at home in moist soil, especially if there is a fair degree of shade. While we are not able to provide shady conditions in a productive vegetable garden, it is not too difficult to maintain a population of earthworms if organic matter is regularly incorporated.

Algae, protozoa and nematodes are among the other prominent soil inhabitants, and their populations also receive a tremendous stimulus with each barrowload of organic material.

Plants can absorb from the soil only those nutrients that are in solution, and it is the varied population of soil organisms that is largely responsible for turning the plant foods in compost, manures and other residues into an available form. In the process of breaking down these materials the organisms respire, giving off carbon dioxide that combines with the soil moisture to form a weak acid that materially assists in dissolving the plant food contained in mineral particles.

A further important benefit of adding organic matter to the soil is that it contains plant food, the nutrient value of which varies considerably according to the type of organic matter used. Nitrogen, one of the essential elements required in relatively large quantities by growing plants, is derived almost entirely from organic matter. Furthermore, because organic matter consists of animal and vegetable residues, it contains a wealth of the trace elements that are so essential in the balanced diet of a healthy plant.

Organic matter is therefore of vital importance in maintaining and improving the condition of the soil. The ways and means of providing it are many and varied, and are dealt with later in this chapter.

PLANT NUTRITION

For satisfactory growth, vegetable crops need several elements, of which the following are essential for most: carbon, oxygen, nitrogen, hydrogen, phosphorus, potassium, calcium, iron, manganese, magnesium, sulphur, molybdenum, boron, copper and zinc. These elements are usually grouped together into 'major' and 'trace' elements, the grouping being based solely on the quantities of each required for satisfactory growth and not on their degree of importance.

Carbon, oxygen and hydrogen are freely available from the air and from water, and no special provision need be made for their supply. Nitrogen, phosphorus and potassium, usually referred to as N, P and K (their chemical symbols), are the 'big three' elements affecting growth, and are required in relatively large quantities by all crops. It is therefore necessary to replenish reserves in the soil regularly, or plant growth will be unsatisfactory and yields will be low.

Nitrogen is the key plant food, or nutrient. Its presence in adequate amounts promotes vigorous vegetative growth of good colour while its deficiency is a limiting factor, especially in the production of cabbage, lettuce and other leaf crops. It is essential in the formation of chlorophyll, the green colouring matter contained in plant tissues, and is also an important constituent of the substances known as proteins. A lack of nitrogen is generally characterized by slow, spindly growth and pale foliage. Owing to

its tremendous influence on vegetative growth, nitrogen must be used with care on root and tuber crops, for excesses promote unbalanced plants with lush top growth and retarded roots and tubers. Excessive amounts applied to any crop will frequently induce soft and flabby growth, which causes the plants to wilt quickly in hot, dry spells and makes them particularly prone to fungal diseases under unfavourable weather conditions. Nitrogen excess can also delay flowering and fruit production, and on onion crops overdoses usually result in thick necks (which impair satisfactory ripening) and in low storage quality.

Phosphorus encourages extensive root development and this makes it particularly important to perennial crops and transplants. Adequate available amounts hasten maturity and, to some extent, reduce the harmful effects of excess nitrogen. Phosphorus is not leached away by rain or irrigation water to any extent and most garden soils have adequate reserves, but most of it is unavailable to plants. Even a high percentage of the phosphorus supplied in fertilizers is rapidly converted into unavailable forms.

The role of potassium in plant nutrition is not quite as obvious as the part played by nitrogen and phosphorus. It appears to be closely linked with nitrogen in several plant processes, including protein formation, and in certain circumstances it can counterbalance the effects of too much nitrogen. Root and tuber crops show a marked response to adequate potash supplies, and the quality of produce grown in such conditions is of a high order.

Calcium is the last of the 'major' group of elements. Because superphospate, which contains about 50% calcium sulphate (gypsum) is the base of most common fertilizers, the plants' requirements are usually met without any trouble. Calcium deficiency does occur in certain circumstances and often results in the death of the growing point. Blossom-end rot of tomatoes is attributed by some to calcium deficiency, although an erratic water supply may also be an important secondary factor. Calcium is one element that is not translocated throughout the plant system to any degree, and consequently a deficiency soon expresses itself in a breakdown of the younger cell tissues. The value of calcium compounds as soil conditioners, and their effect on soil reaction, is dealt with in the discussion on lime (see page 22).

Deficiencies of the trace elements – iron, manganese, magnesium, sulphur, molybdenum, boron, copper and zinc – may also occur in certain soils, especially if the soil reaction is extreme. Vegetables differ greatly in their trace-element requirements and in their response to such deficiencies. Boron deficiency is quite common but the symptoms vary – in beetroots it shows up as deep cracks and cankers on the roots, in cauliflowers as a scaling of the stalk and a brown discoloration of the curd, and in celery as a browning and splitting of the ribs on the

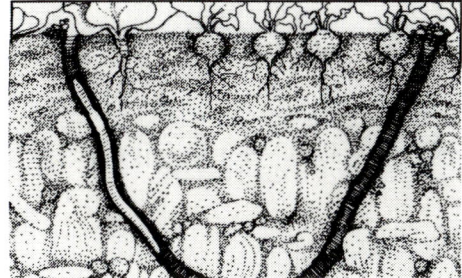

Earthworms are highly beneficial to the soil. They mix and aerate it and introduce organic matter.

PLANT NUTRITION

MAJOR PLANT FOODS

Nitrogen
The key plant food. It promotes vegetative growth and is essential in protein-building and photosynthesis. Nitrogen deficiency leads to slow, spindly growth and pale foliage.

Phosphorus
Phosphorus encourages vigorous root formation. Adequate amounts hasten crop maturity and partly reduce the effects of excess nitrogen.

Potassium
Potassium is linked with nitrogen in several plant processes, including protein formation. Adequate supplies of potash are important for the growth of root and tuber crops.

Calcium
Calcium not only plays an important role in general plant vigour but also affects the reaction and physical condition of the soil, the availability of other foods, and the activity of soil micro-organisms.

TRACE ELEMENTS

Boron

Copper

Iron

Magnesium

Manganese

Molybdenum

Sulphur

Zinc

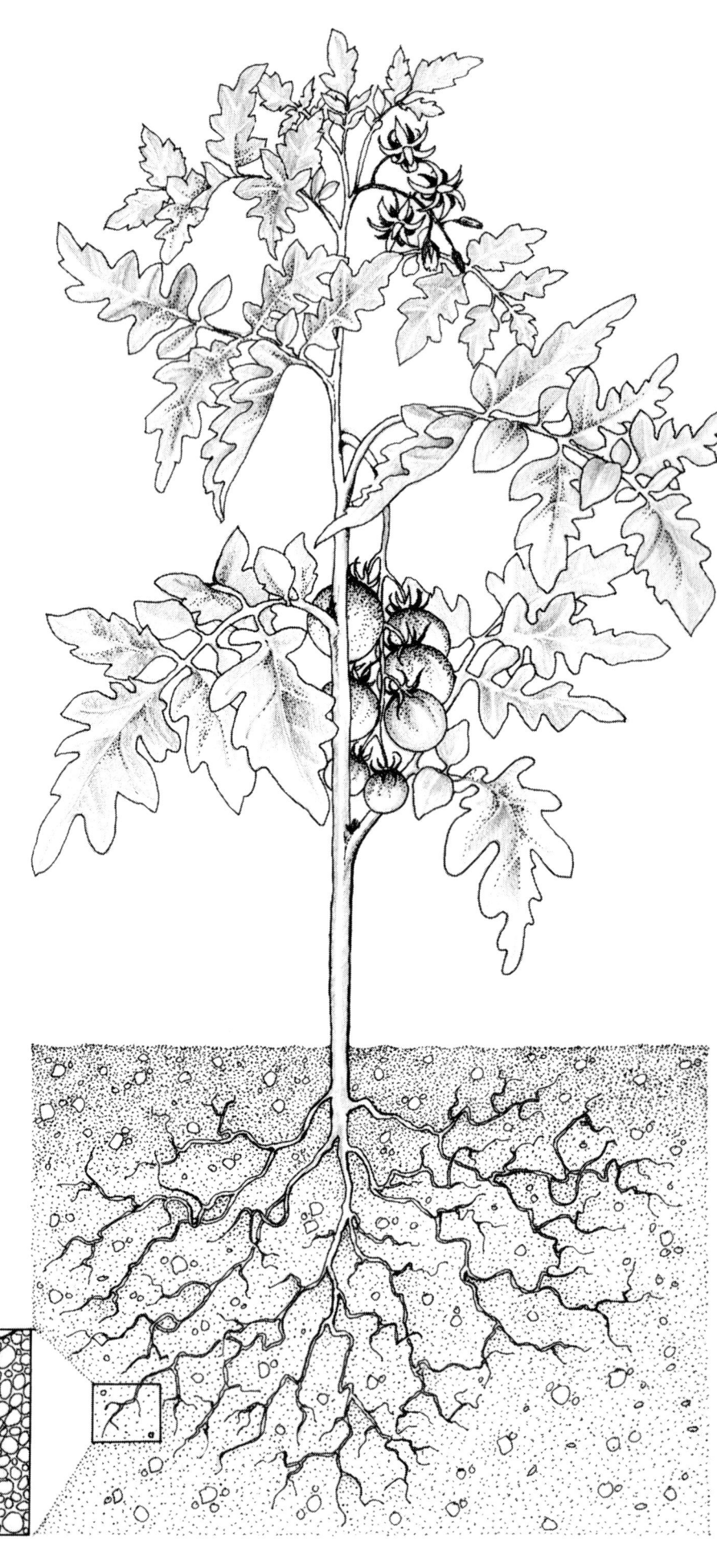

Plants can absorb only those nutrients that are in solution. The organic matter in the soil stimulates the activity of micro-organisms, which play a vital role in turning the nutrients in compost, manure and soil particles into a form that is available to plants.

Mineral salts in solution are drawn up by the fine root hairs of the plant.

stalks. Excessive cracking of sweet potatoes has been reduced by dressings of borax, though several other factors can also cause such cracking.

Certain trace-element deficiencies, as shown by plant symptoms, may be 'induced' deficiencies. Extreme soil reaction and an excess of soluble salts in the soil are the most common causes of such deficiencies.

All these essential elements can be supplied to plants by the regular incorporation of organic residues and materials in the soil, or, if a definite deficiency is pinpointed, by soil or foliar applications of chemical compounds.

MANURES AND OTHER ORGANIC FERTILIZING MATERIALS

Animal and poultry manures are extremely important in maintaining and improving soil condition and fertility. Manure is almost a complete food for plants because it contains fair quantities of nitrogen, phosphorus and potassium, and most of the necessary trace elements. The nutrient value of manures varies greatly, some being particularly rich in a certain element and low in another. The principal factors influencing this variation are the type of animal or bird producing the manure, the kind of food consumed by the producer, the use of litter, and the handling of the manure prior to use. Average analyses, however, place manures in the following order of nutrient value: poultry, sheep, horse, cattle and pig.

Animals fed on lucerne, good quality hay, silage and concentrates, and which have access to established, vigorous pastures, will produce a much better quality manure than, for instance, those animals that get by on veld grazing and poor hay. The latter get barely enough essentials for their own maintenance, and as a result little of value is passed out with the manure. Litter is of great value, for it absorbs urine and therefore contains valuable plant food, particularly nitrogen. Soiled hay and straw are among the better kinds of litter because, apart from having excellent absorptive properties, they break down easily when added to the soil or incorporated into the compost heap. Sawdust, which is often used where horses and polo ponies are quartered, is not an ideal litter despite its great absorptive capacity because it takes a long time to break down and requires a great deal of nitrogen in order to do so satisfactorily.

The value of manure as a source of plant food is often considerably lessened through neglect and careless handling. During wet weather unprotected heaps of manure may lose a considerable portion of their nutrient value through leaching. Most gardeners will have seen the trickle of dark brown liquid that emerges from the base of such heaps during wet periods. This is the most valuable part of the manure, and to check its loss

it is good practice to dig in manure as soon as possible after it is produced, or to store it under cover, or to put it in a well-managed compost heap.

Kraal manure consists of the residues that accumulate in enclosures erected to contain livestock, principally at night after they have been grazing. That which accrues and is removed during dry periods is first-class material, for there is no loss from leaching. It mills easily and is easy to distribute. During wet spells, however, droppings become thoroughly mixed with soil from the kraal floor and much plant food is leached out, resulting in a relatively inferior product.

Average samples of animal manures contain around 1% or less of each of the three major elements, with phosphorus the lowest figure in most cases. Sheep and poultry manures, however, are usually well above this average.

Poultry residues are really in a class of their own, averaging around 2% nitrogen, 1,2% phosphorus, and 0,6% potassium when fresh, and up to double these amounts if carefully collected and dried. A considerable number of egg and poultry producers turn out good quality manure in easy-to-handle packs at reasonable prices. Owing to its relatively high nitrogen content, poultry manure must be used with care. It is best to broadcast it on the rough soil surface after digging, at the rate of 150-200 g per m², and then to incorporate it thoroughly with a garden fork prior to establishing the crop. Its relatively low potash content can be balanced to some extent by adding 500 g of sulphate or muriate of potash to every 5 kg of manure. It should not be incorporated prior to establishing a root crop because it will promote excessive top growth and may disfigure the roots if they come into contact with it. It must also be used with caution in the vicinity of seedlings.

Poultry manure has considerable value as a base for liquid manure. A bucketful placed in a hessian bag and suspended in a drum of water produces a fine stimulant for leaf crops and other plants. After being used in this fashion, the residue can be emptied out

Liquid manure is easy to make and highly beneficial to most vegetables.

and either dug into the soil, used as a mulching material on established crops, or incorporated into the compost heap.

Dried sewage sludge is sometimes available, but its chief value lies in its potential as humus and not in its nutrient content. The greater part of the plant food is removed by the several digestion processes the material normally undergoes before it reaches the innocuous state in which it is offered for sale.

The worth of animal manures must not be judged on their nutrient content only, for their effect on soil condition is equally important. The beneficial effects of organic matter on soil have already been discussed; liberal additions of manure impart all these benefits. For most crops the common practice of placing a 70 mm layer of manure at the bottom of a deep trench beneath each row of plants has little to commend it, for under such conditions it decomposes very slowly and is out of the reach of most feeder roots. It is far better to spread it in a thin layer on the soil surface and to fork it into the topsoil or into the rows of widely-spaced crops. If possible, incorporate manure several weeks before the planting of a crop to allow it to lose its heat and for partial decomposition to take place.

Apart from 'straight' manures, several other organic materials are available, though demand frequently exceeds supply. In coastal areas sufficient seaweed for the home garden is quite easily come by and it contains a wealth of plant food. If it is used in reasonable quantities its salt content is unlikely to have any toxic effect on plant growth. It is best used as a mulch and later incorporated when digging the soil at the end of the season.

Soil additives derived from seaweed are now available in dry, sludge and liquid forms. They are extremely useful, particularly on soils low in organic matter, as they contain a wealth of nutrients. However, they must be used in addition to adequate dressings of NPK materials and not in place of them.

Sawdust is available in some areas at little or no cost except transport charges, and there is no doubt that in the absence of adequate quantities of compost or manure it can be an extremely valuable material. But it must be used with discretion. It is a cheap source of organic matter in an inoffensive and easily-handled form and that is its principal value. But if it is incorporated into the soil generously in its raw state it can spell disaster for several subsequent plantings. To decompose, sawdust needs large quantities of nitrogen and moisture, and if dug in it will obtain its requirements from the soil resources and from fertilizer applied, at the expense of the crops. It is best used by incorporating it into the compost heap in reasonable quantities or by using it as a mulch (50-70 mm deep) for a full season and then digging it in with a generous dressing (150 g per m²) of sulphate of ammonia or limestone ammonium nitrate. Used in this way it can give body to light sandy soils or it can break up soil of a compact, clayey nature.

Blood meal and bone meal are sometimes obtainable in small quantities and should be snapped up when available. Blood meal is a quick-acting nitrogenous fertilizer, averaging 7-12% nitrogen, and is chiefly used as a side-dressing. Bone meal is primarily a phosphatic fertilizer, containing up to 20% P_2O_5 and sometimes a little nitrogen. It is relatively slow-acting but has a long-lasting effect.

Seabird guano consists of the droppings of certain seabirds together with small quantities of corpses and feathers. The name 'guano' is derived from the Spanish word for manure, and its value was first recognized by the inhabitants of Peru, who collected it from islands off the coast. Limited quantities of a similar material are available from time to time in this country and are extremely valuable to the home gardener. Analyses vary, depending on the climatic conditions under which the guano accrues, but it is usually nitro-phosphatic material containing little potash. One good handful per square metre incorporated into the top

150 mm of dug-over topsoil is an adequate dressing before planting. For an organic it is quick acting.

Organic materials in liquid form now command a considerable share of the garden fertilizer market. Most of them are of marine origin, being derived from seaweed or fish residues, but at least one is based on poultry manure. They undoubtedly contain a wealth of plant food, particularly trace elements, and are useful for stimulating and maintaining plant vigour. It must be recognized, however, that they cannot take the place of standard cultivation and fertilizer practices on vegetable crops. Their action is gentle, but they should be used strictly according to the manufacturer's recommendations.

CHEMICAL FERTILIZERS

Nitrogen, phosphorus and potassium are the elements required in relatively large quantities by growing crops, but very often insufficient amounts of manure and other organic materials are available to meet these

requirements in full. It is frequently necessary to look to other possible sources of supply if satisfactory yields are to be obtained.

Chemical or 'artificial' fertilizers are manufactured materials that contain relatively high percentages of these elements. They are available as 'straights', i.e. containing only one element, or as compound fertilizers containing two or three of the NPK trio. Fertilizers have certain distinct advantages over manures and other organic materials: the cost of nutrient per unit is lower; they contain certified quantities of elements; their form makes them easier to transport and distribute; and in most cases they act more quickly. However, they lose out heavily in comparison with the majority of organics in two important respects: they have no ameliorating effect on soil structure, nor do they contain the wealth of trace elements and microscopic life present in organics. Because of the continual and indiscriminate use of chemical fertilizers, many soils have suffered permanent damage. This has led a number of gardeners and others concerned with soils and crops to regard the term 'artificial fertilizer' as distasteful. It is

FERTILIZERS: THEIR NUTRIENT CONTENT AND USE

Category	NITROGENOUS			PHOSPHATIC				POTASSIC		COMPOUND		
Properties	Promotes vegetative growth of good size and colour.			Assists root development. Promotes and hastens flower and fruit formation.				Affects general vigour and disease resistance.		Promotes good all-round growth.		
Type	sulphate of ammonia	limestone ammonium nitrate (LAN)	urea	super-phospate	raw rock phosphate	super and raw phosphate	basic slag	muriate of potash	sulphate of potash	2:3:2 (22)	2:3:4 (24)	2:3:2 (14) (Wonder)
Nutrient content	21% N	28% N	46% N	10,5% P	9,2% P	10% P	7% P	50% K_2O	40% K_2O	6,3% N 9,4% P 6,3 % K	5,3% N 8,0% P 10,7% K	4% N 6% P 4% K
Dressing rate	15-30 g per metre of row	7-30 g per metre of row	15-30 g per metre of row	75-100 g per m²	75-100 g per m²	75-100 g per m²	100-125 g per m²	50-75 g per m²	50-75 g per m²	75-125 g per m²	75-125 g per m²	50-75 g per m²
Specific uses	As a side-dressing to establish crops such as onions, tomatoes, cabbages, cauliflowers, lettuce, spinach and other leaf crops. Can also be used as a supplementary dressing when bulky, undecomposed materials such as sawdust, mulches, straw, etc., are dug in.			As a base dressing prior to sowing or planting. Especially suitable for roots on well-improved soils. Also useful as a base dressing for green manure crops.				Rarely used on its own. Useful, however, to balance poultry manure dressings.		As a base dressing in addition to organic materials, or alone. Also useful as a spring dressing to perennial vegetable crops.		
General remarks	Slowest-acting of this group. Regular applications will tend to increase soil acidity.	Possibly best form for general use. No harmful effect on soil reaction.	Cheapest material per unit of nitrogen. Special grade for foliar application.	Quickest-acting fertilizer in this group.	Slowest acting.	A mixture of two materials.	Slow-acting but long-lasting. Useful on heavy, acid soils because of its calcium content.	Excessive dressings can cause damage to certain sensitive crops such as tomatoes and potatoes.	None	Incorporate thoroughly into topsoil prior to planting.		
Disadvantages	Excessive applications as crops approach maturity can delay flower and fruit formation. Such dressings can also encourage soft growth, which is susceptible to certain diseases.			Excess unlikely.				None		Regular dressings without the addition of compost, manure or other organic materials can harm soil structure, texture and fertility. Avoid direct contact with seed, tubers, etc.		

my belief, however, based on many years' experience on a wide variety of soils, that there is a place for both organic and inorganic materials. If the latter are used judiciously and sensibly in conjunction with, ideally, annual dressings of such organic materials as are available, excellent yields can be obtained consistently with no harmful effect at all on the soil complex.

Nitrogenous fertilizers

Sulphate of ammonia, limestone ammonium nitrate and urea are the forms of nitrogen usually offered for sale in South Africa. As nitrogen is easily lost from the soil by leaching, these fertilizers are used either as split dressings – half at planting time and half as a side-dressing when the plants are well established – or, more commonly, purely as side-dressings to maintain plant vigour.

Sulphate of ammonia (21% nitrogen) is one of the most widely-used forms of nitrogen and is valuable as a stimulant to crops that are not growing satisfactorily. The nitrogen is in the ammonium form and as it has to be changed into the nitrate form in the soil before it can be used by plants its action is somewhat slow.

Limestone ammonium nitrate (LAN) is now being used on an ever-increasing scale in this country as a 'straight' fertilizer. It is known as nitro-chalk or calcium ammonium nitrate (CAN) in other countries. LAN is a most useful fertilizer in that approximately half of the nitrogen is in the nitrate form and the other half in the ammonium form. This means that it combines the quick action of nitrate of soda with the more sustained action of sulphate of ammonia. It also contains sufficient calcium to counteract the acidifying effect of the ammonium nitrogen, and therefore has no effect on the soil reaction. This quality makes it especially useful on soils that are acid in nature. LAN contains 28% nitrogen.

Urea (46% nitrogen) is interesting because, although it is a manufactured material, its nitrogen is in the amide or organic form and, indeed, certain textbooks describe it in the sections on organic materials. Its availability is similar to that of sulphate of ammonia. It is obtainable in both the crystal and 'prill' forms, the latter being most useful on onion and other closely-planted crops as it can be broadcast with little fear of scorching because the 'prills' bounce off the plants on to the soil. Urea is usually the cheapest form of nitrogen but its one slight drawback is that, owing to its high nitrogen content, dressing rates are very low, and even distribution is a little difficult to achieve. This can be remedied if it is well mixed with dry sand or a similar material.

Most nitrogenous fertilizers will scorch the foliage of growing crops, particularly if the leaves are wet, and must therefore be used with care. The usual method of applying a side-dressing is to lift the lower foliage with one hand and to distribute the fertilizer on the soil surface with the other. These fertilizers can also be used as liquid manures, sulphate of ammonia at 15 g to 5 ℓ of water and urea at 15 g to 15 ℓ of water being the most suitable for this purpose.

Phosphatic fertilizers

Superphosphate, raw rock phosphate, super and raw phosphate, and basic slag are the materials in common use for improving the phosphate status of garden soils.

Superphosphate was formerly described as containing 18,5-19,0% P_2O_5, but nowadays it is described by the percentage of water-soluble phosphate it contains, this usually being around 10,5%. It is produced by treating raw rock phosphate with sulphuric acid to make it more soluble. As it contains about 50% calcium sulphate (gypsum), normal dressings (50-75 g per m^2) do not increase soil acidity.

Raw rock phosphate is, of course, not really an artificial fertilizer, but simply crushed phosphate rock that has had no treatment at all. Its phosphoric acid is in a relatively insoluble form and, consequently, this material is slower in action than superphosphate. Leguminous plants are able to utilize its phosphate content more easily than most plants, and for this reason it is perhaps best used as a dressing prior to the establishment of a green manure crop. When legumes fertilized in this way are incorporated into the soil, subsequent crops will benefit from the action of the legumes in converting the phosphate into more readily available forms.

Super and raw phosphate, a mixture of the two materials previously mentioned, combines the relatively quick action of superphosphate with the slower but more sustained action of raw rock phosphate.

Basic slag, a by-product of the steel industry, is dark grey to black in colour and is usually finely ground; indeed, its value depends very greatly on this factor. The grade available in South Africa contains 7% phosphorus. Apart from its phosphate content, basic slag contains appreciable quantities of calcium compounds and this makes it a very useful material on acid soils, especially if these are clayey in nature. Most slags also contain traces of other necessary elements such as magnesium and manganese.

Potassic fertilizers

Potassic fertilizers are rarely applied as 'straights' in normal garden practice because of the general use of compound fertilizers, which contain sufficient potash to meet the needs of most vegetable crops. Their use is warranted, however, as a supplement to poultry manure dressings. The following materials are readily available:

Potassium chloride, or muriate of potash as it is more generally known, contains 50% K_2O and is the material commonly used. However, it contains appreciable quantities of chlorine and is therefore not always satisfactory for use with potatoes (sulphate of potash should be used instead). In addition, muriate of potash contains appreciable quantities of sodium chloride (common salt).

Sulphate of potash is produced by treating muriate of potash with one of several materials. It contains around 40% K_2O and has a low chlorine content.

Wood ash contains quantities of both potash and lime, but if exposed to rain for any period the potash salts are washed out.

Compound fertilizers

Compound fertilizers are materials containing two or three of the NPK trio and are often termed 'complete' fertilizers, although the lack of trace elements renders this something of a misnomer. Until a few years ago these compounds were described by the percentages of N, P and K they contained (e.g. 12:6:12 and 5:13:5), and the change to the new method of description has created confusion in the minds of some gardeners, who still ask for fertilizers under the old code.

Compound fertilizers are now described by what is termed the ratio and multiple-grades method, a system in use in the U.S.A. and some other countries. This gives the ratio of N, P and K to each other and the total percentage of nutrient units in brackets, e.g. 2:1:2(26) is 10,4% nitrogen, 5,2% phosphorus and 10,4% potassium. 5:13:5, one of the oldest mixtures, was altered, and is now known as 2:3:2(22) i.e. 6,28% nitrogen, 9,44% phosphorus, and 6,28% potassium.

Several different mixtures are available to meet the needs of various crops and different soils. These may be slightly changed from time to time by the manufacturers, the changes being the result of extended trials on a variety of soils. The mixtures most suitable for vegetable crops as basic fertilizers are 2:1:2, 2:3:4 and 2:3:2.

Compound fertilizers are usually applied as base dressings prior to the planting or sowing of a crop, but with long-season crops such as cauliflowers a dressing 5-6 weeks after transplanting usually produces a marked response from the plants. With perennial vegetables such as asparagus, chayotes and artichokes the recommended practice is to apply an annual dressing of a compound fertilizer in spring, followed by two or more side-dressings of nitrogenous material.

The mixing of fertilizer requires considerable knowledge if maximum benefit is to be derived from each constituent and should not be attempted by the amateur grower. In addition to the difficulty that may be experienced in obtaining a uniform end-product, the risk of mixing incompatible materials cannot be entirely overlooked.

Apart from the conventional mixtures, usually available in granular form, high-grade fertilizers with a vermiculite carrier have been introduced for use in the home garden and on sports greens. Three mixtures are available – 3:1:5(26), 2:3:2(14) and 4:1:1(21) – and these should cover the requirements of most garden plants and grasses. They are very pleasant and light to handle, but distribution must be carried out carefully if the dressing rates (1 tablespoon per m^2) are not to be exceeded.

Concentrated fertilizers, in the form of salts and liquids and containing varied analyses of NPK, are readily available at most garden shops in packs of 200 g to 1 kg and 200 mℓ to 5 ℓ respectively. They are usually applied as stimulants to promote quick growth in salad crops and are also useful in maintaining vigour in long-season crops such as tomatoes. The recommendations are usually for drench applications to the soil and for foliar sprays. With regard to the latter, it should be stressed that foliar sprays should be regarded only as supplements to basic pre-planting soil fertilization. The quantities of nutrients removed from the soil by even an average crop are far in excess of the amount that can be supplied solely by foliar sprays, however high their analyses may be and however regularly they are applied.

TRACE ELEMENTS

Compounds of boron, magnesium, manganese, zinc, iron and other essential trace elements are used by horticulturists and agriculturists to correct deficiencies that limit growth. However, before any of these 'straight' materials are used it is advisable to obtain a sound diagnosis, as excessive applications can prove just as harmful to plants as deficiencies, and toxicities are much more difficult to correct than deficiencies. Crops react differently when deficiencies occur, and diagnosis by visual symptoms is quite reliable in certain cases. In other instances a test may be necessary.

In recent years new types of compounds have been developed to prevent the 'locking up' of trace elements in the soil. They are known as chelated or sequestered compounds and are usually mixed with water and applied either directly to the soil or as a foliar spray.

Mixtures of trace elements in liquid and powder form are readily obtainable under several trade names. Their analyses usually include elements such as magnesium, manganese, iron and copper. Use only at recommended rates.

Nutrient powders formulated primarily for hydroponic culture are readily available and can be used to advantage on vegetable crops planted in controlled beds and containers. They are well balanced and contain all the major trace elements required for plant growth. Most garden and container plants displaying chlorosis and other symptoms of leaf starvation will respond favour-

ably to two or three successive applications. Hydroponic fertilizers are available in packs of 500 g and upwards.

LIME

Liming materials are applied to garden soils primarily to correct excessive soil acidity and not to meet the calcium requirements of the plants.

The symbol pH followed by a numeral is used by soil scientists to express soil reaction (i.e. acidity, alkalinity or neutrality), which covers a range of values from 0 to 14, the normal range of garden soil falling within the narrower limits 4-10. A soil having a pH of 7,0 is neutral, one with a value higher than this is alkaline or 'sweet', and one with a value of less than 7,0 is acid or 'sour'. Although it would appear that a soil with a pH value of 5,0 is only slightly more acid than one with a pH of 6,0 it is, in fact, ten times more acid. By the same token, pH 4,0 is ten times more acid than pH 5,0 and a hundred times more acid than pH 6,0.

Most vegetables thrive on a soil within the range pH 6,0 to 6,5, i.e. slightly to moderately acid. At such a pH, bacteria of the helpful type will enjoy congenial conditions for their activities, the various soil nutrients will be kept in an optimum state of availability, and the soil will tend to granulate to the right particle size. No exact range can be specified, however, because although the pH value of two soils may be exactly the same, identical crops may fare differently because of other influencing factors in the soil.

Lime is not a fertilizer in itself, but it does have a very considerable effect on the availability of essential plant foods in the soil. When the soil is very acid, phosphates, in particular, are unavailable, while other elements become available in toxic quantities. At the other extreme, in alkaline soils, much the same thing happens, although different elements are unavailable, among them iron and manganese. The regular application of generous dressings of sulphate of ammonia or urea without maintenance dressings of lime is one way of increasing soil acidity.

Apart from its influence on soil reaction, lime may also affect the physical condition of the soil, particularly of extreme soil types. Clay soils, which are hard and compact, can be opened up by lime, thus improving aeration and drainage, while sandy soils can be bound together by similar dressings. By correcting extreme acidity and improving soil conditions generally, lime also stimulates activity among those soil microorganisms that are adversely affected by acidity.

Despite its several benefits, however, lime should never be used unless crop growth or, ideally, a soil pH test indicates that such a measure is necessary. The exception to this rule is that it can safely be used to

counteract the acidifying effect of sulphate of ammonia and urea (1 kg of lime for every kg of sulphate of ammonia, 0,5 kg of lime for every kg of urea). These lime applications should be made some weeks after the fertilizer dressings. It is far, far easier to correct acidity in stages than it is to correct soil alkalinity caused by the indiscriminate use of liming materials.

Forms of lime

Lime is usually added to the soil in one of three forms: calcium carbonate, calcium oxide and calcium hydroxide.

Carbonate of lime, usually called agricultural lime, is the cheapest form and is very easy to handle as it is simply crushed limestone rock, the degree of fineness being an indication of the speed of its action.

When limestone rock is burnt in kilns the product is calcium oxide or unslaked lime. It is a very unpleasant material to handle, being extremely caustic in nature, and is not at all suitable for use in the home garden.

When calcium oxide is slaked by water or rain the end-product is calcium hydroxide or slaked lime, also known as hydrated lime, builders' lime or whitewash lime. Hydrated lime is suitable for the gardener because it is in a finely divided state and is easily distributed on a windless day! It is also an ideal material for incorporation into seedbeds, seedboxes and potting composts. However, it is considerably more expensive than calcium carbonate.

Dolomitic limestone is rock that contains appreciable quantities of magnesium carbonate in addition to calcium, and is a useful material where a deficiency of this element is evident. The properties of basic slag as a soil sweetener have been mentioned elsewhere.

It is quite impossible to recommend definite rates of application of liming materials to bring a garden soil to a desired pH value, for soil types vary greatly and each gives a different response to a similar dressing. Generally speaking, however, heavy clay soils require much heavier dressings than sandy soils to raise the pH by the same value. A dressing of 250 g per m^2 on sandy loams, and up to double this quantity on very heavy soils, should have an ameliorating effect if the need has been established.

Lime, as we have explained, is not a fertilizer, nor is it a panacea for soil insects and diseases, as is sometimes thought. It is a valuable material where acid soil conditions exist, but soils of pH 5,5 to 6,0 rarely require it for profitable vegetable production.

Soil testing

Most agricultural stations and fertilizer manufacturers have sophisticated equipment for doing comprehensive soil tests under laboratory conditions. These facilities were established to assist farmers and other large growers of crops whose livelihood de-

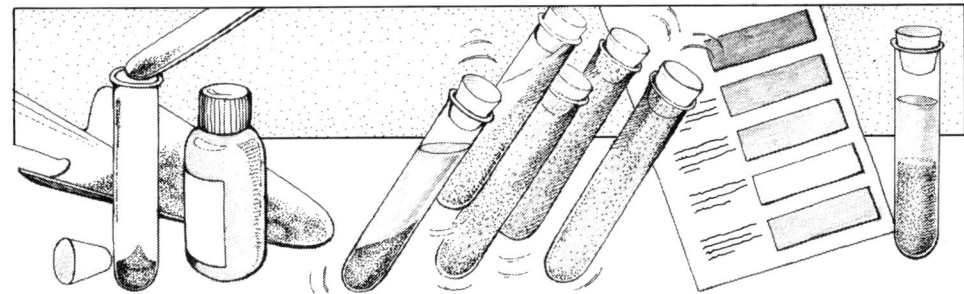

Soil-testing kits for the home garden are all used in a similar way: for example, to determine the pH value of the soil a representative sample of soil is shaken up in a test tube with the chemical provided. The colour of the resulting solution is compared with the colours on the chart supplied with the kit and indicates the degree of acidity or alkalinity of the soil.

pends on the correct use of fertilizing materials. Some extend this facility to smaller growers and home gardeners, and for a relatively nominal fee they will carry out a soil test and make certain lime and fertilizer recommendations.

However, if every home gardener were to forward soil samples for analysis to these agencies it would tax their facilities to the full and thereby delay more important work. Enthusiasts who are really interested in testing their soil should therefore seriously consider purchasing a test kit for themselves. Most garden shops carry three or more different models together with a supply of spare indicator solutions.

The smallest kit is only for lime testing, while the others usually enable one to test for NPK as well. Detailed instructions for use are supplied with each kit, and it is extremely important to carry out the correct procedures to the letter if a meaningful result is to be obtained. The kits consist of test tubes, corks, and chemical solutions, as well as colour charts that indicate any deficiencies and make recommendations for corrective treatment.

Organic soil conditioners

Apart from manures, compost and other organic soil additives, materials described as 'organic soil conditioners' have appeared on the market. The one that is marketed somewhat aggressively in this country is described as being lignitic in nature and is registered as such. At first sight the claims made for this material appear incredible, particularly to one who has spent several decades close to the soil and to plant life. However, in the absence of documented results from a properly supervised series of trials, repeated many times over on a wide range of soils and plant subjects, one cannot make fair comment.

COMPOST

Animal manures are rarely available in sufficient quantities to maintain and increase soil fertility and productivity. Wise farmers will not part with manure for cash because few, indeed, have sufficient to give their own lands adequate, regular dressings. The packing, storage and distribution of bulky animal manures also pose considerable problems. In some areas the milled poultry manures now available in small packs have relieved the situation for gardeners.

Composting is the practice of making the very best use of these meagre supplies of manure by adding them to other organic wastes and providing conditions for their relatively rapid breakdown into homogeneous material suitable for incorporating into the soil. However, excellent compost can easily be produced without manure.

Composting is simply a speeding up of the processes that occur in nature all around us, and involves the same fundamental principles. These are the provision of air, moisture and warmth in order to create an ideal environment for the fungi and bacteria that are responsible for the decomposition and breakdown of the raw materials. If these materials were added direct to the soil and dug in they would, initially, have a deleterious effect on the soil and on any vegetable crops planted immediately after their incorporation. In order to decompose satisfactorily, bulky organic material must have an adequate supply of air and moisture and also of nitrogen, the principal food of the micro-organisms. When fresh and raw materials are turned in, followed quickly by a vegetable crop, there is much competition for these essentials between the two, and the growing plants always come off second best. I have seen several instances of Swiss chard and cabbages planted in this way, and each time the plants made little growth for some weeks. Eventually, when moisture and nutrients became available, the plants grew satisfactorily but did not produce the expected yields despite, in one case, generous side-dressings of fertilizer, and they occupied the ground for a very long period.

Compost is made more easily and with a more satisfactory end-product in a heap above ground than in a hole or pit, although good compost can certainly be produced in a pit if it is carefully managed. In a well-made heap the micro-organisms can more easily obtain their air requirements and the control of moisture is facilitated.

Organic material thrown into a pit in wet weather, especially in clayey soils, either does not break down at all, or it putrifies owing to its saturated condition and gives off a disagreeable odour. Peat is an example of organic material that formed under waterlogged conditions over a period of many, many years. It is potential humus, but until it has been given aerated conditions suitable for natural breakdown it is of limited value.

Further advantages of the heap over the pit are that the stages of decomposition can easily be observed; the temperature and moisture content of the mass can be ascertained without difficulty by simply pushing one's hand into it in various places and levels; and any necessary turning can be carried out more easily and effectively.

Location of the heap

In the tropics and sub-tropics, nature's finest compost is produced in full shade. If you provide this and add partial shelter you have the best spot for the heap. A position under a well-canopied tree or adjacent to a tall hedge is just about ideal. In such a position the heap is sheltered from the sun and wind, which would otherwise dry the outer 150 mm of the heap and prevent this from breaking down satisfactorily. In a shady spot the moisture in the heap is also conserved and much less water need be applied during dry weather than would be necessary if the heap were exposed to full sun. However, care should be taken not to build the heap on low-lying ground, which may be under water for several days during wet weather.

Materials for incorporation

Almost any organic matter can be placed in the compost heap, but the choice for the individual gardener depends not only on the type of material accruing from the house and garden but also on the kind of activator used. If fresh animal or poultry manure is available, it is safe to incorporate vegetable residues provided they are not obviously infected with soil-borne diseases or nematodes. In such heaps, if they are well constructed and managed, a great deal of heat is generated, and temperatures of 75-80°C can be expected. These temperatures are sufficiently high to destroy many parasitic organisms and also some weed seeds, but unfortunately the heat is not uniform throughout the heap, the outer 'skin' being much cooler. No matter how carefully one builds and turns the heap, one can never be sure that all the material has been subjected to such heat.

In the absence of animal or poultry manure the gardener has a choice of several proprietary activators, or accelerators as they are sometimes described. Some of these contain a guaranteed minimum population of several million cellulolytic micro-fungi

Open compost heap.

Compost bin.

Compost box.

Enclosed compost heap.

and cellulolytic and nitrogen-fixing bacteria in suspended animation. They are made into a concentrated suspension that is diluted with water and sprinkled on each new layer of material as the heap is constructed. Other accelerators simply provide a concentrated food supply to stimulate bacterial activity.

Heaps in which these materials are used and to which no manure has been added are usually relatively cool, though lawn mowings and other succulent materials are capable of generating considerable heat. It is advisable to use only leaves, lawn mowings, soft hedge trimmings, unseeded weeds and clean vegetable and fruit residues. In this way there is no risk of perpetuating certain serious diseases, which live over on infected plant residues and which may contaminate 'clean' ground when the compost is distributed. The several wilt diseases of tomatoes and other solanaceous crops, and black rot of cabbages and other brassicas, are examples of this.

Sweetcorn and maize residues are also safe to use, but if they are at all woody they should be chopped and bruised, especially at the nodes, to hasten decay and ease the construction and turning of the heap. There is nothing more exasperating or tiring than turning a heap containing 'long' material such as unchopped maize stalks, for after much effort the fork comes away with little or nothing on it. Unchopped stalks of cab-

bage, cauliflower, broccoli and Brussels sprouts are also troublesome when turning, as the tines of the fork always seem to pierce them and they have to be removed by hand or foot.

If sawdust is available it can profitably be incorporated in reasonable quantities, especially if a handful or two of sulphate of ammonia is thrown over each layer. Residues from fruit and vegetable processing factories can also be incorporated, but, as with sawdust, it is a wise policy not to build a heap entirely with this but to dilute it with the more conventional materials mentioned above.

Lime and wood ash can be used to reduce acidity in the heap, as well as ash from the burning of diseased plant residues. However, do not add lime to a heap if sulphate of ammonia has been applied, as chemical action may result in the loss of nitrogen in the form of ammonia.

Soot is another waste product worthy of inclusion in a compost heap as it contains 3-5% nitrogen. Alternatively it can be applied direct to the soil as a stimulant to established crops and a deterrent to certain insects.

In some towns there are regulations relating to compost heaps, especially to the incorporation of manures as activators. These regulations were introduced primarily to reduce fly breeding in urban areas and should be strictly observed.

Construction of the heap

Most gardeners will be familiar with the multi-layer construction of compost heaps as illustrated diagrammatically in gardening books. This is simply a useful guide, particularly for the new gardener, to the suggested 'mix' of materials and the desirable proportions of the heap.

There are as many recipes for compost making as there are for baking a cake, and it must be emphasized that composting is extremely flexible with regard to the method of construction and the materials for incorporation.

The size of the heap will depend on the volume of material available, but the minimum size for an efficient unit is 1,2 m³. In heaps smaller than this, little heat is generated as too large a proportion of the material is susceptible to drying out by the agencies of wind and sun.

The materials should ideally be mixed as far as possible before incorporation into the heap (i.e. wet and dry material, soft and hard material), and wetted layer by layer as the heap grows. The ideal moisture content for a heap is that of a squeezed-out sponge. During periods of heavy rainfall the crown of the heap can be covered with 150 or 250 micron black plastic sheeting, which can be tethered to pegs in the ground. If the heap gets saturated the decomposition process is slowed down considerably, especially if it occurs once the initial heat has gone and the heap is beginning to compact. If this happens it will be necessary to give the heap a turn to get things going again.

Bottomless compost boxes can be constructed from lengths of treated timber (25 mm x 150 mm), three sides being nailed to uprights and the fourth consisting of loose timbers that are added as the heap grows. Such a box or bin helps contain the heat and ensures that as large a proportion of the material as possible is broken down quickly.

In recent years several types and sizes of manufactured compost bins, made of PVC and other materials, have come on the market. They are very suitable for use in the smaller garden and by those gardeners who have limited quantities of residues. The advantages of these bins are several:

1. Because they are basically round in shape, a more even breakdown of the materials can be obtained as there are no 'cold' spots in the heap.

2. Less manual labour is required to produce a satisfactory end-product.

3. Only a small surface area is exposed (through the air holes), thus limiting egg-laying by flies. An occasional spraying around the bin with Karbaspray or Malathion will control any adults that do emerge.

4. Any necessary wetting of the material presents no problems.

If the garden budget does not allow such a sophisticated piece of equipment, a cheaper, if less effective, substitute can be made from a PVC dustbin with the bottom cut out and several 50 mm holes drilled in the sides.

The only drawback of these bins is that, even in the smallest gardens, the volume of suitable material that accrues necessitates a battery of at least four units in service. With fewer than this the options would be either to lift off the bins as they fill, add more activator, and 'case' the heaps with soil, or to incorporate only selected materials and use lawn mowings and leaves as mulches instead of adding them to the bin.

The concept, put forward by one manufacturer, of adding fresh material at the top and simultaneously removing mature compost at the bottom is both grossly misleading and impracticable.

The sieving of compost, other than when it is used for potting mixes, is quite unnecessary. It is only warranted when materials such as municipal wastes, which usually contain 'foreign' matter such as plastic, metal and glass, are utilized. The sun, soil temperature, and mechanical cultivation by spade or hoe break down compost quickly enough once it has been added to the soil without any assistance from the gardener by way of sieving.

The time taken for compost to reach a state in which it can be distributed in the garden depends upon the following factors: the type of material used, the type of activator used (if any), the method of heap construction, and the season. Generally speaking, however, most of the material should be ready for use in 10-20 weeks. Shredded and bruised material breaks down particularly quickly, and it is pleasing to note that shred-

Electrically-powered shredder for garden residues.

ding units – both power and petrol driven – have become available on the local market. They are relatively expensive but very efficient and will handle coarse vegetable residues with a diameter of 25 mm or more.

GREEN MANURES

Because manures and materials for making compost are not always available in sufficient quantities, other methods of adding potential humus must sometimes be resorted to if soil fertility is to be maintained or improved. Green manuring is the practice of growing a particular crop specifically for incorporation into the soil as an improver, and can be termed 'sheet composting'. In the small garden with just a few rows each of several crops in constant succession green manuring is difficult to apply, but a handful or two of seed broadcast over ground that is to be free of crops for two or three months will be a step in the right direction. On larger properties and smallholdings a crop of green manure can be worked into the rotation programme without too much difficulty.

Benefits of green manuring

A thick stand of succulent material turned into the soil increases the organic content of the soil, thus supplying plant food for succeeding crops and improving soil structure. If a legume is used for the purpose, and this is generally the case, the nitrogen content of the soil is increased because the bacteria that form nodules on the roots under favourable conditions have the capacity to 'fix' atmospheric nitrogen. In addition, green manure keeps the nutrients in circulation and prevents them from being leached out of the root region as can happen on empty ground if heavy rain falls.

Crotalaria juncea (sunn-hemp) and *C. spectabilis* (showy crotalaria) are among the best summer crops for green manure, their soft growth and upright habit making their incorporation into the soil relatively easy. Green manure crops such as velvet beans and cowpeas can be difficult to incorporate by hand because of their vining habits and, in the case of velvet beans, hard growth. Lupins are grown to a considerable extent as a winter green manure crop in the Cape and are frequently followed by beans and sweet potatoes as summer crops.

Lupins and crotalaria contain alkaloids in their tissues that have proved harmful, even fatal, if these crops are fed to stock in quantity, either fresh or as hay.

Establishing a green manure crop

It is essential that a green manure crop be given the same attention as a vegetable crop, especially as regards seedbed preparation and fertilizing. Inorganic fertilizers can indirectly improve the physical structure of

the soil, for on poor ground a dressing of fertilizer will assist in obtaining a good stand and this, after all, is the whole idea. Nitrogen is rarely needed by green manure crops because of the activity of the bacteria in the root nodules, but 75 g per m² of either superphosphate or super and raw phosphate will usually achieve a marked response in plant growth.

Seeding rates vary slightly and depend on the crop used and whether the seed is sown by broadcasting or drilling. It is usual on small plots to broadcast the seed and so obtain a blanket stand. In commercial operations, however, drilling is sometimes practised so as to encourage the development of stronger and more productive plants. A crop that is allowed to run to seed obviously cannot be regarded as a green manure crop even if the stubble is dug in. Much of the plant food is removed in the seed, while the tough, dry residues draw on soil nitrogen in order to break down fully. The following are satisfactory seeding rates:

Bitter lupin: 1 kg to 100 m²
Crotalaria juncea: 600 g to 100 m²
Crotalaria spectabilis: 600 g to 100 m²

After sowing, a thin layer of soil should be raked over the seed. When these crops are grown on a garden soil for the first time it is a good policy to inoculate the seed with the right strain of bacteria to promote nodulization. Inoculants are, however, rarely obtainable in packs suitable for the few kilograms of seed used each year in the average garden, and as they cannot be carried over from one season to the next it is pointless to purchase large packs. The only alternative is to inoculate the seed with soil from ground that has previously carried the crop in question. This can be achieved by scattering a few spadefuls of the soil over the surface of the new area and by mixing the seed with a spadeful of the soil and then broadcasting seed and soil together.

Digging in the crop

Green manures must be turned in when maximum vegetative growth has been attained. In the case of both lupins and crotalaria this is usually when the plants approach 50% flower. At this stage they are rich in nitrogen, and as they are soft and succulent decay commences as soon as they are in the soil. The method of incorporating the material is also important. Do not place it in the bottom of a deep trench and then cover it with soil, for it compacts into a thin layer and breaks down very slowly indeed. Rather chop it into the top 150 mm of soil, where aerated conditions will accelerate decomposition. Alternatively, the 'tidy' gardener can lay it in a shallow trench and cover it with 80-100 mm of soil.

Incorporating the material by hand often requires considerable effort, and the task can be made much easier if the plants are

Cutting a green-manure crop.

Incorporation of wilted material.

severed just above the soil with a grass slasher or sickle a few hours beforehand to allow partial wilting to take place.

Small, powered rotavators and similar implements make a very satisfactory job of incorporating green manures, provided that they are fitted with blades and not tines.

The moisture content of the soil must also be considered before digging in the crop, for any work carried out in conditions that are too wet can cause permanent damage to the soil. On the other hand, little immediate breakdown will take place if the soil is too dry.

After incorporation it is advisable not to plant vegetables for at least four weeks in order to allow the initial stages of breakdown to take place.

In an emergency I have, on occasion, used the green manure material for mulching, but have thereby completely sacrificed its value as a soil improver.

MULCHING

Mulching is one of the least arduous and yet most rewarding and beneficial practices in the home garden. It is therefore quite remarkable that so few gardeners make use of mulches. One frequently sees a gardener cheerfully watering several times a week during hot weather, while close at hand there is a wealth of material that would save him a great deal of time and halve his water bill.

Mulching can be defined quite simply as the practice of covering the surface of the soil between growing crops with a layer of material. A mulch can be of inestimable value during hot, dry weather when soil temperatures frequently soar above the optimum for satisfactory growth. Brassicas, leaf crops and root crops, in particular, appreciate mulching. It is a practice that can be carried out on any size of enterprise, from windowboxes upwards.

Benefits of mulching

The benefits of mulching are almost as numerous as the materials that can be used for

the purpose. The most outstanding property of a mulch is that it reduces evaporation from the soil, thereby ensuring that the moisture content of the topsoil does not fluctuate too widely and consequently preventing damage that can be caused to tomatoes, potatoes and root crops as they approach maturity.

In addition to conserving moisture it prevents or reduces the compaction and crusting of the soil caused by watering, rain and treading, thereby increasing water penetration and preventing runoff and erosion.

A further important property of a mulch is that it suppresses weed growth. A layer 50-75 mm thick will prevent the emergence of most annual weeds and will certainly weaken the growth of the more vigorous annuals and the more stubborn perennials, making their control by hoeing or hand-pulling relatively easy.

A mulch also insulates the soil to a considerable extent from extreme day and night temperatures. Root and tuber crops derive most benefit from this property.

By regulating the moisture content and temperature of the topsoil a mulch not only creates favourable conditions for root development but also ensures an ideal environment for both the microscopic and macroscopic flora and fauna in the soil.

If compost or manure is used as a mulch,

A good mulch consists of fairly coarse material.

watering and rain wash a steady supply of nutrients down to the roots.

Finally, a mulch can appreciably reduce the 'greening' of roots and tubers, which results from their exposure to prolonged sunlight, and will also facilitate the harvesting of these crops as they can be pulled or dug without great effort.

In my experience there are two possible drawbacks to using a mulch. Firstly, in certain circumstances it can harbour cutworms, slugs, snails and other pests and make their detection and control extremely difficult. Secondly, if mulches are employed too early in the spring while the soil is still cold they can cause unsatisfactory germination and, in certain cases, rotting of the seed of early summer crops, cucurbits being extremely vulnerable.

Mulching materials

A variety of materials can be used for mulching, ranging from sawdust to polythene sheeting and flat stones. However, as with composting, it is obviously sensible to use materials that are obtainable at little or no cost. Grass cuttings, leaves, soft hedge-trimmings, seaweed, deep-litter material and kraal manure are all extremely useful organic materials, which have the advantage that when their life as an effective mulch is spent they need not be removed but can simply be worked into the soil. Before a mulch is dug in it should ideally be in a fairly advanced state of decay otherwise the growth of the subsequent crops may be retarded through nitrogen deficiency. If the mulch is very woody, add a light dressing of nitrogenous fertilizer. With sawdust and pine needles, two other useful mulches, a liberal dressing should be applied.

Ideally a mulching material should not absorb too much moisture (this is where sawdust is somewhat unsatisfactory), otherwise a copious amount of water must be applied before any reaches the soil. In theory the maximum benefit would be derived from a mulch if it were raked aside prior to each watering or irrigation and then replaced immediately afterwards, but this is impracticable in most cases. The maximum depth for a sawdust mulch is 50 mm.

The use of polyethylene film as a mulch is dealt with in the chapter 'Plastics in the Vegetable Garden'.

The 'dust mulch' (created by constant cultivation of the top few centimetres of soil to produce a layer of loose, dry soil in an attempt to prevent the escape of moisture from the lower soil regions) has fallen out of favour. Such a practice is only of benefit when the water table is within a metre of the surface. In conditions other than these it can actually increase the rate of evaporation and harm feeder roots.

The value of a mulch in seedbed practice is discussed in the chapter 'Seed, Sowing and Transplanting'.

3

GARDEN PLANNING AND CROP ROTATION

GARDEN PLANNING

Once the location and size of the area to be devoted to vegetables have been determined there is still a great deal to be done before a profitable vegetable garden becomes a reality. The small, intensive, but extremely productive gardens we sometimes encounter and which make us stop in admiration do not just happen: they are the result of knowledge, hard work and careful planning.

To get consistent, satisfactory yields with a variety of vegetables over a period of several years it is necessary to make careful plans well in advance of planting time. The aim of every home gardener should be to produce a constant supply of fresh, top-quality vegetables throughout the year. In our climate this is not too difficult a task. It can be achieved with thorough soil preparation, the selection of suitable crops and cultivars, the early recognition and control of pests and diseases, and an adequate supply of water during dry periods. Perhaps the most common mistakes I encounter when visiting gardens, or when judging garden competitions, is that there tend to be too many vegetables or, worse still, too many of one particular type maturing simultaneously. Often this period of plenty is followed by a long period of scarcity, during which vegetables may have to be purchased. A garden is not producing to full capacity unless it is producing all the year round.

Before a cropping plan can be decided upon, however, the following points must all be considered:

1. The area of ground available.
2. The likes and dislikes of the family.
3. Soil type and depth.
4. The experience of the grower.
5. Features such as permanent windbreaks and unavoidable shade.
6. Presence of perennial weeds.
7. Presence of persistent diseases and plant nematodes.
8. Allocation of ground for any permanent crops.

The size of the area available for vegetables has a considerable bearing upon the type of vegetables it will be most profitable to grow.

For instance, large gardens can comfortably accommodate potatoes, pumpkins, sweet potatoes and sweetcorn, which are all widely-spaced crops and in some cases of spreading habit, but in smaller gardens such crops take up too much room. However, they are all crops that keep reasonably well, apart from sweetcorn, losing little of their nutritive value if held over on the greengrocer's shelf for a day or two. On the other hand, beans, Swiss chard, spinach, peas and salad crops deteriorate rapidly once they have been picked, and it is on these and on closely-spaced root crops such as beets, carrots and turnips that the grower should concentrate.

The personal tastes of the family must also be considered. It is useless to produce a big crop of cabbages simply because they are relatively easy vegetables to grow, if cabbages are not popular with your family.

Soil type is an important factor determining the kind of crops that can be grown. Clayey soils are most unsuitable for root crops, which find such soils too hard and compact during dry periods and consequently develop misshapen roots. But if these soils are supplied with liberal dressings of compost and manure, and devoted to cabbages, tomatoes, and other 'top' crops, they will gradually open up so that in a few seasons the growing of good quality roots will be possible. A sandy soil, on the other hand, is suitable for root and tuber crops – the loose character of the soil allows these vegetables to swell easily and facilitates harvesting. Most root crops are sown direct where they are to mature, and sandy soil is an ideal medium for the germination and emergence of seeds. On shallow soils that overlie clay subsoils it is advisable to restrict sowings of root crops to globe beet cultivars, turnips, and carrot cultivars such as Shorthorn, Nantes and Oxheart. I have frequently seen long cultivars such as Cape Market and Imperator produce strange roots in these soils. The top 100 mm of the root, from the shoulder downwards, was perfectly shaped, but from there to the tip the root was flat like a spear point.

In big gardens there may be two or more soil types and the grower must plan his crops accordingly, until he has worked up a

reasonably uniform topsoil. Another characteristic of a sandy soil is that it warms up much more quickly in spring than a heavy soil. Therefore, where one has a choice of soil types, the lighter one should be used for early sowings and the heavier one for main-crop and late sowings.

Certain crops, such as cauliflower and celery, require quite a lot of skill to be grown successfully in some areas, and often they are the cause of great disappointment. The inexperienced grower would therefore be well advised to leave these crops for a season or two and concentrate initially on easier crops such as cabbages, leeks, carrots, beets, radishes, peas, kohlrabi, Swiss chard and beans. After gaining experience on these crops he can proceed to widen his range until, eventually, he is able to handle everything in the seedsman's catalogue. He would also be wise, in the beginning, to grow crops only during the most favourable seasons because, while some vegetables will grow satisfactorily during most months, many are specific in their climatic requirements. Early and late sowings usually require considerably more attention than main-crop sowings. The difficulty with early sowings is to get satisfactory germination and initial growth. With later plantings, pests and diseases are often a problem, especially aphids, caterpillars, pumpkin fly and mosaic of certain cucurbits.

The presence of perennial weeds, such as oxalis, water grass and couch grass, can make ground totally unsuitable for the growth of certain crops. On such 'dirty' ground it is almost impossible to grow, with any success, directly-sown crops such as beets, peas, beans, parsnips and carrots, because the weeds with their underground resources always get off to a flying start as soon as moisture is provided, while the crop seeds, which germinate later, produce weak seedlings as a result of competition from the weeds. Clean ground is also required by onions, because of their slow early growth, even if transplanted, and the close planting normally practised with this crop. Couch and water grass are particularly difficult weeds, for attempting to remove them by hand disturbs all the young tender seedlings. Such weedy ground can only be used for transplanted crops such as cabbages, cauliflowers and tomatoes, which can be set out when they are on the big side and whose beds can, if necessary, be cleaned by hand or hoe a day or two after transplanting.

In Europe the potato is regarded as a cleaning crop because under favourable conditions it produces a dense canopy of foliage, which shades the soil and suppresses weed growth. In addition, the 'earthing up' required by this crop severs and smothers many weeds. This is a sound theory as far as most annual weeds are concerned, and the 'cleaning' label is warranted. However, where water grass and couch grass are the enemy the potato comes off a poor second best.

Several plant diseases are able to live over in garden soils for years, notably those causing 'wilts', and it is essential that outbreaks of these diseases be recorded to assist future planning and prevent crop losses. For this and other reasons it is a good idea to keep a garden diary, in which sowing and planting dates, sources of seed, maturity dates and the appearance of insects and diseases can be entered. Rainfall figures can also be recorded to give a fuller picture when the season's results are analyzed.

There are few permanent crops among vegetables, but if such crops are to be grown a special site must be set aside for them. Asparagus, rhubarb, globe artichokes and pole lima beans are among the more usual permanent and semi-permanent crops, and if attention is given to their diet they will justify their choice by giving profitable yields over several seasons. These crops are best placed together at one end of the vegetable garden, or on its perimeter, where they will not interfere with seasonal planning. Some of them, notably asparagus, require a distinct resting season, and in the warmer parts of the country this can be brought about only by withholding water, a procedure that is impossible if they are surrounded by annual subjects that need watering regularly.

A relatively minor point, but one worth attention, is that it is far better to have two or three short rows of a tall-growing crop than one long row. In a single row, crops such as sweetcorn and staked tomatoes are vulnerable to strong winds, heavy downpours and other mechanical damage.

CROP ROTATION

Crop rotation is best described as a system of crop production in which the various crops are grown in a certain sequence in order to economize on the resources of the soil. Soil in which the same crop, or a closely related one, is grown season after season without a break tends to deteriorate rapidly in both nutrient content and structure. In smaller home gardens it is often extremely difficult to avoid doing this, but if the bed method is followed, rotation and planning are facilitated.

Botanically and by habit vegetables can be grouped as follows:

Cruciferous crops: Cabbages, cauliflowers, Chinese cabbages, broccoli, Brussels sprouts, kale.
Solanaceous crops: Tomatoes, potatoes, peppers, egg plants.
Root crops: Carrots, turnips, beetroots, parsnips, salsify.
Cucurbitaceous crops: Cucumbers, pumpkins, squashes, vegetable-marrows, melons, watermelons.
Leguminous crops: Beans and peas of all types.
Miscellaneous crops: Swiss chard, spinach, radishes, okra, leeks, kohlrabi, celery, onions, sweetcorn, sweet potatoes, lettuce, endive, artichokes.

For the average gardener, even if he grows two or more crops per year, formulating and implementing a rotation based on six groups may be difficult. Therefore, to simplify matters, vegetables can be re-arranged into four groups without defeating the objects of crop rotation. These groups are:

Group 1: Cabbages, cauliflowers, Chinese cabbages, broccoli, Brussels sprouts, onions, leeks, celery.
Group 2: Carrots, beetroots, parsnips, salsify, turnips, kohlrabi, sweet potatoes.
Group 3: Tomatoes, potatoes, peppers, egg plants, lettuce, Swiss chard.
Group 4: 'Snap' beans, Lima beans, broad beans, peas.

Cucurbits, although a family of considerable consequence in most South African gardens, have not been grouped because they are not troubled to any degree by specific soil-borne diseases and can be included anywhere in the rotation. They are essentially warm-season crops that respond favourably to a forkful of manure or compost worked into the rows or planting stations. Miscellaneous crops not grouped include okra, sweetcorn, radishes and endive, but, again, they can be slipped into the rotation at any point without difficulty.

Group 1

The cruciferous crops, often called brassicas (the generic name of most types) or cole crops, are heavy feeders and must be supplied with liberal quantities of manure or compost to produce satisfactory yields. The other vegetables in this group also respond to such feeding. In general this group prefers cool growing conditions, with cabbages and onions as they approach maturity being most tolerant of high temperatures.

Group 2

The 'roots' are a well-defined group and their requirements are all similar, sweet potatoes being by far the most tolerant of high temperatures. Turnips rightly belong to the cruciferous group as do kohlrabi, but for the purpose of planning a rotation they have been re-allocated.

It is undesirable to add manure to the soil prior to the establishment of a root crop. Such manuring causes roots to become irregular in shape with much 'forking' and it encourages the rooted subjects to throw out an abnormally high number of fibrous roots. Manure, which contains considerable nitrogen, also induces excessive top growth at the expense of root development.

Group 3

Of this group tomatoes, egg plants and the several types of peppers like warm to hot conditions, while the others prefer somewhat cooler temperatures. All these crops will respond to dressings of manure or compost, but such treatment is not essential if the soil is in good heart and if a generous fertilizer dressing is incorporated during soil preparation.

Group 4

The legumes, or pod-bearing plants, are represented in the vegetable garden by the several types of peas and beans and are usually given a spot in any system of crop rotation and land usage. However, legumes only improve the soil to any degree when the *complete* plant is returned to the soil while it is in a succulent state. When treated as vegetables, that is when the pods are removed for eating purposes, or as a seed crop, they can hardly be classed as soil-improving crops from a nutrient point of view. They are relatively undemanding in their food requirements and rarely require additional nitrogen. Most legumes develop extensive root systems under favourable conditions and these appear to have an ameliorating effect on the physical condition of the soil.

Lime and crop rotation

Apart from manure or compost dressings, another point to decide is when to apply lime in the rotation should occasional or regular maintenance dressings be considered necessary. Generally speaking, legumes and brassicas will benefit the most from applications, while potatoes, cucurbits and roots usually show the least response. In the case of potatoes, a dressing prior to planting is definitely undesirable on the majority of soils, while cucurbits will make very satisfactory growth on soils with a low pH. Thus, the best time to incorporate a liming material is before the establishment of crops in Groups 1 and 4, or before planting a green manure crop.

Pest and disease control

An equally important reason for practising crop rotation is that it helps to control diseases and pests. As far as certain diseases

CROP ROTATION

cucurbits and miscellaneous crops not grouped above

are concerned it is, except for total soil sterilization (which is impracticable in the home garden), the only method of control.

Solanaceous and cruciferous vegetables are particularly susceptible to certain soil-borne diseases and must receive first consideration when a rotation is devised. Black rot, a widespread bacterial disease of cabbages and related crops, is able to live over in the soil for up to 3 years once the affected plants have been removed. When a 3-year rotation between these crops is practised, the causal organisms in the soil are starved out through lack of an accommodating host plant. If such a long rotation is impossible, susceptible crops should be grown on affected ground during the cooler months, when the disease is less likely to cause serious damage.

Bacterial wilt and fusarium wilt are two crippling diseases affecting solanaceous crops, and a long rotation between members of this group is desirable to effect control. Anthracnose and halo blight, which affect dwarf beans, and various root rots that attack peas and beans, are also controlled to some degree by rotation.

It is useless to try to work out a rotation with the specific aim of controlling eelworms or nematodes of the root-knot species (*Meloidogyne* spp.) on vegetable crops, for all are hosts to one or more species or strains of these microscopic pests.

The rotation suggested in the diagram is an extremely simple one. It can be modified to include crops that are more to the grower's taste, but care must be taken not to alter the position of the solanaceous and cruciferous groups, otherwise diseases may become a problem. Manure or compost can be incorporated before planting any crops, except the root crops, but when these materials are in short supply Group 1 should have first call on available supplies with Group 3 second.

INTERCROPPING

This practice, sometimes termed 'companion cropping', requires a very considerable knowledge and experience of vegetable growing to be successful. It is a system based on the different growth rates of crops. Radishes, lettuce, turnips, beets and other relatively fast-growing vegetables are planted between slower maturing crops, such as cauliflowers, sprouts and drum-head cabbages, or between widely-spaced crops such as pumpkins, in order to get the maximum quantity of produce from a limited area. Another form of intercropping is when early sowings of summer crops are established between maturing winter crops and vice versa. My main objection to the practice is that damaging pests and diseases are legion in our climate, making the spraying and dusting of crops a regular necessity. When two or more vegetable types are grown so intimately it is impossible to get satisfactory coverage of the one that requires spraying without also wetting the crops that are ready for harvest. If the catch crop is lettuce or Swiss chard, for example, it means that harvesting must be delayed for at least a week with most pesticides and the produce must be washed thoroughly afterwards.

Another demerit, in my experience, is that intercropping often complicates watering, for newly-sown seeds and seedlings need very regular watering until they are established, while maturing crops such as potatoes and onions need little, if any, in the final stages. Excessive watering here could cause serious disorders in potatoes and lower the storage qualities of both crops.

SUCCESSION AND CONTINUITY

Continuity should be the keyword in every home garden and 'successional' sowings is one way in which this can be achieved. With crops such as dwarf beans and peas, which can be picked over a period of only a few weeks, it is necessary to make small but regular sowings every 3 weeks or so to ensure a continuous supply of young pods. This is successional sowing. Lettuces, which shoot to flower and seed rapidly once the heads are firm, particularly during hot weather, are also subjects for this practice, as are radishes, which soon become 'woody' or pithy. Successional sowing entails much more work and planning than large, single sowings and plantings, but it is most rewarding.

Continuity can be achieved with certain crops from a single sowing. With lettuce and beetroots, for example, if they are carefully thinned, the removed thinnings can be used to plant out further rows, which, with the inevitable check from the move, will mature slightly later than the 'mother' rows. With cabbages, continuity can be achieved by simultaneously sowing two or three cultivars with different growing rates. Early Jersey Wakefield, Golden Acre, Copenhagen Market, Cape Spitzkool and Flat Dutch are all popular cultivars, which mature in that order. Care should be taken to plant the different cultivars alongside each other to facilitate any spraying or dusting.

I have also found it possible to obtain continuity from a single planting of a crop such as tomatoes by pushing some rows and retarding others through fertilization and other cultural operations. This usually results in lower yields over the plot as a whole, but it can be useful, especially when one is growing for show and exhibition.

4 TOOLS AND EQUIPMENT

The range of garden tools on the market today is bewildering, and each season sees new additions and gadgets. Some of these are simple, some are sophisticated, some are cheap, some are expensive, some are practical and some are designed for obscure functions.

Fortunately, in most vegetable gardening enterprises, only a small range of relatively simple tools is necessary. It is therefore a wise policy to buy a few basic tools of high quality to start with, and to add to the range as the need arises and the pocket permits.

Over the years there have from time to time been advocates of 'no digging', a current example being the manufacturers of certain organic soil-conditioners. Perhaps a 'no digging' system might be productive with certain crops in a vegetable garden that has a few small beds, and where regular and generous dressings of manure and other bulky organic additives are used. But in my experience there is no substitute in the average vegetable garden for the spade and the physical effort needed to use it properly. The only acceptable alternative, used in more tropical areas, is the plantation hoe.

The six basic tools in the vegetable garden are the spade, the fork, the Dutch hoe, the rake, the trowel and the dibber. To this can be added the garden line, which is hardly an expense. A wheelbarrow, a hand-fork, a miscellany of hoes, a watering-can, a hosepipe and pest control equipment, can be acquired as the project develops.

Most garden-tool manufacturers of repute base the design of their products on the results of extensive field trials conducted by practical people on soils which vary greatly in type and condition. The fact is, though, that few basic tools have changed at all in pattern over the years.

Spade. A spade is an absolutely indispensable tool, and expense should not be a consideration when this purchase is made. The blade is usually 300 mm long and 210 mm wide and (most important) should have a tread of at least 15 mm. A wide tread allows maximum weight and pressure to be used on the blade with little or no damage to the instep of the boot or shoe.

The spade should be used in as upright a position as possible to get optimum results. My training was of the formal kind and fol-lowed meticulously the practices of single spit digging, bastard trenching and deep trenching, accompanied by the addition of manure and compost. After some 40 years, however, I am convinced that on most soils in this country, provided that drainage is not a limiting factor, the top 200-250 mm of soil is all that needs attention. If this is properly dug, fertilized, enriched regularly with organic material and given a surface application of lime, as indicated by a soil test, maximum yields will be achieved.

The standard spade has a D-type handle that ensures a comfortable grip and maximum leverage. A smaller version, described as a ladies' spade, is smaller all round and has a T-shaped handle. It is useful for the intermediate turning over of light soils and small beds and for scoffling. It is necessary to keep spades clean and sharp, and the latter can be achieved by using a 250 mm or 300 mm flat file on the cutting edge from time to time.

Garden fork. The fork to select for general use is the digging fork, which has 4 tines, usually square in section. Because of its size it is used, like the digging spade, in preparatory work before the ground is sown or planted. It is used for removing weeds, roots and any foreign matter from the soil after it has been dug over, and for breaking up any clods in the same operation. It is also useful for the incorporation into the topsoil of materials such as fertilizer, compost, ma-nure and granular soil fumigants. For stacking or turning the compost heap or collecting material for loading on to the wheelbarrow the fork is, unquestionably, without peer.

The smaller fork with a T-shaped handle can be used for a similar range of functions on light soils and, in addition, it can be put to good use between growing crops if care is taken to work as shallowly as possible.

The potato fork has flat tines and is useful, as its name implies, for lifting potatoes and other roots. It is also extremely useful on heavy, clayey soils.

Hoes. Just as there are enthusiasts who advocate 'no digging' there are, remarkably enough, individuals who argue that weed growth is desirable. However, researchers and practical gardeners throughout the world acknowledge that weeds are detrimental to crop growth and should be destroyed regularly if worthwhile yields are to be obtained. There are several types of hoe which can be used for this purpose, the most effective being the Dutch hoe, the Paxton hoe or 'skoffel', and the push-pull hoe.

The Dutch hoe has a flat blade 125-175 mm wide, the cutting edge of which should be sharpened regularly. In experienced hands it is, on light to medium soils, the most suitable tool for inter-row cultivation. The Paxton hoe is a similar tool with a blade 175-225 mm wide and is usually of much heavier construction, which makes it

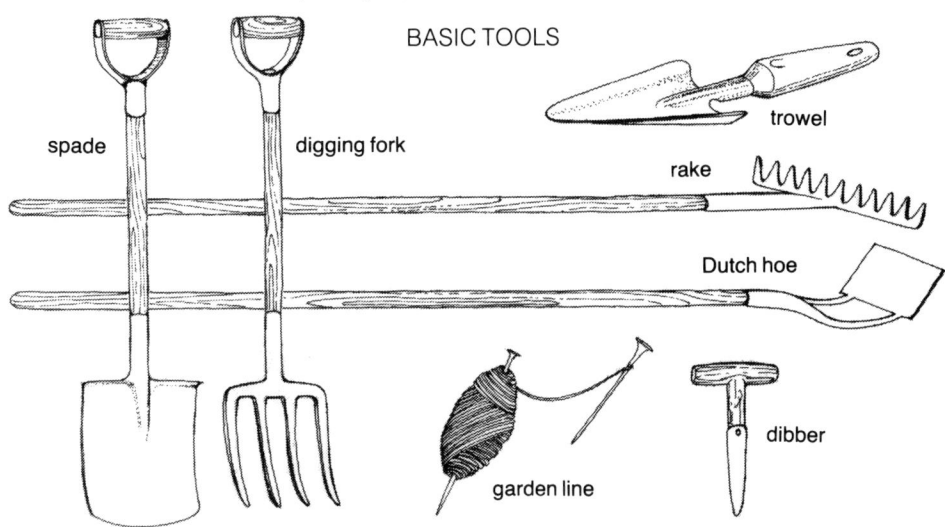

BASIC TOOLS

spade   digging fork   trowel   rake   Dutch hoe   garden line   dibber

The spade should be used in an upright position and should be pressed in with the ball of the foot, not the instep. During use, the blade should frequently be cleaned with a piece of wood.

particularly suitable for larger gardens and smallholdings and for heavier soils. Both these tools are used by scraping the soil surface with a forward jabbing action or by pushing them shallowly into the soil, thereby severing the weeds just below the surface. They are best used on the retreat (i.e. by walking backwards) to prevent unnecessary compaction of the soil. Working on the retreat also prevents weeds that have been severed from being 'heeled in' again, which would allow them to root adventitiously.

The African hoe is a smaller version of the plantation hoe, mentioned previously. Several sizes are available, the lighter ones (1,0-1,5 kg) being most suitable for the home garden. The blade is roughly at right-angles to the handle, and the tool is used with a chopping action. Inter-row cultivation, ridging and earthing-up are but some of its many uses.

The draw hoe and swan-neck hoe are very similar in design. Both are smaller and lighter versions of the African hoe (except that the blade is narrower) and they perform a similar range of functions but on lighter soils. In addition they can be used in conjunction with the garden line to make drills for sowing seeds or transplanting.

The push-pull hoe is similar to the Dutch hoe except that both edges of the blade are sharp and are usually wavy in profile instead of straight.

The Canterbury hoe or vine hoe has three broad prongs at right angles to the handle and is useful for working over ground that is hard and compact or stony. When reversed (i.e. with prongs upwards) the ring on the head can be used as a hammer to break up clods. The African hoe can perform the same function. In heavy ground the use of the Canterbury hoe requires considerable physical effort.

The tined cultivator is, strictly speaking, not a hoe but is used in a similar fashion for a similar purpose. This cultivator usually has 3 or 5 tines, and on lighter soils it can be an effective tool. It is, however, inclined to cultivate too deeply, particularly in inexperienced hands, which is most undesirable where the rows are closely spaced.

Rake. A rake, made of high-quality steel for durability, finds ample employment in the vegetable garden. I favour the kind that is pressed from a single piece of metal. A 12-tooth one is adequate for the average garden, although larger ones, having 14 or 16 teeth, are usually also available. The type with individual teeth riveted or welded on are too light for most soils.

The rake is used to finalize the preparation of the ground prior to sowing or planting. The way it moves through the soil gives an indication to the experienced gardener of the condition of the soil for these two operations. It can also be used, teeth upwards, to close off drills after sowing, and, with the handle in a vertical position and the head downwards, to tamp the ground lightly over the seeds.

Trowel and dibber. The principal uses of these two items, the latter unkown to many gardeners, is to set out transplants and to plant crops such as potatoes and Jerusalem artichokes.

With so many seedlings being raised in individual mini-containers such as Jiffy 7s and soil cubes, or in sectionalized seed-trays, the trowel is required to set them out in open ground.

The dibber is used for bare-root transplanting, and a range of different sizes can easily be made from spade, rake and broom handles. A commercially manufactured one with a steel point is available.

Garden line. This is simply a length of stout mason's line, thin rope or nylon fishing line tied to a sharpened stick at each end. It is pulled tightly along the ground between the two sticks and serves as a guide for making drills. When not in use it should be kept clean and dry with the line wrapped around the two sticks.

Cleanliness is an important factor in the life expectancy of garden tools. A sharpened piece of wood is the ideal instrument for removing soil from spades and forks. If the tools are not to be used for a few days, they should be allowed to dry properly and then rubbed with an oily rag.

ADDITIONAL TOOLS

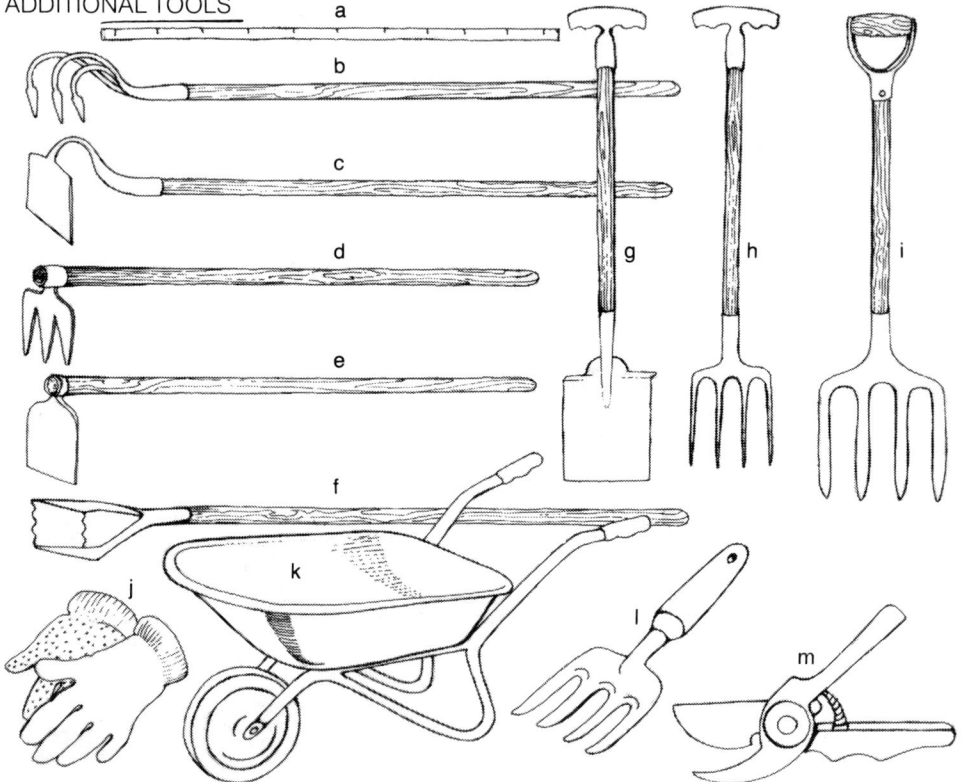

(a) Measuring stick. (b) Tined cultivator. (c) Swan-neck hoe. (d) Canterbury hoe. (e) African hoe. (f) Push-pull hoe. (g) Ladies' spade. (h) Ladies' fork. (i) Potato fork. (j) Gardening gloves. (k) Wheelbarrow. (l) Hand-fork. (m) Secateurs.

5 WATERING, CULTIVATING AND WEED CONTROL

WATERING

Most cultivated plants consist, by weight, of about 90% water. Vegetables are no exception, and it is necessary during dry periods to supply water in order to maintain plant vigour and health. Established crops will survive for several weeks without water, but with young seedlings even a few days can be disastrous. An adequate supply of water enables plants to make rapid growth, and a shortage can check growth and have serious consequences for certain crops. A check induces peas, tomatoes and other fruiting crops to flower and set fruit before sufficient vegetative growth has been made, and consequently yields are low. Leaf crops, such as lettuce and endive, become tough and bitter and tend to flower prematurely when subjected to similar conditions.

Plants lose great quantities of water by transpiration, particularly plants with large leaf surfaces such as pumpkins and squashes, which are often the first to wilt in hot weather. If the root system cannot replace the moisture as fast as the leaves are losing it the plant tissues lose their turgidity and the plant wilts. Wilting usually occurs during the middle of the day and by evening the plants have recovered temporarily. Prolonged wet spells cause plants to become soft and flabby, with the result that when there are a few days of sunshine they soon show signs of wilting although the soil may still be quite moist. This soft growth is also susceptible to fungal diseases, for example late blight of potatoes and tomatoes and powdery mildew of marrows and cucumbers.

On the whole, vegetable crops are a little more drought-resistant than the average home gardener imagines, and overwatering is just as common as underwatering. A few seasons ago I set out a few beds of tomatoes in April and, owing to a breakdown, discontinued watering a month later. Yet in September the plants were still alive although no rain had fallen. Admittedly they were dwarfed and hard, and had set only a few tiny fruits, but at least they had survived, despite being without water for 16 weeks.

How much water?

The average gardener waters too frequently and too lightly. While daily watering may be necessary for young seedlings and also for a short period after transplanting, it is totally unnecessary and undesirable on established crops even during hot weather. It is of course impossible to set down hard and fast rules for watering as there are a number of influencing factors, which include the following: the nature of the topsoil and subsoil, the prevailing weather conditions, the type of vegetable, the degree of maturity of the crop, and whether or not a mulch is being used.

Crops require much more water in hot weather, for in such conditions the rate of moisture loss from the plants by transpiration and from the soil by evaporation is high. Winds also have a considerable drying effect on the soil and on plants.

Vegetable crops vary greatly in their water requirements. Cabbage, spinach and lettuce are particularly thirsty, and because quick growth is essential if sweet, succulent produce is to be harvested, water should always be plentiful. Root and tuber crops do not require quite so much water, but it is essential to maintain a constant level of moisture in the soil, particularly when the crops approach maturity. Carrots and beets frequently have a pale internal colour when soil temperatures are high.

The stage of maturity of a crop must also be taken into account, for erratic watering can cause the appearance and quality of certain crops to deteriorate quickly, especially in the cooler months. The splitting of cabbages can be reduced considerably if watering is gradually decreased once the heads are firm. The splitting of carrots can also be reduced if they are treated in the same way when they approach market size. The cracking of tomatoes and 'hollow heart' and 'second growth' of potato tubers are all common disorders that can be directly attributed to excessive or irregular watering at critical stages of growth.

It is up to the individual gardener to learn by experience how much water to give his crops. As a guide, 25 mm of water every 4-8 days should be sufficient to maintain plants in healthy growth during hot periods, although on extremely sandy soils with good drainage up to double this amount may be necessary. On light soils 25 mm of water may penetrate 200-250 mm but on heavy soils and on soils containing much undecomposed organic material it may penetrate only 75-100 mm. On heavy soils it is therefore advisable to give heavier waterings at greater intervals.

The light watering of a garden every day is a dangerous practice that encourages plants to develop surface root systems. The tender feeding roots are easily damaged or destroyed by drying out and are also liable to be severed by cultivating tools. This once again emphasizes the great value of a good organic mulch whereby soil moisture is conserved, soil temperature is reduced and weed growth is suppressed, making cultivation unnecessary.

Methods of applying water

Nowadays the gardener has a choice of many different methods of applying water, some simple, some sophisticated, some cheap, some relatively expensive. Soil type, garden layout and aspect, type of crop, stage of growth, and whether or not a mulch is used, are all factors to be taken into consideration when deciding upon a watering system or combination of systems.

Soil type. As discussed in Chapter 2, soils vary greatly in their moisture-holding capacity. Clayey soils and those with a high organic content hold large quantities of moisture for long periods. Topsoils overly-

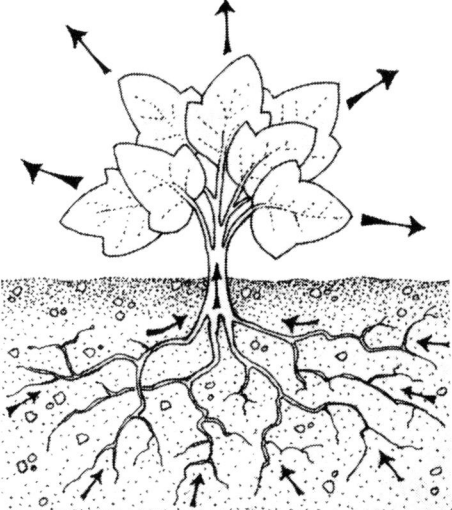

Moisture loss by transpiration.

ing subsoils that are similar in nature exhibit similar characteristics to a degree.

Garden layout and aspect. During the hot summer months, in particular, high raised beds will require much more water than low beds or beds constructed on the flat or slightly below path level. Gardens laid out on a north-facing slope will require more water than those with the opposite aspect, but offer some compensation in that they warm up earlier in spring, can be planted earlier, and will produce mature vegetables a week or two earlier.

Stage of growth. All seedlings and young transplants are very dependent on a frequent and adequate water supply, which must ideally be distributed in as fine a spray as possible to avoid mechanical damage to the plants. A heavy spray also affects the soil surface, particularly on soils that tend to crust easily. Crusting prevents water penetration and makes the emergence of seed-

lings somewhat difficult, resulting in patchy stands.

Watering-can, hosepipe and sprinkler

The watering-can, the hosepipe (with or without spray attachments) and the standing sprinkler (either rotating or stationary) have long been the common media for applying water and are all satisfactory if properly handled.

The watering-can is still a reliable method of distributing water in the smaller garden, but the physical effort it entails has brought it into disfavour in recent years. With a fine rose on the spout, and I have the oval Haws pattern in mind, it can be used for the very smallest seedlings such as parsley and celery in seedboxes or seedbeds. Without a rose it can be used for watering-in transplants. It is particularly useful, as well as economical, for spot watering widely-spaced plants such as tomatoes, egg plants and cauliflowers, as it allows adequate

quantities to be given to the growing crop and allows none for the inter-row weeds! In addition, liquid-manure stimulants can be mixed in and distributed by a watering-can most economically. Before liquid manure is applied, however, the soil should be thoroughly wetted to ensure a uniform distribution of the material throughout the root area.

A hose can be used with a spray nozzle, or by putting the index finger over the delivery end to create a coarse spray, or by laying it on the soil surface and allowing the water to flood among the plants. I prefer the last method once the plants are established, provided that water is plentiful and the ground fairly level, and I usually place the end of the hose in a tin can, lying on its side on a tuft of grass, to reduce the force of the water.

If the rows are very long and the slope appreciable, better penetration will be obtained if temporary barriers are put up at intervals to halt the flow a little and increase penetration. These can be made with a

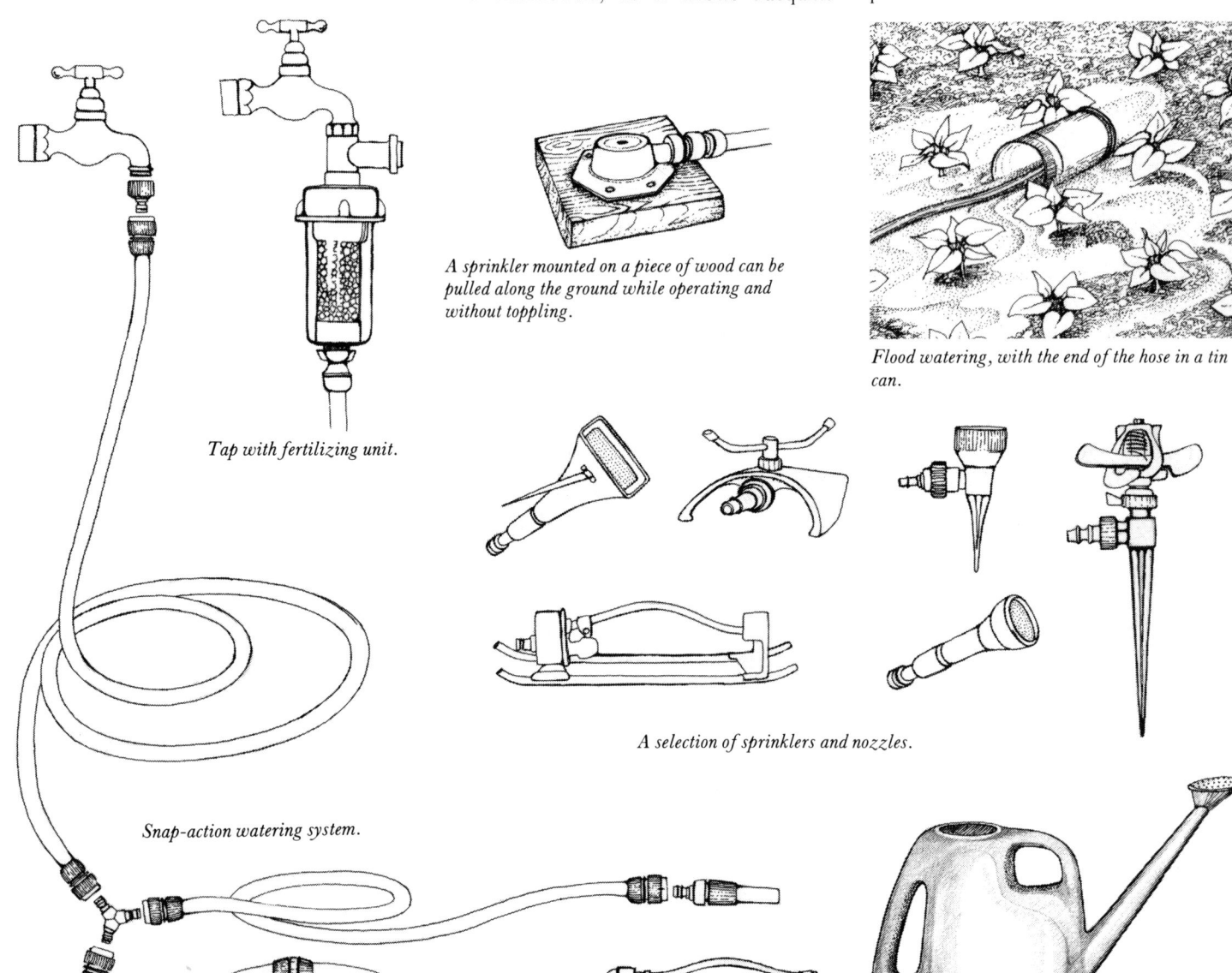

A sprinkler mounted on a piece of wood can be pulled along the ground while operating and without toppling.

Flood watering, with the end of the hose in a tin can.

Tap with fertilizing unit.

A selection of sprinklers and nozzles.

Snap-action watering system.

Watering-can with Haws-type rose.

spadeful or two of soil, but an empty grain bag is just as effective once it is saturated. By using a hose in this way the water requirements of the plants are met without the foliage being repeatedly wetted.

A recent addition to the garden range, and one that is· used in conjunction with the garden hose, is a fertilizing unit that screws directly on to the hose tap. It consists of a round glass bottle with a screw top in which fertilizer cartridges of varying formulae are placed. As the water flows through the unit the cartridges slowly dissolve, thereby distributing the fertilizer throughout the garden in much the same way as the regular mix-nozzle. This method of fertilizing can be used with spray nozzles and sprinklers of all types.

The main drawback of sprinkling continually is that under certain climatic conditions it can assist in the establishment and spread of diseases such as late blight of potatoes and tomatoes and black rot of cabbages and related crops by creating a high

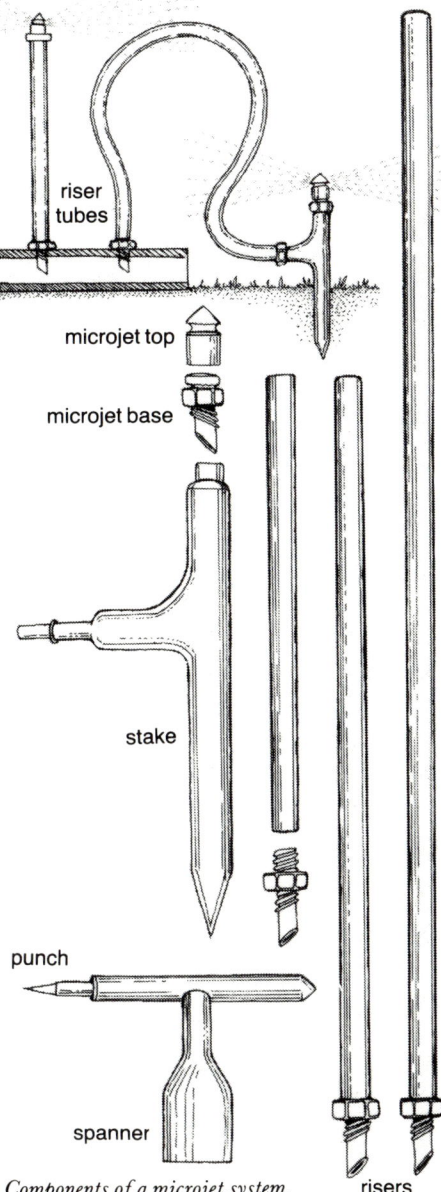

Components of a microjet system.

relative humidity among the plants. With the last-named disease 'splash' is also a contributory factor in its establishment, particularly on land that has carried affected crops in previous seasons. With a sprinkler system it is also extremely difficult to maintain effective deposits of fungicides or pesticides on the plant surfaces unless the spraying programme is co-ordinated with the watering operation.

My observations indicate that the activities of aphids and red spider may be slightly reduced when sprinkling is used, for they prefer dry foliage.

Microjet systems

Microjet irrigation systems have been used for some years in several overseas countries and they are now gaining favour in South Africa. These systems are particularly suited to the average home garden as they use water resources economically, are extremely flexible, are easy to install, and are relatively inexpensive. The systems consist of lengths of black plastic piping laid underground, in a pattern to suit the garden, to which are fixed a number of riser pipes and micro-nozzles as required. The latter are available in spray patterns ranging from 40° to 360° to suit each gardener's requirements. Basic kits are available in several sizes and these can be added to or modified as the need arises. These systems can be used in conjunction with timing devices, filters and foliar fertilizers and are worthy of consideration, especially since they allow one to get on with other garden chores!

When to water

The watering of established crops is best carried out in the late afternoon, when the plants will obtain maximum benefit from the quantities supplied. With seedbeds and seedlings it is better to water earlier in the day to enable the soil surface to dry out a little by evening. This considerably reduces the chances of damage by damping-off fungi, while a dry surface also slows down the movements of slugs and snails. If sprinkling is the only possible method of watering mature crops of tomatoes and potatoes, it should be done earlier in the day so that the foliage will dry off by evening, thus reducing the chances of disease establishment.

Watering with waste water

During periods of drought and water shortage, some gardeners use waste water from the house to supplement their meagre allocation. Most vegetables do not take kindly to this, preferring a slightly to moderately acid soil. Waste water can easily upset the soil reaction and can also disturb the microbiological soil population. It is best used sparingly on lawns and shrubs, alternating with irrigations of clean water if possible.

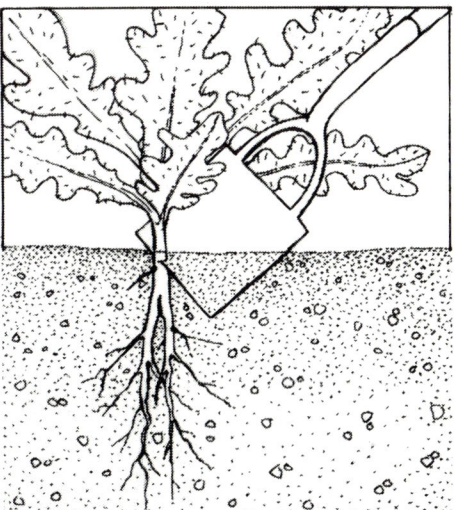

The correct use of the Dutch hoe: weeds should be severed just below the surface.

CULTIVATION AND WEED CONTROL

Although in its wider sense the word 'cultivation' covers all gardening and farming operations, the term is usually reserved for the tillage of the soil after the seeds have been sown or the transplants set out. The four main reasons put forward in support of cultivation are: weed control; increased infiltration of rain or irrigation water; improved soil aeration; and reduced evaporation. Weed control is by far the most important, and only in exceptional circumstances is cultivation for the others justified.

To define the term 'weed' is difficult, for a plant that is regarded as a weed in one part of the world may be treated as a cultivated crop in another. Examples of this are purslane and water grass. 'Volunteer' plants of tomatoes, pumpkins, sweet potatoes and potatoes, which spring up from fallen fruits or from small pieces of root or tuber left in the soil, must be regarded as weeds in any subsequent crop and treated accordingly. Their removal is more important in one respect than the removal of acknowledged weeds, for these 'volunteers' can defeat the objects of crop rotation, especially by carrying over diseases and pests. When speaking of weeds we usually refer to the wide variety of plants, both annual and perennial, that appear in profusion on most garden soils and compete seriously, and usually most successfully, with crop plants for moisture, plant food, light and air.

If moisture supplies are limited, a common occurrence nowadays, weeds will draw their requirements to the detriment of the crop plants. Together with the moisture, the weeds take up plant foods in considerable quantities, including nutrients that have been added in one form or another during soil preparation. Consequently, if weeds are allowed to grow to any size before they are removed, the crop will show little response to fertilizers or manures.

Within the microjet diagram labels: riser tubes, microjet top, microjet base, stake, punch, spanner, risers

SOME COMMON WEEDS
(see photographs on pages 77-80)

Amaranthus spp. (pigweed)
Several species of this genus are regarded as weeds, while others are cultivated as garden plants. *A. spinosus* and *A. deflexus* are perhaps the most common weeds, and mature plants are best removed by hand. However, unless gloves are worn this can be a very painful experience with the former species because of the spines in the leaf axils. Throughout the continent, African people relish the young leaves of many species, and recent research in the U.S.A. has revealed that the young foliage and the seeds of several species are highly nutritious.

Bidens pilosa (blackjack)
This common nuisance is a relatively tall annual of branching habit with small flowers that have white ray-florets. The foliage resembles that of the African marigold, as do the seeds. The latter have barbs, which adhere tenaciously to clothing and to the coats of animals, a characteristic that accounts for its widespread distribution.

Capsella bursapastoris (shepherd's purse)
An annual weed of cultivated land, bearing very characteristic seed-cases. It seeds readily, and must be removed by hand or hoe before seeding takes places.

Cynodon dactylon (couch grass)
This hardy grass, often used for turfing recreational areas because it can take a lot of traffic and withstand drought, is a difficult customer once it becomes established in cultivated beds. I have often seen potato tubers penetrated by its strong shoots.

Cyperus esculentus (water grass)
This plant, also known as 'uintjies', is one of the worst weeds of garden soils, particularly if they are poorly drained. It is a sedge with small bulbs that can remain dormant in unfavourable conditions for an extended period and still be viable. Water grass is best controlled by removing all parts of the plant from the soil at every opportunity.

Cyperus rotundus (nut grass)
A close relative of *C. esculentus*, but not as difficult to control.

Datura stramonium (stinkblaar or thorn apple)
This plant is perhaps more of a nuisance on the farm than in the home garden. It is of soft upright growth, attaining a height of 1,5 m, and can easily be identified by the disagreeable smell it gives off when bruised or severed.

Galinsoga parviflora (quickweed)
A very common annual weed 150-450 mm in height. Its tissues are soft and its growth weak and leggy. It is not difficult to control if it is removed by hand or hoe before seeding takes place.

Nicandra physaloides (apple of Peru)
A quick-growing but soft annual weed of upright habit with pronounced ribbing of the stalk, which becomes hollow when the plant reaches a height of 1,5-2,0 m, as it does under favourable conditions. Its specific name was probably chosen because the fruits resemble those of the Cape gooseberry (*Physalis edulis*). In recent years this plant has received considerable publicity in the United Kingdom as a pot plant with the property of repelling house-flies, and is catalogued as the Shoo-Shoo Plant!

Oxalis spp. (sorrel)
Two species of this weed are commonly encountered, the yellow sorrel (*Oxalis pes-caprae*) being the bigger problem. It is a particular nuisance when it becomes established in the soil of pot plants, the bulbs often being quite deep and thus extremely difficult to remove without doing damage to the pot plant.
O. semiloba is a much taller, softer plant. Both species are best dealt with by persistent cultivation and hand-pulling, while those in pots are best removed when the plants are being divided or repotted.

Portulaca oleracea (purslane)
This is a fleshy, reddish weed with a prostrate habit in most situations. Its long taproot makes it one of the worst of all garden weeds to remove. It is an annual, rising from the tiny black seeds distributed from the fruit capsules. Its flowers are relatively insignificant and it reaches the seeding stage very quickly. The seeds are produced in large quantities, making the regular removal of the plants a necessity. Improved strains of this plant are catalogued by seedsmen in Europe, where it is classified as a potherb.

Sonchus oleraceus (sow thistle)
An annual weed 1,0-2,0 m high, with a soft upright habit. The leaves are covered in 'bloom' and the flowers are yellow. All parts of the plant exude a milky latex when the tissues are broken. It is easily pulled by hand when the soil is moist.

Stellaria media (chickweed)
A common weed 100-150 mm high with soft pale-green growth and producing insignificant white flowers. It is easily removed by hand or hoe.

Certain weeds produce a large canopy of leaves while others have a spreading, prostrate habit. The former, if allowed to grow, modify the micro-climate between the plants to such a degree that they will assist in the establishment of fungal diseases. In addition, many weeds are hosts for diseases, insects and nematodes. Certain viral diseases are able to live over on weeds and are transmitted to young crops through the agency of insects. The role of weeds as suitable hosts for nematodes is dealt with fully in Chapter 8.

Weed control measures must begin as soon as possible after vegetables have been sown or planted. They can even be started earlier than this by preparing the soil a week or two before the crop is established in order to allow annual weeds to germinate and be destroyed by a shallow going-over with a Dutch or Paxton hoe. Ground that is infested with couch grass or water grass should be forked over once or twice before planting or sowing, as any serious attempt to remove them later will inevitably disturb and check, or even destroy, the crop plants. This is a particularly worthwhile practice if carried out during hot, dry weather.

When to cultivate

The time to cultivate is governed by two factors: the amount of weed growth and the condition of the soil.

Weeds should be destroyed as soon as the seedling rows can be seen in directly-sown crops, and as soon as the transplants have become established in other cases. With crops such as carrots and onions, which get off to a a slow start, it is good practice first to weed by hand for 40-50 mm on either side of the rows so that the seedlings can easily be seen, and then to follow this up with the Dutch hoe between the rows.

Weeds should *never* be allowed to seed before they are removed, otherwise your work will be increased a hundredfold the following season. Many weeds have inconspicuous flowers and produce viable seeds in a short time, purslane being one of the main offenders. If weeds are allowed to get too big before they are removed by hand, their removal may damage the feeder roots of the crop plants. Unseeded annual weeds need not be removed from the plot after they have been severed by the hoe or pulled by hand. They can simply be shaken free of soil and dropped on to the ground between the rows. However, this is not good practice with water grass, couch grass or rapoko grass, all of which are extremely hardy and begin to grow again once the plants are watered.

With potatoes and sweet potatoes, which are grown on the ridge, all cultivating with tools for weed control should cease when the tubers or roots begin to swell, or damage may result. It is sometimes necessary, when these crops approach maturity, to bring up a little soil to close off soil cracks and thus prevent damage from the potato tuber moth and the sweet potato weevil, which lay eggs on the tubers and roots. This operation will also prevent 'greening' of the tubers and roots, which lowers their quality considerably. Among cucurbits, too, cultivation should cease when the vines begin to spread, otherwise damage to the vines themselves and to the newly set fruits may result.

Soil, especially clayey soil, should never be cultivated when it is wet, or the tilth may be damaged permanently. If there is a prolonged wet period, remove only prominent weeds by hand, and await drier conditions before using a hoe. It is also unwise to work among plants when they are wet, for several diseases affecting potatoes, tomatoes, cucurbits and beans are easily spread in this way.

How deep to cultivate

The first cultivation can be deep to loosen the soil that has become compacted by the sowing or planting operations, but all subsequent cultivations should be shallow to avoid disturbing and damaging the roots of the crops. A too frequent cultivation of the soil in the irrigation season also increases evaporation, and in hot weather it helps to burn up valuable organic matter in the top 100 mm of soil. In addition, each deep cultivation brings to the surface another batch of weed seeds, which germinate and necessitate further cultivation.

In a previous chapter we discussed the benefits of mulching. The suppression and weakening of weed growth is certainly one of the most outstanding of these benefits.

Chemical weed control

In recent years certain oils, chemical weed-killers and herbicides have been marketed, of which 2-4D has probably received the most publicity. Some are selective, while others destroy all vegetation. 'Selective' is, however, an extremely relative term, and the stage of growth of the crop is critical, as plants that are too small or too advanced may get severely damaged. The materials 2-4D and MCPA, specifically formulated for use on lawns, are dangerous to all broad-leaved plants, including most vegetables of commerce. For this reason they should never be used on windy days in case the spray drifts on to nearby flower borders, vegetables or shrubs.

Sodium chlorate and sodium trichloracetate (TCA) are materials used for controlling weeds and grass on paths, driveways, tennis courts and other places where growth is undesirable. They not only kill standing weeds but partially sterilize the soil and suppress plant growth for several months.

Again care should be taken when applying these materials.

Certain soil fumigants, such as DD and EDB, may destroy a small percentage of weed seeds in addition to nematodes. However, they are not specific for the purpose, are all comparatively expensive, and require heavy rates of application to achieve any degree of weed control.

A great deal of research is constantly being carried out to discover economic and effective materials for use in controlling weeds among vegetables and other crops. Numerous products have already been registered for use on vegetables, but several factors unfortunately make them prohibitive for the home gardener. Most can only be used on specific crops at particular stages of growth and in some cases in certain regions. Soil type, condition and temperature, and prevailing weather conditions, must also be considered. In addition, these materials are only available in relatively large and expensive packs. As yet there is therefore no alternative for the home grower to hand-pulling, hoeing and good cultural practices.

Many troublesome weeds are introduced to the garden in topsoil and certain manures, and the origin of topsoil, in particular, should be ascertained before it is purchased. Weed seeds can also be imported in soil adhering to transplants obtained from outside sources. The laws relating to the production, certification and selling of seed have fortunately been tightened considerably in recent years and there is now very little chance of importing weed seeds when purchasing seed either in packets or in bulk.

6 SEED, SOWING AND TRANSPLANTING

Most vegetables are propagated from seed, and because few nurserymen specialize in raising the wide variety of subjects that can be grown in the home garden, it is usually necessary for the gardener to produce his own plants. In any event, raising one's own transplants provides great satisfaction and enables one to use any of the numerous cultivars and hybrids that are now readily available. Many vegetables, too, do not transplant well, particularly root crops such as carrots, turnips, radishes and parsnips, and must be sown *in situ* for optimum results. Legumes such as peas and beans require similar treatment, as do sweetcorn, cucumbers, squashes and pumpkins, although the last group can be sown early in containers for setting out later.

The 'coming to life' of seed from the dormant stage is known as germination, although this term is more generally used to describe the appearance of the young plants above the soil. Viable seeds are those that have the ability to commence growth when suitable conditions are provided. Seeds possessing vitality are those that not only germinate but continue to grow with considerable vigour.

GERMINATION

In order to germinate satisfactorily, seed must have air, warmth and moisture. When seed is sown at the correct depth in soil of average texture and tilth, it can easily obtain its oxygen requirements from the soil air. However, if it is sown too deeply, particularly in wet, heavy soils, it may not be able to obtain adequate supplies and will fail to germinate and simply rot.

Moisture is probably the most important of the three factors influencing satisfactory seed germination because it can also influence the soil temperature to a marked degree. The seed of warm-season crops such as squashes, pumpkins and cucumbers, sown in late July and August in anticipation of warmer weather, frequently rots and produces uneven and uneconomic stands because the soil is too cold and wet. Excess water in a seedbed or seedbox also encourages injurious soil fungi to attack the seed before, or shortly after, it has germinated. Old seed should be given water more spar-

ingly than fresh seed, for although it may germinate it does not possess the vitality of the latter and is much more susceptible to harmful soil organisms. Again, in my experience, old seed is best used when weather conditions are most favourable, and should be sown slightly shallower than usual to avoid soil problems.

Most vegetable seed germinates satisfactorily within the temperature range 16-24°C, and by careful use of shade, moisture and temporary mulches it is often possible to keep the top 75 mm of soil around this optimum range for several months of the year. Winter crops, especially brassicas, will germinate satisfactorily at temperatures below this ideal range, while tomatoes, egg plants, peppers and a few other summer crops will tolerate slightly higher temperatures.

The age and degree of maturity of seed also affect the germination percentage. The age of seed is particularly important but it is impossible to formulate an accurate table of seed longevity because there are other influencing factors, such as the degree of maturity at harvest and the conditions under which the seed is packeted and stored. High relative humidity is the principal enemy of seed in storage (the fact that so much seed is now packed in plastic and foil packets and

in hermetically sealed tins is adequate testimony of this). Nevertheless it can broadly be said that most cruciferous, solanaceous and cucurbitaceous vegetable seed should remain viable for 2-4 years (tomato seed being amongst the longest-lived), but parsnips, onions, carrots and leeks may remain good for only 1-2 years (the first-named being the shortest-lived).

If there is any doubt at all about the viability of the seed left over from the previous season, it is advisable to carry out a small-scale germination test indoors a month or so before the crop is sown. Using the 'rag doll' method, about 20 seeds (or half this number of beans and cucurbits) are rolled up in a piece of surgical lint or similar absorbent material and kept moist in a warm place. They can be carefully examined from the third or fourth day onwards and the approximate germination percentage can be established from the number of seeds that germinate quickly and uniformly. Any that are appreciably slower to germinate than the majority should not be included in the count as it is unlikely that these stragglers would have made the grade in the more demanding conditions of the vegetable garden.

Seed testing, as described, may appear to be a rather laborious and time-consuming exercise, but it is wise to carry it out with old

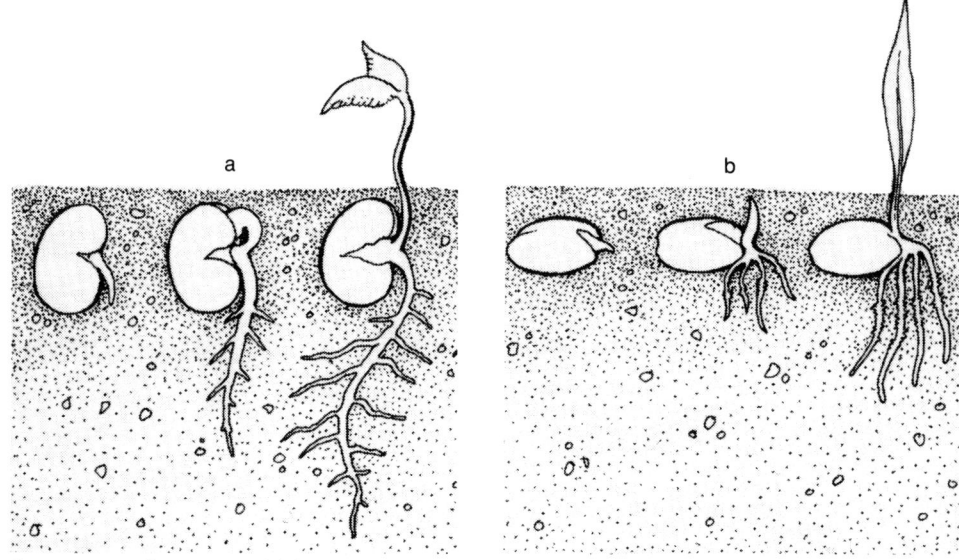

Germination and emergence of (a) a dicotyledon and (b) a monocotyledon.

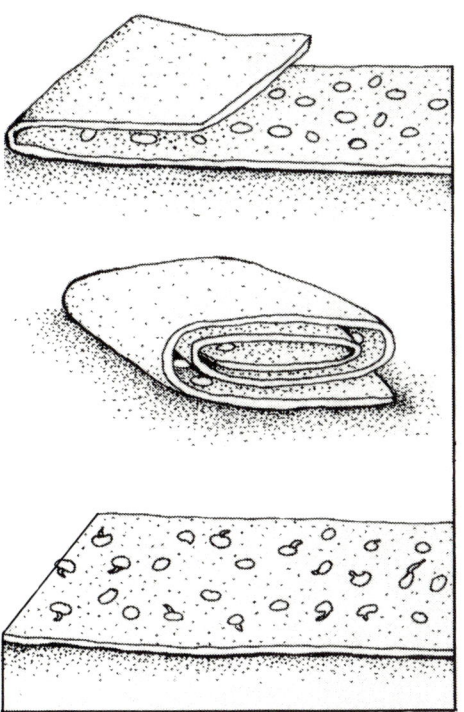

Germination test using the 'rag doll' method.

seed. There is nothing more exasperating than waiting for 2 or 3 weeks for seed to germinate and then finally, when it is obvious that the seed has failed, to have to purchase new supplies and resow. Such a break can also upset the continuity of supplies to the table. In addition, certain crops can only be sown over a relatively short period because of their exacting climatic requirements (for example onions, cauliflowers, Brussels sprouts and sweet melons) and it is essential to have seed of good germinating power otherwise reduced yields or total crop failure may result from a delay. A very thin stand, especially of directly-sown subjects, should be abandoned and the area dug over and re-sown, for it will require the same amount of labour and water as a successful planting.

The seed of certain vegetables, including peas, onions and sweetcorn, has the ability to stop growth and regerminate several times under fluctuating soil moisture conditions. However, this regermination requires much energy and, as the reserves in the seed are small and rapidly depleted, the resultant seedlings are usually very weak.

KEEPING SEED

The production of good vegetable seed of good viability and vitality is a highly specialized job and it is unwise for the gardener to collect and save his own seed if the same cultivars are easily available from seedsmen. An allowable exception to this rule, perhaps, is when the vegetable is of an uncommon or rare kind that is not usually catalogued. Even then, however, seed should only be kept from 'clean' plants and

should be selected for size, fullness and freedom from blemishes.

It is useless to keep the seed from lettuces that shoot to flower during hot, dry weather, or from odd specimens of beetroot, cabbage, celery or Swiss chard that run to seed prematurely. Plants produced from such seed will invariably show these same undesirable characteristics and result in unsatisfactory yields.

In addition, certain serious diseases of tomatoes, cabbages and peas are seed-borne and may, quite unknowingly, be carried over from one season to another. In the second season they will be far more damaging as they get at the plants at an earlier stage of development. The 'black rot' disease of brassicas comes immediately to mind in this context.

A final point to remember is that plants kept for seed very often occupy the ground for a long period, during the latter half of which, with their declining vigour, they receive the unwelcome attentions of pests, diseases and nematodes. In this way they act as between-season hosts to these organisms and are a hazard to young plants.

BUYING SEED

The planning of a sowing and planting schedule should be completed some weeks before the season so that seed of the required cultivars can be obtained in good time. In most large centres there are garden shops that specialize in seed, plants and other garden sundries, and they usually ensure, as do their suppliers, that the seed they sell is fresh and of good quality. Most supermarkets and chain stores, too, have garden departments from which fresh supplies can be obtained. In smaller centres, seed occasionally gets carried over from one season to another. If local supplies are unreliable, it is sensible to order one's requirements from a seed catalogue. Many such catalogues are extremely comprehensive and contain much valuable gardening information.

Most suppliers nowadays offer seed in foil packets, on which is endorsed the date of packing and the date of expiry. Their representatives service the seed stands regularly and replace all expired packets.

It is advisable to purchase certified seed when this is available, for the plants from which the seed was taken were inspected regularly during growth by trained technical personnel and found to be true to type and free from serious diseases. Such seed is usually a little more expensive but the few extra cents are well spent.

It is an offence to import vegetable seed into South Africa without a permit. Anyone wishing to import seed can obtain an application form from:

Division of Plant and Seed Control
Private Bag X179
Pretoria 0001

This procedure is a very necessary precaution to prevent the introduction of certain diseases into this country. Unfortunately there are irresponsible individuals who knowingly contravene these regulations when returning from overseas. Although this is usually in a very small way it could jeopardize crops of economic importance.

Gardeners need never resort to these measures, as high-yielding disease-free cultivars are bred in South Africa. Already some extremely valuable introductions are freely available through the agency of the leading seed merchants. It must be remembered that a new cultivar is not bred overnight – it is the result of the selection and re-selection of several generations of progeny and is only released to the trade after consistently satisfactory performances in a series of trials spread over several seasons.

CULTIVARS

The term 'cultivar' is a contraction of 'cultivated variety'. A cultivar is the sub-division of a species that has acquired, in cultivation, certain characteristics that distinguish it from other forms of the species.

The growing of unsuitable cultivars is a common cause of disappointing yields, particularly with vegetables such as bulbing onions, which respond to exacting photoperiods. Cabbages, too, are of many types, some quick-maturing, some slow-maturing, some cone-shaped, some ball-headed and so on. The cultivars recommended in Part 2 of this book are, in the main, vegetables that have performed satisfactorily on a wide variety of soils over several seasons, though here and there I have included some recent introductions and some of the newer hybrids. They are also cultivars whose size and planting distances are well fitted to the average home garden.

HYBRID SEED

In recent years plant breeders in all parts of the world have produced quantities of hybrid vegetable seed, particularly of tomatoes, cucumbers, Chinese cabbage, squashes and Brussels sprouts. Many of these are now as familiar to us as the older cultivars.

Hybrid seed is produced by cross-pollinating two true-breeding species or cultivars of vegetables or flowers. The breeders have definite objects in view when carrying out this work, including better form or colour, increased disease or nematode resistance, improved quality and yields, earlier maturity, and greater uniformity. The breeding of hybrids for purposes such as canning and for particular climatic conditions is also receiving attention. One possible drawback for the home gardener is that hybrids tend to mature too uniformly, resulting in a glut. But this characteristic can be used to advantage with vegetables that can be frozen.

Hybridization is only possible between plants having a relatively close relationship with one another. The majority of crosses are between cultivars of the same species, while species-hybrids (i.e. crosses between different species of the same genus) are also numerous. With tomatoes, for example, the hybrid seed is produced by emasculating the seed-bearing parent, i.e. removing the stamens and pollinating the pistil with pollen collected from the other selected parent. The first generation from such crosses is known as the first filial or F1 generation, and provided that the same pure parent stocks are used, the progeny should be uniform in every way. Seed catalogues always clearly identify F1 hybrids.

Hybrid seed is relatively expensive, because in most cases the emasculation and pollination are carried out by hand. Apart from the desirable characteristics that are bred into hybrids, the technique also usually imparts a new vigour to the plants that arise from the cross. With a crop such as sweet-corn, however, where both male and female flowers are produced separately on the same plant, much easier methods of hybridization can be employed.

Seed should never be saved from hybrid plants, for in the second generation the various characteristics of the parents segregate out among the individual plants and there is no uniformity. Hence the F2 generation will not possess all the desirable characteristics that were present in the F1 generation, and it is therefore necessary to produce fresh F1 seeds every season.

SEED TREATMENT

Seed disinfecting is quite a difficult job for the home gardener because it entails soaking the seed in solutions of poisonous chemicals such as bichloride of mercury, or hot water treatment, which demands carefully controlled conditions. The seeds of different vegetables react differently to these treatments, and if they are not carried out carefully they may fail to destroy the injurious fungi or bacteria that are carried in or on the seed, or they may reduce the viability of the seed. Old seed, in particular, often gives disappointing results following such treatment, even if it is carefully controlled.

Seed protectants are much easier to handle, for they are usually in the form of dusts that are shaken up in the packet or tin with the seed. This places a thin deposit of the material on the seed-coat. Unfortunately there appears to be a dearth of such materials in this country, so it may be necessary to resort to adding a pinch of Dithane M45 and shaking it up with the seed. The seed of certain vegetables is treated with a seed protectant before packing, and the packets are marked clearly to this effect. Peas, beans, sweetcorn, squashes and cucumbers are the vegetables most often treated in this way. The material used is usually pink or red in colour and on no account should such seed be used for salad sprouts. The hands should be well washed after handling treated seed.

PELLETED SEED AND SEED TAPES

Pelleted seed of flowers and vegetables appeared on the South African market several years ago after extensive trials in the USA, Australia, and Europe.

Initially there were certain problems with the coating, which, although dissolving to a degree, clung to the tips of the emerging shoots like a cap and inhibited germination. The moisture content of the soil, both in seedbox and seedbed, also appeared to be more critical with pelleted seed. These two factors plus the fact that only a limited range of flowers and vegetables was available were, I believe, responsible for their lack of appeal and consequent disappearance from the seed racks.

Seed tapes, in which seeds are properly spaced and embedded in soil-degradable plastic, and which are simply laid in shallow furrows and covered with fine soil, also appeared for a season or two some years ago. But they, too, appear to be off the market.

I believe that a similar fate awaits the pre-seeded trays that appeared on the market recently, which apparently need only water to germinate and produce transplants. Again, the range of cultivars available lacks depth, excluding as it does some popular names and including others that are not popular at all.

PREPARING THE SEEDBED

There are several vegetable crops that are sown only *in situ*, i.e. where the plants are to grow and mature. Many others are usually raised in seedbeds and seedboxes and later transferred to permanent quarters. Several crops can be produced by either method, onions, Swiss chard, beets and lettuce being among the most important.

The average garden soil is not an ideal medium for raising seedlings, especially from the point of view of tilth, and so it is usually necessary to set aside a small portion of the garden and to give it special treatment for the express purpose of raising healthy and vigorous transplants.

The site of the seedbed should be very carefully chosen if strong, healthy seedlings are to be produced. Seedbeds should preferably be in full sun; temporary shade can be provided during particularly hot periods by erecting hessian or shade cloth. In such a situation the seedlings, if spaced correctly, will develop into strong, stocky specimens better able to withstand the transplanting operation and the open ground conditions than the pale, leggy seedlings produced in heavy shade.

The seedbed need not be deep if the drainage is good. The soil for the bed must not crust and must be of a loose nature to encourage good root development. Seedbeds can be worked up by thoroughly incorporating mature compost, peat moss and milled kraal manure prior to the sowing date. A handful (60 g) of 2:3:2(22) per m², worked into the top 100 mm of the bed, should assist in getting the plants off to a flying start.

If soil-borne diseases and nematodes are a problem, and in older gardens they often are, it will be necessary to take certain precautions before sowing the seed. Damping-off fungi and other parasitic disease organisms can be destroyed by sterilizing the soil with a 4% formalin solution. Commercial formalin is 40% formaldehyde, but for the purpose of dilutions it is regarded as a 100% solution, which means that it should be used at the dilution rate of 1 ℓ to 25 ℓ of water. The 4% solution is used as a soil drench applied by watering-can, at the rate of 10 ℓ per m², and should be applied only after the soil has been given a good soaking with water to ensure an even distribution of the disinfecting liquid. Immediately after drenching, the soil should be covered with wet sacks for 36-48 hours to allow the toxic fumes to diffuse slowly through the soil. If sacks are not readily available, and this is often the case these days, a piece of plastic laid on the surface and weighted down with a few pieces of light timber is equally effective. After the covering material has been removed the beds should be allowed to air for 10-14 days, otherwise the persistent fumes will inhibit germination or damage the emergent seedlings. When formalin is used it should not be allowed to come into prolonged contact with the hands for it quickly dries out the skin and leaves it rough for days. Jeyes Fluid is also a useful sterilant, used at a strength of 2 tablespoons to 5 ℓ of water. It is applied in the same way as formalin.

Although drenching with formalin and Jeyes Fluid may destroy a number of nematodes, they are not regarded as specific materials for the purpose and further measures must be taken where these organisms are troublesome. The procedure for fumigating seedbeds (described in some detail in the chapter on pests) can be carried out once the sacks or plastic have been removed after drenching. When Methyl Bromide is used as a soil fumigant, drenching with formalin is unnecessary.

It is most important when using soil sterilants and fumigants to incorporate all compost, manure and bulky organic materials *before* treatment, otherwise re-infection may take place. Equally important is the removal of all old roots, crop residues and perennial weeds.

If cutworms are likely to be troublesome, and they often are if organic amendments have been incorporated, a dusting of BHC hoed in shallowly a few days prior to sowing should effect control. Karbaspray or Malathion used as a soil drench are just as effective. White grubs, wireworm and millipedes will also be controlled by these materials as will, unfortunately, any earthworms in the top 50 mm of soil.

SOWING THE SEED

When the seedbed has been dug over, and all bulky improving materials incorporated, it should be trodden lightly to avoid undesirable subsidence once the seeds have been sown. This initial work should, ideally, be completed 2 weeks or so before sowing to allow any annual weed crop to germinate and be destroyed before sowing takes place.

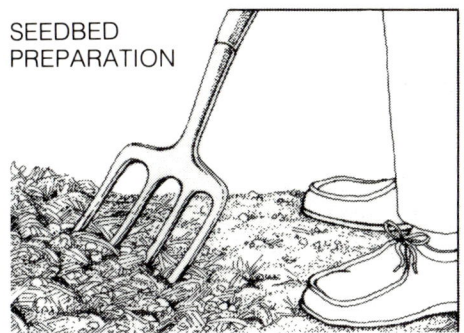
SEEDBED PREPARATION

(a) Incorporate manure or compost.

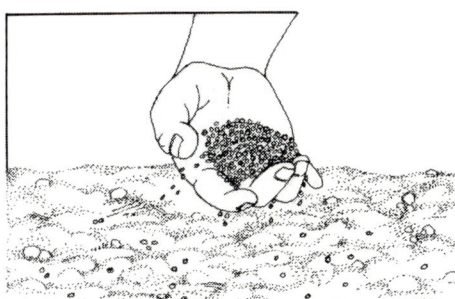

(b) Apply fertilizer dressing.

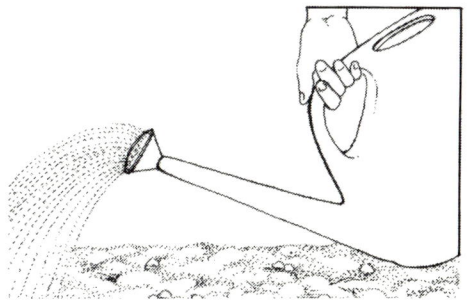

(c) Apply soil sterilant.

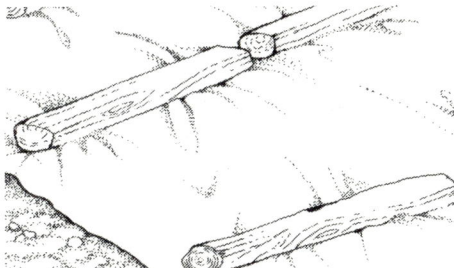

(d) Cover seedbed with plastic sheeting to allow sterilant to penetrate.

Prior to sowing, the soil surface should be raked to a fine tilth. This operation should only be carried out when the surface is sufficiently dry. During raking, all clods should be broken up and any stones, plant residues and coarse organic material removed.

Broadcasting (i.e. scattering) the seed in a seedbed is not advisable; sowing it in shallow drills gives much better results. However, drilling takes up more seedbed space for a given number of plants, and where space is very limited broadcasting may be warranted. Drilling is the sowing of seed in furrows 100-150 mm apart; with the individ-

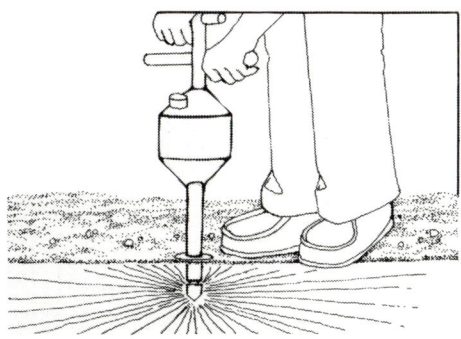

(e) Fumigate for root-knot nematodes.

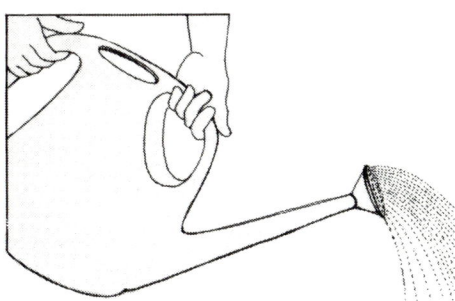

(f) Drench soil with pesticide for cutworms, white grubs, etc.

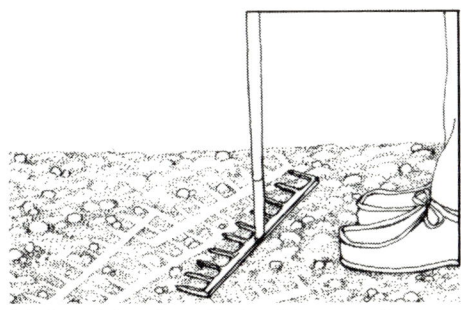

(g) Consolidate the soil by breaking up surface clods.

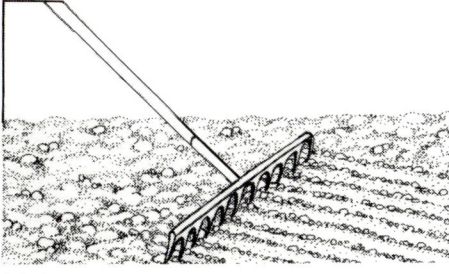

(h) Rake to a fine tilth.

ual seeds spaced as evenly as possible in the drills. The principal advantages of drilling are that the plants have much more room to develop, leading to a more even stand; weeding is facilitated; damping-off is less troublesome; and any pest and disease control measures are easier to carry out. The depth is also more easily controlled, for with broadcast sowings the seed can only be raked in and it settles at various depths.

Sowing depth is extremely important, and many poor and patchy stands of seedlings can be attributed to sowing too deeply. When seeds are sown too deeply they may not germinate at all, particularly in cold, wet soil, and even if they do germinate the young shoots find the journey to the surface most exhausting and arrive in a weak condition. Larger seeds (e.g. sweetcorn, beans and pumpkins) can be sown 30-50 mm deep, depending on soil type and condition, and on the season. Finer seeds (e.g. carrots, parsley and celery) need to be placed much more shallowly, even under favourable soil conditions. In seedbeds it is difficult to make a drill less than 15-20 mm deep. This is a suitable depth for most seedbed subjects and is somewhat reduced if the rows are tamped down with a spade after sowing. This shallow drill can easily be made by simply scraping the soil surface to the required depth with a sharpened stick drawn along a tightly stretched garden line or against a straight piece of light timber.

The seed should be sown thinly either out of the corner of the packet or, and this is more satisfactory, by putting the loose seeds in the palm of the hand, taking pinches with the other hand and rubbing the seed between finger and thumb along the drill. With a little practice a very even distribution can be achieved by the latter method. More even stands of tomatoes, Swiss chard, beetroot and other vegetables with irregularly-shaped seeds are obtained if a little more time is taken in placing the seeds 15-20 mm apart in the drill.

After sowing, the seed should be lightly covered with fine soil drawn over with the back of a rake, or with clean river sand, and the bed should then be tamped down lightly with the back of a spade to ensure close contact between seed and soil. If the seed is broadcast it should be raked in shallowly and the bed should again be lightly tamped down with the back of a spade. Finally, the seedbed should be thoroughly watered with as fine a rose or spray as possible and covered with a thin layer of dry grass, preferably without seedheads. Clean straw is an alternative cover. This grass or straw acts as a temporary mulch, which will greatly reduce evaporation and thereby ensure an even supply of moisture to the seeds, break the force of any water that need be applied and prevent crusting of the soil surface.

From the fourth day onwards the grass should be lifted daily to examine the soil moisture and to watch out for the emergence of the seedlings. As soon as germination is apparent and an even stand of seedlings has emerged, the grass should be removed completely, especially during cold and wet weather. In very hot weather it can be lifted on to a temporary light frame 450 mm high and maintained for 10-14 days until the seedlings need to be hardened-off by full sunlight. Shading, unless it is completely waterproof, is most undesirable during wet weather, for the 'drip' which will occur is considerably worse than direct rainfall and combined with the shade may cause damping-off. If the mulching grass is of the fine, wiry type without leaves it can be chopped into lengths not exceeding 200 mm and scattered loosely in a criss-cross pattern on the beds after sowing, and allowed to remain. It can be thinned out if necessary after the seedlings have emerged so that the plants grow through the mulch.

Cabbages, tomatoes, lettuces and most other crops reach transplanting size in 4-6 weeks, depending upon the season, but onions, leeks and celery may take up to 8 weeks to reach a similar stage. If the stand of seedlings is too thick it can be thinned out, the earlier the better, to allow the plants to stand 20-25 mm apart. Throughout their spell in the seedbed a watch should be kept for caterpillars, aphids and grasshoppers, which can be controlled with BHC or Malathion, in dust or spray formulations. With tomatoes and onions, in particular, it is advisable to give the plants one or two sprays, depending upon the season, with Dithane M45 or copper oxychloride (which is sold under several trade names). A drench with Karbaspray will control cutworms and deter snails and slugs, although the latter are more effectively controlled with met-aldehyde/carbaryl preparations or with Mesurol.

Seedbeds will require watering every 2-4 days, depending upon soil type, weather conditions and whether or not the beds are mulched. This should be co-ordinated, as far as possible, with any dusting, spraying or drenching that may be necessary.

Fluid sowing

Fluid sowing is a relatively new technique developed to assist growers in obtaining satisfactory stands of early-season vegetables.

The kits on the overseas market consist of several shallow, clear plastic incubators or jars, absorbent paper pads, a soft plastic bottle or applicator with 2 or 3 different nozzles and some sachets of gel powder.

The seeds are sown on the moistened pads in the jars, the lids are put on, and the jars are placed in good light indoors. When the seeds have germinated satisfactorily they are stirred into the prepared nutrient gel, poured into the applicator, and sown in the open ground by gently squeezing as one does a liquid detergent bottle.

The advantages claimed for this technique are that a more even early-season germination is obtained, the seed spacing can be more easily controlled, the seedlings emerge satisfactorily in a soil too cold for normal germination, and the crop matures 2-3 weeks earlier.

Seedboxes and containers

With vegetables such as tomatoes, egg plants, peppers and celery, only a dozen or so plants are needed at a time in the average home garden. Seedlings for these crops are usually raised in seedboxes or seed-trays.

While there has been a decided swing in horticulture generally to the use of soil-less mixtures for seedboxes, I feel that these mixtures are only really needed for the fine seeds of flowers, pot plants and other ornamentals. A suitable mixture for vegetable seeds can be made up of:

2 parts garden soil,
1 part peat or sieved compost,
1 part coarse sand.

SEEDBED SOWING

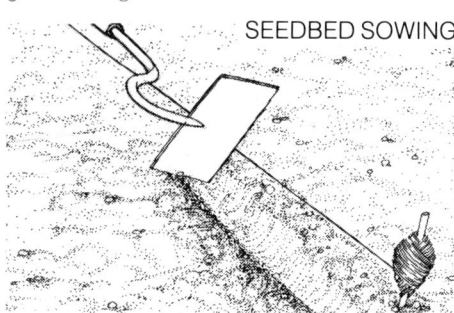

(a) Make drills against garden line.

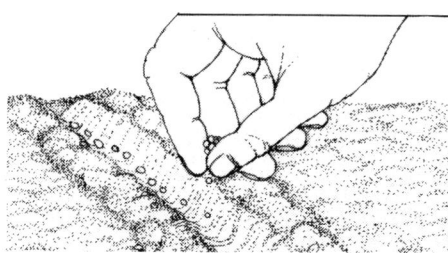

(b) Sow seeds by rubbing them carefully between thumb and forefinger.

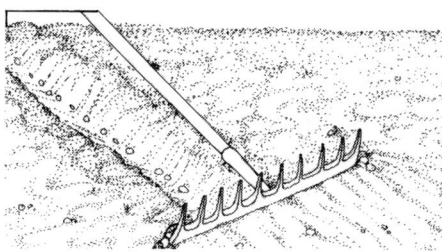

(c) Close the drills.

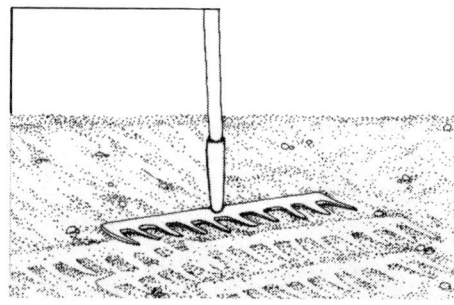

(d) Firm soil over seeds with rake head or back of spade.

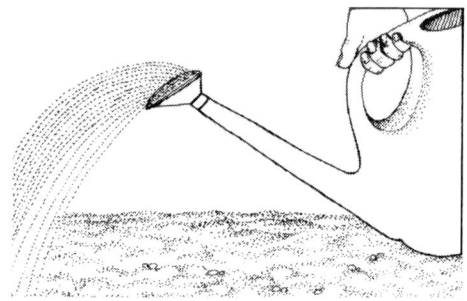

(e) Water carefully using a fine rose.

(f) Cover seedbed with fine grass or straw.

(g) Lift mulch to check for seedling emergence.

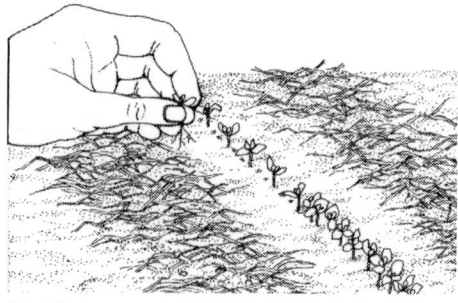

(h) After emergence, thin out seedlings if necessary.

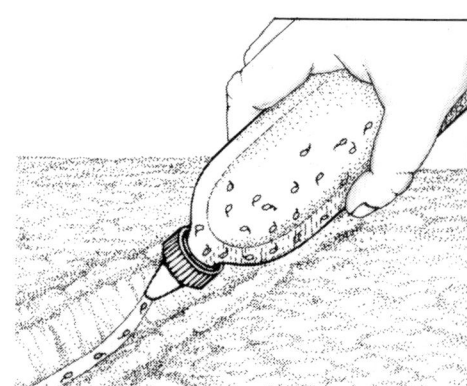

The fluid sowing of germinated seeds.

SEEDBOX SOWING

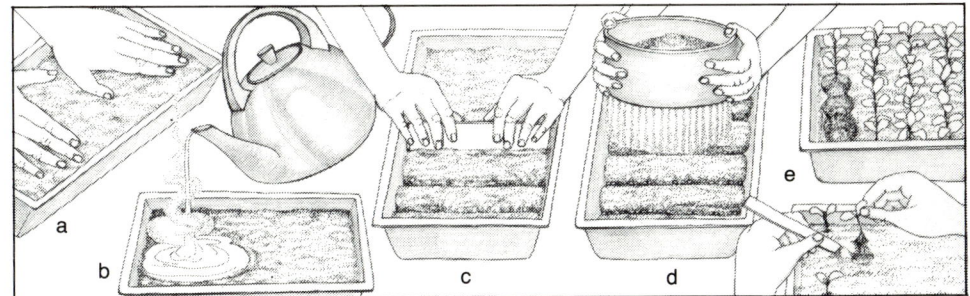

(a) Firm the soil. (b) Sterilize the soil with boiling water. (c) Make shallow drills. (d) After sowing the seeds, cover the drills with fine soil. (e) Prick out seedlings to allow more room for development.

If the soil has a light texture, then the mixture should contain more peat and less sand, and vice versa if the soil is heavy. A handful (60 g) of 2:3:2 and of superphosphate can be added to every 10 ℓ of mixture (the capacity of an average-sized plastic bucket). All the material should be rubbed through a 6 mm sieve and mixed thoroughly. Should your soil be too heavy, or in some other way unsuitable for seedbox use, a simple soil-less mixture can be made up of:

2 parts coarse sand,
3 parts peat moss,
2 parts vermiculite.

To this can be added superphosphate and/or 2:3:2 as before. Both of the above mixtures will benefit from the addition of 60 g of dolomitic limestone.

The seedbox can be made of asbestos, plastic, wood or metal and must have holes in the bottom for drainage. It should be filled to a depth of 20 mm with coarse drainage material, some of which can accrue from the sieve, or with a layer of crocks or small stones. The prepared mixture can then be added to within 10 mm of the top. The soil should be firmed with the fingers, particularly in the corners, and then levelled off and firmed again, this time with a firming board (which is much like a plasterer's wooden float).

The seedbox can then be sterilized by standing it level and pouring boiling water over it. One standard kettleful of boiling water should be sufficient for sterilizing 3 or 4 black plastic seed-trays.

The seedboxes should be allowed to cool off completely before the seed is sown. In seedboxes, as in seedbeds, drilling is preferable to broadcasting the seeds and for precisely the same reasons. The drills should be 5-6 mm deep and 30-40 mm apart, and can be made by simply pressing the edge of a thin piece of wood of a suitable length into the soil. The seed should then be sown thinly, covered with sterilized soil, river sand or fine vermiculite, firmed, watered with a fine spray, and placed initially in a shady location.

Several types of segmented seed-trays are now available, some rigid and some very flexible, and they are particularly useful for crops such as tomatoes, egg plants and peppers of all types. The trays are filled with a suitable well-drained mixture and two seeds are sown in each segment by dibbling in. The seedlings can later be thinned out to one plant per segment if satisfactory germination is obtained.

Although the majority of seeds are sown in seedbeds and seed-trays, early sowings of tender summer vegetables, normally sown *in situ*, can be made under protection in small containers. Cucumbers, squashes, tomatoes and peppers are some of the crops that lend themselves to this practice. The ideal container is perhaps the Jiffy Pot, made of compressed peat, of which both square and round forms are available in various sizes. These pots can be filled with a prepared mixture and packed together to support each other in a seedbox. They should then be watered and allowed to drain before sowing takes place. With cucurbits, two seeds can be dibbled into each container and, if germination is satisfactory, the weaker seedling can be carefully removed. With tomatoes, peppers and egg plants, the seeds can either be sown directly in the containers or they can be sown in seedboxes and the seedlings can be pricked out into the individual pots once they have produced two true leaves.

As with seedboxes or trays, the containers should be subjected to a high light intensity for at least 2 weeks before setting out to encourage the development of sturdy plants. By the time they are ready for outdoor planting the roots will, in most cases, have grown through the peat pot. Thereafter, transplanting consists only of making a hole with a trowel, dropping the pot into it so that the rim is slightly below soil level, covering in and firming. A thorough soak should follow.

Jiffy 7s are compressed peat discs 40-50 mm in diameter and about 7 mm thick, having a nutrient content and covered with a fine membrane except at the top, where the seed is to be sown. When placed in a shallow tray filled with water they slowly swell to six or seven times their initial thickness and thereby become excellent containers for the early starting, under protection, of vegetables such as tomatoes, egg plants, peppers, cucumbers and squashes. They are of course also useful for tip-cuttings of jasmine, fuchsias and other ornamentals, but are, I find, unsuitable for large softwood cuttings of plants such as pelargoniums and hydrangeas.

Although the rootlets grow through the membrane I always carefully peel it off before setting the plants in their permanent quarters, but this is just a personal preference. The one problem I have experienced with Jiffy 7s is that in warm, humid conditions they are apt to green over with moss. When this occurs, a spraying with a material such as Fungisprey is effective in clearing it up.

Although peat pots and discs are ideal for the early starting of plants, very good results can be obtained by using ice-cream tubs, cream cups and similar containers with a few holes punched in the bottom. With these containers, transplanting should be carried out at a slightly earlier stage and the cup must of course be peeled off to allow the roots free access to the soil.

The soaking and chipping of vegetable seeds prior to sowing is rarely necessary or desirable, the seed of New Zealand spinach with its hard coat being the only one that really requires soaking. Improved results have also been achieved by soaking parsley seed.

A final point about sowing is that the rows in the seedbed or seedbox should be labelled clearly with the type of vegetable, cultivar and date of sowing. This information can also be entered into the garden diary together with the source of the seed and any other relevant information that may be of value when results are analyzed and future sowings planned.

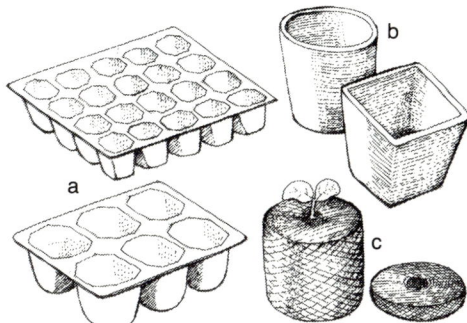

(a) Segmented plastic seed-trays. (b) Jiffy pots. (c) Jiffy 7, before and after expansion.

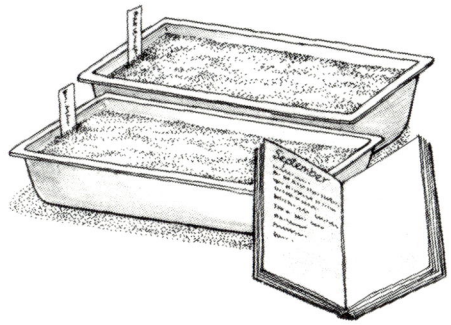

Label seedboxes and record all information in a gardening diary (see Appendix 6).

DAMPING-OFF

Damping-off is a condition that shows up on young seedlings as a darkening and shrivelling of the stem near the surface of the soil, followed by the dramatic collapse of the plant. It is caused by several species of soil fungi, which may also attack and destroy young plants before they emerge from the soil. This is known as 'pre-emergence' damping-off. However, the former is the more common and more easily observed condition.

Prolonged cloudy and wet weather with warm temperatures is conducive to the development and spread of this disease, but too thick a sowing is a very important contributing factor. Thick stands of seedlings should therefore be thinned out when climatic conditions as described above are prevailing or expected. Poor drainage is also often associated with this problem, while watering too late in the day certainly does not assist in keeping it in check. Should a serious outbreak occur after emergence, a thorough spraying of the plants with a fungicidal/pesticidal mixture such as Dithane/Malathion, followed if possible by a partial drying out of the beds or boxes, should arrest its progress. Thereafter this same spray can be used at weekly intervals until the seedlings are ready for transplanting.

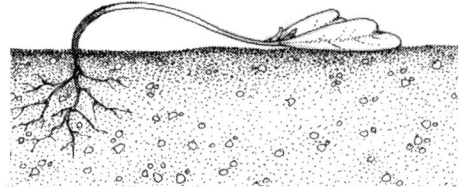

Damping off.

TRANSPLANTING

Transplanting or setting out is the operation of lifting seedlings from their seedbed or containers and transferring them to prepared quarters in open ground where they will grow and mature. Contrary to general belief, transplanting does not, in itself, stimulate the plant or improve its growth; in fact, in most cases growth is temporarily checked. However, as a result of the procedure, a plant is given more room for development. The main aim during transplanting should be to interrupt growth as little as possible, and if the operation is not carried out carefully it can severely check growth or, in extreme cases, cause the death of the transplants.

Most vegetable seedlings are ready to be moved when they are 75-100 mm high, a stage usually reached 4-8 weeks after sowing. (Onions and leeks, of course, reach a height of 150-200 mm before transplanting, although they are usually trimmed back a little during the operation.) This is a very broad guideline and it is only by experience that a gardener will know when to trans-

plant each of the crops in his garden. If the seedlings are too small when they are moved they can easily be destroyed by careless watering or heavy rains. However, if they are too big, especially when planted 'dry root', they receive a severe check and seldom develop into a uniform stand.

Transplants must be 'hardened-off' so that they can withstand the transition from a relatively sheltered and protected environment to a sometimes harsh, open situation. Seedbox plants are particularly sensitive to the change. Hardening-off seedbox plants is achieved by gradually exposing them to the lower (or higher) temperatures and the higher light intensity prevailing outdoors. Watering should also be gradually reduced as the seedlings approach the transplanting stage.

In the seedbed watering should also be reduced, starting 10 days before the move, and unless the weather is extremely hot should be withheld completely for the last 4 or 5 days to harden the plants further. However, 6-12 hours before the plants are to be set out the seedbed should be given a thorough soaking. This ensures that the plants regain their full turgidity and that the roots retain plenty of soil when the plants are lifted. The ground to receive them should be given a similar soaking at the same time so that the planting holes can be opened up easily with dibber or trowel and the plants firmed without difficulty.

The equipment needed for setting out plants in the home garden is quite simple: a trowel or dibber, a fork, a rake, a garden line, a measuring-stick and a hose or watering-can. A measuring-stick is simply a straight piece of timber approximately 900 mm x 25 mm x 25 mm, planed all round, with notches at 50 mm intervals. The seedlings should be lifted with a fork, a few at a time, and laid out singly along the tightly-stretched garden line at the recommended distance apart, using the measuring stick to ensure even spacing. As the gardener gains experience he will be able to use his trowel or dibber as a spacer in place of the measuring stick.

If a good ball of soil can be lifted with the plants, then the trowel is the most suitable tool for both lifting and planting out. If the plants have been growing close together in the seedbed and need teasing apart, then the dibber is superior. A dibber can easily be made from a piece of broom handle 200-250 mm long and sharpened to a point at one end. A broken spade handle 250-300 mm long is equally effective and more comfortable when a large number of seedlings are transplanted. The hole to receive the plant is made to the required depth, the plant is lowered into the hole with the other hand and the dibber is then pressed into the soil again, close to the hole and at an angle, to force the soil against the plant and firm it. This method usually leaves a hole near the plant but this soon fills up after a watering or two.

TRANSPLANTING

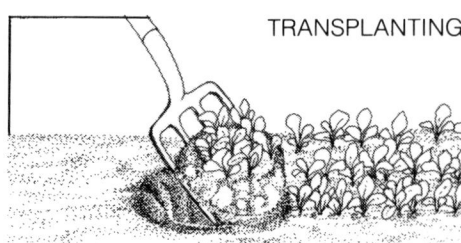

(a) Lift seedlings from seedbed with a garden fork.

(b) Lift seedlings from seedboxes with a trowel.

(c) Lay seedlings along garden line at recommended intervals.

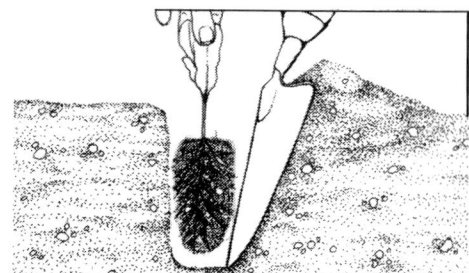

(d) Plant out using a trowel.

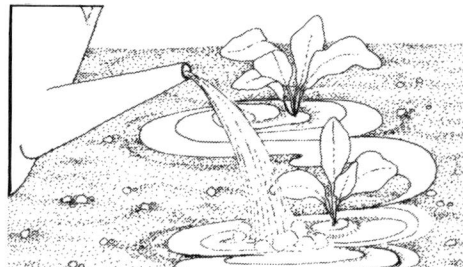

(e) Water the transplants well.

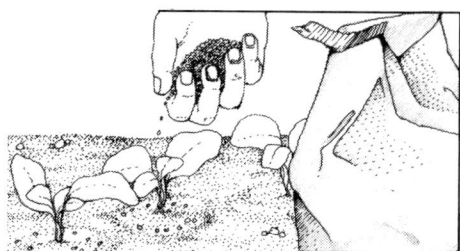

(f) Distribute bait for snails, cutworms etc.

When the first row is finished the ground should be raked over, the next row marked out and planted, and so on, until the whole bed or area has been planted. The seedlings should then be given a thorough watering, even if rain is imminent or actually falling, for it takes more than a light shower to settle the soil around the roots. Starter solutions are not often used in this country by home gardeners. For those who are interested, 30 g each of 2:3:2 and superphosphate, or 60 g of the former, stirred into 5 ℓ of water and distributed at the rate of 125-200 mℓ per plant, should get them off to a good start. Alternatively one can use a proprietary preparation such as Supranure, which has a similar analysis.

An alternative transplanting method, especially useful for widely-spaced plants and when water is scarce, is the puddling method, which ideally requires two pairs of hands. The one operator has a garden trowel and the other a bucketful of water or starter solution and an empty 500 mℓ container for pouring. The planter makes a hole with his trowel, his assistant pours a cupful of water into the hole, the planter then *quickly* places the transplant in the hole so that the roots are in the water and, with the other hand, pulls soil around the roots. The water can, alternatively, be dispensed from a watering-can without the rose. This may appear a rather difficult and complicated operation but in practice it is extremely simple and quick. Yet another method, if water is scarce and the permanent area is on the dry side, is to dip the roots before transplanting into a slurry of clay and water. This will greatly assist the seedlings during the critical transplanting period.

If cutworms are likely to be troublesome, Karbaspray can be incorporated into the transplanting water or starter solution to give immediate protection. If aphids or small caterpillars are in evidence when the seedlings are lifted from the seedbed, it is wise to mix a small quantity of Malathion or Karbaspray with water and douse the tops of the plants before setting them out. With tomatoes fungal diseases are a constant hazard, and to get instant protection the transplants should be treated in a similar way with a fungicide solution such as Dithane M45. This fungicide is compatible with Malathion or Karbaspray, i.e. they can safely be mixed with each other, if necessary.

The best time to carry out transplanting is in the late afternoon or early evening, for this allows the plants 12 or 15 hours to get partially re-established in their new quarters before having to face the heat of the day. Cool, cloudy weather is ideal for transplanting. Provided that the plants are lifted from the seedbed or seedbox carefully and are given a good watering-in by any of the methods detailed there should be little check to growth and few losses.

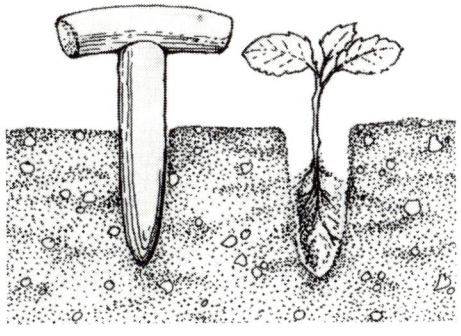
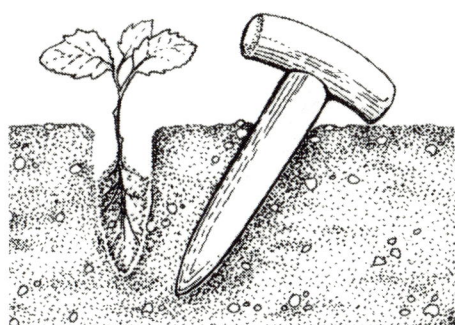
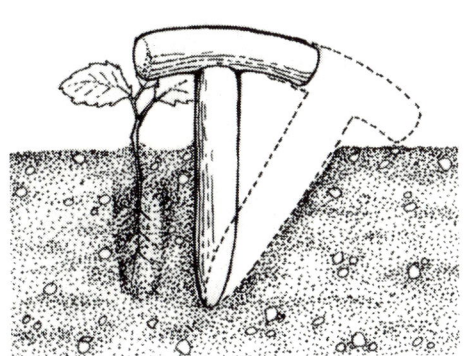
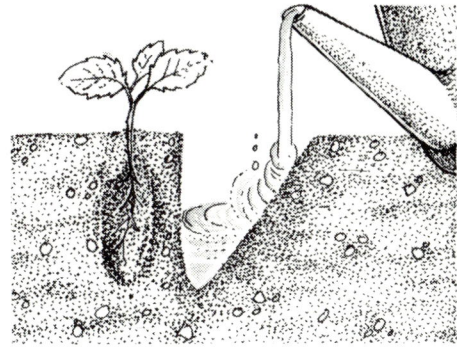

Transplanting with a dibber.

It is always wise to raise about 30% more plants than are actually required so that any weak or 'blind' plants can be discarded and any casualties replaced. If the seedbed or seedbox is needed for subsequent sowings, the spare plants can be moved to temporary quarters, for example at the end of one of the rows. It cannot be overemphasized that only *strong* plants should be set out even if this means reducing the number of rows planted, for a patchy stand needs just as much watering, cultivating and spraying as an even stand of vigorous plants.

When there are only a few transplants it is worthwhile using protectors or hot-caps of the wigwam type to shade the plants for a few days if it is extremely hot, but this is not absolutely essential. If these protectors are used it is important to ensure that each has a hole or vent in the top so that plants do not get damaged by a build-up of heat. A few large leaves bent over will give equal protection, as will a handful of grass dropped on each plant, although in certain circumstances this could encourage and obscure cutworm activity.

The 'topping and tailing' (i.e. leaf and root trimming) of transplants is unnecessary and, indeed, inadvisable with most vegetables. However, onions and leeks are much easier to handle if this is carried out, and they appear to suffer no ill-effects from the practice. Beetroot and Swiss chard seedlings, if transplanted, get off to a better start if the leaves are trimmed back a little (but *not* the roots!).

If cutworm activity is evident a few days after transplanting, Karbaspray can be sprayed around the base of each plant. Alternatively, an eggcupful or so of this suspension can be poured over the crown of each plant so that it runs down the stem and into the soil around it. A third method of control is to dust BHC on the soil and work it in shallowly with a Dutch hoe. Cutworm bait can also be scattered.

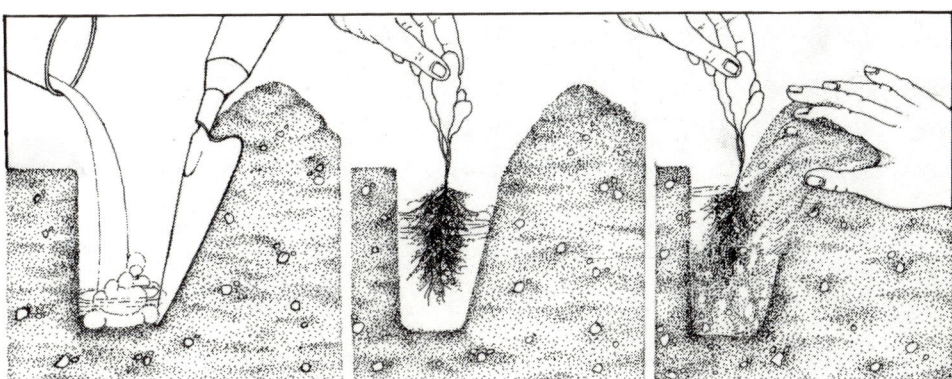

Transplanting using the puddling method.

DISEASES

1. A progamme of spraying for disease prevention is an important aspect of successful vegetable gardening.
2. Tomatoes: early blight and iron deficiency
3. Tomatoes: late blight, leaf symptoms
4. Tomatoes: late blight, fruit symptoms
5. Beans: bacterial blight (grease spot)

1

2

3

4

5

6. Potatoes: early blight
7. Potatoes: leaf roll (and plants with healthy leaves)
8. Potatoes: late blight, tuber symptoms
9. Peas: pod spot (dark lesions) and downy mildew (yellow patch)
10. Brussels sprouts: black rot

6

7

8

9

10

7 DISEASES AND THEIR CONTROL

In the detailed discussion of each vegetable in Part 2, the diseases that commonly occur in Southern Africa are described, together with suitable control measures. However, to control diseases effectively over an extended period it is essential for the grower to have some idea of the organisms he is up against. This knowledge can mean a saving of money spent on useless materials and can help prevent the spread of disease from crop to crop.

Wherever vegetables are grown, diseases cause serious damage and losses at certain times. Broadly speaking, high-value crops are affected the most by diseases and low-value crops the least. It is therefore strange that while most gardeners do not hesitate to dip into their pockets to purchase seed, plants, fertilizer and manure, relatively few make any serious effort to protect their investments by commencing, *in good time*, an effective disease control programme using suitable materials and methods. Plant breeders all over the world are doing excellent work in producing crops that have some resistance to certain diseases, but they are still a long way from their goal in many cases. One of their greatest difficulties is that of combining resistance with productivity and market acceptance.

Before the amateur grower initiates any disease control measures, however, it is essential that he knows something of the nature of diseases and of the capabilities and limitations of the spraying and dusting materials on the market. Plant diseases can be divided into two classes – parasitic and non-parasitic. Parasitic diseases are caused by the activities of microscopic organisms such as fungi, bacteria and viruses. Non-parasitic diseases are not true diseases and no organisms are responsible for their appearance. They are abnormal developments of foliage, fruits, tubers and roots that appear when soil and climatic conditions are unfavourable, when certain essential nutrients are in short supply, and when cultural operations are carried out incorrectly or haphazardly.

FUNGAL DISEASES

Fungi are parasitic plants that possess two characteristics – they reproduce by means of spores and are devoid of chlorophyll, the green substance contained in higher plants. Fungal diseases affecting the foliage, stems, flowers and fruits are usually most troublesome in conditions of low light intensity and fairly high relative humidity. While certain fungi restrict their activities to one plant or plant family, others attack a wide range of plants. In addition, some fungi can exist only in parasitic form while others can live as either parasites or saprophytes, which means that they can exist on both fresh and dead material. Some of the latter cause the most troublesome diseases for they are able to live over in the soil for long periods.

The spores by means of which fungi reproduce are tiny bodies easily distributed by wind and water and by such common, but often unsuspected, agencies as boots, stockings and trousers. In addition, several fungal diseases are transmitted on and under the seed-coat of true seeds, while others are distributed in seed potatoes. Several diseases, notably late blight, the scourge of tomato and potato growers, can only reach epidemic proportions if certain specific climatic conditions prevail. Overcast skies for long periods, warm weather, and high relative humidity, are essential for the rapid development of this disease, the spores of which can only germinate on the plant surfaces if free water, caused by rain, watering or heavy dew, is present. In the United Kingdom there is a forecasting service that studies these climatic conditions and warns farmers, by telegram, if late blight is likely to appear within a few days. This forecasting is apparently also being done in certain parts of South Africa with some success.

Overcrowding is a common mistake made by home gardeners, and while most vegetables grown in this way will remain 'clean' when the weather is dry, the incidence of disease is often high when conditions become generally wet. Giving the plants adequate spacing allows them to dry off quickly after rain and heavy dew and also facilitates dusting and spraying. Tomatoes, potatoes, carrots and beans, in particular, need to be adequately spaced.

Fungal diseases that cause plants to wilt, such as fusarium wilt of tomatoes, cannot be controlled by spraying or dusting, and affected plants should be removed, with their root systems, and destroyed. Long rotations between related crops should be practised when such diseases occur.

BACTERIAL DISEASES

Bacteria are microscopic single-celled organisms that reproduce by simple fission or breakage.

Bacterial diseases of plants take on many forms and can cause wilting of the plants, spotting of the leaves, cankers on the stems with accompanying fruit and leaf symptoms, and rots of roots and tubers.

Most bacterial diseases attack the vascular system of the plant and spraying is of little value as the causal bacteria travel rapidly throughout the plant. Certain diseases of this class, such as black rot of cabbages and related crops, are in many cases introduced into the garden in or on seed-coats. When this happens the seedlings make poor growth, rarely mature, and contaminate the soil. Some bacterial diseases, including the one just mentioned, can also be introduced on seedlings, and here again poor growth and soil contamination are the result.

Bacterial wilt of solanaceous crops, described in Part 2 in the entry on tomatoes, lives over in the soil for several years and attacks the plants through their root systems, particularly if nematodes and soil insects have damaged the roots to any degree.

With all bacterial diseases, infected plant material should be removed carefully, roots and all, and destroyed. Fallen leaves and other residues of affected plants should be similarly treated. Apart from total soil sterilization, which is in most cases impracticable, crop rotation is the only answer to the problem and should be practised rigorously once a disease of this nature has been identified. As with nematodes, ignorance has played a major part in the build-up of bacterial diseases in garden soils.

VIRAL DISEASES

Viruses are infectious agents of minute proportions. Owing to their general invisibility, they are usually identified, classified and described by the symptoms they produce on the host plant. The more common symptoms of attack are mottling, stunting, crinkling and other distortions of the foliage, while the flowers of certain crops show colour 'breaks'. Potatoes, peas, peppers, tomatoes, sweet potatoes and a wide range of cucurbits are the main sufferers in the vegetable garden.

Although some viral diseases are spread by the gardener touching diseased plants and then healthy ones, and others are carried over on true seeds, the majority are spread by pests. Sucking pests such as aphids, thrips, white flies and mites are the main culprits, but leaf hoppers and some beetles are also capable of transmitting certain diseases. These pests feed on the tissue of affected plants and then move on to infect 'clean' plants. In some cases the virus needs to undergo an incubation period of several days within the pest before it can be transmitted, while in others it is believed that the pest loses its power of transmission within 36 hours. It will be seen, therefore, that it is very desirable to control pests on vegetable crops even if they do not appear to be doing a great deal of direct damage by their feeding. Some annual and perennial weeds also act as hosts of viral diseases and are capable of harbouring pests and carrying the disease over from one crop to a later one even when all crop residues have been removed and destroyed. In some cases, the symptoms on weeds may be quite different from the typical symptoms on the crop, and very often they are relatively insignificant.

SPRAYING AND DUSTING FOR DISEASE CONTROL

Of the three different types of parasitic plant diseases, those caused by fungi are the only ones that can be directly checked or controlled by spraying or dusting, and then only if suitable measures are taken at an early stage. Whether to spray or dust for plant diseases is something of a controversial issue. Perhaps the points that weigh heavily in favour of spraying are that, firstly, the deposits on the foliage last much longer than dusts, especially in wet weather when a single sharp shower can completely remove the dust from the upper leaf surfaces and stems; secondly, with liquid sprays a much better coverage of the foliage can be obtained; and thirdly, a much larger range of materials is available in the form of wettable powders and emusifiable concentrates.

To be really effective, spraying must begin either before the disease appears, which means that the gardener must, by experience, anticipate attacks, or as soon as the first signs of disease are observed. The whole idea behind the use of fungicides is to place a thin protective layer or deposit of the material on all aerial plant surfaces, i.e. leaves, stems and fruits. This ensures that when the disease spores alight from the air or from some other agency, they are destroyed before they can germinate and penetrate the plant tissues. It is obvious, therefore, that as good a coverage as possible must be obtained, for patchy spraying is useless. Indeed, the effectiveness of any

dusting or spraying programme depends as much on the efficiency of the apparatus and the proficiency of the operator, as on the material used.

With sprays, an effective coverage can be obtained only by building up a good pressure, by using a fine nozzle, and by creating considerable turbulence among the plants (this is achieved by directing the spray at the plants from all angles while constantly moving the lance around). Maintaining an effective deposit on foliage is difficult, but must be attempted. In wet weather this means spraying after every heavy downpour. Control is almost impossible once a disease gains entrance into the leaves, for however complete the subsequent coverage of fungicide is, the disease can spread internally through the tissues.

There is a bewildering variety of spraying apparatus available, those with plastic pumps and containers being the cheapest and easiest to operate. However, some of the cheaper models have a life expectancy of only a few months at best and, being solvent welded, are almost impossible to repair. The apparatus to purchase is that which delivers a fine mist, preferably adjustable, and which has a lance of reasonable length. Those with a capacity of 5 ℓ are perhaps the most suitable because of the volume and because many spray materials are formulated to a 5 ℓ module.

The range of dusting apparatus is considerably smaller; in fact there are occasions when it is difficult to find a suitable duster in even the most comprehensive garden centre.

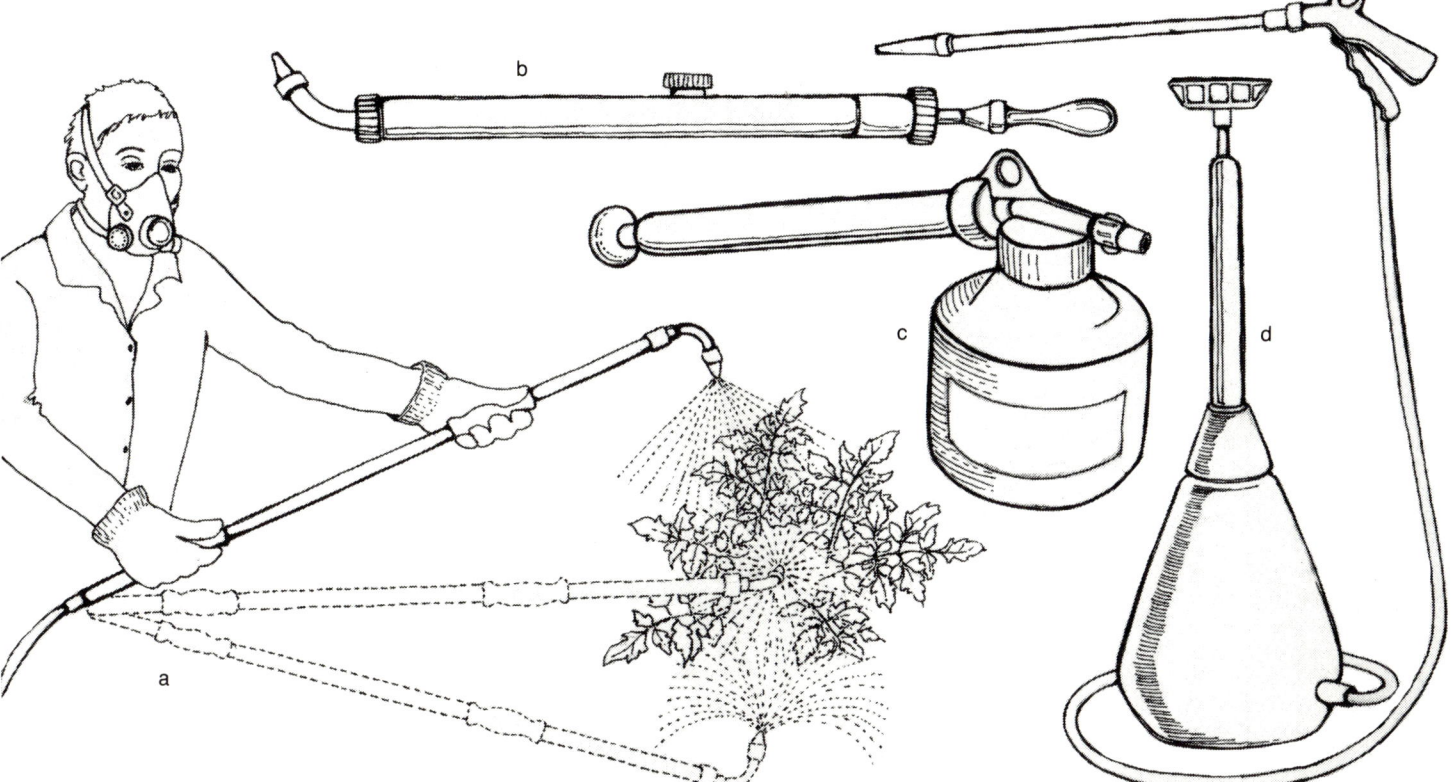

(a) To ensure complete coverage of fungicides, create turbulence by directing the spray at the plants from all angles while constantly moving the lance around.
(b) Syringe. (c) Continuous sprayer. (d) Pressure sprayer.

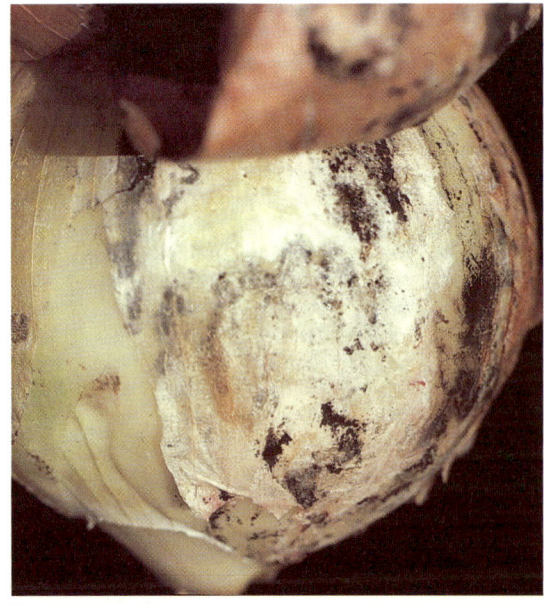

1. Onions: *Aspergillus* infection (very common at certain times of the year, especially in storage)
2. Swiss chard: *Cercospora* leaf spot
3. Squashes: powdery mildew
4. Pumpkins: powdery mildew
5. Pumpkins: downy mildew

PESTS

1. Cabbage aphids
2. Green aphid and young
3. Adult thrips
4. Fruit fly
5. Red spider mites and
eggs on lower leaf surface

Puffercan packs, small trigger sprays and plant aerosols are more suitable for clearing up local insect infestation (e.g. aphids) in the flower garden and on patio and indoor plants, than for use in the vegetable garden.

Certain spraying materials do not remain in suspension for long and the liquid must be stirred or agitated constantly to obtain an even deposit. Where wettable powders are concerned (and these appear in general to be more effective for fungi control than liquid concentrates), it is better to 'cream' the powder with a small quantity of water and then to add to it the full quantity of water, stirring briskly. The efficacy of most spray materials can be greatly increased, particularly on vegetables such as cabbages and related crops that have 'bloom' on their leaves, by adding a very small quantity of a proprietary 'wetter', or some dishwashing liquid, to the spray mix.

The fungicides in the box below are extremely effective if used as described above and according to the manufacturer's recommendations. They are compatible (can be mixed) with most other fungicidal and insecticidal materials, but for safety the mixing should be carried out immediately prior to use.

All-purpose dusts containing fungicides such as mancozeb, sulphur and copper, and pesticides such as mercaptothion and carbaryl, are available under several trade names. However, their relatively high cost limits their use to pot plants and small infestations of aphids and caterpillars. When fungal diseases are likely to be troublesome it is much more economical to use effective fungicides at frequent intervals.

These, then, are some of the materials that are currently available to the home gardener in small packs to combat fungal diseases. However, this situation is never static and older materials are regularly withdrawn and replaced by allegedly more effective ones. Finally, it must be stressed that fungicides are, in general, protective and not curative, and are only effective when a proper programme of spraying is formulated and carried out to the letter. Weather conditions must of course be considered when deciding how often to spray, but it is always best to err on the safe side, particularly if wet and overcast weather is being experienced. Again, plants such as cucurbits and tomatoes, which visibly produce new foliage every day in summer and which are susceptible to several serious diseases, will require more regular spraying to protect the new growth.

NON-PARASITIC DISEASES

As was mentioned earlier, non-parasitic diseases (or functional disorders) are not caused by any organisms. They are brought about mainly by unsuitable environment or climate, by nutrient deficiency, by improper placement of fertilizer or manure, by poor drainage, by accidental exposure to non-selective weed-killers, and by faulty watering practices. Potatoes and tomatoes are among the main sufferers, although many crops are affected in different ways.

'Second growth' of potato tubers is one of the most common disorders and is caused either by heavy watering or by heavy rain after the soil has been rather dry for a considerable period when the crop is approaching maturity. When a soil is allowed to dry out the skin of the tubers loses its elasticity and becomes tough. If the soil is then saturated suddenly, the tubers are unable to

SOME NON-PARASITIC DISEASES

Beetroot: boron deficiency.

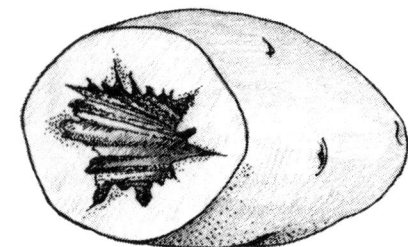

Potato: hollow heart.

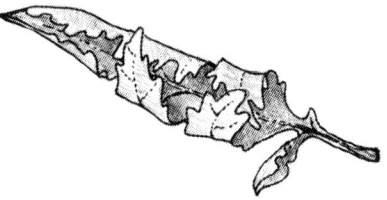

Tomato: leaf-roll.

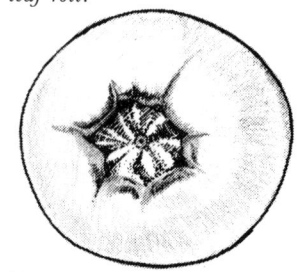

Tomato: blossom-end rot.

Tomato: concentric cracking of small-fruited types.

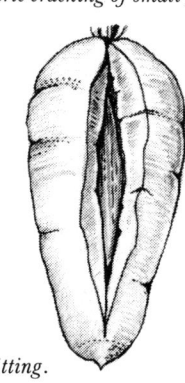
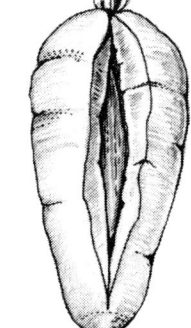

Carrot: root splitting.

FUNGICIDES

Bayleton: A systemic fungicide which, like Benlate, gives satisfactory control of powdery mildew on cucurbits and peas.
Benlate: A relatively expensive systemic material that has proved effective against powdery mildew. It is available as a wettable powder.
Copper oxychloride: Copper has long been used as a broad-spectrum material on vines, vegetables and ornamentals. Originally it was only available in a mixture with lime under the label Bordeaux Mixture, which is still obtainable. However, because this can in certain circumstances cause damage to various plants and is incompatible with pesticides and other fungicides, its use is limited. Copper oxychloride, marketed as Cupravit, Virikop, or under its true name, has proved to be a more effective and easily handled material. It should only be used at recommended strengths, as should all spray materials.
Dithane M45: This is a broad-spectrum

material i.e. it can be used on a wide range of plants to control several fungal diseases. Its satisfactory control of early blight, late blight and other diseases of tomatoes and potatoes has established it as an essential material on the gardener's shelf. It is a wettable powder compatible with most pesticides.
Fungisprey: A new systemic material marketed as an emulsifiable concentrate. It is based on triforine and is recommended for the control of powdery mildew and rust on vegetable crops.
Sulphur: Sulphur, in one form or another, has long been used as a base for fungicidal sprays and dusts. It is still widely used, particularly in country areas, by older gardeners, who each summer dust regularly for 'roes' on tomatoes and potatoes. It also has some pesticidal properties, being a satisfactory material for mite control. One of its limitations is that it has occasionally caused damage to young foliage.

swell uniformly and the skin simply ruptures at the weakest points, usually around the 'eyes', and little knobs are formed. Affected tubers are often bound to be 'glassy' when cut across. Round cultivars appear to be less susceptible to this condition than oval-shaped ones such as Up-To-Date and Arran Chief. Waisting of the tubers is another expression of the same condition.

Hollow heart is a condition of potato tubers in which cavities form in the centre of the tubers, often accompanied by a darkening of the tissue, and it is impossible to detect which tubers are affected until they are cut across. It is also thought to be caused by fluctuating moisture conditions in the soil and when growth is resumed following a check. The disorder appears to be most common in large-sized tubers.

Leaf-roll, sun scald and 'greenback' of tomatoes are brought about by cultural methods such as excessive pruning and improper fertilization, and some cultivars appear more prone to damage than others.

Cracking of root crops such as carrots, parsnips, turnips, sweet potatoes and radishes, and also of tomato fruits and cabbage heads, is yet another disorder that can be directly attributed to faulty watering practices or unfavourable climatic conditions. Blossom-end rot, a rather common disorder that can be caused by a combination of two or more factors, is described in detail in Part 2 under tomatoes.

It should also be remembered that not only do these non-parasitic upsets cause root, tuber and fruit defects that render the produce unattractive, but they also pave the way for the entrance of parasitic diseases, principally fungi, that are themselves unable to penetrate healthy skin tissues. The cracking on tomatoes, which causes the juice to appear, is also favoured by several insects as an egg-laying site.

GENERAL CONSIDERATIONS

The appearance and spread of diseases can be reduced very appreciably if the gardener provides the plants with favourable soil conditions and pays attention to the removal and destruction of old plants, weeds, and 'volunteer' growth of any kind. Garden sanitation is one of the most effective and cheapest methods of controlling plant diseases and yet it is one of the least practised.

Usually it is the smaller and weaker plants that first succumb to diseases and pests, with one or two notable exceptions, and correct plant nutrition can go a long way towards keeping the plants in a healthy and vigorous condition. Growing vegetable crops only during the most favourable seasons also keeps serious outbreaks of both parasitic and non-parasitic diseases to a minimum.

The benefits of practising crop rotation as a method of controlling diseases are described in a separate chapter.

Gardeners who have trouble diagnosing specific diseases from the descriptions and photographs in this book are advised to purchase a copy of *Vegetable Diseases*, a Department of Agriculture publication. Specimens can, of course, be submitted for examination to the regional headquarters of the Department of Agriculture, but this should not be done unnecessarily as the Department has a great deal of routine work to get through. As much as possible of an affected plant, the foliage of which must be dry, should be wrapped in several thicknesses of newspaper or placed in a plastic bag, and packed in a stout cardboard box. Specimens should be posted to arrive early in the week; those that lie unopened for a weekend may be in a sorry state when finally examined. The following details should always accompany the specimens: name and address of sender, name and cultivar of plant, brief description of the disease, symptoms and number of plants affected, fertilizer and manure given, prevailing weather conditions, and whether or not any pesticides or fumigants have been used. This information is most important and may save the pathologist handling the specimen much time and trouble, particularly where non-parasitic diseases are involved. In many cases it is useless to despatch specimens without this detailed and vital information.

THE TWELVE GOLDEN RULES FOR YOUR PROTECTION

1. Before using any pesticide, fungicide, fumigant or weedkiller read the manufacturer's recommendations for use *twice*.

2. Store all spray materials out of the reach of children and animals and away from foodstuffs.

3. Do not spray when there is an appreciable amount of wind.

4. When mixing spray materials, and when spraying or dusting, avoid inhaling excessive amounts of the smog. It is wise to wear a protective mask when using these materials.

5. Cream wettable powders with a little water before bulking up.

6. Always be conservative in observing the safety period recommended for the particular product being used.

7. Wear rubber gloves and protective clothing.

8. Do not eat, drink or smoke during application.

9. Thoroughly wash all exposed parts of the body (e.g. face, hands and arms) with soap and water after spraying and before eating, drinking or smoking.

10. Discard empty containers carefully: glass bottles should be broken; plastic containers should be perforated and flattened. (Do not puncture aerosols!) Never re-use these containers for any other purpose.

11. Always empty and flush out all spraying apparatus and mixing containers with clean water.

12. Prevent contamination of streams and other water sources.

1. Slug
2. Garden snails
3. Snail eggs
4. Locust
5. Grasshopper
6. Mating grasshoppers on cauliflower
7. White grubs (the larvae of chafer beetles)
8. Cutworm (the nocturnal-feeding larva of an owlet moth)
9. Tomato roots showing damage from root-knot nematodes
10. Roots with typical symptoms of nematode infestation
11. White fly
12. Leaf miner on tomato leaf

7

8

9

10

11

12

8 PESTS AND THEIR CONTROL

As with diseases, it is desirable for the gardener to have some knowledge of the main insects and other pests that attack vegetable crops, and of the pesticides available and the theory behind their application, before control measures are undertaken. In Part 2 a number of important pests and their control are mentioned, but this is meant only as a guide to what the gardener should look out for on each vegetable.

Some pests occur in definite cycles, while the appearance of others is influenced by climatic conditions. For example, slugs and snails are prevalent when the ground and plants are continuously moist; during dry periods they rarely cause damage. On the other hand, aphids and red spider mites enjoy hot, dry conditions, the former having a particular liking for young flushes of growth.

Although some pests feed on others, and birds, frogs and lizards account for a few more, this activity is only of consequence in natural bush, veld and vlei. Within the confines of the home garden the grower frequently has to resort to the use of pesticides to keep his crops clean and free from damage. It is claimed by some that purely organic fertilizers such as compost and manure enable plants in some way to develop a resistance to attack. This contention would not, I feel, be substantiated by results obtained in a *carefully conducted* field trial, with artificially fertilized control plots. It is true that vigorous plants are often unscathed by pests and diseases, but whether the nutrients responsible for the vigour were obtained from a forkful of compost or a handful of 2:3:2 is surely of little consequence.

Pests that attack vegetable crops can generally be divided into four groups: chewing pests, sucking pests, stinging pests and soil pests (including nematodes). Of these, the bean-stem fly, the sweet potato weevil, the potato tubermoth and the corn earworm require rather different methods of control to the majority and are discussed under their respective host plants in Part 2. Scale insects, which are often quite a problem on shrubs, ornamentals and fruit trees are, fortunately, not a problem on vegetables.

PESTICIDES AND THEIR USE

Pest control on crops was originally achieved solely by dusting or spraying with materials of organic origin such as pyrethrum, nicotine and derris, all of which occur naturally in the tissues of certain plants. Some of these materials are still obtainable, but in the last two decades there has been a definite swing to synthetic materials. This swing appears to have been influenced by several factors, the most important of these being the broad-spectrum nature of most of the synthetics, their longer residual effect and the fact that in most cases they are considerably cheaper. However, as with fertilizers, I believe there is a place for both organic and inorganic products, although it is not always easy to obtain suitable garden formulations of the organics. Where edible crops are concerned, the fact that the organics have relatively little residual effect can be regarded as advantageous.

In this chapter the materials recommended are those that are most effective and readily obtainable. Some pesticides, particularly one or two of the organo-phosphate group (e.g. parathion), are extremely toxic to humans and warm-blooded animals and therefore cannot be recommended for use in the home garden on ornamentals, flowers or vegetables. Some of these materials necessitate the wearing of respirators and protective clothing and the problem of their leaving toxic residues on food crops is a very considerable one. All pesticides are poisonous to some degree, and during dusting and spraying operations and when wettable powders are mixed one should avoid inhaling any quantity of dust or spray. The storing of these materials also carries considerable responsibility, and they should be kept well away from children, pets and food-stuffs.

With most pests dusting is quite as effective as spraying, provided that good coverage is obtained. In addition, dusts have the advantage that they are ready for use when purchased and do not need diluting or mixing. They are also more easily removed from edible leaf crops than spray deposits if control measures are necessary shortly before harvesting.

As with fungicides, the efficiency of pesticidal sprays is greatly increased if a 'spreading and sticking' agent is also used, or if a little soap or liquid detergent is added. This is particularly true when one is attempting to control aphids on cabbages, cauliflowers, broccoli or kohlrabi, for both the insects and the leaves have a waxy coating that causes the spray to run into large globules, resulting in poor coverage.

Apart from the several pesticides and fungicides recommended in this book there are many others available to the larger grower and farmer. Some of these are materials formulated specifically for use on one crop or against a particular pest or disease. Many of these materials are available only in large commercial quantities and some of them must be used under very strictly controlled conditions with expensive apparatus. The materials mentioned throughout this book can be used perfectly safely in the home garden if the manufacturers' recommendations for use are followed and the necessary precautions taken.

Pesticides must be used with care when crops approach maturity. Although the occasional product (e.g. Malathion) can be used to within a few days of harvesting certain crops, home gardeners should observe a minimum period of 7-10 days between spraying and harvesting.

SPRAYING AND DUSTING EQUIPMENT

As was mentioned in the previous chapter, there are different types of spraying and dusting equipment available, most of which are also suitable for pest control. Some dusts are available in shaker packs with perforated lids and are suitable for local infestations of aphids, caterpillars and beetles. A makeshift method of distributing dusts is to put a quantity of the material into a small bag made of muslin or mutton cloth, or even into an old sock or stocking, and shake it over the plants.

The brass garden syringe is one of the most serviceable and useful of spray applicators. The better ones have interchangeable fine and coarse nozzles, and can easily be dismantled and changed, and can be used with any plastic bucket or other container. Cheaper plastic syringes are also useful for the occasional spraying of small areas.

CHEWING PESTS

Chewing pests can conveniently be split into two groups, the first comprising snails and slugs of several species, the second cut-worms, caterpillars, grasshoppers and various species of beetles, including the CMR beetle. Apart from the last-named, their presence does not go unnoticed for very long. Slugs and snails often play havoc with young seedlings and maturing crops, especially those such as lettuces and cabbages that have much of their bulk either close to, or lying on, the soil surface. The habit of such plants provides shade, moisture and daytime protection for these voracious feeders. Slugs and snails are somewhat unique in that they are hermaphrodites, i.e. each individual possesses both male and female reproductive organs. They can easily be controlled by the regular use of proprietary baits and also, to a considerable degree, by strict sanitary practices around seedbed areas, in particular the removal of weed growth and crop residues.

Chewing insects from the other group obtain their food by eating foliage, stems, flowers and fruit. The usual method of control is to place a thin, poisonous deposit on all plant surfaces, so that when the insects feed a quantity of the poison is ingested. Materials used for this purpose are known as stomach poisons and those listed below are the most effective. On all packs the active constituent is detailed together with its percentage, and the maker's recommendations for use are clearly displayed and should be followed to the letter. In recent years many of the materials with long residual properties (e.g. the chlorinated hydrocarbons) have been withdrawn and replaced by materials that break down more quickly.

Cutworms are the larvae of several species of nocturnal moth. Like snails and slugs they do most of their damage after dark and can devastate a good stand of seedlings or transplants overnight. In addition, they browse on the shoulders of root and tuber crops such as carrots, beets, potatoes and sweet potatoes. I always associate severe attacks with heavy applications of coarse organic materials, particularly those with a manure content. A preplanting dressing of Bexadust or a drenching with a weak solution of Malathion are useful practices. Cutworm bait in the form of granules based on sodium fluosilicate are also most effective, and for maximum control I prefer to strew the bait the night before transplanting.

SUCKING PESTS

Aphids, thrips, spider mites and mites are the principal sucking pests that cause damage to vegetable crops. They usually make for the undersides of the leaves where they cannot easily be seen, and very often the damage goes unnoticed until a sizeable infestation has built up. Their sucking causes a backward curling of the leaves, or a silvering or bronzing of the foliage. Aphids are sometimes called plant lice, green fly or black fly, and are particularly partial to cabbage and related crops, globe artichokes, beans of all types, cucumbers, carrots and bush squashes. However, if the leaves of almost any vegetable crop are examined, particularly on the undersides, aphids of some type can usually be found. They reproduce very quickly (live birth being usual in warm climates such as ours) and produce winged forms when overcrowding occurs. There is an interesting relationship between ants on the one hand and aphids, scale insects, Australian bugs and other honeydew-secreting insects. Quite often the first indication of the presence of these damaging pests is the increased activity of ants up and down the plants.

Aphids cannot be controlled with stomach poisons for they ingest little, if any, of the surface tissue. They simply penetrate the plants with their 'beaks' and suck up the cell sap as if through a straw. They are, however, very soft-bodied insects and can easily be controlled with specific contact dusts or sprays such as nicotine or with all-purpose materials such as Malathion and Thiodan.

The control of sucking pests, especially aphids and red spider mites, was revolutionized a few years ago when systemic pesticides were released for use on vegetables, flowers, fruit trees and ornamentals. These are materials that are sprayed on the foliage or, in one or two cases, applied to the soil in granular form. Thereafter they are absorbed into the plant tissues and translocated throughout the top growth. Several are now on the market, but only one or two of these can be recommended for use on vegetable crops within the confines of the home garden. Probably the two great advantages of the systemics are that, firstly, they cannot be removed by heavy rain or by watering once they have been absorbed into the plant tissues; and secondly, the pests can be controlled wtih less than a 100% coverage of the foliage, a factor that is especially important when aphid infestations are sufficiently severe to cause curling of the leaves, which would otherwise protect the aphids from the poison.

PESTICIDES: CHEWING PESTS

BHC: This is just about the only chlorinated hydrocarbon registered for use on vegetable crops in the home garden. The usual formulation, a dust, can be used to control a wide variety of sucking and chewing insects on a wide range of crops. It can also be used to control soil insects such as cutworms and certain household insects.

Dedevap: Another material that gives satisfactory control of aphids and caterpillars on several vegetable crops. Its usual formulation is an emulsifiable concentrate.

Karbaspray: Based on carbaryl, this material is a relatively safe stomach poison aganst beetles and caterpillars.

Malathion: A relatively safe member of the organo-phosphate group. It is a broad-spectrum material having very considerable value as a stomach poison and as a contact pesticide on soft insects such as small nymphs, larvae and aphids. The usual formulation for the home garden pack is a 50% emulsifiable concentrate. Because of its relationship to the extremely toxic parathion many gardeners appear to be afraid to use this material, and it is indeed right that they should have considerable respect for all spray materials, particularly pesticides. As far as Malathion is concerned, some idea of its relative safety can be gauged from the fact that commercially it is used to within a few days of harvesting crops such as lettuces and beans.

Mesurol: A pelleted material based on methiocarb, which has given excellent results under a wide range of conditions. Unfortunately baits have rather a limited life, particularly on wet soil, and need to be replaced every 48 hours or so in such conditions.

Metaldehyde: This material, which gives excellent control of slugs and snails in most conditions, is available in ready-to-use bait forms, which have superseded the old mixture of Meta and bran. These preparations are distributed very easily, for they are pellets that usually contain 4% metaldehyde. The baits, best distributed in late afternoon (as in all but cloudy, wet conditions slugs and snails are more active at night), kill by contact, although they also act as a stomach poison. Contact with the bait causes slugs and snails to exude an abnormally high quantity of the slime they use for locomotion, and this trail can be seen quite clearly on the soil surface in the morning. This effort causes the slugs to dehydrate, and in many cases also results in their exposure during daytime. More recently, carbaryl has been incorporated into snail baits to good effect.

Liquid formulations of snail baits are now available and although they have little application in the vegetable garden they are extremely useful on perennial flowers and ornamentals, on which slugs and snails often spend much of their lives.

Thiodan: This material, based on endosulfan, also has a short safety period and has given good control of aphids, thrips and caterpillars. Its usual formulation is a 50% wettable powder. A wetting agent is particularly necessary when it is used for onion thrips.

1

2

3

4

1. Millipedes
2. Astylus beetles
3. CMR beetle
4. Chafer beetles
5. Potato snout beetle
6. Potato with snout beetle damage
7. Looper caterpillar on tomato leaf
8. Common molerat

5

6

7

8

Mites of several species were controlled long ago with sulphur dusts and sprays, while Malathion has proved effective in many cases. Kelthane is a material produced specifically to control these insects and is described as a miticide or acaricide. It has proved extremely effective against the tomato russet mite and is to be recommended when these pests appear.

The following materials are suitable for controlling sucking insects on vegetable crops:

PESTICIDES: SUCKING PESTS

Aphicide: A systemic material based on dimethoate, an organo-phosphate that is safe to handle if used as directed. It can be used on edible crops until a week or two before harvesting.

BHC: A 'straight' insecticidal dust available under several trade names. It is useful for controlling aphids on seedlings, and for infestations that are exposed and easily accessible.

Insecticide Granules: These granules are normally incorporated into the soil at sowing or planting time and give good aphid control for 6-8 weeks. They should be used with great care because of the long safety period, which should be observed rigidly on edible crops.

Kelthane: A specific miticide that kills all stages of red spider mite and tomato russet mite. It is a contact preparation to which a wetter should be added for maximum effect.

Malathion: This broad-spectrum material, described earlier, gives satisfactory control of aphids and red spider if used with a wetting agent. It is a contact material and requires good coverage to ensure maximum effect.

Metasystox: Another organo-phosphate, with similar capabilities and limitations to Aphicide, having a safety period of 10-21 days.

Sulphur: In dust or wettable powder formulations, sulphur is effective against mites as well as having certain fungicidal properties. A limitation of the dust is the difficulty in obtaining a high-percentage coverage.

Thiodan and **Dedevap:** These will also give some control of aphids and thrips and are excellent stomach poisons.

To clear up aphid infestations with contact preparations it is advisable initially to spray or dust twice, 4 days apart, for there may be odd survivors the first time. Not only can these survivors multiply very quickly and so create further problems, but they can build up some resistance to the spray materials and can pass this on to their offspring.

On certain crops attacked by aphids and white fly, the leaves and stems become black with 'sooty mould'. This is not a disease in itself, but a black fungus that grows in the honeydew secreted by these insects. It will disappear if the infestation is destroyed, and is a condition more common on ornamentals and fruit trees, where aphids, mealy bugs and scale insects secrete large quantities of honeydew.

SOIL PESTS

Among the most troublesome garden pests are cutworms, wireworms and white grubs, all of which are the larval stages of moths and beetles. Some species of small millipede are occasionally also destructive on young seedlings. Cutworms are the larvae of nocturnal moths of several species, and are voracious feeders. As their name suggests, they do most damage by cutting off young seedlings and transplants at or around soil level, but they also do damage to potato tubers, asparagus spears, and root crops such as beetroot and carrots. Heads of celery and leeks also receive a certain amount of attention when the soil is drawn up to the plants. They are most troublesome in soils containing an abundance of manure, compost or other organic matter, and appear to favour moist conditions.

Wireworms are the larvae of click beetles and often spend several seasons developing in the soil by a sequence of moults. The worms are segmented, yellowish-brown in colour, have three pairs of legs just behind the head, and may be up to 30 mm long.

White grubs are the larvae of chafer beetles and, like wireworms, may live in the soil for a few seasons, depending upon the species. The larvae are dirty white or cream in colour with a medium brown head and three pairs of legs on the front section. When disturbed by the spade or fork they usually curl up. They do not appear to do very much damage to vegetable crops in general, although damage to roots is of course difficult to detect.

Millipedes usually attack tubers, bulbs, roots and other parts of the plant that are below ground. However, on several occasions I have found them damaging young seedlings in seedpans and seedboxes placed in a cold frame. During the daytime they can often be found underneath the containers, as can slugs.

The withdrawal many years ago of chlorinated hydrocarbons such as Aldrin and Dieldrin from the range of materials readily available for the control of soil insects on a wide range of crops left a gap which has never been filled successfully. Low-percentage BHC dusts have been obtainable for many years, but the possibility of their tainting root and tuber crops have led to their being used less and less. However, the general availability of new BHC materials based on the gamma isomer has changed the picture somewhat. These dusts can be used in a broadcast application incorporated shallowly before sowing or planting, or as an inter-row post-planting application hoed in shallowly between established plants.

Carbaryl-based materials such as Karbaspray can be used as drenches a day or two before sowing or planting, or as heavy sprays or drenches along the rows only, or as a blanket treatment after sowing and again after emergence. Excellent control of cutworms on transplants can be achieved by pouring a small quantity (e.g. an eggcupful) of the suspension over the transplants when they have been watered in.

On established plantings some relief can be obtained from cutworm attack by distributing small quantities of bait among the rows in the late afternoon. Suitable ready-mixed baits, usually based on sodium fluosilicate, are now available at any garden shop.

Where only small plants are concerned, some control of cutworms can be achieved by digging *carefully* with the finger, or with a small dibber, around the base of severed or damaged plants or around adjacent plants, and removing the worms. This is best carried out early in the morning before they move away.

STINGING PESTS

The cucurbits, including chayote, are the only vegetables that are troubled by fruit fly. The species attacking these crops is usually referred to as melon fly or pumpkin fly. If no control measures are carried out damage can be very severe, especially to later plantings. There are two methods commonly used to control these insects, each based on a different theory. The older of the two is the baiting method and is extremely effective if the control programme is begun when the first flowers appear and is repeated every 7-10 days, particularly if heavy rain is experienced. To attempt control with this method once damaged fruits are detected is rarely successful. The method of baiting is to make up a thin, attractive, but poisonous syrup, and to syringe it into the air above the plants, using as coarse a nozzle as possible. The large drops fall on the leaves and the water soon evaporates, leaving behind poisonous crystals to which the adult flies are attracted. If no syringe is available the material can be distributed quite satisfactorily with an old whitewash brush, which is dipped in the mixture and then shaken or flicked here and there over the foliage. With some crops it is quite easy to see the effectiveness of this method. On bush marrows, for example, the leaves stand like hands with partly opened fingers, and in the cup at the base of the leaves I have frequently found considerable numbers of dead adult flies, which had fed on the bait. There are several recipes for this bait, the following being one that I have found most effective:

15 g Malathion W.P. or Dipterex,
500 g sugar,
5 ℓ water.

Fruit fly attractants are sometimes available and these, instead of sugar, can be mixed with the active constituent.

PLANT NEMATODES

Plant parasitic nematodes or 'eelworms', as they are generally called, cause an enormous amount of damage to garden crops and to certain farm crops each year. With the tremendous host range of the majority of species, they are the most damaging organisms the gardener in South Africa has to contend with. For this reason a detailed discussion of their activities and of available control measures is very necessary.

Plant nematodes are roundworms, similar in form to the intestinal worms of domestic animals, but of microscopic dimensions. There are many hundreds of species in the soil, but less than fifty or so are plant parasitic. Some of these are ectoparasitic, i.e. they move around in the soil and feed on the roots externally, while others are endoparasitic and enter the roots, feeding there and laying their egg batches either in the roots or on the surface. Although the spiral nematode, the stubby root nematode and the root rot nematode are all found in soils in different areas, by far the most widespread and damaging is the root knot nematode. It is this pest that will be dealt with in some detail here, although the recommended control measures will also take care of most other species.

Most gardeners will at one time or another have noticed plants which, despite being given generous amounts of fertilizer, manure and water, make little or no growth, are of poor colour, and wilt even in moist soil. If one of these plants is carefully lifted from the soil, complete with roots, it will in many cases be found that instead of the roots being smooth and even they are disfigured with lumps or galls. The galls vary in size according to the degree of attack and the species of root knot nematode involved, but they are usually very conspicuous on affected tomatoes, pumpkins and Swiss chard. Nematode damage should not be confused with the beneficial bacterial nodules that are found on most leguminous plants and discussed in an earlier chapter. Bacterial nodules are appendages that can easily be pulled off without damaging the roots, whereas the nematode galls are actually swellings of the roots themselves.

On very susceptible root crops, such as beetroot and carrots, the swellings are very noticeable, and if the plants are attacked during the early stages of growth the roots will be little more than strings of galls. If such crops get away to a good start, however, they will develop normal roots, but if they are left in the soil for any length of time after maturity, particularly when the soil is wet, they will eventually become disfigured.

With potatoes the root system is attacked in the usual way and shows the characteristic galling, but the tubers display rather different symptoms. The nematodes cause the normally smooth skins of the tubers to become warted or pustulous, and when this tissue is cut with a knife it has a grey, water-soaked appearance. The nemas rarely penetrate more than 10 mm into the tubers, but by causing the pustules they make the potatoes unattractive, reduce their keeping qualities, and make them susceptible to attack by certain soil fungi that cause rotting.

On sweet potatoes the symptoms are again different. The smaller roots have raised lumps that are rather paler than the surrounding skin tissue and the larger roots are often deeply cracked, although this can also be caused by boron deficiency and by fluctuating moisture conditions in the soil. The cracking makes the roots unattractive and also makes them susceptible to certain soil fungi that are unable to enter the roots unless the way is opened for them by other organisms or by mechanical damage.

Form and life cycle

Root knot nematodes are, in most stages, visible only with the aid of a lens, but in the roots of certain plants the adult females can clearly be seen with the naked eye. If a heavily-galled root of pumpkin, cucumber or tomato, for instance, is broken open by *twisting* and carefully examined, a number of pearly-white bodies, about a quarter the size of a pinhead, will be seen in the tissues, especially close to the axial cylinder or core. These bodies are somewhat pear-shaped and are the adult female nematodes that have become sedentary and have probably begun egg-laying. The adult males and young larvae, which cannot be seen without magnification, are eel-shaped, i.e. long and narrow. It is almost impossible to see adult females in carrots and beetroot because of the hard tissue and the colour of these vegetables.

When the young larvae hatch and make their way into the soil, they move around in search of a root belonging to a suitable host plant. Having found one they enter it and inject into the tissue, by means of a hollow, needle-like stylet, a substance that causes abnormally large cells to develop. It is collections of these cells that give affected roots their characteristic galled or knotted appearance. This distortion of the root tissues interferes very greatly with the translocation of moisture and plant foods, and the upper portions of affected plants suffer accordingly; it is rather like tying a knot in a hosepipe.

Once a young female larva is established in the root tissue she becomes sedentary, and after further growth and development (which under favourable conditions may take only 3-4 weeks) she begins to lay eggs. An egg batch may contain between 100 and 1 000 eggs, depending upon the host's suitability and the soil temperature. The eggs are deposited in a yellowish-brown, jelly-like sac that prevents them from drying out in adverse soil conditions. On most plants these sacs are produced within the root tissues, but on peas and the fine roots of sweet potatoes they can often be seen on the outside and can be picked off easily. Normally the eggs hatch quickly, but if the soil is very dry and therefore unfavourable for movement they simply remain in the sac until conditions improve, making this the most resistant stage of the parasite.

The life cycle may be completed in 30 days in warm, wet weather, but in winter it could take considerably longer. However, it is quite possible that in irrigated soils, planted with a succession of susceptible vegetable crops, 8-10 generations may be produced in a single year.

Distribution

Root knot nematodes are indigenous to most parts of the world that have tropical or subtropical climates. They are favoured by hot summers and cool, mild winters, and are found in greater numbers in light sandy loams than in heavy clay. In natural veld, infestation seldom builds up to any degree, because of the lack of accommodating host plants and also because of the long, dry season experienced in many parts of the country. Severe infestations are, however, rapidly built up under intensive gardening practices, where susceptible crops follow each other in quick succession and where watering, or irrigation, is carried on throughout dry periods.

For many years nematodes carried on their activities unsuspected, and poor yields and crop failure were attributed to nutrient deficiency, unfavourable climatic conditions and to other soil pests and diseases. Because of this ignorance the situation was allowed to worsen and severe infestations built up. Residues of affected crops were frequently either turned into the soil or incorporated into the compost heap, which, in the average home garden, seldom generates the temperatures necessary to kill these organisms. Later this material was distributed all over the garden, thereby contaminating previously 'clean' ground. In many parts of South Africa this routine is still carried out by unenlightened gardeners, and when one politely points out the dangers one is often greeted with disbelief. It is only when the activities of the nemas render crop growing disappointing and unprofitable that one is taken seriously. Prior to the post-war introduction of economic control measures, whole farms were abandoned because of the unprofitability of raising crops on nematode-infested land.

Nematode larvae do not travel far of their own volition and even the most energetic amongst them probably never manage more than a metre a year. However, they are all too easily given transportation in soil adhering to boots and tools and in storm water. Careless watering and irrigation also result in their distribution. They are often introduced into a garden in imported topsoil and in plants from outside sources. Registered nurseries are regularly inspected by personnel experienced in insects, diseases and nematodes, and it is therefore wise to purchase all plants from such sources.

Susceptibility of plants

All root knot nematodes belong to the genus *Meloidogyne*. *M. javanica* and *M. incognita* var. *acrita* are two of the most common species found in Central and Southern Africa, the former being particularly troublesome to tobacco growers.

The number of plants that are confirmed hosts to at least one species of root knot nematode runs into thousands, and the list grows daily as fresh specimens are submitted for examination. Plants can conveniently be classified as 'susceptible', 'tolerant', 'resistant' and 'immune'. Susceptible plants are severely attacked and suffer greatly, tolerant plants make satisfactory growth despite severe attack (this group includes many weeds), resistant plants are not heavily attacked, and immune plants are not attacked at all. The majority of vegetables are excellent hosts to several species, a few being attacked by only a single species.

The following vegetables have a high susceptibility rating to one or more species of root knot nematodes: beans, beetroot, carrots, celery, cucumbers, egg plants, parsley, peas, peppers, potatoes, pumpkins, squashes, Swiss chard, tomatoes, watermelon.

Vegetables that are really cool-season crops and can often be grown in infected soil during the winter months, particularly if they are generously treated with manure or compost, are cabbage, broccoli, turnips, onions, leeks and kohlrabi.

Apart from vegetables, certain flowers, sub-tropical fruits, weeds and field crops are also hosts and must be considered before any control scheme is formulated.

The following flowers have been confirmed as hosts: amaranthus, antirrhinum, calendula, centaurea, cyclamen, dahlia, delphinium, lobelia, lupin, nasturtium, nicotiana, pansy, shasta daisy, sunflower, sweet pea, zinnia.

Pawpaws, pineapples, bananas, granadillas, tree tomatoes and peaches are among the most common fruit hosts. Soya beans, Rhodes grass, maize, sorghum, velvet beans, tobacco, sugar cane and certain clovers are also hosts to these nematodes, although many of them can be classified as tolerant. Nevertheless, this tolerance means that they allow reproduction to take place in their roots and, therefore, increase the degree of soil infestation and jeopardize companion plants and later crops. Among the most prominent weed hosts are most species of amaranthus, oxalis, galinsoga, nicandra, uintjies and blackjack. In certain cases these weeds can be used by the experienced gardener to judge whether or not fumigation will be necessary for the succeeding crop.

Control of nematodes

The word 'control' is a carefully chosen one, for it is quite impossible to eradicate nematodes in the open garden. Although the majority of these organisms dwell in the top 250 mm of soil they have frequently been found in roots 1 m and more below the surface, which is way beyond the effective range of any practical control measures, be they cultural, biological or chemical.

CULTURAL CONTROL

For very many years it was thought that root knot could be controlled effectively and economically by cultural methods only. Long rotations between highly susceptible crops, bare fallow, the use of immune and trap crops were some of the recommendations.

Attempting control by crop rotation, i.e. by planting highly susceptible crops at very long intervals and using less accommodating hosts in between, is of little value in the home garden. A glance at the list of susceptible vegetables shows quite clearly that there are few crops of consequence remaining for use in any rotational sequence, particularly during the summer months. Again, the relatively few rows per sowing or planting of each vegetable makes the application of this theory impracticable.

A bare fallow, in which the ground is kept free of any sort of vegetation by continual light cultivations, has to be maintained for a very long period if any real benefit is to be derived from it, for susceptible crops such as tomatoes have become badly affected after 18 months of this treatment. In the home garden it cannot be regarded as a satisfactory and practical method of control. Another method, which has met with some success on field scale in Zimbabwe, is that of having a bare fallow and cultivating the soil quite deeply and frequently during the hot, dry months in an attempt to kill off the nemas by desiccation. In the home garden this method has little future and even on field scale it can be practised only at the risk of destroying the soil structure. It is also believed by some researchers that in areas with regular wet and dry seasons the nematodes have developed the ability to move downwards as the general moisture content of the topsoil drops and to make their way to the surface again when the rainy season commences. In addition, of course, any system of bare fallow means that nothing can be planted or harvested for extended periods, while the main aim of any home vegetable garden should be to keep in full production throughout the year or at least for as many months as possible.

The question of root knot control by trap-cropping is a very complex one indeed because the behavioural pattern of these organisms with regard to host relationship can change in different geographical locations. Trap-cropping is a system in which a crop that is known to be susceptible to root knot is sown or planted and subsequently turned into the soil early in growth, after an invasion of the roots has occurred but *before* the nemas have reached the mature, egg-laying stage. Anyone with common sense will immediately see that this practice demands an intimate knowledge of the complete life cycle of the nematodes. Failure to turn the crop in and destroy the plants in good time could result in an increase in the nematode population instead of a decrease.

Over the years several articles have been published containing claims that nematode populations can be reduced considerably by turning into the soil thick stands of certain types of marigold (*Tagetes* spp.). It would appear that the nemas attack the roots in large numbers and enter the root tissue but do not develop beyond the second larval stage and so the plants, in a way, act as a trap crop, as does sunn-hemp if sown thickly. A drawback in using crops such as marigolds and sunn-hemp in this way is that because they are usually seeded by the broadcasting method it is impossible to obtain a pure stand of the plants, and the weeds that will inevitably appear may be very susceptible host plants.

BIOLOGICAL CONTROL

The short life cycle and high reproductive capacity of these parasites would enable them to multiply astronomically if they were left unchecked. Fortunately the majority are destroyed by bacteria, fungi and protozoa, as well as by other nematodes, insects and mites. One leading American researcher believes that predatory organisms destroy more than 95% of the plant parasitic nematodes at the larval stage.

Desirable microbiological activity that reduces the nematode population is only found in soils that are kept in good heart by intelligent management, and particularly by practices that build up the organic content. The value of manure, compost, mulches, clean crop residues and green manures in stimulating and maintaining a thriving soil population must again be stressed. Although the incorporation of such materials is definitely a step in the right direction, an overnight reduction in the nematode population should not be expected. Of course, such amendments not only stimulate the beneficial soil populations but also create improved moisture and nutrient levels, which lead to more vigorous crop plants that possibly have an improved resistance to nematode attack.

RESISTANT CULTIVARS

In recent years a great deal of research has been carried out in an effort to breed vegetable cultivars and hybrids that have a degree of resistance to root knot nematodes. So far some success has been achieved with peppers, tomatoes and sweet potatoes. Not only do resistant cultivars grow on in infected soils, but many young larvae that attack the plants fail to develop properly inside the roots and die.

CONTROL BY HEAT

Any potting soil sterilized with steam or baked should be free from nematodes, provided that a uniform heat is obtained throughout the material. A small quantity of soil for seedboxes can be sterilized to a degree by pouring a kettle of boiling water over it in the seedboxes or by putting the material on a steel tray and baking it in the oven. Temperatures of 93-95°C for two hours should be effective for soil treatment if these temperatures are sustained throughout the material. Small packs of sterilized compost are available at some garden shops and are most useful for seedboxes.

CHEMICAL CONTROL

Although cultural and biological control may bring about some reduction in the nematode population, soil fumigation of one sort or another is the only assured method of control and then only if the application is carefully carried out. It is also important that the fumigation be done in good time, before the crop is established, as no suitable material has yet been formulated for *general* application after the planting of annual crops.

The materials in the box below are used in soil fumigation.

Many amateur gardeners use other insecticides and even lime in an attempt to control root knot. Most of the modern insecticides and related materials, as well as a host of other chemicals, are ineffective against these organisms, and it is therefore a waste of time for the home gardener to try them out. As far as lime is concerned, nematodes can tolerate a far wider pH range than any crops of commerce.

Soil conditions. To get maximum benefit from the use of soil fumigants, certain important points must be understood before the materials are used.

The temperature, porosity, moisture content and level of organic matter of the soil are all factors that can markedly affect the efficiency of soil fumigants. Volatilization of the material is rapid when the soil temperature is high, whereas in cold soil it is slower and consequently a less uniform penetration is obtained. Porosity can similarly affect penetration. In light-textured, sandy soils the gas moves quickly and it is often necessary in such areas to seal the soil surface by watering to prevent the fumes from escaping before they have done their job. Heavy clays are difficult to fumigate, whether wet or dry, and a higher rate of application may often be necessary to achieve any measure of control.

Free-moving forms of root knot nematode live in the films of moisture surrounding soil particles, and even in what might appear to be fairly dry soil these films exist. However, if there is excessive moisture in the soil the spaces between the soil particles are completely full and this creates a barrier that makes it difficult for the toxic vapours to diffuse. In wet, clayey soils the spread of the fumes will therefore be minimal, and very small pockets of soil will get an overdose while the bulk will remain untouched.

Soils with a very high organic content are also difficult to fumigate because this material absorbs much of the vapour, thus reducing its effective spread. Consequently, as with clay, higher levels of fumigant have to be used to ensure adequate control.

Soil preparation. Before fumigation is carried out the soil must be well prepared. The following points, in particular, must receive careful attention:
- The soil must be free from any undecayed organic matter, especially root systems of previous crops. The fumigant may destroy nematodes in the outer tissues of these roots but it will not penetrate to the core, where infestation is often most severe.
- Any manure, compost or other organic material needed to improve the soil must be added *before* fumigation, as there is a real danger of reinfection if it is added afterwards. In addition, it must be well decayed and free of very large lumps.
- The soil must be well worked to a depth of at least 250 mm and all clods must be broken up as they do not allow penetration of the fumes.
- The soil should be in planting condition, i.e. quite moist. If it is too dry the fumes will escape rapidly instead of diffusing slowly through the soil and doing a thorough job.

Methods of application. DD and EDB are best injected into the soil with a special injector gun, of which there are several models. These guns are all based on the same design and can be calibrated to deliver the recommended quantities of fumigant by moving the top of the plunger spindle and thereby lengthening or shortening the stroke. From 6 to 12 mm per injection is the usual rate of application depending upon the material and the formulation used. Before each fumigation the gun, especially the piston washer, should be checked for any signs of wear, and the stop should be tightened or it will shift up the spindle and increase the quantity of fumigant delivered per stroke. Calibrating is best carried out with paraffin rather than with the actual fumigant. The guns also have an adjustable flange that rests on the soil surface and regulates the depth, and this can be moved up and down the injector spike. The ideal depth is 200-250 mm, which is possible in most soils. The injector head is around 50 mm long, usually has 6 holes to give an even coverage, and contains a spring-loaded ball.

There are two methods of covering the area to be treated. The first is to give it overall or blanket coverage and the other is to inject only the planting rows or stations. The overall method is rather expensive, but should definitely be used in seedbeds. Where the bed method of crop production is practised, overall treatment is also recommended for closely-spaced, directly-seeded subjects such as carrots, lettuces and beetroot. Treating only the crop rows and planting stations is a satisfactory and economical

---

NEMATODE FUMIGANTS

Basamid: This is one of several granular soil fumigants introduced in recent years. It contains dazomet and is readily available in 500 g containers.

DD: This dark brown, volatile liquid is a mixture of dichloropropene and dichloropropane. It is always sold under this name and should not be confused with DDT.

EDB: Ethylene dibromide is another excellent material and is one of the few suitable preparations available in 5 ℓ containers. Several formulations are obtainable, some of which need to be mixed. It is important *not* to mix these in a galvanized container.

Methyl bromide: Apart from controlling nematodes very well, this material also accounts for many parasitic fungi and weed seeds. It is a gas at ordinary temperatures and is kept under pressure in sealed containers.

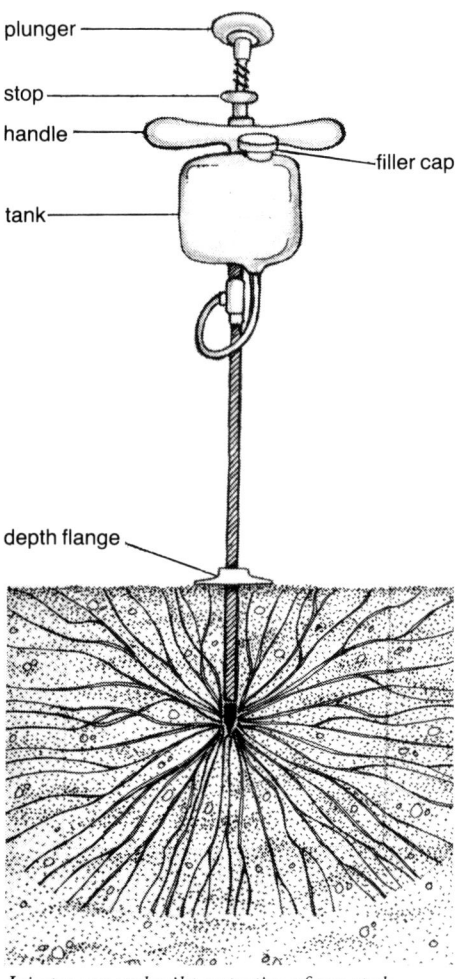

plunger
stop
handle
filler cap
tank
depth flange

Injector gun and soil penetration of nematode fumigant.

the soil after each injection, the hole it leaves should be closed off firmly with the heel to seal it and prevent the fumes from escaping too rapidly. At the end of every row or two the gun should be tried out above ground to check that all the delivery holes are still open, but care should be taken not to splash the legs or trousers. If any holes are blocked with soil they should be opened with a large safety-pin or a piece of thin but strong wire.

On completion of the whole operation, the ground can be wetted lightly with a fine spray to seal off the surface and contain the fumes for a period, but this is not essential if the ground is moist enough for planting. After use the gun should be completely emptied and flushed out with paraffin to which a little clean oil has been added. Most fumigants are corrosive, particularly DD, and neglecting to flush out properly will appreciably reduce the life of the injector gun.

Not everyone may wish to go to the expense of purchasing an injector gun, but two or three gardeners could acquire one together. The alternative to the injector gun is to use a long-stemmed funnel and a teaspoon. This method is effective if carried out carefully, but back-breaking when a large area has to be treated. A hole is made to the required depth with a stick or dibber, the funnel is placed in the hole and the fumigant poured in, 1-2 teaspoonfuls (5-10 mℓ) being a satisfactory rate of application. The funnel is then withdrawn, the hole sealed off, and the procedure repeated until the area has been covered. It is essential that a long-stemmed funnel (200 mm or so in length) be used, otherwise the bulk of the dosage will never reach the required depth but will adhere to the walls of the holes.

After using DD and EDB, the ground should be left for 2-3 weeks before sowing or planting is carried out, the longer period being advisable during wet periods and in heavy ground. It is always advisable to dig over the soil very carefully when rows or planting stations have been treated, to allow any remaining fumes to disperse. With root and tuber crops a full month should elapse during wet weather before sowing or planting is undertaken. I have sometimes harvested carrots and potatoes that have had a distinct off-flavour after a fumigation.

Methyl bromide is a little more expensive than DD and EDB but has the advantage of controlling soil fungi and some weed seeds and allowing sowing or planting to take place 48 hours after the treatment has been

completed. The usual formulation is methyl bromide 98% and chloropicrin 2%, the latter being added as an indicating agent because methyl bromide is relatively odourless when pure.

Methyl bromide requires a different method of application from the other two fumigants. A plastic cover is laid over the area to be treated and is tucked in all round to prevent the escape of the gas. The cover is not laid flat on the soil but is supported by sacks of grass or boxes with *no sharp edges*. Underneath the cover is placed an evaporating tray (or trays if necessary), consisting of a 20 ℓ tin with a depth of 30-50 mm. A piece of garden hose is placed under the cover with one end in the evaporator tray and the other buried in the soil and emerging *outside* the cover.

The methyl bromide is released from its container, usually a 500 mℓ pack, by means of a special applicator attached to a thin plastic tube that is inserted into the hose for a metre or so. When the applicator handle is closed the tin is punctured and the methyl bromide, which is under pressure, is released and runs into the evaporator tray. Here it quickly resumes its gaseous form and penetrates into the soil. Care should always be taken to see that the thick rubber washer around the applicator's puncturing device is in place and in good condition. After application the tube can be removed from the hose and the end of the latter can be sealed with a wooden stopper to prevent gas from escaping. After 48 hours the plastic cover can, if necessary, be moved to another spot. The usual rate of application is 500 g per 10 m^2.

Methyl bromide can also be used for fumigating large quantities of potting compost or soil. The material is spread out to a depth of 300-350 mm and covered wth a plastic cover, supported as before, with the evaporating tray on top of the levelled heap. In this case 500 g per m^3 is an effective rate. Plastic covers should be checked carefully between applications to ensure that they have not been punctured.

With all fumigants care should be taken not to operate too close to permanent features such as hedges, trees and shrubs, for serious damage may result. In addition, the manufacturer's recommendations for use, including application rates, should be strictly adhered to, as these chemicals are all extremely poisonous and in some cases highly inflammable.

method for the open garden, particularly with widely-spaced crops such as tomatoes, cucumbers, squashes and pumpkins. This method allows the plants to get away to a flying start, particularly if they are well fertilized, and although the younger feeder roots may later become affected, the yield is seldom reduced to any degree.

In overall applications the whole area is injected every 300-350 mm, depending upon the manufacturer's recommendations, and in row treatment each row is injected at 300 mm intervals for crops such as beets, carrots and lettuce. With tomatoes the injections can be 400-450 mm apart, depending upon the spacing of the plants, and with subjects such as pumpkins and squashes each planting station can be given two injections.

When the spike has been removed from

Fumigation using methyl bromide.

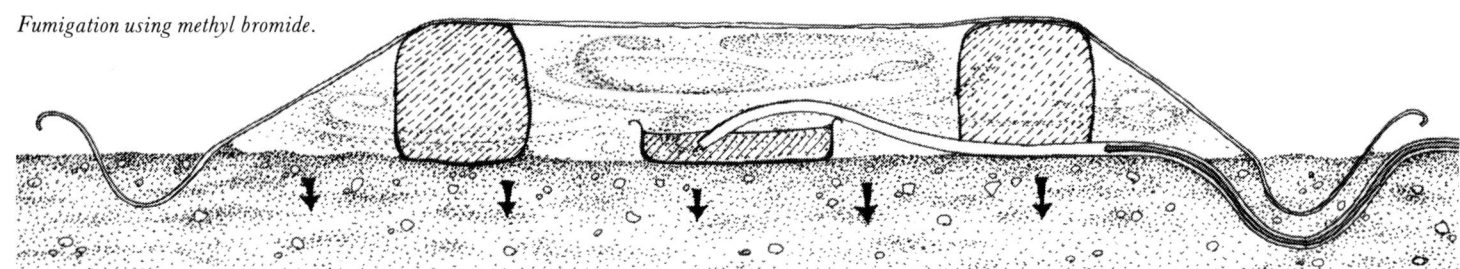

GENERAL CONSIDERATIONS

The chemical and physical control measures recommended for pests will only be completely effective if they are carried out in conjunction with the maintenance of a high standard of garden sanitation. So often relatively expensive materials and valuable time are used in the spraying and dusting of crops while, close by, breeding continues unchecked on weeds or other plants in the garden. One also frequently encounters vegetable gardens in which the plants have been left standing after harvest or after they have failed to develop properly. Cabbage, broccoli and cauliflower are among the more common subjects neglected in this way. Such plants soon become infested with caterpillars, aphids and leaf hoppers. 'Stung' fruits of the cucurbit family should also be removed and destroyed regularly to reduce similar trouble on later plantings.

The destruction of all weeds and refuse is of very great importance because pests such as cutworm moths often lay their eggs on these materials. And old seedboxes, flower pots, bricks, pieces of timber and other materials lying on or close to the ground offer protection to such unwelcome guests as slugs, snails, cutworms and millipedes.

Weak plants often suffer most, initially, from infestations, especially of aphids and caterpillars. The gardener should therefore endeavour to keep his crops in a vigorous condition by thorough soil preparation, using fertilizer and manure when appropriate, and by applying organic or inorganic side dressings when necessary.

As far as nematodes are concerned, a high standard of garden hygiene is again essential if control measures are to be completely effective. All affected plants should therefore be removed, together with their roots, and either incinerated or destroyed by spreading them out in a *thin* layer in very hot, dry weather and turning them occasionally. This will kill most active stages of the organism. On no account should such plants be turned under or added to the compost heap. Care should also be taken to lift them in good time, otherwise the roots will rot and disintegrate, spilling the egg sacs and young larvae into the soil. After they have been removed, the ground should be forked over and any small sections of root removed.

No affected roots or tubers should be saved for propagation purposes because such material can easily contaminate 'clean' ground. Any seedlings obtained from outside sources should be carefully inspected and, if affected, should be discarded together with the soil in which they were growing. I believe it is important for the recipient to inform the supplier that the plants were affected, for it is only by a concerted effort that the problem will be contained.

MOLES

Some mole species are insectivorous while others feed on roots, bulbs and tubers. In general, however, it is their disturbance of the soil rather than their feeding habits that causes hostility among gardeners. Traps of several different kinds are currently on the market and if set regularly and correctly they can claim many victims in a short time. There are, in addition, several proprietary chemical formulations available that have given satisfactory mole control, but it would appear that they must be used regularly to ensure mole-free gardening. The following products have gained considerable support:

MOLE FUMIGANTS

Arrex: This product is of French origin and is a cartridge that is ignited and then quickly placed in the tunnel. Its effect thereafter is similar to that of Phostoxin. With both products it is important that soil should not be allowed to run in and close off any portion of the tunnel when the hole is sealed.

Phostoxin: This material is in tablet form and when placed in the burrow it reacts with the soil humidity and gives off fumes, which permeate the tunnels and surrounding soil and either kill the moles or drive them off.

SSB: This is an emulsifiable concentrate that is mixed with water to obtain a 2,5% solution, which is poured generously into the burrows.

The creeping mole, which just breaks the soil surface, is extremely difficult to control with gaseous products as they immediately lose their effectiveness. Of the above preparations perhaps SSB, because it is in liquid form, is most likely to be successful.

The following are some of the materials mentioned in this chapter and in Part 2, and some of the trade names under which they are sold:

PESTICIDES

Carbaryl: Karbadust, Karbaspray, Wurmsprey, Extermacarb
Carbaryl-BHC: Blue Death (powder)
Demeton-s-methyl: Metasystox
Diazinon: Dazzel
Dichlorvos: Dedevap
Dicofol: Kelthane
Dimethoate: Rogor, Protecta 'A', Aphicide, Insecticide Granules, Aphicide Granules
Endosulfan: Thiodan
Fenthion: Lebaycid
Gamma BHC: New Bexadust, Bexadust '5'
Mercaptothion: Malathion, Malasol, Gardicide, Extermathion, Musko
Mercaptothion-mancozeb-sulphur: General Protekta (powder)
Metaldehyde: Disa Liquid Snail Bait
Metaldehyde-carbaryl: Sluggem, Snailban, Snailflo
Metaldehyde-copper: Pestex Snail Bait
Methiocarb: Mesurol
Sodium fluosilicate: Cutworm Bait
Trichlorfon: Dipterex, Danex

FUNGICIDES

Benomyl: Benlate
Copper oxychloride: Cupravit, Virikop, Koppersprey
Copper sulphate-lime: Bordeaux Mixture
Mancozeb: Dithane M45
Mancozeb-sulphur: Milrust
Sulphur: Vine and Dusting Sulphur
Triadmefon: Bayleton
Triforine: Funginex, Fungisprey

SOIL FUMIGANTS

Dazomet: Basamid
Dichloropropene-dichloropropane: DD
Ethylene dibromide: EDB, Agrifume EDB
Fenamiphos: Nemacur
Methyl bromide: Methyl Bromide, Brom-o-Gas

9 VEGETABLES AND HERBS IN CONTAINERS

Not everyone is fortunate enough to have an area of suitable ground for a conventional vegetable garden. Limiting factors include rocky outcrops, hard pot-clay, precipitous building plots and excessive shade, while many town houses do not have gardens at all. However, there are very few people who do not have a patio, balcony or verandah that enjoys several hours of sun each day. In such situations container gardening is of course regularly practised, though in most cases this is limited to flowers and shrubs.

Vegetables and herbs that adapt themselves well to container culture include tomatoes, radishes, onions, spring onions, carrots, beets, lettuces, cucumbers, green peppers, courgettes, parsley, sage, thyme, marjoram and chives. Mustard and cress in containers are discussed in Part 2. Even a single tomato plant in a suitable container placed in a sunny spot can be an interesting and worthwhile project, particularly for a city dweller.

Containers have certain advantages over the open garden: the soil mixture warms up more quickly in spring, drainage is better (provided that a suitable potting mix is used), and feeding and fertilizing are easier. In addition, containers can be placed so that they get maximum sunlight and protection from strong winds. Drawbacks to be considered are that the soil, in smaller containers especially, can get rather hot in summer, the plants have a restricted root run, and the moisture content of the soil must be monitored more regularly.

CONTAINERS

Nowadays the range of plant containers offered is bewildering in terms of size, shape, material and cost. Concrete, asbestos-cement, wood, earthenware, expanded polystyrene and a wide range of plastics are but some of the materials used for the purpose.

The containers can be both functional and decorative, as can the crops grown in them. Some containers, such as those made of asbestos-cement, can easily be painted with PVA or acrylic paint in whatever colour blends in with the surroundings or suits the grower's taste.

The size of container for this kind of gardening depends principally upon the extent of the area available, the situation, and the requirements of the subjects to be grown (root area being critical). The depth of the containers is important, and I would suggest 150-175 mm for radishes, spring onions, lettuce and herbs, and 200-300 mm for larger and heavier-feeding crops.

Larger plant containers need not be placed on the ground, but can be situated on suitable supports if the gardener has some limitation in bending. Permanent brick flower boxes can be set up so that the soil level is at waist height or higher, but care must be taken to provide weep holes.

Container vegetables can even be grown on the balcony of a flat.

Most nurseries and garden centres offer a wide range of containers.

DRAINAGE

As in the open ground, drainage is an important consideration. More container plants of all types have been lost through poor drainage and overwatering than by any form of parasitic disease. Most containers when purchased have a few holes in the base but very often they are too small or too few and have to be enlarged or increased in number.

The size of the pot will determine the depth of the drainage material. This layer can be between 15 and 50 mm deep and can consist of pot shards (scarce these days), stones, broken bricks or coarse gravel. Larger containers can have a 20-25 mm layer of coarse river sand on top of the drainage material to prevent the soil 'fines' from washing away. It must be remembered that with large containers drainage problems cannot be rectified once sowing or planting has been carried out, and it is therefore essential that adequate provision be made before the container is filled with the potting mix.

LIGHT

The best place for containers is a sheltered spot, with a north or north-east aspect, that receives at least 6 or 7 hours of sunlight each day. Some herbs will make satisfactory growth with less direct sunlight. In many situations the plants receive a good deal of reflected light from adjacent walls, which are usually white or pale in colour, and this can be an important consideration when placing the containers for it also affects temperature. It is always a good plan to observe the position one has in mind on a few sunny days before finally establishing the container garden. Containers fitted with castors are also available and are useful for moving plants at midday to increase the number of sunlight hours. Alternatively 'dollys' can be made, similar to the ones used by garage mechanics when working on their backs under cars. Planted containers placed on these can be moved around, thus giving the gardener more flexibility in difficult and confined areas and broadening his scope.

SOIL MIXES

However good a garden soil may appear to be it is not a suitable material for filling containers. After poor drainage and incorrect watering the use of garden soil is probably the most common reason for failure in container gardening.

The essential requirement of any soil mix is that it be porous and well drained, yet able to retain a fair amount of moisture. The root systems of the plants must be able to develop properly and penetrate easily so that they can breathe and make maximum use of soil moisture and nutrients.

There are several proprietary potting soils on the market and their quality varies greatly from centre to centre, even when they are sold under the same label, for they are costly materials to transport and often the manufacturing plants are regional. Some of them are no more suitable for serious container culture than the average garden soil, for they are fine and compact easily. At the other end of the scale there are soil-less mixes consisting of materials such as imported peat, perlite, vermiculite and washed river sand. These are suitable for vegetable growing but tend to be rather expensive.

Proprietary materials sold in bulk can be used as a 'clean' base for building up a suitable potting mix. I would recommend the following as an economical yet satisfactory mix for vegetables and herbs:

2 parts potting soil or garden soil,
1 part river sand or perlite,
1 part sieved (6-10 mm) compost, leaf mould or peat.

Containers should have sufficient drainage material and adequate drainage holes. Fertilizer sticks, shown in position here, are ideal for container gardening.

To this should be added (per 20 ℓ volume) a handful of 2:3:2, a handful of hoof and horn meal, and half a handful of lime. If milled kraal manure is available, 3-4 handfuls can also be incorporated. Large volumes can be mixed with a shovel on a flat surface outdoors, while smaller quantities can be prepared by hand on the potting bench. When filling the containers it is best to firm the mix a little with the fingers as one goes along, and it is essential that the final soil level is 20-25 mm below the rim.

FERTILIZING

The regular watering required by container-grown plants removes considerable quantities of plant nutrients from the soil and these must be replaced more regularly than in the open garden, where, quite often, rainfall and waterings do not penetrate beyond the more extensive root region. The growth of the plants will indicate when replacement nutrients are required. Plant growth in containers should always be steady and vigorous and supplementary dressings must keep in line with this and be light and regular. Nowadays there is, in addition to conventional granular fertilizers, a wide range of ready-mixed, easy-to-use materials formulated for container gardening. Some of these are quick-acting while others release their nutrients slowly. Let the plants be your indicator by their growth and colour, and use the material of your choice strictly according to the manufacturer's instructions on rate and frequency of application. I have found Chemicult, seaweed and fish preparations, and slow-release stick fertilizers particularly effective.

SOWING AND PLANTING

Several vegetables and herbs can be sown directly in containers while others need to be raised in seed-trays. Generally, the in-row planting distances recommended in Chapter 6 can be reduced a little, for quite often the plants in containers do not attain the size of those in open ground. With a little experience the gardener will be able to establish the optimum spacing for different crops. Vegetables such as tomatoes, cucumbers, peppers and courgettes can, as before, be raised under protection in Jiffy pots or segmented seed-trays and then set out in permanent containers when the weather warms up a little. Herbs and carrots, radishes, beets, New Zealand spinach and lettuces are best sown directly where they are to mature and then thinned out if necessary.

WATERING

The most common factors in container gardening that lead to poor growth and plant loss are incorrect watering and inadequate drainage. Most gardeners tend to over-water container plants, a fault that has particularly serious consequences if the soil is compact or if the container has no crocking material and few drainage holes. Plant roots easily become suffocated in dense, wet soil and either die as a direct result of these conditions or succumb to attack by soil fungi that are unable to penetrate healthy tissue. An optimum watering programme for containers is even more difficult to formulate than one for the open garden. Factors such as weather, situation, soil drainage capacity, size of the plants in relation to container size, and stage of plant growth all need to be considered.

With freshly-sown seed and small seedlings, the top 50-75 mm of soil must be kept moist by means of a temporary mulch of sea-grass or dry lawn mowings. With established plants, the top 40-50 mm may be dry provided that the bulk of the soil is moist. It is a good practice in container culture to open the soil surface regularly with a dibber or daisy grubber to ensure that when water is applied it penetrates evenly and does not run down the inside wall of the container.

CONTAINER VEGETABLES

A range of vegetables suitable for containers was mentioned in the introduction to this chapter. In general the conventional cultivars and hybrids grown in the open garden can be grown successfully in containers with, perhaps, a little more pinching out of the growing points of tomatoes and cucumbers to induce more compactness, though this inevitably leads to smaller fruits. Early cultivars are more suited to containers than larger, later ones.

In recent years considerable research has gone into the breeding of cultivars and hybrids specifically for containers. While overseas catalogues mention quite a number, especially tomatoes, few are yet available in South Africa. Small Fry tomatoes and Pot Luck cucumbers are hybrids that are at present listed locally. Of the regular cultivars the following, by virtue of their size, quality and earliness, are suitable:

Beans: Seminole, Top Crop, Contender
Beets: Detroit Dark Red
Cabbages: Early Jersey Wakefield

Carrots: Nantes, Little Finger, Oxheart, Amtou
Cucumbers: Marketer, Crystal Apple
Lettuce: All The Year Round
Spinach: New Zealand
Squashes (courgettes): Blackjack F1, Ambassador F1
Tomatoes: All determinate cultivars

SUCCESSIONAL PLANTING

With containers, as with any other form of vegetable gardening, regular replanting should be undertaken to ensure a succession of fresh produce. To achieve success, however, it will be necessary to replenish the soil mix with fertilizer and organic amendments. Small containers can easily be emptied and refilled with a fresh mix for each crop, ensuring, of course, that the drainage material is replaced. But when larger containers are involved it will be necessary to re-use the bulk of the mix for several successive crops, and this can be quite successful provided

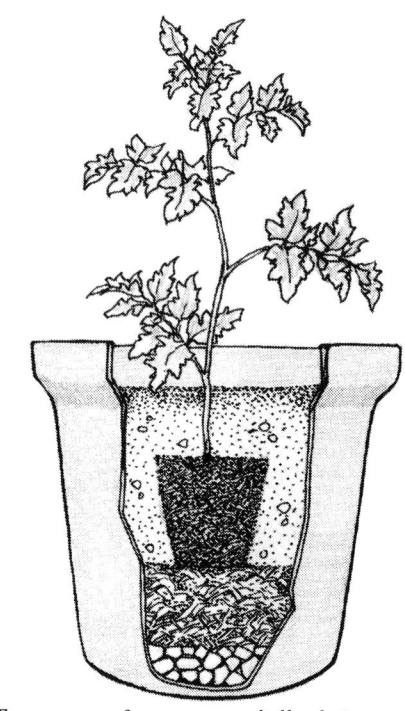

Tomatoes are often grown too shallowly in containers. When they are potted the soil should reach up to the first true leaf.

that nematodes or fungal and bacterial disease organisms are not evident. In any event, it should be standard practice each time to remove the preceding crop residues, particularly the root systems, which should be carefully examined as a routine measure.

The soil should be opened up as deeply as possible, especially against the walls of the container, and a handful or two of milled kraal manure and of hoof and horn meal, together with a light dressing of 2:3:2, can be mixed in thoroughly with the loosened soil. Manure should, of course, not be added before planting a root crop. Between crops the soil can periodically be given a drench with a solution of Jeyes Fluid, or if nematodes are evident Basamid can be worked in as a sterilant. An annual light dressing of lime will counteract the effects of organic and inorganic amendments.

PESTS AND DISEASES

While container-grown vegetables and herbs are in theory subject to the same range of pests and diseases as crops in open ground, they in fact appear to suffer less. This is possibly because they get more individual and regular attention and because growing conditions are more favourable. On occasion, however, aphids, white flies and caterpillars can be troublesome, while damping-off and mildew on certain seedlings can cause problems. The multipurpose pesticide/fungicide dusts in shaker and puffer packs are eminently suited to this sort of situation. Bexadust is another useful pesticidal material, while garden aerosols are most convenient for controlling local infestations of pests. Caterpillars and beetles should regularly be picked off by hand, care being taken to examine both surfaces of the leaves. Soap suds can be used to control aphids.

Slugs and snails may also be a problem from time to time and can ruin a promising stand of seedlings overnight. Bait pellets broadcast lightly on the surface in the evenings will effect control in most cases. When containers are placed on gravel-covered benches, slugs can usually be found nestling in the cool, moist crocks above the drainage holes. They can quickly be destroyed from below with a sharpened stick or dibber, if the containers are small enough to lift.

10 PLASTICS IN THE VEGETABLE GARDEN

In horticulture and agriculture plastic products are used increasingly for a wide variety of purposes. In South Africa constant research is being carried out by at least one major company to improve the quality of existing products and to find new applications for them, particularly for plastic sheeting. Farmers already use this material on a large scale to modify the environment and to create optimum conditions for plant growth, and it can also be used to great advantage by home gardeners.

TUNNELS AND OTHER PLASTIC-CLAD STRUCTURES

Several manufacturers offer plastic-covered tunnels of various sizes, the smallest being about 2-3 m long. The keen gardener with sufficient space would derive a great deal of pleasure as well as a steady flow of fresh produce from such a facility. It would considerably extend the growing season for summer crops such as tomatoes, cucumbers and peppers, and enable him to propagate by seed, cutting or other means under protection.

Those with less space can, with a little ingenuity and care, construct their own plastic greenhouse or modify an existing structure. However, this is not as easy as it might appear, for wind, stability, structural strength, aspect and rust proofing (where metal supports are used) all have to be considered. Perhaps the most important factor when constructing one's own greenhouse is the method of attaching the cladding to the framework. The failure of the plastic at this vulnerable point is often caused by the heat of a metal framework or the roughness and sharp angles of timber supports.

The following points should be borne in mind when constructing a greenhouse:
- Choose as sheltered a location as possible.
- Position the structure north-south if possible.
- Locate it in full sun and well away from possible damage by falling tree branches and other debris.
- Locate it near a water supply.
- Choose well-seasoned timber that will not twist and place stress on the plastic covering, causing it to fail. The timber should be planed all round.
- Ensure that all sharp edges are rounded off and that the timber is generally free from splinters.
- Ensure that the timber is impregnated with a wood preservative, and that this is not injurious to the plastic covering.
- Use a rafter spacing of 600-900 mm.
- Provide adequate ventilation.
- Only use a proven material such as Uvidek 602 as a covering.
- Choose a windless day for cladding and fix the plastic tightly but without stretching. Several pairs of hands may be necessary to achieve the optimum tension.
- Cover the points of contact between framework and covering with a strip at least 15 mm wider than the rafters to prevent heat building up in these areas. This will significantly prolong the life of the plastic.

Most clear plastics commonly available are quite unsuited to exterior use in general and to exposure to hot sun for long periods. They tend to become brittle after a few months if subjected to these conditions. Uvidek 602, which is used widely for covering tunnels and other outdoor structures, is a material that possesses exceptional qualities and is obtainable from leading garden centres and hardware stores, usually by the metre. It contains an ultraviolet inhibitor and has a light transmission factor of 90%. Its life expectancy is about 2 years, although geographical location presents variables that have a bearing on the longevity of the sheeting. Altitude, relative humidity and the way the structure faces are some of the influencing factors.

The cold frame, rarely encountered in the South African garden, is a useful facility if well managed. It can be used for growing-on and hardening-off seedlings, it can improve the growth of crops such as lettuce, radishes and other salads in winter, and it can be used for early direct sowings of summer crops such as squashes and cucumbers. Once the warmer weather is apparent and the plants are growing away, the 'lights' or plastic covers can be taken away completely and stored. Most of the points detailed above apply in the construction of frame covers. Frames should also be in full sun and should ideally face north. Plastic frame covers should be anchored well, especially when they are half open for ventilation, as they lift easily and can be damaged.

MINI-TUNNELS

Another application of clear plastic film in vegetable production is in the construction of mini-tunnels. The design of these is based

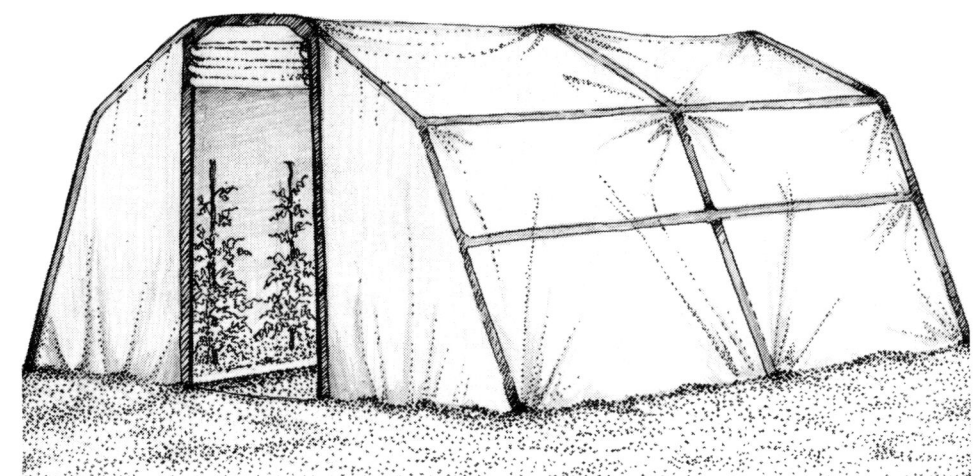

A metal-framed plastic tunnel.

A cold frame.

on the cloche, which has been a feature of European gardening practice for many years. The original cloches were made of glass squares clipped to a wire frame and were placed in the open garden, usually in series, to provide a modified and favourable micro-climate for starting rows of early, directly-sown and transplanted crops and for raising seedlings. Once the plants were growing the cloches were moved on and another row or two were planted or sown.

The plastic tunnels have a framework of galvanized wire hoops (4 mm being the recommended thickness) set in the soil over the rows at 650-750 mm intervals. The plastic is secured at one end and then carefully drawn over the hoops, to which it is fastened by lengths of string or line that hook on (see illustration). Full rolls of film are 100 m long and 2 m wide, but cut lengths may be obtained. One of the products used for mini-tunnels is known as Rydek film and comes in two grades: 3 months and 6 months (indicating its life expectancy under field conditions).

These mini-tunnels are extremely useful for starting early tomatoes, squashes, mel-ons and other cucurbits. Once the weather has warmed up and the plants are beginning to fill the space available the plastic can be rolled back partially or fully to allow the crops to grow on to maturity. The galvanized hooks can then be lifted, cleaned off and stored until they are again required.

MULCHING

Until fairly recently mulches were always thought of in terms of organic residues such as leaves, grass mowings, straw, compost and manure. However, because of availability, transport and labour (among other factors) it is not always possible to use these conventional materials.

In recent years plastic film or sheeting has revolutionized mulching in commercial agriculture and horticulture. In South Africa, vines, pineapples, citrus fruit, apples and a range of vegetables have performed extremely well in growth and yield when mulched with plastic film. There is therefore no reason at all why it should not also be used in the home garden. Plastic mulches can modify soil temperature, conserve soil moisture, suppress weed growth (thus preventing possible damage to plants by hand weeding or hoe cultivation), prevent crusting of the soil, and create improved conditions for beneficial soil organisms.

One of the products on the market, Gunmulch, is available in both clear and black versions, the latter being more commonly used as it has the ability to suppress weed growth. The clear film, however, does allow the soil to warm up a little earlier in spring. Gunmulch is thin (40 microns) compared with the thicker materials of similar appearance that are used in dampcoursing and other building applications. The rolls are 1 m wide and although a full roll is 500 m long, most suppliers of gardening materials will sell it by the metre to the home gardener. If the use of Gunmulch is envisaged when the ground is being prepared, the beds or planting system should be designed so as to use the material economically and to maximum effect. This means that an allowance should be made on each side of the bed to enable the plastic to be tucked into the soil.

The following is the recommended procedure for laying the mulch: anchor the film with soil in a shallow trench at one end of the row and roll it out over the formed bed. Then press the remaining three edges into shallow trenches and fill these with soil. Approximately 100-150 mm of plastic should be allowed for anchorage on either side of the bed. No edges should be left exposed as this will permit lifting by the wind. To prevent weed germination and maximize soil warming, the film should be fitted as closely as possible to the surface, with as few air gaps as possible. Should the mulch need to be joined, both ends should be buried in a shallow trench across the bed and covered with a layer of soil.

Leave the mulch in place for 2 or 3 days before cutting the planting holes. Round holes are more effective than slits because they are less likely to tear or cause damage to young plants by rubbing against the stems. Before laying the mulch, prepare the ground well and incorporate any fertilizer and manure. If fumigation is required it should be carried out beforehand and the

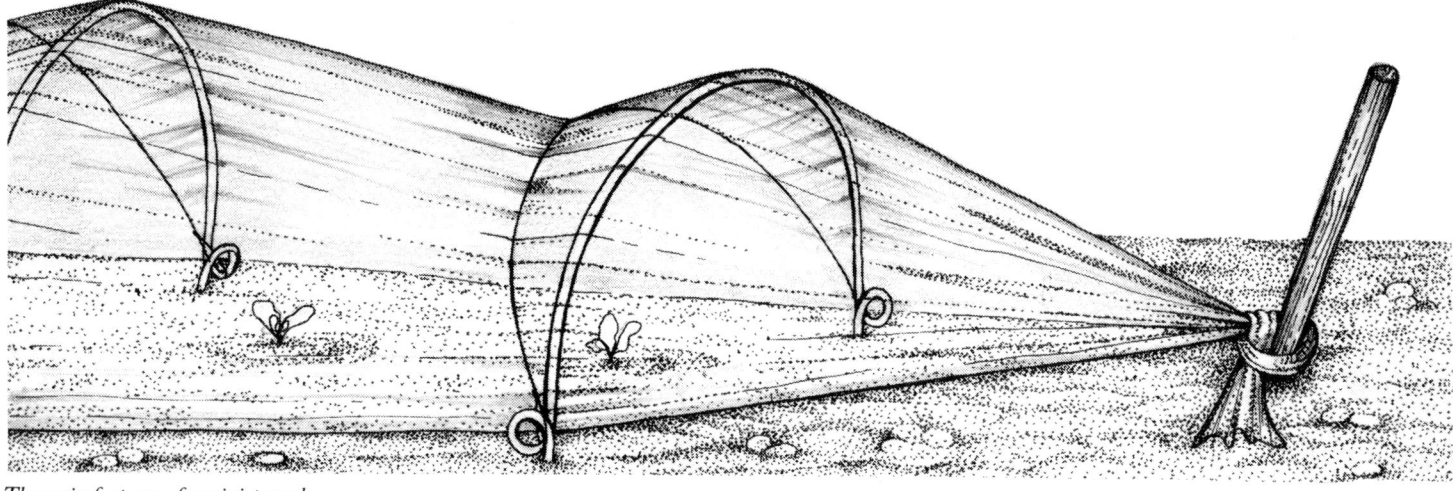

The main features of a mini-tunnel.

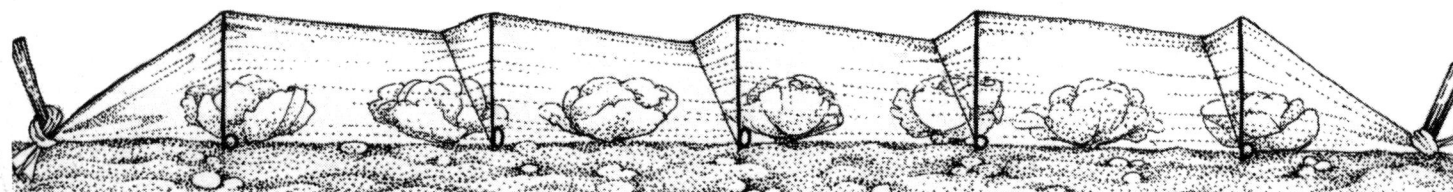

Mini-tunnels make earlier crops possible.

ground should be aerated for 2-3 weeks. The bed should then be raked off carefully and *given a heavy watering before the mulch is applied.*

In sandy soils water moves almost directly downwards, whereas in heavier soils there is an appreciable amount of lateral movement. It is therefore advisable to cut larger planting holes on light soils to allow more infiltration of water.

These, then, are some of the ways in which plastic sheeting can be used to considerable advantage on vegetable crops, the result being higher yields of better quality produce. Shade cloth of many grades, fruit tree nets and various microjet systems are other plastic products that can reduce the labour involved in vegetable gardening and make it more profitable and interesting.

When laying a plastic mulch ensure that all the edges are securely anchored with soil to prevent lifting by the wind.

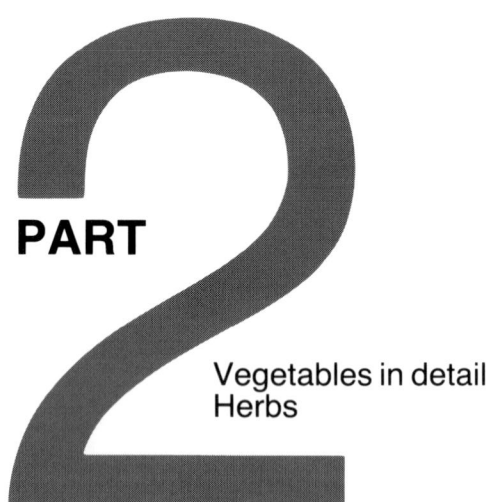

PART

2

Vegetables in detail
Herbs

11 VEGETABLES IN DETAIL

ARTICHOKES, CHINESE
Far East
Stachys sieboldii
Optimum pH 6,0-6,5

The Chinese artichoke does not appear to be widely known in South Africa, possibly because of the scarcity of planting material. However, like the Jerusalem artichoke, it yields in abundance once it is established and the ground must be thoroughly cleaned to avoid unwelcome 'volunteer' growth the following season. It is a tuberous rooted perennial but is usually treated as an annual crop.

Cultivars. No named cultivars are on record. The tubers are ivory or white in colour.
Soil preparation. This crop demands a fertile but light-textured soil, ideally one that has been enriched for a previous crop with generous applications of compost and manure. A handful or two of 2:3:2 (30-60 g) per m² will assist in getting the plants off to a good start. When this crop is relegated to a poor corner of the garden, and this often happens, the tubers produced are small and hardly worth the trouble of preparing for the table.
Propagation. This is by tubers only, which may be extremely difficult to obtain if the crop is being grown for the first time.

Chinese artichoke tubers.

Planting. The seed tubers can be planted with a hand trowel or in a drill opened to a depth of 75-100 mm with a spade or hoe. A distance of 225-300 mm should be allowed between plants in the row and 450 mm between rows. October to early December is the best period for planting.
Further Treatment. This is not a demanding crop once it is established. Routine weed control and a slight earthing up of the plants are about the only activities necessary. However, a liquid feed once the crop is growing will assist the plants to achieve their full height of around 450 mm. A mulch will ensure that the soil is kept moist and thereby assist in the production of good-sized tubers that are up to 75 mm long and 25 mm thick. Hot, dry ground often results in small, shrivelled and bitter tubers.
Harvesting. The tubers should mature from late February onwards, and should be lifted with a fork and used as required. They will shrivel quickly if left out of the ground for any length of time.

Because of their shape it is impossible to peel or scrape them satisfactorily and they are best prepared by scrubbing.
Pests and diseases. No specific pests and diseases are on record.

ARTICHOKES, GLOBE
Southern Europe
Cynara scolymus
and Mediterranean
Optimum pH 6,5

The globe artichoke is not widely grown, partly because it is unknown to many gardeners but also because of the difficulty in obtaining selected planting material. Its low yield per square metre also counts against it. In larger gardens, however, a row of 8-12 plants situated on the edge of the garden will provide something different for the table and will at the same time, owing to its habit and height (1,2-1,5 m), provide a protective and attractive border. Apart from good planting material, the three main factors influencing success are maximum sunlight,

well-manured soil and good drainage. The globe artichoke is a herbaceous perennial and the edible portion is the immature flower bud, particularly the fleshy lower scales and the base.

Recommended cultivars
Large Green
Scarlet Globe: A cultivar with a purplish tinge.
Soil preparation. Although plantings in other parts of the world may remain productive for 4-5 years, in South Africa they are rarely worth keeping for more than about 3 years, the second and third years being the most productive. As the plants need wide spacing in order to develop fully it is more economical on manuring and fertilizing materials to prepare separate planting stations for each plant, especially since only a few plants are usually maintained. The planting stations, which should be 1,0-1,2 m apart and well dug over to a depth of 250 mm, should each be improved with a good forkful or two of mature compost or manure plus a handful (60 g) of 2:3:2. These materials should all be thoroughly mixed in with the topsoil and each station should be shaped like a shallow dish, trodden lightly, watered and then allowed to settle for a week or so before the plants are set out.
Propagation. If no good vegetable planting material is available, the initial planting stock will have to be raised from seed. Unfortunately the globe artichoke is one of those difficult vegetables that does not produce seed that is uniformly true to type. Therefore, once the first seedlings have matured, it is advisable to make subsequent plantings from the suckers of plants bearing desirable characteristics in terms of vigour, yield, size and shape. Out of a dozen plants or so, perhaps only one will be worth propagating from. November to December is the best sowing period.
Planting. The seedlings are usually large enough to be moved to their prepared planting stations 3-5 months after sowing. Suckers or off-shoots can be removed from the

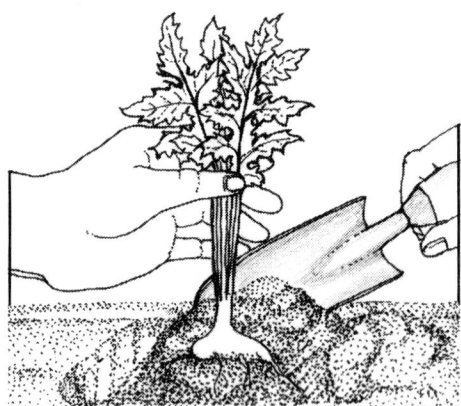

Globe artichokes are grown from the rooted suckers of selected plants.

Harvest globe artichokes before the buds open.

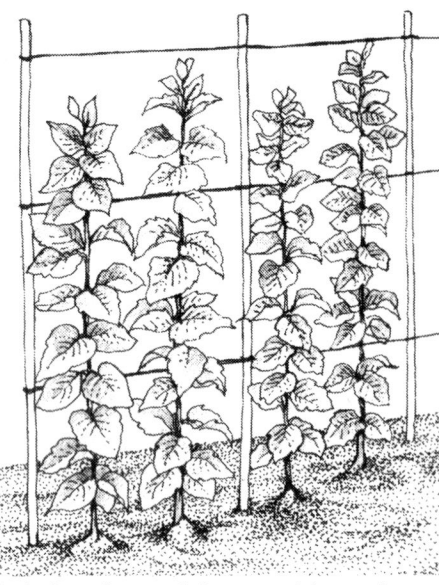

Stake Jerusalem artichokes to avoid damage by wind and heavy rain.

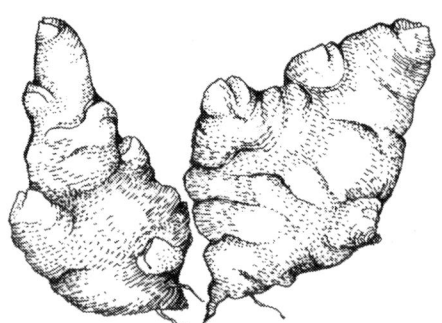

Jerusalem artichoke tubers.

parent plant with a portion of root, trimmed back to 250 mm if necessary, planted firmly and watered thoroughly. March/April plantings give consistently good results. The removal of 2-3 suckers from the parent plant does not appear to have any effect on subsequent growth and yield. It is always best to discard only half the mature plants at a time so that one always has a continuity of supply from vigorous plants.

Further treatment. Once established, the plants require much less attention than most vegetables. Almost all that is necessary is the regular removal of weeds and of dead lower leaves. An effective mulch will reduce even further the attention required. After all the buds from a stem have been harvested, the stem should be cut back to soil level to encourage further growth to develop and thereby extend the season. Dressings of compost or manure are perhaps the best materials for maintaining plant vigour over several seasons, although an application of nitrogen or 3:2:1 at the rate of 60-90 g per plant in spring will invariably bring a favourable response from the plants. The fertilizer should be broadcast in a wide band 150 mm away from the plant and should be hoed in shallowly.

Harvesting. At the end of the first year's growth from seed, or 6-7 months after propagating from suckers, a few edible buds may be produced. These can be harvested when young or cut and discarded. The second and third years usually produce the heaviest yields and the buds should be cut with secateurs, taking with the bud 75-100 mm of stem, before the scales open to any degree. Should the buds be allowed to develop they will grow into purple flowers up to 150 mm across. Like all vegetables they are best when eaten fresh, but surpluses can be stored by deep-freezing or bottling.

Pests and diseases. *Aphids*, usually black in colour on this crop, are frequently troublesome during hot weather. They congregate in large numbers on the furry undersides of the leaves, particularly the lower ones, and large infestations often build up before damage is apparent. Malathion and dimethoate are effective control materials.

Diseases are unlikely to be troublesome.

ARTICHOKES, JERUSALEM

Helianthus tuberosus   North America
Optimum pH 6,0-6,5

The Jerusalem artichoke is, as can be seen from its generic name, a member of the sunflower family. Indeed, its common name 'Jerusalem' is thought to be a corruption of the Italian 'girasole', which means 'turning to the sun'. It is not related to the globe artichoke. The edible portion is the tuber, the flavour of which is said to be best when it is cooked whole and not peeled. However, like the parsnip, the flavour is not to everyone's liking, and in some countries this vegetable is regarded as pig food!

Cultivars. Little if any work has been done in this country to develop new strains and cultivars, but by careful selection of the tubers and plants the gardener himself can improve to a considerable degree the material generally available. It is often extremely difficult to procure planting material, particularly now that the advertising of such material is strictly controlled. Both white and purple types are encountered from time to time, the former being more common and desirable because of its delicate flavour.

Soil preparation. This vegetable grows to a height of 1,8-2,1 m in favourable conditions and has large leaves 150-200 mm in length. It should therefore be allocated accommodation on the perimeter of the garden where it cannot shade other plants. The soil should be well dug over and compost or manure, plus 1 handful of superphosphate per m², should be incorporated. In the absence of organic material, at least 60-75 g of 2:3:2 per m² should be worked in.

Propagation. This is by tubers, replanted annually. Material for initial plantings can be difficult to obtain. Once a crop is established, however, there will be a plentiful supply of planting material.

Planting. This is usually done in October/November. The planting procedure is very similar to that of potatoes. The tubers can be set out 300-400 mm apart in the row at a depth of 75-125 mm, depending upon soil type. About 1 m should be allowed between rows.

Further treatment. Little further attention need be given apart from the routine task of removing weeds by hoeing shallowly. As the plants grow some soil can be drawn up to them. Because of their height and habit the plants need to be staked to avoid damage by wind and heavy rain. Any damage to the stems before the plants are mature will reduce yields appreciably.

Harvesting. The tubers can be lifted, as required, from February/March onwards, depending upon planting time and growing conditions. Smooth tubers around 70 g (those the size of a small egg) can be selected and set aside in a cool, dry place to provide planting material for the following season. The selection of seed tubers from high-yielding plants producing good-sized tubers, nicely shaped, is a worthwhile exercise that will help to ensure the success of future crops.

Pests and diseases. No specific pests or diseases appear to trouble this crop.

ASPARAGUS

Asparagus officinalis   Eastern
Optimum pH 6,5-7,5   Mediterranean

This is a perennial maritime plant of the lily family, and is a relative of the several species of decorative asparagus 'ferns'. Cultivated asparagus is dioecious, i.e. the male and female flowers are borne on separate plants, although occasionally plants are encountered that produce flowers containing both male and female organs. Investigations by many research workers have shown that male plants usually produce a greater number of spears per plant than the female but that the spears of the latter are bigger and heavier. At the end of the cutting season the females are easily recognizable as they show flowers and then fruits, which are red when ripe.

Recommended cultivars

California 500

Connover's Colossal: An old cultivar with slender pointed buds.

U.C. 72: Large green-tipped spears. This cultivar has some resistance to fusarium wilt.

Soil preparation. If they are given an adequate resting period each winter, followed by a good feeding programme when in growth, plantings will remain productive for a very long time, 10-15 years being the average life expectancy. It is therefore sensible to put a little extra time and effort into the selection and preparation of the area to be planted. Ground severely infested with perennial weeds such as water grass should not even be considered when selecting a site, for the weeds will almost certainly win the battle for the soil and its nutrients.

The soil should be loose and well drained, for the plants must develop extensive root systems if they are to grow away each spring and withstand the setback of a cutting season. I mentioned in an earlier chapter that deep trenching is unnecessary for most vegetables, but asparagus is one of the exceptions and will reward the gardener generously for such treatment before planting. The trenches should be 450 mm wide, 250-300 mm deep and of any convenient length. When the topsoil has been removed, the bottom of the trench should be loosened with a spade, fork or hoe and improved with liberal quantities of well-decomposed manure or compost, plus a handful (60 g) of 2:3:2 per metre of trench. The soil that is removed should be improved in the same way and well mixed. During the preparation all stones should be removed, clods broken up and old roots disposed of.

Propagation. Seeds can be sown singly 100-125 mm apart in well-prepared seedbeds during the period September to December and covered with 25-30 mm of soil. Soaking the seed overnight in lukewarm water gives improved germination according to some reports. The seeds germinate rather slowly, particularly in early sowings, but once they have emerged the seedlings grow quickly and should be encouraged to make as much growth as possible before cooler and perhaps drier weather comes along and the tops brown off. The plants can be removed to their permanent quarters 10-12 months

after sowing, but only good-sized crowns should be selected; any weak, undersized specimens must be discarded at this stage.

Growing plants from seed need only be by choice and not necessity, for several reputable nurserymen specialize in raising asparagus crowns on a large scale. Both one- and two-year-old crowns are usually offered and most of the time the stock is selected and of a high quality. Strong one-year-old crowns are perhaps the best investment, for two-year-old crowns are more expensive and do not always re-establish themselves as well as the younger plants.

Planting. The crowns, whether raised by the gardener or purchased, can be set out in their permanent quarters by one of two accepted methods. The first, which is very widely used, particularly in the home garden, consists of replacing some of the removed and improved soil and treading it lightly so as to leave a trench 150 mm deep. In heavy soils this can be shallower. A slight ridge is then drawn up down the centre of the trench and on this the crowns are set out 450-500 mm apart with the roots spread as evenly as possible around the crown, care being taken not to damage them as they are somewhat brittle. The crowns can then be covered carefully with about 75 mm of soil, gently trodden and watered in. During the growing season the trench can be closed completely to bring it up level with the ground.

The second method is used on deep fertile ground where no trenching is required. Here the improving materials are laid 40-50 mm deep and 450 mm wide in a band where the rows are marked out and thoroughly incorporated into the topsoil with a fork or African hoe. When this has been lightly trodden and watered it should be allowed to settle for a week or more. The planting procedure is to push a garden spade vertically into the soil to its full depth, and to lever it back to create a narrow, wedge-

shaped hole behind the blade. The crown is then carefully inserted into the hole behind the spade with the roots fanwise and the crown 75 mm or so below ground level. The spade is then withdrawn and the ground firmed with the boot on both sides of the slit. After planting, a good soaking should be given. July/August is the most favourable planting period in most areas. At least 1,0-1,2 m should be allowed between rows.

Further treatment. Once the plants are established, the ground should be kept free of weeds by hand-pulling between plants in the row and by shallow cultivation between the rows. Deep cultivation is damaging even when well away from the crown, for the roots of plants in rows 2 m apart can bridge the gap completely within a few years.

A dormancy period of at least 3 months is very necessary if the planting is to remain vigorous and productive for many years. Dormancy is brought about naturally by very low temperatures, a dry period or a combination of both. In certain areas, winter rains and mild temperatures prevent true dormancy and the resulting year-round growth taxes the strength and vigour of the plants very severely.

After the cutting season, the plants should be allowed to go to grass and thereby replenish their spent reserves. A mulch of mature compost or manure can be spread in a band on either side of each row and can be covered with soil from the ridge when the tops start yellowing. When the top growth has yellowed off at the beginning of the dormancy period it should be cut as closely as possible to soil level and removed from the site. Any 'volunteer' growth should be removed as it appears.

When the plants are required to resume growth a handful of 2:3:2 per metre of row can be broadcast. A flattened ridge of soil 150 mm high and 400-500 mm across at the base should then be drawn up over the rows and a thorough watering given. The soil in-

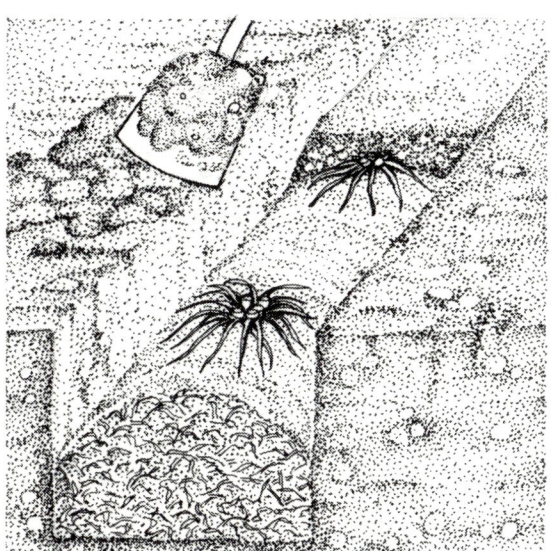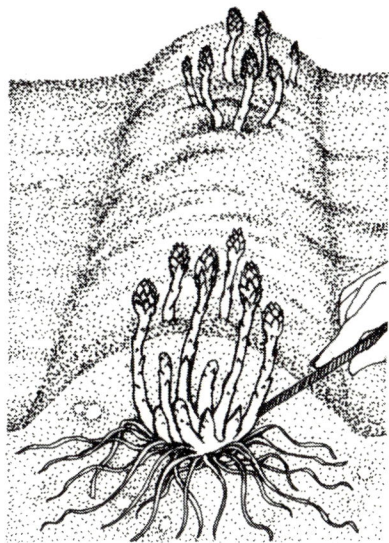

When planting asparagus in trenches, ensure that the crowns are placed on a ridge with their roots spread evenly. Harvest asparagus by inserting the cutting tool into the base of the ridge at a 45° angle.

corporated into the ridge should be as free as possible from clods and stones otherwise few straight spears will be harvested. Do not draw up the ridge if green asparagus is required.

Harvesting. A short cutting season of no more than 2-3 weeks is permissible 12 months after planting out, provided that the crowns are vigorous and have made satisfactory growth. However, better long-term yields can be expected if the gardener can be patient for another year before starting to harvest. Thereafter the cutting season can be extended by a week or so each year to a maximum of 10-12 weeks on vigorous, healthy plantings. However, the gardener must use his discretion and shorten the season if spear size declines appreciably. On mature plants a spear diameter of 12 mm is the minimum that is acceptable. During the cutting season all spears, large and small, should be harvested, otherwise those that go to grass will draw heavily on the plant's resources.

The spears should be cut as soon as the tips protrude through the ridge cap and the cutting should be carried out carefully, otherwise damage to younger, unseen spears may result. A special asparagus knife is manufactured but they are often difficult to find. A serviceable substitute can be made from a thin piece of steel 250-300 mm long and 30 mm wide. It should be sharpened at one end so that it has a cutting edge similar to that of an ordinary wood chisel and at least as sharp! This knife is then jabbed into the base of the ridge below the protruding spear at an angle of 45° to sever it. The cutting of green asparagus is quite straightforward and requires no special tool or technique. Asparagus must be cut regularly, even daily during hot weather, if unnecessary losses are to be avoided. When cut, the spears can be left for some days in water in the refrigerator or they can be bunched and stood upright in a flat dish containing about 30 mm of cold water.

Pests. *Cutworms* can be a permanent prob-

lem on asparagus and often feed on the young spears. They can be controlled with carbaryl and BHC formulations or with a bait containing sodium fluosilicate.

Asparagus beetle, a regular pest wherever asparagus is grown, feeds on the foliage during the summer months. Dusting with BHC should give satisfactory control.

Slugs and *snails* can be controlled with bait pellets.

Diseases. *Rust* has been a very serious problem on both commercial and home-garden plantings for very many years. Light infestations can be reasonably well controlled with Dithane M45 or copper sprays early in the season. However, the use of resistant cultivars is the only real answer and those of the Washington strains appear to be in the forefront in this regard.

AUBERGINES: see EGG PLANTS

BEANS, BROAD   Mediterranean
Vicia faba
Optimum pH 6,0-7,0

The broad bean, a most nutritious vegetable extensively grown in England, enjoys limited popularity in South Africa but deserves to be known more widely for it is relatively easy to grow. It is essentially a winter vegetable that enjoys cool, moist growing conditions. During very mild winters and in warmer areas the set of pods may be disappointing even if the plants are good in size and colour. Being a legume, a giant vetch in fact, the broad bean can be sown alongside peas in the winter rotation and is a much safer crop during June, July and August than the dwarf bean, which is much more tender. The broad bean is also called the fava bean in some countries.

Recommended cultivars. There are two principal types of broad bean – 'long pod' and 'Windsor' – and most cultivars fall into

these classes. The former is a more consistent performer in sub-tropical areas and most seedsmen catalogue only this type, of which the following are examples:
Aquadulce: A long-podded, white-seeded cultivar. The pods tend to grow away from the stem at an upward angle.
Longpod: There are several strains of this cultivar and most are prolific bearers in ideal conditions. The pods are pendulous.

Soil preparation. Broad beans are perhaps the heaviest feeders among legumes and although they will grow satisfactorily on a wide range of soils, they prefer heavier ones and demand generous treatment. Ground well improved with compost or manure for a previous crop is ideal and can be brought up to scratch with a base dressing of 60-120 g per m^2 of 2:3:2. On poorer and unimproved soils mature compost can be incorporated together with a similar fertilizer dressing.

Propagation. Like all leguminous vegetables, the broad bean is propagated by seed sown where the plants are to mature.

Sowing. March to June is the most favourable period for sowing, April and May being the most satisfactory months for large sowings. Broad beans are of upright habit, attaining a height of up to 1 m under good growing conditions, and it is advisable to sow in double or even triple rows. Widely-spaced single rows usually end up lying on the ground, but in closely-sown double or triple rows damage from wind and heavy rain is much less likely to occur, and pollination is improved.

The seeds can be sown singly 150-200 mm apart in the row in holes 50 mm deep. Alternatively, a drill of similar depth can be made and the seeds can be dropped in singly, the same distance apart, and covered with soil. Double rows should be 250-300 mm apart, allowing at least 600-750 mm between each set of double or triple rows to facilitate cultural activity.

Further treatment. Once the seeds have germinated and the plants are growing away, they should be kept clean and free from weeds. Regular watering or rainfall is a must with this crop, especially during the flowering and fruit-setting period, when a check would be disastrous. Low humidity appears to be a factor adversely affecting fruit set. In this respect double- and triple-row plantings are at an advantage because close planting encourages a moist micro-climate.

In exposed situations it is worth running a single or double string, depending upon growth, along each side of the double row to give some support when the pods begin to fill and the plants become top-heavy. Light-gauge galvanized wire (2 mm) will also do the job, as will plastic-coated washline. Earthing up the rows will complete the job by providing basal support.

Once a good number of pods have set on a plant the growing point should be removed to discourage aphids.

Harvesting. The pods are usually ready for

Broad beans need support in exposed situations. Once sufficient pods have set, pinch out the growing point to discourage aphids.

1

2

WEEDS

3

4

5

6

1/2 *Amaranthus* spp. (pigweed)
3/4 *Bidens pilosa* (blackjack)
5/6 *Cynodon dactylon* (couch grass)

1. *Cyperus* sp.
2. *Cyperus esculentus* (water grass)
3. *Cyperus rotundus* (nut grass)
4/5 *Datura stramonium* (stinkblaar, thorn apple)
6. *Galinsoga parviflora* (quickweed)
7. *Nicandra physaloides* (apple of Peru)
8/9 *Oxalis* spp. (sorrel)

2

1

3

4

5

7

6

8

9

1

2

3

1/2 *Portulaca oleracea* (purslane)
3. *Sonchus oleraceus* (sow thistle)
4. *Stellaria media* (chickweed)

4

VEGETABLES

1. Well-grown Jerusalem artichokes.
2. In spring and summer, dwarf beans mature quickly enough to satisfy even the most impatient gardener.
3. Runner beans need firm and adequate support to ensure maximum yields and prevent wind damage.
4. Beetroot can be grown successfully for most of the year. The tops need not be discarded but can be used as a spinach substitute.

1

2

3

4

1

2

3

4

1. Broccoli prefers cool, moist conditions, which assist in the development of compact heads.
2. Sprouts should be picked from the base of the plant upwards as soon as they are firm. The lower sprouts in the photograph have been left too long on the plant.
3. Gloria Osena, a ball-headed cabbage, is an F1 hybrid that shows great uniformity and a high resistance to bolting.
4. Chinese cabbage is a high-yielding, quick-maturing vegetable with a delicate flavour.

5

6

7

8

9

5. Because they take up little room and give high yields, carrots are particularly suited to the home garden.

6. Cauliflowers need a constant and plentiful supply of plant food and soil moisture, and prefer cool growing conditions.

7. The celeriac root, which grows partly out of the soil, should be kept free of side-shoots and suckers throughout growth.

8. Green celery, as shown here, has a higher nutritive value than blanched celery and is becoming increasingly popular.

9. Chayote, a little-known perennial vegetable, is a member of the cucurbit family.

1

2

3

4

5

1. A sunny situation is essential for the successful growing of frame or 'English' cucumbers.
2. The fruits of egg plants should be removed before they lose their lustre.

3. Like other leaf brassicas, kale will perform satisfactorily on most soils that have been improved organically.
4. Endive prefers to follow a well-manured crop in the rotation programme. The photograph shows an unblanched curly-leaved plant, which would be suitable for use as a spinach substitute.

6

7

9

5. Kohlrabi is grown for its swollen, edible stem, which develops above the ground. The photograph shows a white cultivar.
6. If a steady supply of moisture is available, leeks will tolerate a wide range of soil types and climatic conditions.

7. Crisphead lettuce is still the most widely-grown type in South Africa.
8. Butterhead lettuce.
9. Cos or romaine lettuce.

1

2

3

4

5

6

7

8

1. Honeydew, a winter melon with considerable keeping qualities.
2. Imperial 45, a popular melon that is densely netted in most strains.
3. Okra, a species of hibiscus, is grown for the edible pods that are produced singly in the leaf axils.
4. Their versatility in the kitchen and their excellent storage qualities make onions an ever popular vegetable with home gardeners.
5. Parsnips require a fairly deep soil in order to produce smooth roots of good shape.
6. Peppers, a useful addition to summer salads, are warm-weather vegetables related to tomatoes and egg plants.
7. A satisfying experience for any home gardener is to produce well-shaped and blemish-free potatoes.
8. The earthing-up of potatoes to prevent greening also facilitates furrow irrigation.

1. Ironbark pumpkins stand and store well.
2. There are now several strains of Flat Boer, the most popular pumpkin cultivar in South Africa.
3/4 Radishes are particularly suited to the confines of the home garden and are among the easiest vegetables to grow.
5. Rhubarb is a perennial that requires very little attention; half a dozen well-selected crowns will provide a regular supply of succulent sticks for many months of the year.

6

7

8

9

6-9 Squashes are an important summer vegetable and vary greatly in size, shape, flesh texture and keeping qualities. The cultivars shown here are, in numerical order, Ambassador, Butternut-type, Green Hubbard and Little Gem.

10. Freshly-picked sweetcorn is far superior in quality and nutritive value to the finest produce offered by the greengrocer.

11. Sweet potatoes do not store easily and the home grower should lift them only as required.

10

11

1

2

3

4

5

1. Swiss chard is grown mainly for its leaves, but the leaf stalks can be used in a variety of dishes.
2. A good truss of small-fruited tomatoes.
3. Tomatoes trellised along galvanized wire to improve yield and quality.
4. The fruits of a typical multi-celled cultivar such as Heinz 1370 or Homestead.
5. Turnips should be harvested before the texture of the roots deteriorates.

HERBS

1. A carefully-planned and well-stocked herb garden.
2. Chives
3. Fennel
4. Mint *(Mentha spicata)*

1. Borage

2. Parsley

3. Sage

4. Tarragon

5. Sweet Marjoram

6. Thyme

7. Rosemary

8. Basil

9. Bay

picking 3-4 months after sowing and the rows should be gone over twice a week. Removing pods regularly as they mature allows the younger pods to fill before plant vigour flags.

Pests. *Aphids*, black on this crop, are a scourge wherever broad beans are grown. They usually appear as the plants flower and set fruit, congregating in large numbers in the flowering area. A severe infestation weakens the plant and reduces yields. Removing the growing points of the plants, as has been mentioned, is often sufficient to prevent severe infestation. Should further control measures be necessary Malathion is a useful spray, while even a soap solution is better than nothing.

Diseases. *Chocolate spot* can be destructive in the Cape, especially during prolonged wet periods. Both leaves and stems are affected. Dithane M45 and copper oxychloride will give some measure of control if used in good time.

Rust can be a problem, especially on late sowings. Dithane M45 and copper oxychloride are suitable for this problem also.

Mosaic, a viral disease, occasionally appears. The removal and destruction of affected plants are the only measures that can be taken.

BEANS, DWARF
Central and South America

Phaseolus vulgaris
Optimum pH 6,0-7,5

Dwarf beans, also known as green beans, snap beans, French beans and bush beans, are one of the most profitable crops for the home gardener. They can be closely spaced where only a few rows are involved and yield heavily in relation to the area they occupy. Dwarf beans are tender, and even where temperatures do not reach freezing point the growth is always poor and uneven and the pods tough and misshapen. In spring and summer, however, they mature quickly enough (7-10 weeks) to satisfy even the most impatient gardener.

Recommended cultivars. There are many cultivars, but recent years have seen a definite preference for the round-podded, stringless type. Flat-pod cultivars such as Long Tom have all but disappeared from seedsmen's catalogues.

Contender: An outstanding stringless cultivar with buff-coloured seed.

Golden Wax Pod: This cultivar bears well and is reasonably stringless, even when the plants are past their prime.

Seminole: Produces heavy crops of dark green pods and has dark brown, speckled seed.

Top Crop: Similar in most respects to Seminole, even having seed of a similar colour.

Soil preparation. Most soil will produce a satisfactory crop of dwarf beans as long as it is loose and friable and provided that drainage is good. Heavy soils and those that crust easily should be avoided, for they interfere with germination and particularly with the emergence of the seedlings. In such soils, unless they are kept uniformly moist until emergence is complete, the seeds may germinate but the young brittle stems find the task of pulling the fleshy cotyledons to the surface, beyond them. Consequently a large percentage of the stems usually snap, resulting in a poor stand of plants.

Beans grow particularly well when they follow heavy feeders such as cabbages, cauliflowers or potatoes, for which the ground was generously improved. Frequently the residue of fertilizer and organic matter remaining in the soil after these crops have been removed will carry a quick-maturing crop such as this through to maturity. However, to ensure that the necessary quick growth occurs, an application of 2:3:2 at the rate of 60 g per metre of row or per m^2, depending upon the planting pattern, can be made. Quick growth is essential, and slow growth usually results in a low yield of tough and misshapen pods.

Propagation. Beans are propagated by seed that is almost always sown where the plants are to mature. The seed should be carefully examined before sowing to see that it is free from weevils and from the scars caused by halo blight. Shrivelled seed, too, should be avoided, and the hands should be washed well after sowing seed that has been treated.

Sowing. Seeds should be sown singly 75-100 mm apart in the row in holes made by a dibber against the planting line or in a drill opened up along the line. The depth of sowing must be carefully watched, particularly for early sowings, if an even stand of plants is to be obtained. In light to medium soils, 40-50 mm is a reasonable depth, but in heavier soils 30-40 mm is sufficient. On heavy soils a more even stand will be obtained if the rows are given a temporary mulch of fine grass or lawn mowings, or if the drills are filled in with sand, loose soil or fine compost to prevent crusting.

In larger plantings, 400-450 mm should be allowed between rows. Alternatively, double rows 150 mm apart can be planted, with 450-500 mm between each set of rows. In intensive bed culture 300 mm between the rows will give higher yields if there are only 3 or 4 rows, without markedly reducing plant development. As the harvest period of beans rarely exceeds 4 weeks it is essential for continuity of supply that sowings should be made every 3 weeks or so.

Further treatment. Owing to their short growing and harvest period beans require relatively little attention, and on clean ground 1 or 2 shallow cultivations should suffice from sowing to maturity. Ground that has been well prepared usually contains sufficient nutrients to carry the plants through. However, if after 3 weeks or so growth is unsatisfactory a dressing of 2:3:2 at the rate of 30 g per m^2 should improve growth and lengthen the picking period. Watering should be carried out carefully, especially during the germination period and with early sowings before the soil warms up. As with most plants, watering is extremely critical during the flowering and fruit setting period, and with beans a shortage once the pods have set will cause them to be small and stringy.

Beans are very shallow rooted, and under favourable growing conditions the lush top growth, particularly in wet weather and when the plants are heavy with pods, becomes a bit much for the stems to support. This makes the plant prone to damage by rain and wind. Drawing a little soil up to the stems while there is still room to work with a hoe between the rows will assist the plants to withstand bad weather. A mulch with short material to a depth of 50 mm will also have a beneficial effect.

Harvesting. The pods are usually ready for picking 7-10 weeks after sowing, depending upon the season and the cultivar grown. The pods should be removed while they are still young and tender and before any swelling of the seeds occurs. In hot weather the plants should be cleared of pods twice a week, even if this means putting surplus quantities in the deep freeze. If a few pods are allowed to become coarse and stringy, the picking of uniform pods is extremely difficult and the strain on the plants shortens the picking period appreciably. As bean plants are very brittle, particularly at this stage in their development, and are easily damaged if pulled around roughly, the plant should be held with one hand while the pods are removed with the other.

If a row or two are to be kept for seed, dry beans or sprouts, all the pods should be left on the plant until they yellow and become dry. The plants can then be removed in their entirety and hung up in an airy shed or laid thinly on trays. When they are thoroughly dry the pods can be shelled and the beans stored.

Pests. *Cutworms* are often a problem. Drenching the young plants with carbaryl or dusting the soil with BHC usually effects control, as does cutworm bait broadcast along the rows.

CMR beetles are large conspicuous flying beetles, yellow and black in colour, that at-

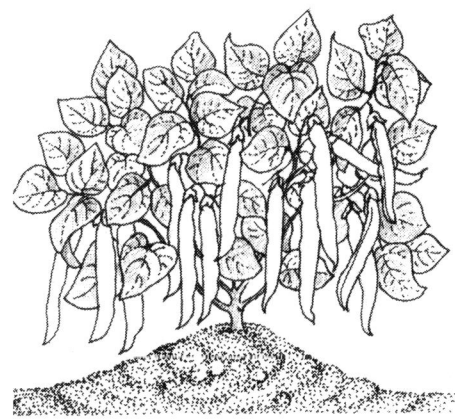

Support dwarf beans by drawing up soil to the stems.

tain a length of 30 mm. They are also known as blossom or pollen beetles because they eat only the flowers and buds, leaving the foliage untouched. This frequently results in their activities remaining unnoticed until the pods fail to develop on strong healthy plants. When there are only a few rows of beans, hand-picking in the early morning as the beetles cling to the plants is a simple and effective method of control. Malathion and BHC are useful materials if further measures are necessary.

The *bean-stem fly* occasionally causes trouble. Although it rarely kills plants outright it stunts growth, makes stands uneven and lowers yields. The adult flies, black in colour and extremely small, lay their eggs in the tissue of the lower leaves, usually near the leaf stalk or petiole. The larvae tunnel down the petiole and the main stem until they reach a point at or just above soil level, where they pupate in the outer stem tissue. In most instances a swelling develops, especially where several larvae are involved, and sometimes the pupae can be seen in slits on this swelling. Malathion is, again, a suitable material for effective control.

Diseases. Diseases are usually only troublesome when there is wet and overcast weather with warm temperatures.

Anthracnose is a fungal disease causing browning and blackening of the veins on the underside of the leaves, angular spots on the upper surface, and reddish-brown or black sunken spots on the pods themselves. It is common on ground that has carried several crops of beans within the space of a few years and its establishment is assisted by prolonged cool and wet weather. Brown sunken spots appear on diseased seed and this is the major method of infection, although the disease can overwinter in diseased material left on the ground. If possible, only certified seed should be used. Plants can be sprayed with Dithane M45 at 7-10 day intervals if necessary.

Brown rust is a common disease, especially during wet periods and on late sowings. It is recognized by the small brown pustules that mostly occur on the underside of the leaves, each pustule having a yellow halo. Spraying with Dithane or Funginex may arrest its development during dry spells.

Bacterial blight is a disease that has similar pod symptoms to anthracnose but it produces small water-soaked spots, like grease spots, with green or yellow halos, on the foliage. Clean seed and crop rotation are the only methods of control, although the cultivar Seminole is said to have some degree of resistance to one of the bacteria responsible.

BEANS, LIMA
South America

Phaseolus lunatus
P. Limensis
Optimum pH 6,5-7,5

Lima beans, sometimes called butter beans (although this term is often used for the bush types only), are not grown to the extent they merit. This is mainly because seed of named cultivars is extremely scarce and is only catalogued intermittently by one or two seed houses. The seeds, when young, are delicious and surpass, to my mind, even the finest broad beans in both texture and flavour.

Recommended cultivars. There are both bush and pole types of this perennial bean, with the bush type usually regarded as an annual even in warm areas. The pole type, which in clean, well-prepared soil can be treated as a perennial for 2 or 3 seasons, is usually catalogued as Pole Lima. The following bush cultivars are the ones usually offered:

Burpee's Bush: A later, large-seeded cultivar of good quality.
Bush Fordhook: An early type with medium-sized seeds.
Henderson Bush: An early, small-seeded and extremely productive cultivar.

Soil preparation. Like dwarf beans, lima beans prefer a well-improved light soil, which is retentive of moisture and yet well drained. If there is still evidence of compost and manure residues from a previous crop, 60 g per m² of a complete fertilizer (e.g. 2:3:2) can be applied and incorporated before sowing. Compost or decayed manure and a similar fertilizer dressing will be necessary on less fertile soils to produce sufficient vegetative growth for high yields. This applies especially when a planting of pole limas is established. In good soil the pole lima produces a dense cover of vines and leaves and therefore requires a strong support. A solid fence with a treated pole framework is ideal for the purpose, particularly as it is usually placed on the perimeter of the garden where the beans will not shade other crops.

Propagation. All cultivars are grown from seed usually sown where the plants are to mature. Early plantings of pole limas can, however, be started under protection in Jiffy 7s or Jiffy Pots.

Sowing. Seed for dwarf cultivars can be sown when all danger from frost is over and sowings can continue till early February. The drills should be 450-600 mm apart with the seeds spaced at 100-150 mm intervals to allow the plants to develop fully. The sowing depth can be 25-40 mm, depending on soil and weather conditions.

The seeds of pole cultivars usually encountered are large, and the seed-coats, when fresh, are white with a maroon spot at one end. October to December is the most favourable period for sowing in most areas, as it allows a crop to be reaped before cold weather or even frost come along to cut back the tops. It also allows the plants to develop a strong root system before these unfavourable conditions stop growth. At the base of each support 2 or 3 seeds can be sown 100 mm apart and thinned out later to leave the two strongest plants to grow on to matur-

ity. The seeds should be sown at a depth of 30-50 mm.

Further treatment. Throughout growth the bush lima requires similar treatment to the dwarf bean. The pole lima, which may bear satisfactorily for 3 years in fertile and nematode-free soil, needs little attention apart from the removal of dead tops and an occasional thinning, in areas experiencing a mild winter, if growth becomes too thick. A side dressing with 2:3:2 in spring at the rate of 60 g per metre of row or a mulch with mature compost or manure will encourage vigorous growth. In December a nitrogenous side dressing will maintain plant vigour and prolong the picking season appreciably.

Harvesting. Dwarf limas are usually ready for the pot 2½ months after sowing, while the pole cultivars generally need 3 or 4 weeks longer to mature. Only the seeds of lima beans are eaten and not the pods, which are tough and fibrous, especially in the case of pole cultivars. The pods should regularly be removed from the plants when seeds are fully swollen but before they turn yellow. At this stage the seeds should still be succulent and the seed-coats light green in colour. However, as with many crops, only experience can teach the gardener when to harvest.

Lima beans are shelled more easily if the pods are allowed to wilt for a day or two after picking. If they are to be kept for a few days on the vegetable rack before being used they should be stored shallowly, especially if picked when wet, for they soon heat up otherwise.

Pests and diseases. Lima beans of both types are considerably more attractive to *aphids*, usually grey in colour, than dwarf beans, and severe infestations can build up within a few days during hot, dry weather. Malathion or Aphicide in the form of a spray will give good control provided that a wetting agent is used and provided that another application is given after 5-7 days. Bexadust will assist when small local infestations appear.

There are no recorded diseases specific to this crop.

BEANS, RUNNER
Central and South America

Phaseolus vulgaris
P. multiflorus
Optimum pH 6,5-7,5

Most cultivars of runner or pole beans belong to the first-named species, as do dwarf beans, but Scarlet Runner, Kelvedon Wonder and one or two others belong to the species *Phaseolus multiflorus*. The growing of all cultivars is identical, the only difference between the two species being that the former are true annuals while the latter are true perennials treated as annuals in the garden. The flavour of runner beans is usually stronger and coarser than that of dwarf beans and they are preferred to the latter by many gardeners for that very characteristic.

They usually take 10-14 days longer to mature than dwarf beans but their picking season is considerably longer.

Recommended cultivars. *Abundance:* A leading cultivar that produces high yields of tender pods up to 200 mm long.
Blue Peter: This is something of a novelty and is sometimes catalogued as Blue Coco. It bears clusters of long purple pods that turn green after several minutes of cooking.
Lazy Housewife: A very popular cultivar, bearing flat, curved pods. In my view it is inferior to the other cultivars.
Scarlet Runner: This old cultivar has red flowers and produces coarse-textured pods of top quality and flavour. The seeds are dark brown and speckled and are extremely large.
Witsa: A white-seeded, disease-resistant cultivar bred in South Africa. It bears stringless pods.

Soil preparation. If the plants are to develop properly and provide a steady supply of tender pods over an extended period, the soil must be thoroughly prepared and even shallow trenching is warranted on poorer soils. The trenches can be taken out to a depth of 200-250 mm after which the bottom can be loosened up with a fork to facilitate root growth. The removed soil should be mixed with as much manure and compost as can be spared and then replaced in the trench, trodden lightly and given a dressing of 2:3:2 (which should be worked in) at the rate of 60 g per metre of row.

Supporting the plants. It is a good idea to erect the support before the seeds are sown so that the root systems of the seedlings are not disturbed or injured. If there is a suitable permanent feature such as a substantial fence with a suitable aspect it can easily be used as a base for support. In the absence of such a support, runner beans are best grown in double rows 750-850 mm apart and the plants trained up bamboos or similar stakes with a uniform length of around 2 m. The usual method, and a very satisfactory one, is to place the stakes 300-450 mm apart with the two rows leaning inwards so that the stakes cross about 150 mm from their tips and can be tied in pairs. Horizontal stakes of a similar size can then be dropped into the V formed by the uprights and tied in to give the structure sufficient rigidity. A second method is to use similar stakes and place them to form a tepee-like shape 750 mm to 1 m in diameter. Whatever method is used, the stakes can of course be placed in position after the seedlings have emerged, provided that it is done carefully and the plants, which are very brittle at this stage, are not damaged.

Propagation. Propagation is by seed, sown where the plants are to mature.

Sowing. September to January is the most favourable sowing period in most areas. The seeds can be sown 75-100 mm apart around each set of stakes at a depth of 30-40 mm and thinned out later, if necessary, to leave two plants to mature at each station.

Runner beans can also be grown without support by continually pinching out the growing points, thereby restricting their natural spreading habit so that they form into bushes 350-450 mm high. In this case the rows or double rows should be at least 750 mm apart with the seeds spaced 100-150 mm apart in the row. A disadvantage of this method is that it results in bent and twisted pods, which are difficult to handle in the kitchen. Other negative factors are: damage to plants while picking; a high incidence of diseased pods, particularly on old ground; and a susceptibility of the pods to insect attack.

Further treatment. Once the vines have reached the top of the support they should be pinched back to encourage flowering and pod development. A side-dressing of LAN or 2:3:2 (or 1 or 2 applications of liquid manure) as the first pods set will keep the plants growing vigorously and thereby extend the picking season. Mulching the rows with compost, manure, lawn mowings or seaweed is also particularly beneficial with this crop.

Harvesting. Runner beans should be ready for picking 9-10 weeks after sowing and should continue to yield for up to 6 or 7 weeks if picked regularly and fed properly. Again, care should be taken to hold the plants firmly when the pods are pulled.

Pests and diseases. *Aphids* and *CMR beetles* often appear and can be controlled as described in the entry on dwarf beans.

Rust is often a problem, particularly on late sowings. Control measures are as described in the entry on dwarf beans.

BEETROOT   Europe and Asia Minor
Beta vulgaris
Optimum pH 6,0-7,0

Beetroot, one of the most popular root crops, is an ideal subject for the home garden. Swiss chard, sugar beets and mangelwurzels also belong to the same species and they readily cross with each other. Although the garden beet is really a cool-season crop it can be grown for most months of the year, September to March being the most favourable sowing period. Beets are not especially sensitive to heat, provided that soil moisture is adequate, and although they are resistant to cold their growth is extremely slow in winter. During hot, dry weather, however, and on poorer soils, the plants appear to grow well, but the roots produced are frequently poor in colour and quality with marked white zoning in some cultivars.

Garden beets are of course grown primarily for the swollen roots that are used, when cooked, in the preparation of several salad dishes. But the foliage or 'greens' need not be discarded for they can be used as a spinach and, indeed, for several hundred years they were grown specifically for this purpose.

Recommended cultivars. The red globe or round cultivars are the only ones grown to any extent in the home garden, although golden-yellow and white sorts are catalogued overseas, while one or two long cultivars have appeared locally in recent years. The flat cultivars have all but disappeared from local catalogues as they are less tolerant of heat.
Crimson Globe: In the main this has similar characteristics to Detroit but shows more zoning, even when grown under the same climatic and soil conditions.
Detroit Dark Red: A globe-shaped beet with more than one strain. It is the leading cultivar in most areas and displays a deep colour with little or no zoning.
Formanova and *Long Canner* are cylindrical cultivars that are well worth a trial by the home gardener.

Soil preparation. Beets can be produced satisfactorily on a wide range of soils but, like most roots, they prefer deep, friable soils

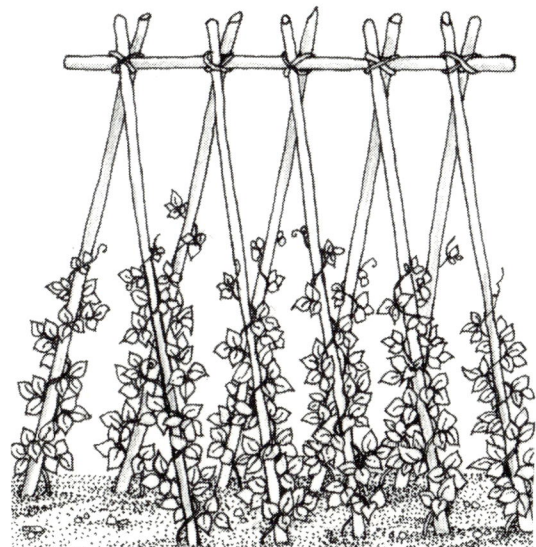
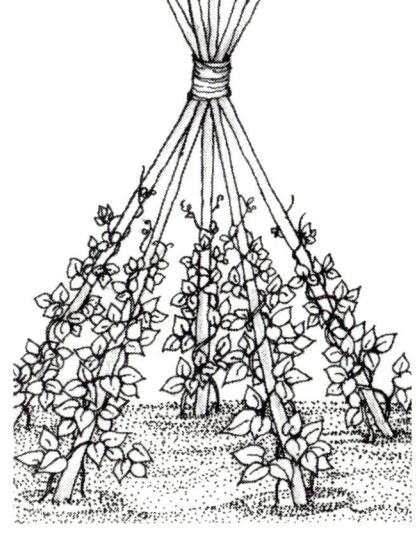

Two methods of supporting runner beans.

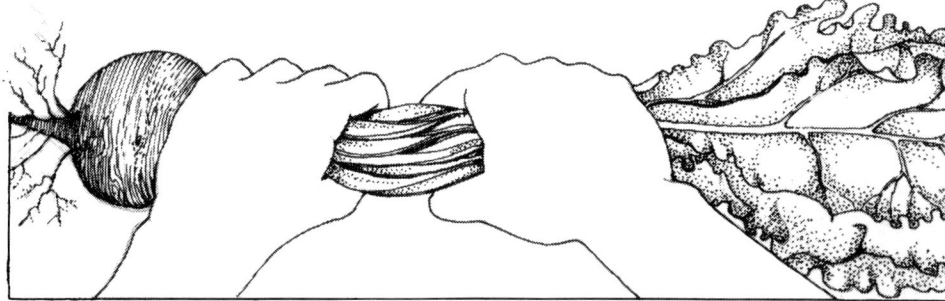

Twist off beetroot tops to prevent bleeding.

rich in organic matter. Hard compact soils should be avoided if possible, especially for long cultivars, as they do not allow the roots to develop symmetrically and growth is often slow. Soils improved with compost or manure for potatoes, brassicas or tomatoes produce the best roots, and on such soils 60 g per m² of superphosphate should be an adequate base dressing. On poorer soils a dressing of 2:3:2 at a similar rate should be regarded as a minimum requirement.

Beets, because of their maritime origin, will not thrive on strongly acid soils, which, in any event, are frequently clayey in nature. They are extremely sensitive to boron deficiency and are in fact a good indicator for this condition. Blackened areas and cracking of the roots are the usual expressions of this deficiency, which can be rectified by distributing commercial borax at the rate of 50 g per 10 m² at the same time as the basic fertilizer dressing. The ground for beet plantings, as for all directly-sown crops, should be free from perennial weeds.

Propagation. Beets are propagated by seed, usually sown where the crop is to mature, although seedlings can be raised in nursery beds and later transplanted. This move, however, retards the crop considerably. The 'seeds' as purchased are actually seed clusters containing 2-5 seeds, and this should be remembered when sowing takes place. Monogerm cultivars containing only 1 seed are currently being developed.

Sowing. After the ground has been well dug over and amendments added the soil surface should be brought to a fine tilth with a rake and all clods broken and foreign matter removed. The seeds should be sown 50-60 mm apart in shallow drills and covered with 20-25 mm of soil. An adequate distance between rows in bed culture and where only 3 or 4 rows are concerned is 250-300 mm. During hot weather grass can be laid thinly on the rows as a temporary mulch to prevent crusting and drying out, and to assist emergence. It should be removed completely or moved to the inter-row spaces as soon as the seedlings emerge.

Transplanting. Plants raised in seedbeds can be moved to permanent quarters when they are 80-100 mm high and should be set out 75 mm apart in the row. Trimming off a third of the foliage facilitates planting out and appears to assist in obtaining an even stand of transplants.

Further treatment. As with all directly-sown crops, weed control is essential during the early stages if the seedlings are to have a chance to grow away. Because of the nature of the 'seeds', thinning out is usually necessary, even in the most carefully-sown rows, otherwise there will be tremendous competition for light, moisture, nutrients and space. Unthinned rows are completely useless for anything except leaf spinach, because under such conditions the roots tend to become woody even when young. The first thinning can be carried out when the seedlings are 30-40 mm high, followed, if necessary, by a second when they are 70 mm high. The second thinning, if carried out carefully, should provide planting material for a row or two or 'greens' for the table. This thinning should leave the plants 75-100 mm apart. Drawing up a little soil to the plants after the final thinning will give the remaining plants welcome support, and this can be repeated again if necessary.

Harvesting. This is a simple and pleasurable activity. Beets can be pulled from the time they are 50 mm in diameter, which should be 8-9 weeks after sowing or 7-8 weeks after transplanting. The cylindrical cultivars will require another 2-3 weeks to be ready. After pulling, the tops should be twisted off 30-50 mm above the root crown. Care should be taken not to damage the taproot, or bleeding and consequent loss of colour will result.

Pests. *Cutworms* often feed on the young seedlings and on the shoulders of the mature roots. BHC and carbaryl applications in the early stages of growth, and baiting as the roots approach maturity, should reduce damage appreciably.

Refer to Chapter 8 for advice on measures to prevent root knot *nematode* infestation in the soil.

Diseases. *Cercospora leaf spot,* a fungal disease that is extremely common on beets, Swiss chard and related crops, is particularly prevalent during wet periods. High humidity and medium temperatures appear to stimulate its development. The spots are small (3-4 mm in diameter) but appear at an alarming rate under favourable conditions. Crop rotation and the use of clean seed are basic to long-term control, while Dithane M45 and copper oxychloride are useful once the disease has become established.

BRINJALS: see EGG PLANTS

BROCCOLI, SPROUTING
Brassica oleracea var. *italica*
Optimum pH 6,0-7,0

Western
Europe

In Europe the term 'broccoli' is used primarily to describe plants that are, to all intents and purposes, hardy, late-maturing, winter cauliflowers. Some sprouting types, purple and white in colour, have been cultivated for many years, including one that is a true perennial with an economic life of 3-4 years. The sprouting broccoli that we are going to discuss here produces central heads 150-200 mm across (depending upon the cultivar), which are green to bluey-green in colour, followed by a succession of smaller bud-clusters of equal quality. Broccoli of this type has been grown in the U.S.A., commercially and in home gardens, for very many years, and it definitely deserves more popularity among home gardeners in South Africa because its culture is relatively easy. It is easier to grow than cauliflower for it is not so specific in its temperature requirements or so demanding in soil preparation. Broccoli is a close relative of cabbage and cauliflower and, like them, it prefers cool, moist conditions, which assist in the development of compact heads.

Recommended cultivars. *Calabrese:* One of the older open-pollinated cultivars, the name of which is often loosely used to describe green sprouting broccoli regardless of cultivar.
Green Duke: A hybrid that is extremely uniform in its development. Many other excellent hybrids have been introduced in recent years but these are directed primarily at the commercial grower and the seed is not available in small packets.
Premium Crop: Often used in commercial planting, this hybrid matures 65-70 days after transplanting.
Soil preparation. Like most brassicas, broccoli needs a fairly high level of fertility to grow and yield satisfactorily. Poor soils lead to growth that is frequently stunted and of poor colour, to premature maturing, and to a low yield of inferior heads. As much ma-

Harvest broccoli when the buds are fully swollen but unopened and the heads still compact.

nure or compost as can be spared should be thoroughly worked into the topsoil, together with a dressing of 60-75 g of 2:3:2 per m². In the absence of compost or manure, the basic fertilizer dressing should be increased to 100-120 g per m². Because brassicas of this type prefer a firm footing the ground should, if necessary, be trodden to meet this requirement.

Propagation. Broccoli is propagated by seed sown in seedbeds or, where relatively few plants are required, in seedboxes. Plants in seedboxes must be hardened-off properly before setting out. Very often this important point is overlooked, leading to great disappointment when the plants are set out in midsummer.

Sowing. The seeds should be sown thinly in shallow drills, covered with 10-15 mm of fine soil, firmed and watered. December to February is the best period for sowing, although March sowings can be successful in cooler areas.

Transplanting. The plants should be large enough to move to prepared quarters 4-5 weeks after sowing. They should be set out in rows 600 mm apart allowing 450-500 mm between plants in the row. Seedlings that become too tall and 'leggy' before they are set out often receive a check when transplanted, making little growth for some weeks and then producing small heads prematurely. Throughout the seedbed period, a close watch must be kept for chewing insects that may destroy the 'eye' or growing point, although 'blindness' can also be caused by an inherent weakness. Only strong plants should be set out even if this means planting fewer rows than intended.

Further treatment. Shallow inter-row cultivation with a Dutch hoe should be carried out whenever necessary to destroy weed growth. A month or so after transplanting and again when the central heads are cut, the plants will usually respond to a side-dressing of LAN at the rate of 1 handful to every 4 plants. Earthing up the plants also appears to give positive results.

Harvesting. The central head is usually ready for cutting 8-10 weeks after transplanting, and should be removed together with 150 mm of the main stem when the buds are fully swollen and the head is still compact. If cutting is delayed for just a few days, losses will occur because the buds will open, giving way to yellow petals. Once the central head is removed, the plants throw out a profusion of axillary shoots with much smaller heads. These should be cut at the same stage of development, together with 100 mm of stalk. On vigorous plants sprouts may continue to appear for several weeks in cool weather, but as soon as production ceases the plants must be removed and not left to provide shelter for aphids and caterpillars. Once cut, broccoli turns yellow very quickly and surpluses are best blanched and put into the freezer.

Pests. *Aphids*, usually blue-grey in colour, are often a problem, particularly on un-

thrifty plants. Malathion and dimethoate will effectively control these insects provided that a wetting agent is incorporated.

Several types of *caterpillars* find broccoli an accommodating host and make their home in the growing point, on the foliage generally, and in the framework of the developing head. Malathion and Karbaspray are stomach poisons that give good control. When the plants are young, Bexadust is effective.

Diseases. *Downy mildew* is occasionally a problem in the seedbed in warmer areas. The undersides of the young leaves and the cotyledons become covered with a white mildew, while upper leaf surfaces show small black markings plus a general yellowing. Spraying with Dithane M45 at the rate of 10 g per 5 ℓ of water often gives satisfactory control.

Black rot is a bacterial disease that is not very widespread on this crop because of the upright habit of the plants. However, it may give trouble at the seedling stage if diseased seed is used. On mature plants any leaves showing severe marginal discoloration should be removed. A fuller discussion of black rot may be found under cabbages.

BRUSSELS SPROUTS Western Europe
Brassica oleracea var. *gemmifera*
Optimum pH 6,0-7,0

Brussels sprouts are not among the most popular garden vegetables in this country, although their unique flavour is being appreciated by more and more people daily through the medium of the frozen pack. Their long growing season, susceptibility to attack by pests, and frequently unsatisfactory yields are the main reasons for their lack of attraction. However, new hybrids and pesticides have improved the prospects and sprouts are now well worth a trial if they are a family favourite. They prefer cool, moist growing conditions, performing disappointingly in hot weather, and can stand lower temperatures than cabbages or cauliflowers.

Recommended cultivars. Open pollinated cultivars are cheaper than hybrids but should not be considered by the home gardener. They are unquestionably inferior to hybrids in performance in all but the most favourable conditions of climate and soil.
Jade Cross Regular and *Jade Cross E:* These appear to be the only hybrids available in small packets. They set tight sprouts more uniformly than straight cultivars and are more tolerant of heat.

Soil preparation. Success with this crop can only be achieved if the ground is well prepared and improved with liberal dressings of mature compost or manure. In addition, a complete fertilizer such as 2:3:2 should be added because the growing season is a relatively long one and the plants need to be started and maintained in a condition

of vigorous growth. Sprouts are even more demanding of a firm soil than broccoli and cauliflowers, and it will be necessary to tread soil firmly that has been dug over and loosened to any depth.

Propagation. Propagation is by seed sown in seedbeds and seedboxes from late December until the end of February.

Sowing. The seed should be sown thinly in shallow drills covered with 10-15 mm of soil, firmed and watered. The soil should be kept moist after sowing to promote rapid germination and emergence, which should take place 6-10 days after sowing. As with all members of the cabbage family, insect and disease control in the seedling stage is of great importance.

Transplanting. The seedlings should be 75-100 mm high 4-5 weeks after sowing and are ready to be transplanted to their prepared quarters. Where only a few rows are involved, the rows can be 600 mm apart, with 450-600 mm between plants in the row.

Further treatment. Throughout the growing period weeds must be destroyed by regular, shallow hoeing, taking care not to damage the lower stalk. A side-dressing with LAN, 2:3:2 or 3:2:1 a month after transplanting and again a month later will maintain plant vigour and increase yields. Liquid manuring can also be carried out at intervals of 2-3 weeks.

Although sprouts develop substantial root systems they will benefit from having the soil drawn up to them once or twice during growth. This operation also keeps weeds in check.

Harvesting. Sprouts can be picked from the base upwards as soon as they are firm and of good size. This should be 90 days or more after transplanting. As they are picked, the lower leaves, which are usually beginning to

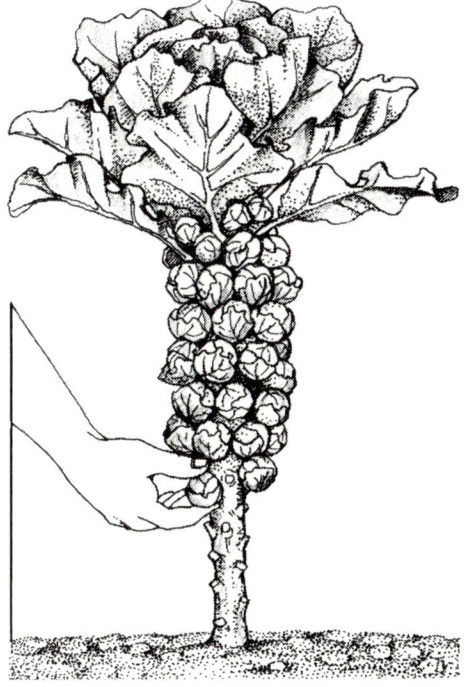

Pick Brussels sprouts from the base upwards.

yellow-off at this stage of maturity, can be removed. The picking season may extend to 2 months or so in the home garden if the plants are well nourished and provided that aphids and caterpillars do not take over. The final boiling can include the tops, which should not be removed before this stage. The tops, however, do not have anything like the distinct flavour of the sprouts themselves. When picking ceases, the plants should be removed completely without delay otherwise plantings of cabbages and other related crops may suffer from any pests present.

Pests and diseases. The pests are the same as those described for broccoli. Spraying or dusting should cease 14 days or so before harvesting commences.

Although in theory Brussels sprouts are susceptible to most diseases of the cabbage family, in practice few of these are troublesome if the plants are kept growing vigorously. *Downy mildew* may be a problem in the seedbed and *black rot* may affect the plants if it is seed-borne. The former can be controlled as described under broccoli, while any lower leaves that yellow prematurely and have wedge-shaped brown areas at the leaf margins should be removed at an early stage.

CABBAGES

Mediterranean

Brassica oleracea var. *capitata*
Optimum pH 6,0-7,0

The cabbage is one of the most widely-grown of all vegetables, both commercially and in the home garden, mainly because it is relatively easy to grow but also because it will perform extremely well on a wide range of soils and in greatly differing climatic conditions. Although by preference a cool-weather crop, cabbages can be grown pretty well throughout the year in most areas. However, plantings that mature in the hottest months are sometimes disappointing, while May and June sowings face a difficult seedbed period in the cooler areas.

Recommended cultivars. The several types can conveniently be grouped into the following categories according to the shape of the head: conical or sugarloaf-headed, ball-headed and drum-headed. Apart from Cape Spitzkool, of which there are several strains and which is possibly the top cabbage in quality, colour and texture, the conical cultivars are quick-maturing, of good quality and an ideal size for the average household. The ball-headed group, too, contains several excellent cultivars for the home garden. Drum-headed or flat-headed types are generally not ideal subjects, for they need wide spacing, are slow to mature, and their texture and colour when cooked do not compare with that of the smaller sorts. In addition, the mass of the heads is frequently too much for the stalks and as a result they lie on the soil, which leads to all sorts of problems.

Savoy cabbages have little appeal for most South Africans, their main virtue being extreme hardiness, a quality that is of little value in this country.

Cape Spitzkool: Several distinct strains are available, some of which will withstand summer temperatures while others are much more at home during cooler months. A cultivar of top quality and colour with conical heads.

Copenhagen Market: A larger version of Golden Acre, which takes 10-14 days longer to mature and which produces medium-sized heads.

Early Jersey Wakefield: One of the earliest-maturing cabbages with a big following in the Western Cape. It produces smallish, conical heads of good quality.

Gloria Osena: An F1 hybrid similar in shape and size to Glory of Enkhuizen. However, it shows greater uniformity and possesses greater resistance to 'bolting'.

Glory of Enkhuizen: The 'big daddy' of straight ball-headed cultivars. It is a little coarser in texture than Copenhagen Market and has pronounced mid-ribs in some strains. A heavy yielder.

Golden Acre: One of the earliest ball-headed

cultivars of the Primo type. It is a short-stemmed, compact cabbage, light in colour with few outer leaves.

Perfection: This appears to be the only Savoy cultivar catalogued.

Red Rock and *Niggerhead:* These are reliable red cabbages that are slower to mature than their green ball-headed counterparts but which have heads of extreme hardness and density.

Several hybrids available to commercial growers are not obtainable in small packets. However, cabbage is an example of the desirability of using straight cultivars in the home garden, for they will not all mature together and thus a succession of heads will be ensured.

Soil preparation. Although cabbages are not too particular about basic soil type, they are gross feeders and it is essential that the ground selected should be deeply dug and prepared thoroughly. Although nitrogenous side-dressings and liquid manure applications are of considerable value in the overall fertilizer programme, nothing can compensate for poor soil preparation. This applies not only to cabbage and its hungry relatives, but extends right across the range of vegetables that produce a lot of top growth. Cabbages thrive on soils rich in organic matter and retentive of moisture. To meet this demand, as much compost or manure as can be mustered should be worked in thoroughly, accompanied by a dressing of lime if a soil test indicates that the soil is very acid. Prior to planting, a dressing of 60-90 g per m^2 of 2:3:2 may be regarded as a minimum to ensure that the plants get away to a good start.

Propagation. Cabbages are easily raised in seedbeds or seedboxes, prior to being transplanted to permanent quarters.

Sowing. Cabbages can be sown throughout the year in several areas and for most of the year in the remainder. The seeds should be sown thinly in shallow drills covered with 8-10 mm of soil and tamped down with the back of a spade. During very hot periods a temporary mulch or some light shade for up

Conical, ball-headed and drum-headed cabbages.

to 10 days after emergence will be beneficial. Shading should not be overdone, however, otherwise soft plants of poor colour will be produced that will fold up when set out in the open ground.

Transplanting. The planting distances for cabbage are very flexible and depend upon the cultivar and the growing method. I would say that, on the whole, cabbages are given much more room than they require. Where only a few rows are concerned, as in bed-culture, 350-400 mm each way is adequate for Early Jersey Wakefield and Golden Acre, while 450 mm intervals in rows 600 mm apart is the maximum necessary with the larger cultivars. As the plants are being lifted from the seedbed, which should have been well wetted beforehand, plants that are weak, 'blind' or affected with 'wire-stem' should be discarded. ('Wire-stem' shows up as a constriction and hardening of the stem just above soil level, often accompanied by a darkening of the stem tissue in this area.) If such plants are overlooked and transplanted, they will make little or no growth and will simply become a haven for aphids, caterpillars and other pests.

Cabbages usually reach the transplanting stage (i.e. 100 mm high) 4-5 weeks after sowing, although a further 14 days may be necessary in winter in cold areas. The plants should be set out with a dibber and firmed, or with a trowel if they are from segmented seed-trays, and given a thorough soaking with water or with starter solution at the rate of 250 mℓ per plant. They should be set out a little deeper than they stood in the seedbed, care being taken not to cover the 'eye' or growing point.

Further treatment. As cabbage plants are set out when they are quite big and are much stronger at this stage than many other vegetables, shallow cultivation can begin a few days after transplanting, if necessary. Thereafter the plants will respond to a side-dressing of nitrogen every 3 weeks or so, or to a series of liquid manure applications, inorganic or organic, at similar intervals.

Although maximum yields can be obtained only if the plants have adequate moisture throughout growth, water should be applied with caution once the heads are firm. A heavy fall of rain or a heavy watering at this stage may cause a great deal of splitting of the heads. Ball-headed cultivars are particularly prone to this trouble, followed by the conical cultivars. The drum-heads are least susceptible. Again, mulching will assist in keeping losses from this cause to a minimum. Insect control throughout all stages of growth is particularly important with this crop.

Harvesting. There is nothing difficult about harvesting this crop, a sharp knife or cane knife being all that is required. Ideally, of course, the heads should be cut when they are firm, and for market this is essential. In the home garden, however, heads can be cut, if required, 10-14 days before this stage

is reached so as to extend the season from a single sowing and to prevent a glut later on. The cabbage should be cut with 3 or 4 outer leaves and every week or so the stumps should be pulled up and disposed of. Leaving the stumps in the ground in the hope of getting a few loose secondary heads is most unwise, for this growth invariably becomes infested with aphids and other pests, whose progeny move on to later plantings. Severely bruising and chopping the hard stalks with a spade or hatchet will markedly hasten their decomposition if they are to be added to the compost heap.

Pests. *Aphids* favour Savoys, Cape Spitzkool and the drum-headed cultivars, and controlling them on the underside of the lower leaves can be difficult. Dimethoate and Metasystox are specific aphicides that are available to the home gardener, while Malathion and Karbaspray are useful for controlling *caterpillars* and other chewing pests.

Diseases. *Black rot* can play havoc with cabbage plantings, especially during wet weather and on soils that have carried this and related crops in succession for some years. The disease is initially seed-borne but once a crop has become severely affected the responsible organisms will live over in the soil for several years. The disease, if seed-borne, shows up as unthriftiness in the seedbed, and if the stems of one or two seedlings are carefully split longitudinally with a sharp knife, affected plants will show a black internal discoloration just above soil level. This stage frequently goes unnoticed and the plants rot off at intervals during later growth. In well-grown plants, black rot can usually be identified by marginal discoloration of the lower leaves. These discoloured areas are yellow to light brown in colour, V-shaped, and there may be several on one affected leaf. The disease then makes its way down the ribs, causing internal blackening, and into the stem. If the plant is badly affected it becomes stunted, leaves drop off, and it makes one-sided growth. Black rot is a bacterial disease and is usually accompanied in the later stages by 'soft-rot', a fungal condition that causes the stalk and head to decay internally, accompanied by a most disagreeable odour.

Downy mildew: the symptoms and control measures are described under broccoli.

Club root is a disease caused by a slime fungus found in soils that are cool, wet and acid. Symptoms are general unthriftiness of the plants, yellowing of the leaves, and swollen and stubby root systems. Heavy lime applications and long crop rotations are the only recommended control measures.

CABBAGES, CHINESE

Asia and
Brassica pekinensis — Eastern China
Optimum pH 6,0-7,0

This vegetable is very popular in Japan and other Eastern countries, where it is also known as Shantung cabbage, but is of rela-

tively minor importance in South Africa. It is a high-yielding, quick-maturing crop with a delicate flavour and is, particularly in the case of some cultivars, very similar in appearance to cos or romaine lettuce but usually larger and with more fibrous leaves. Chinese cabbage will tolerate a certain amount of light shade.

Recommended cultivars. Seedsmen in South Africa usually offer the following:
Chihili: A more recent introduction than Pe Tsai and Wong Bok.
Pe Tsai: A slender, semi-heading cultivar of medium height.
Wong Bok: A later, heading cultivar 250-300 mm high and 200-225 mm in diameter.

Soil preparation. Chinese cabbages require a well-improved and moisture-retaining soil to make quick growth, which is essential if the leaves are not to become tough and bitter. If Chinese cabbages follow a well-manured potato or tomato crop, 60 g per m² of 2:3:2 should be an adequate basic dressing if it is worked into the top 150 mm of soil. On poorer soils a dressing of compost or manure will be necessary to obtain satisfactory growth and yields.

Propagation. Where only a few rows are required the seed is best sown where the plants are to mature, for sometimes transplanting results in rather uneven stands. In addition, transplanted seedlings are inclined to shoot to flower in hot weather without forming sizeable heads.

Sowing. The seed can be sown from February to April, with March being the best month in most areas. The seed should be sown thinly in rows 350-400 mm apart and covered with 10-15 mm of firmed soil. A temporary mulch over the rows will assist in obtaining an even stand of seedlings. When sown in seedbeds, the plants may be moved to permanent quarters when they are on the small side (i.e. 75-80 mm high). Allow 300 mm between plants in the row.

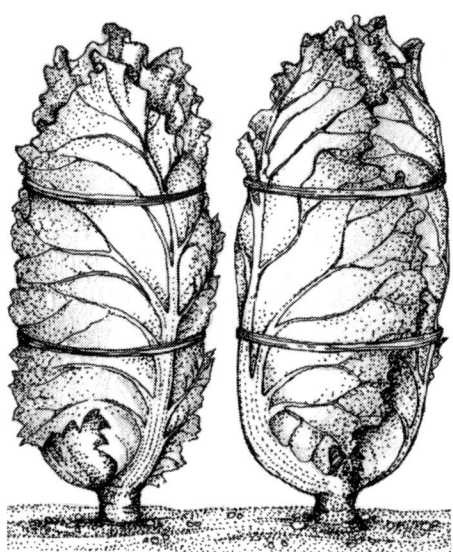

Loosely tie up the leaves of Chinese cabbage with raffia to encourage blanching.

Further treatment. Thinning is usually necessary in directly-sown rows and can be carried out in one or two stages, leaving the plants 250-300 mm apart, depending upon the cultivar. A light side-dressing of nitrogenous fertilizer or a generous liquid manure application should prove beneficial 5-6 weeks after sowing. As the plants heart up, the outer leaves can be lifted and tied loosely with raffia to encourage blanching. From this stage onwards a shortage of water may prove disastrous.

Harvesting. Chinese cabbages are usually ready for cutting about 2½-3 months after sowing, and the heads should be cut without delay once they are mature. In hot weather any delays in cutting may lead to severe losses from 'bolting' and to internal discoloration of the heads.

Pests and diseases. There are no diseases of real consequence if the crop is grown during the most favourable period, but *cutworms, snails, slugs, aphids* and *caterpillars* may necessitate control measures.

CARROTS
Eastern Europe
Daucus carota
Optimum pH 6,0-7,0

Carrots are, together with beetroot, among the most important root crops of commerce and hold the same position in the home garden. Together with celery, parsley and parsnips they belong to the Umbelliferae family and are true biennials, treated as annuals. They take up very little room as their development is mainly downwards, and therefore give high yields in relation to the area they occupy. Like most root crops they prefer cool growing conditions, but, provided that adequate moisture is available, they can be grown during most months in all but a few areas. In very hot weather the roots are often strong in flavour and pale in colour.

Recommended cultivars. The range of carrot cultivars is very wide and includes long, short, tapered, cylindrical and blunt-ended roots. So far few, if any, F1 hybrids are being grown on any scale. The short cultivars such as Oxheart are extremely useful in shallow soils and in containers, but must be pulled 8-9 weeks after sowing. Failure to pull at this stage can result in their becoming woody with pronounced green cores. The most suitable cultivars for the home garden are the intermediate sorts, of which the following are among the best:

Cape Market: A rather cylindrical cultivar, larger all round than Nantes and more pointed at the tip.

Chantenay: A very reliable cultivar of which there are many distinctly-named strains. It has a tremendous following among home gardeners and is the one usually sold by greengrocers. This is perhaps the heaviest yielder if allowed to grow to full maturity.

Nantes: This has good shape and is of extremely high quality. It is a slender, cylin-

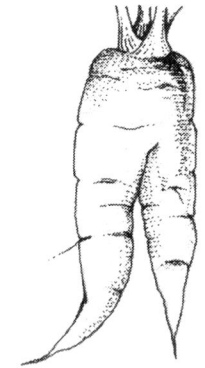

Fresh organic matter incorporated prior to sowing causes malformation of carrots. Cover carrot shoulders with soil to prevent 'greening'.

drical and stump-rooted cultivar possessing a rich internal colour in most soils and a rather undefined core.

Soil preparation. Soil texture is a very important factor affecting the production of smooth, well-shaped roots. Heavy compact soils should be avoided at all costs for they adversely affect germination and emergence, do not allow roots to develop freely, and make harvesting extremely difficult. Deeply-worked sandy loams that have been improved with generous dressings of compost or manure for a previous crop such as cabbages or cauliflowers are just about ideal. On such soils carrots of top quality can be produced with ease. Under no circumstances should heavy dressings of compost, manure or other organic matter be incorporated before establishing a carrot crop, for two reasons. Firstly, the nature of the material itself can have a deleterious effect on the roots, causing them to fork, grow crooked, have a rough skin and throw out excessive numbers of coarse side-roots. Secondly, the addition of such material almost inevitably introduces a quantity of weed seed, which is the last thing required by any directly-sown crop. If longer cultivars such as Cape Market are grown on shallow topsoils overlying a hard and compact subsoil, the roots produced are often perfect in shape for the first 75-100 mm but are flat and rough lower down. In some cases they will even lift out of the soil because downward development is impossible. The root shoulders are then susceptible to cutworm damage and are likely to become green, as are the cores, despite continual earthing up.

On well-worked, friable soils in extremely good heart, carrots will yield satisfactorily if 60 g per m² of superphosphate is incorporated. A more desirable application is 60-100 g of 2:3:2 per m². A side-dressing of nitrogen is rarely given to carrots, but 2:3:2 at the rate of 1 handful per metre of row may be worthwhile if applied about 6 weeks after sowing. During digging, forking over and raking, all clods, stones and roots of water grass, coarse oxalis or onion weed should be removed. Such weeds can cause havoc once the carrots have germinated.

Propagation. Propagation is by seed in rows where the crop is to mature.

Sowing. The soil surface should be raked to a fine tilth. Carrot seed is quite fine and should be sown thinly if fresh, and much more thickly if it is seed carried over from a previous season. The drills can be 250-300 mm apart when there are only a few rows, or 300-450 mm apart when larger areas are being seeded. I find that seed is best sown by putting a quantity into the palm of the one hand, taking a substantial pinch of it with the other, and rubbing it between finger and thumb forwards and backwards along the drills until the desired sowing rate has been achieved. The seed should then be covered to a depth of 10-12 mm, firmed and watered. In hot, dry weather, covering the rows with a thin mulch of grass until emergence is evident will assist germination. The grass can then be laid thinly between rows if so desired. Germination may take 7-14 days, depending upon cultivar, soil type and season.

Further treatment. Weed control, watering and thinning are the three major chores once the seed has been sown, apart from pest and disease control when necessary. If any of these is neglected, yields and quality will suffer. Carrots grow away very slowly at first and should be given a shallow cultivation as soon as the rows can be seen and if weed growth warrants it. The first step is carefully to handweed for 40-50 mm on either side of the row of seedlings and in the rows themselves if necessary. The inter-row spaces can then be scoffled carefully with a Dutch hoe or small, tined cultivater to kill the weeds and loosen any compaction of the soil caused by treading. Selective weedkillers have been used most successfully for many years on carrots, but several factors, discussed in an earlier chapter, preclude their use in the average home garden.

Thinning is usually necessary however well the rows have been sown, yet some gardeners are reluctant to remove surplus seedlings. If the stand is very thick the first thinning should take place as soon as 2 or 3 true leaves are well-developed, followed by further thinnings as the crop grows away. Failure to begin thinning at an early stage results in the roots becoming entwined and misshapen and rather difficult to handle in the kitchen. The operation should be carried out when the ground is moist, preferably late in the afternoon. This allows the remaining plants to have some respite after the ordeal before having to face up to the heat of the day. It is advantageous to earth up the rows a little after thinning to replace the support provided by the removed plants, and to give the rows a light soaking.

Most carrots will mature satisfactorily if thinned to 30-50 mm apart, but 50-60 mm should be allowed for Oxheart and for Chantenay if it is to be allowed to grow to full maturity. The final thinnings are usually large enough for the table.

Throughout growth the shoulders of the carrots should be lightly covered with soil to prevent 'greening', for even if only 10 mm of the root is exposed to sunlight the internal greening often extends more than twice this distance down the core. This is most undesirable as it makes the roots bitter in taste and less succulent.

Carrots require a steady supply of moisture throughout growth and prefer a cool soil. During hot weather, therefore, mulching with lawn clippings or similar short material will have a beneficial effect. As the crop approaches maturity, watering can gradually be decreased to prevent longitudinal splitting of the roots.

Harvesting. In the home garden carrots can be harvested as soon as they reach the preferred size. This may be 8-10 weeks after sowing, although a further 3-4 weeks may be necessary for full size to be reached. Harvesting is best started early, as with all roots, by removing the biggest and so making room for the remainder to develop. Very large roots are coarse and woody and usually have a poor flavour. Those left in nematode-infested soil often become disfigured, especially during wet periods.

Pests. *Aphids*, usually grey in colour and having a mealy and waxy appearance, often congregate in large numbers at the base of the foliage during hot, dry spells. On mature carrots they can do very little damage, but they may migrate to later sowings and cause severe injury. Spraying with pesticides such as Rogor or Metasystox usually gives excellent control. As the crop approaches maturity, Malathion (plus a wetting agent) is a more suitable material.

Cutworms can cause problems throughout growth. They sever young seedlings after emergence and feed on, or around, the carrot shoulders later in growth. Dusting with BHC is effective on young seedlings; a drenching with Karbaspray gives good control later on. Cutworm bait is also a useful material, best applied late in the afternoon.

Refer to Chapter 8 for a discussion of measures to control *nematodes*.

Diseases. *Leaf blight*, which attacks the foliage and causes it to brown off and curl up, is very common indeed and is especially troublesome during wet periods. Spraying at 7-14 day intervals, depending upon weather conditions, with Dithane M45 or copper oxychloride is usually quite effective in arresting the spread of the disease.

CAULIFLOWERS

Mediterranean

Brassica oleracea var. *botrytis*
Optimum pH 6,0-7,0

The cauliflower is one of the aristocrats of the vegetable world in general and the cabbage family in particular. It is much more difficult to grow than cabbage, however, being similar to Brussels sprouts in its all-round requirements but on the whole giving much better results than sprouts. Cauliflowers require a constant and plentiful supply of plant food and soil moisture and prefer cool growing conditions, especially during the later stages of growth. High temperatures prevent satisfactory heading, causing the heads to 'bolt' before they have reached a decent size. Cauliflowers are therefore a very demanding crop in terms of soil preparation, water requirements, climatic conditions and the attention they require from sowing to harvest. Nevertheless, if these factors are given due attention most gardeners with a little experience should achieve satisfactory results.

Recommended cultivars. Few hybrids are available in small packs, but they should each be given a trial as they appear. However, there are several fine open-pollinated cultivars with proven track records from which to choose.

Canberra: An Australian cultivar that performs well in milder areas. A heavy yielder.
Snowball: An early cultivar suited to the home garden because of its compact habit. Several strains are available.
Snowcap: Slightly later and larger than Snowball and more at home in warmer areas than most.
Snowdrift: An outstanding second-early cultivar that produces deep, meaty heads of fine quality and colour.

Soil preparation. Like cabbages and broccoli, this crop is a heavy feeder. While the physical character of the soil is relatively unimportant (heavier soils being preferred), the degree of fertility is of great consequence. Compost or mature kraal or poultry manure should be worked into the soil in liberal quantities, ideally some weeks before the plants are set out, together with a dressing of lime on soils known to be acid. This can be supplemented a few days before transplanting with a dressing of 2:3:2(22) at the rate of 60-100 g per m², which should be broadcast and forked in. Lighter soils should then be trodden to create the firmness essential for good yields. Cauliflowers do not appreciate the incorporation of raw manure immediately prior to transplanting, and it is said that when such a dressing is given the heads have a distinct off-flavour.

Propagation. Cauliflower is best raised by seed sown in seedbeds. As only one packet of seed is usually sufficient for an average planting it is a wise policy to buy the very best that is available. With this crop and Brussels sprouts, cheap seed is false economy.

Sowing. November to March is the best period for sowing, February and March being the best months in hotter areas because plants can then make much of their growth in the cooler months of winter. The seed should be sown thinly and covered with 10-12 mm of fine soil. Should the resultant stand be too thick, the seedlings can be thinned out to 20 mm apart in the row to allow them ample room for development. Pest control is important during the seedling stage, cutworms, caterpillars and grasshoppers being particularly damaging at times.

Transplanting. The plants should be 100 mm high and ready for transplanting 4-5 weeks after sowing. Those held over too long in the seedbed become leggy and are rarely productive when set out. The degree to which transplanting checks growth depends upon the amount of injury to the root system, and seedlings should therefore be lifted carefully and handled by the leaves, not the stem, to help prevent damage. The plants should be set out with a dibber or trowel, at 450 mm intervals in rows that can be 600-700 mm apart, depending upon the cultivar. When there are only 2 or 3 rows they can be 350 mm apart if they are check planted (i.e. staggered). As the plants are being set out, all 'blind' and weak specimens should be discarded.

Further treatment. A month or so after setting out, the plants will benefit from a nitrogenous side-dressing. LAN is the most suitable material, at the rate of 1 handful to 3 or 4 plants, and should be worked in shallowly. This can be repeated 3 weeks later. Cauliflowers should never be allowed to take on autumn (i.e. red and purple) tints, as these indicate a nutrient deficiency from which the plants will never recover sufficiently to produce good-sized heads. Such plants will have small, discoloured heads, will 'bolt' prematurely and will succumb to pest infestation.

Any necessary hoeing, which should always be shallow, is best carried out late in the afternoon when the leaves are less brittle and therefore less prone to damage.

Fold a few outer leaves over the developing curds to prevent cauliflower heads from discolouring.

Water should be given generously once good growth is made. Earthing-up the plants a little and mulching with any available material are beneficial practices with this crop.

Once the developing curds are 75-100 mm across, a few of the larger outer leaves should be brought up and tied together to exclude sunlight and prevent the discoloration of the head. Alternatively, 3 or 4 of these leaves can be broken, by snapping the mid-rib, and folded over the developing head. Tying up *does not* encourage heading and should not be done until the correct stage has been reached. After tying or covering, the heads should be examined every 3 or 4 days and cut as soon as they are fully developed. On large plantings coloured tape or string can be used for tying, each colour being used for 2 or 3 days. This will give the grower an idea of which plants are ready for harvesting at the same time.

Harvesting. The condition and texture of the head and *not* its size will determine when it is ready to be cut. Indeed, many home gardeners lose several heads by not observing this rule. Cutting should be carried out when the head is fully developed but before any branching, as indicated by the lifting of certain sections of the head, occurs. In hot weather this can happen very quickly. The plants should either be pulled from the soil completely or cut with a cane knife together with their foliage. The heads can then be trimmed carefully without damage to the curd, which is very brittle. The small, blanched inner-leaves have a delicate flavour and should be cooked, not discarded.

Pests. *Aphids* and *caterpillars* are often troublesome, especially in hot weather and on late plantings. The plants should be cleaned up thoroughly with Aphicide, Malathion or Dedevap as a spray, or by dusting with BHC, the final applications being just before tying or covering.

Diseases. *Downy mildew* is sometimes troublesome in the seedbed. Spraying with Dithane at the rate of 10 g per 5 ℓ should effect control, as should copper oxychloride.

Black rot is often a problem during wet periods. Clean seed and long rotations between susceptible cruciferous crops are the only practical remedies.

Club root is a disease caused by a slime fungus found in soils that are cool, wet and acid. It occurs in most areas but is very common in the south-west Cape. Heavy lime applications and long rotations are the recommended control measures.

Non-parasitic diseases. Discoloration of the curd is common, especially on unthrifty plants. Strong sunlight will lower the quality of unprotected heads by causing them to turn cream to light yellow in colour. Covering as recommended will ensure that the heads are white and succulent. Browning of the curds is usually caused by boron deficiency, the affected areas usually being somewhat sunken. Scaling on the stalks is another symptom of this condition. Ferti-

lizer borate at the rate of 40 g per 10 m² or borax at half this strength should be incorporated before planting beetroot, celery or cauliflower, three susceptible crops. Many cauliflower heads are spoiled by pinking and purpling of the curd. Although strong sunlight may be a contributing factor, nutrient deficiency would also appear to play some part. Therefore, from the outset, cauliflowers should be kept growing vigorously and should never be allowed to stand still.

CELERIAC   Mediterranean
Apium graveolens var. *rapaceum*
Optimum pH 6,0-6,5

Celeriac or, as it is sometimes called, turnip-rooted celery, is of minor importance but it makes a welcome change and a few rows should be tried occasionally. It is a type of celery developed principally for the swollen roots, although all parts of the plant have the authentic celery flavour. It is a rather slow grower, needing 5-5½ months from sowing to harvest.

Recommended cultivars. World-wide the choice of cultivars is narrow, with *Giant of Prague* being about the only one offered in South Africa. In Europe the cultivar *Globus* is gaining in popularity.

Soil preparation. Like celery, celeriac requires a well-prepared soil with a high organic content for moisture retention. It will perform reasonably well on soils that have been generously improved for a previous crop if a dressing of 60-90 g per m² of 2:3:2(22) is added before planting. Where such a place in the rotation is impossible, a dressing of compost plus the above fertilizer will be necessary to see the plants through their long growing period.

Propagation. Propagation is by seed, usually sown in seedbeds or seedboxes. The seedlings are set out into permanent quarters at 6-8 weeks.

Sowing. The seed, which is fine, should be sown thinly, covered with 6-8 mm of fine soil, firmed down and watered with a fine spray. Germination is slow, as with most members of this family, and may take up to 18 days in cool weather. February/March is the most favourable sowing period in most areas but spring sowings may also be successful.

Transplanting. When the seedlings are a good size they can be set out in rows 300-350 mm apart with 150-200 mm between plants in the row. Care should be taken to set them out shallowly, like bulbing onions, to allow for root development.

Further treatment. The swollen root, which is produced more out of the soil than in, should be kept free of side-shoots and suckers throughout growth. Although not quite as thirsty as celery, celeriac needs plenty of water to keep on the move. A side-dressing or two of LAN or sulphate of ammonia at intervals of 3-4 weeks will also assist in this di-

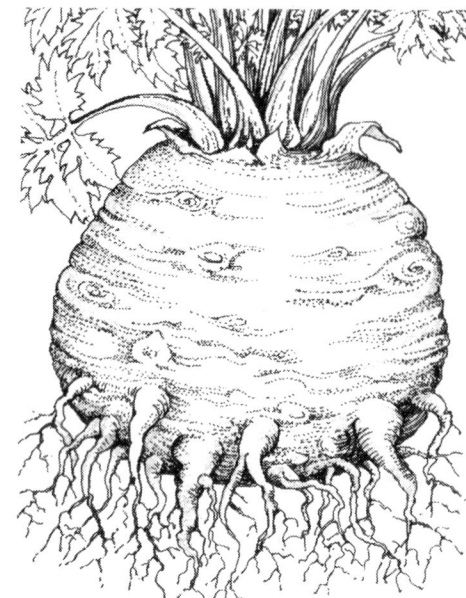

Before use, celeriac needs to be peeled rather deeply to remove all external fibres.

rection. Liquid manure applications at similar intervals will prove equally beneficial. As the roots approach maturity, soil can be drawn over the rows to avoid 'greening' and improve the flavour.

Harvesting. The roots are lifted when they are 70-100 mm across and are peeled before use. Unlike potatoes and turnips, it is necessary to peel rather deeply to ensure that all the external fibres are removed. Although it is usually cooked before eating, it does, if grated finely over a salad, impart an interesting tanginess to the dish.

Pests and diseases. In theory celeriac is susceptible to all the problems associated with celery, but in practice it is rarely troubled to any degree. However, a watch should be kept for *aphids*, which may congregate at the crown. Malathion, with a wetting agent, should check any infestation.

CELERY   Mediterranean
Apium graveolens
Optimum pH 6,0-6,5

Celery is not an easy crop to grow, even if self-blanching cultivars are used, and needs much care and attention from sowing through to cutting if heads of good quality are to be obtained. It will only mature satisfactorily in cool, moist conditions. An odd plant or two set out on the perimeter of the garden, or among the herbs if necessary, will provide a steady supply of greens for flavouring soups and other dishes.

Recommended cultivars. Only seed of white and self-blanching celery is catalogued in South Africa. The following are recommended cultivars:
Golden Self-Blanching: One of the most popular cultivars, eminently suited to the smaller home garden. It is of American ori-

gin and appears to perform better in warmer conditions than the blanching type. It is of compact habit with relatively short petioles and requires little or no blanching if set out closely. The flavour is somewhat milder than that of blanched celery.

Pascal and *Tall Utah:* These are classical tall-growing cultivars that require blanching to be crisp, succulent and free from strings.

Soil preparation. Celery is a gross feeder and develops a very extensive, if somewhat shallow, root system if soil conditions permit. It requires a fertile soil containing an abundance of organic matter, which will ensure that soil moisture is never in short supply. On sandy loams liberal quantities of compost or manure, together with a dressing of 2:3:2(22) at the rate of 100-125 g per m², should be incorporated before planting. Land with peaty, fibrous soil that retains an abundance of moisture at all times is particularly suitable for this crop (but such land is, of course, seldom encountered in urban areas).

The deep-trench method of growing celery, widely practised overseas, is rarely successful in our climate. The crop can, however, be grown in well-prepared shallow trenches with good results. The trenches, which should each be 300-350 mm wide, can be taken out to a depth of 150-250 mm. The bottoms should be dug over and 50-75 mm of mature compost should be well worked in together with a fertilizer at the rate of 60-75 g per metre of trench. Between 50 and 75 mm of the removed topsoil should then be replaced, trodden a little, and watered. The seedlings can be set out at a later date, check planted (i.e. staggered) in double rows.

Growing celery on the flat is suitable for the self-blanching cultivars. A bed 1 m wide is marked off and given overall, or blanket, treatment with compost, manure and a compound fertilizer to support a thick stand of plants.

Propagation. Propagation is by seed, sown in seedbeds or seedboxes. The seed is very fine, some cultivars producing 2 000 to the gram.

Sowing. The small seeds and seedlings can be handled much more easily in seedboxes than in open beds, one seedbox providing enough plants for the average planting in a home garden. The seeds can be sown thinly in shallow drills in the seedbox and covered with 6-8 mm of soil. If sown in the seedbed, 8-10 mm is the maximum depth. Temporary shade will assist in obtaining a quick and uniform germination, which should take place within 10-21 days. It must be stressed that fresh seed is essential with this crop.

When the seedlings show 3 true leaves they should be thinned out in the seedbed to stand 40 mm apart or pricked out from the seedbox into others, again allowing 40 mm between plants. Pricking out actually benefits celery seedlings, for during this operation the taproot is usually severed and this promotes the development of a more branched root system, which is to the plant's advantage when it is set out in permanent rows. February/March is the most favourable sowing period in most areas, but success can be achieved with spring sowings if the plants are harvested quickly.

Transplanting. The seedlings should be check planted 225 mm apart in double rows in shallow trenches if they are to be blanched, allowing 300 mm between the rows. Where the bed method is used, and this is ideal for self-blanching types, the plants should be square planted 200-225 mm apart each way, or 150-175 mm apart in poorer soils where smaller growth can be expected. Using this method, only 4-5 rows should be allowed per bed. This might appear to be very close spacing for the self-blanching types, but the thick growth and good canopy of foliage greatly assist blanching.

Whichever planting method is used, the seedlings should be set out a little deeper than they stood in the seedbed but with the growing point above soil level. Early watering should be carried out with care to avoid washing soil over the growing point.

Further treatment. Once established, celery is a crop that responds to generous applications of water during dry periods and to side-dressings and liquid manure applications. Sea-Gro and inorganic stimulants are both suitable when used at medium and full strengths.

Most people prefer blanched celery, although green celery contains more vitamins and minerals and is becoming more popular. Blanching can be carried out by one of several methods, depending to a large extent on the planting pattern. In trenches the heads can be tied up loosely with raffia or twine, when the plants are half grown, and a collar of strong paper or cardboard can be tied around the bottoms. (Newspaper is unsuitable as it will rot before the plants are ready for use.) After this the remainder of the soil that was removed when making the trench can be replaced. As the plants grow taller the collar can be extended and more earth can be brought up around and between the plants with a draw hoe. Lengths of builders' dampcoursing can also be used for blanching. Drawing up soil to any height against uncovered plants is rarely successful, for the stalks often become 'rusty' from contact with the soil and are susceptible to attack by cutworms and other pests.

When self-blanching celery is grown using the high-population bed method, better blanching of the outer rows will be achieved if the whole bed is cased in during the final stages of growth with planks 200-225 mm wide.

Harvesting. When the plants are mature, blanched celery should be lifted carefully with a fork and the root system removed with a sharp knife. The self-blanching type can simply be cut off at ground level, as required. Split sticks should be discarded and

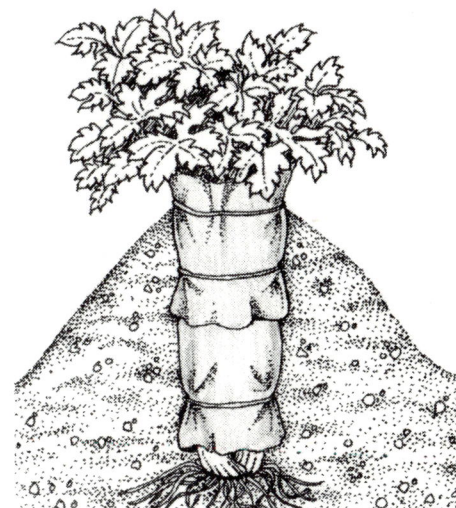

Plant self-blanching celery on a grid, not in rows. To blanch celery, loosely secure the heads with raffia, tie collars around the stalks and earth-up the plants. Extend the collars and bring up more soil as the plants grow.

the very long leaves trimmed back if they are not going to be used for flavouring. The stalks of plants left to stand for long in hot weather rapidly become pithy. Dryness in the final stages will also bring about this condition and accelerate 'bolting' or running to flower.

Pests. Like all vegetables with a long growing season, celery must be closely watched throughout for infestation by various pests.

Aphids, usually blue-grey in colour, are often a problem on this crop, especially when the plants begin to heart up. Because it is almost impossible to control them once the plants are tied up, any infestations must be dealt with before this stage is reached. In the earlier stages pesticidal granules containing dimethoate are effective, while Metasystox and Malathion can be used in the final stages provided that the safety periods are rigidly observed.

Leaf miner, which is also common, can be controlled by using the above-mentioned materials.

Cutworms, slugs and *snails* can be controlled by a drenching with Karbaspray after transplanting, followed by regular baiting. The destruction of any overgrown areas adjacent to the celery will help to reduce the slug and snail populations.

Diseases. *Leaf spot* on celery and celeriac is caused by several fungi, all of which can be seed-borne. Apparently after 2 or 3 years any form of the disease carried on the seed will be dead, but as the seed is not noted for its longevity this is of little help. Hot-water treatment is used by commercial growers but this impairs the viability of the seed. Thus the home gardener has only fungicidal sprays as a weapon, and of these copper oxychloride and Dithane M45 are the most effective if applied regularly.

Heart rot is a non-parasitic condition that appears to be caused by fluctuating moisture levels in the soil, cloudy weather with high relative humidity, and excessive nitrogen. Blanching for as short a period as possible in cloudy and humid weather is a measure that might help to prevent the condition.

CHAYOTE Central America
Sechium edule
Optimum pH 5,5-6,5

Chayote, often called sou-sou in Southern and Central Africa, is also known as choko or christophine in other sub-tropical and tropical regions. It is related to the loofah and is seldom encountered in home gardens. Because it is not a vegetable of commercial importance, planting material may be difficult to obtain. Although it is a cucurbit and has foliage typical of the family, its fruits are very different from those of its relatives. The plant is climbing in habit and the fruits, which are yellow to cream or green in colour, are pear-shaped and often wrinkled. Like the pole lima bean the chayote is a per-

ennial and is useful for covering a fence or trellis. It prefers a wind-free situation in full sun, and 2 or 3 plants will take up little space and will introduce some variety to the table.

Cultivars. The different types do not appear to have been clearly identified and named, and are described entirely by their fruit characteristics. At first glance the fruits appear to be made of wax, the most common colour being light cream, although green as well as green and cream variants are found in South Africa.

Soil preparation. Because so few plants are usually grown in one garden, it is a good plan to prepare separate planting stations at the base of a trellis or other support. Holes can be dug, 300 mm in diameter and 225 mm deep, the bottoms loosened and the removed soil mixed with one or two forkfuls of compost or well-decomposed manure and a handful of 2:3:2. This material can then be returned to the holes, trodden lightly, and the surface fashioned into shallow dish-like depressions to facilitate planting, watering and feeding.

Propagation. The chayote is propagated by planting the whole fruit, for there is only one large seed inside.

Planting. Good-sized fruits, which may weigh 500 g or more, should be selected for propagation purposes. In heavier soils they should be planted with the broad base 30-40 mm below ground level and the stem end just a little above it; in lighter soils the fruit can be covered completely with 50 mm of soil. The new plant arises from the deep 'dimple' in the base of the fruit. The fruits can be planted whenever they are available, but as chayote is a warm-season plant it makes little or no growth during the colder months.

Further treatment. Once the new plants are growing away, there is little to do except keep the planting station free from weeds and apply water when necessary. When the first flowers appear the plants can be given a light side-dressing of nitrogenous fertilizer or an application of liquid manure. A mulch with decayed manure will also be welcome.

In warmer districts the plants will continue to grow, flower and fruit for many months of the year, although the main flush of growth is usually in late spring. In other areas the plants may die back. When this happens the dead growth should be removed and the plants cut back to a height of 100-150 mm above soil level. When growth recommences each year from the tuber in the soil, the plants will benefit from a dressing of 30-60 g of 2:3:2 and a forkful or two of compost or manure worked into the top 50-75 mm of soil.

Harvesting. Although fruits may be produced 4-6 months after planting, depending upon the time of year, it is only in their second season that the plants bear to full capacity. The fruits are best removed with a pair of secateurs.

Pests. Like most of its relatives the chayote attracts the attention of certain species of *fruit fly,* which 'sting' the fruits. Lebaycid is a material specifically formulated for the control of these insects. The regular removal of affected fruits, particularly those that have fallen to the ground, is an important additional control measure.

Aphids can be sprayed with Metasystox and Malathion.

CHICORY Europe
Cichorium intybus
Optimum pH 6,0-6,5

This little-known relative of endive rarely appears on the greengrocer's shelves and is well worth a trial. South Africans who grew up in Europe are extremely appreciative of its flavour, especially the flavour of the blanched 'chicons' sometimes described as Belgian or French endive.

Recommended cultivars. *Magdeburg:* Similar to endive, the leaves are useful for adding to salads, especially when lettuce is scarce. *Witloof:* There are several strains of this cultivar, which is used for producing chicons.

Soil preparation. Like other roots, chicory

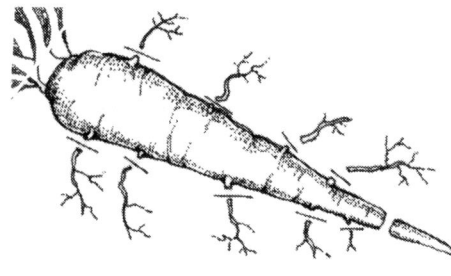

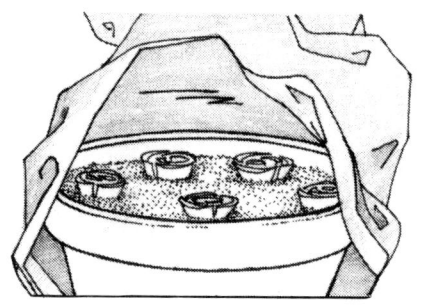

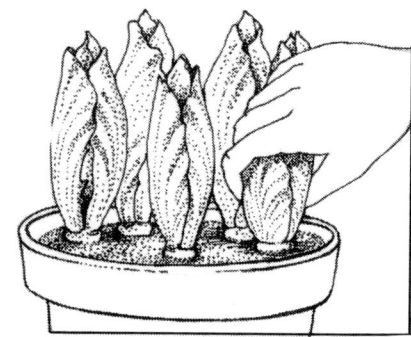

To obtain chicons, plant trimmed chicory roots in deep pots or boxes and cover these with black polythene or inverted containers to exclude light. If the resulting chicons are carefully snapped off, a second growth may occur.

prefers lighter, well-dug soils that have been generously improved with compost and manure for a previous crop. A dressing of 2:3:2 at the rate of 60 g per m^2 should be adequate on such soils.

Propagation. Propagation is by seed, sown where the crop is to mature. August to October is the most favourable period for sowing.

Sowing. When the soil has been raked over, drills can be made 225-300 mm apart. The seed should be sown thinly at a depth of 10-12 mm and the rows should then be firmed and watered. Germination usually takes 8-14 days.

Further treatment. Thinning is necessary in almost every case. This should be carried out carefully when the seedlings are 40-60 mm high and should leave the remaining plants 150-200 mm apart in the row. The Magdeburg type can be picked green for salad when the plants are large enough.

Witloof chicory should be kept free of weeds throughout growth until sizeable roots (40-50 mm in diameter at the shoulder) are produced. Any flower stalks that appear before this stage should be cut off low down as they will reduce the ability of the root to produce chicons.

Harvesting. When the roots are of good size they should be lifted, at which stage the foliage is usually deteriorating. The tops should be cut back to 20-25 mm from the shoulder, the root tip trimmed back a little and any side roots removed. The roots can then be stored in a cool airy place. When chicons are required the roots can be replanted a few at a time in deep pots or boxes filled with moist (*not wet*) sand, peat, light soil, vermiculite or any mixture of these, ensuring that no soil pests are present to cause damage. The shoulders should be covered by the mixture but the crowns should be left above the surface. The boxes or pots are then covered with black polythene or with containers of equal size and depth so that all light is excluded. (Light causes greening, which results in a bitter taste.) After 2½-3 weeks the chicons should have reached a height of 150-200 mm and are ready for use. If they are carefully snapped off, shorter second growth may occur, but these chicons are usually not as tight. Chicons deteriorate very rapidly and should be used as soon as possible.

Pests and diseases. Chicory appears to be singularly free from pests and diseases, but an eye should always be kept open for snails, slugs and chewing insects.

CRESS: see MUSTARD AND CRESS

CUCUMBERS   India

Cucumis sativus
Optimum pH 5,5-7,0

Cucumbers are salad vegetables of considerable importance and have apparently been

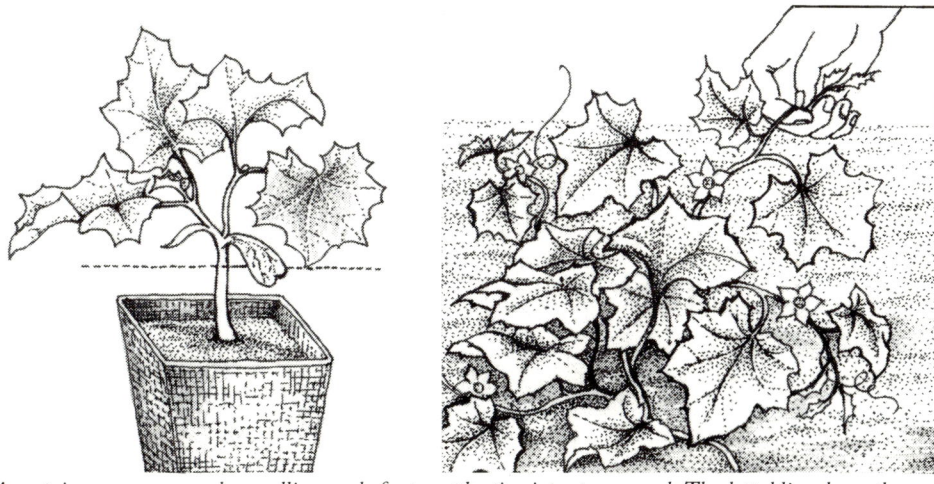

A container-grown cucumber seedling ready for transplanting into open ground. The dotted line shows the correct planting depth. Pinch out the growing points of cucumbers to induce the production of laterals.

in cultivation for thousands of years. Unlike several other salad crops, including lettuce and celery, cucumbers actually thrive in the summer months when cold dishes are in demand. In the home garden this crop, like most other cucurbits, is frequently disappointing, with few clean fruits of good shape being harvested. This can usually be overcome if an early and earnest effort is made to control fruit flies.

Recommended cultivars. Cucumbers can be divided into two distinct groups: 'frame' or 'English' cucumbers and 'ridge' cucumbers.

Frame cucumbers are so called because they are climbing in habit and require to be trained up a framework to grow well and produce desirable, straight fruits. The Japanese climbing cultivars and hybrids include some short-fruited kinds similar in fruit characteristics to ridge cucumbers. Ridge cucumbers are cultivars that are grown, in most cases, on ridges or 'hills', although there is no reason at all why they should not be planted on the flat. They are usually grown without support and are the cultivars most often used for commercial and domestic plantings in this country.

Ashley: A relatively early cultivar having, allegedly, some resistance to downy mildew.
Marketer: An excellent cultivar producing fruits that are 200-250 mm in length and of good colour and shape.

There are numerous other cultivars of both types and it is up to the individual grower to try them out and establish the merits of each by practical growing experience.

The true West Indian gherkin, prized for pickling, is actually a distinct species, *Cucumis anguria.* Seed is rarely catalogued, but those wanting fruit for pickling can try the cucumber *Chicago Pickling* or the F1 hybrid *Cherokee 7.*

Soil preparation. Ridge cucumbers can be grown either closely planted in rows with a wide spacing or in planting stations. When grown in rows, which should be at least 1 m

apart, it is economical to place compost or manure in a layer along the demarcated rows, add 60-90 g of 2:3:2(22) per metre, and then incorporate the improving material fully with a fork or digging hoe.

Where planting stations are used, and this I believe is the better method for the average home garden, they can be 750 mm to 1 m apart, centre to centre, and 300-350 mm in diameter. Compost can be worked into each station plus a handful of 2:3:2. The stations can be on the flat or in the form of mounds, depending upon the expected rainfall conditions during the growing season.

Propagation. Propagation is by seed, usually sown where the crop is to mature, although seedlings can be raised in Jiffy 7s, Jiffy pots, or segmented seed-trays under protection and then set out into open ground when the weather and soil warm up.

Sowing. Seed can be sown in the open ground from August to December in most districts, although September may be the earliest one can sow in colder areas. Cucumbers grown in containers under protection may be started earlier, but in most cases a 3 week difference in sowing time closes to a 7-10 day difference in picking time as more favourable weather prevails. Very late sowings are occasionally successful, but all too often, while plant growth is satisfactory, the plants succumb to the build-up of pests and diseases emanating from early sowings. In addition, nematodes are much more active at this stage.

At each planting station 5 or 6 seeds should be sown, and the seedlings should later be thinned to the 4 strongest plants. If planted in rows the seeds should be 150-200 mm apart at a depth of 15-20 mm. Early sowings should be a little shallower (12-15 mm) while the soil is still cold, and should be watered with extreme care otherwise the seed will rot in the cold wet soil. Later sowings (i.e. from November onwards) can be covered with a thin mulch of lawn mowings that should be moved aside once the majority of the seedlings have emerged.

Further treatment. Thinning the rows or

stations may be necessary if germination is good, for crowded plants do not develop properly and produce small fruit. Hand-weeding and careful hoeing should be carried out until the growth of the vines covers the soil. When the growing points have reached 600 mm the tops should be pinched out to induce the plants to produce laterals, for it is on this growth that most of the fruits are produced.

Once the first flowers show, the plants will benefit from a stimulant. Liquid manure should be applied carefully under the foliage in the root area after watering. The plant's vining habit makes the cucumber difficult to side-dress with granular fertilizers.

Cucumbers, like most cucurbits, are monoecious, i.e. the male and female flowers are separate but are produced on the same plant. The male flowers are usually the first to appear, followed by the female flowers, which can be identified by the small fruits behind the calyx. Most frame cucumber hybrids now being introduced are 'all female', i.e. they bear very few or no male flowers at all, and this obviates the necessity of removing the male flowers, as formerly. Insect pollination is unnecessary and undesirable as it leads to misshapen or bulbous fruits and also causes them to be bitter. Frame cucumbers are allowed to grow without stopping until they have reached a height of 2,0-2,5m. Feeding frame cucumbers is easy, for the ground can simply be drenched with liquid manure and in addition a manure mulch can be applied a few weeks after setting out the plants.

Cucumbers of all types must be kept growing if they are to make the vegetative growth necessary to produce high yields of top-quality fruits. Frame or greenhouse cucumbers are much more susceptible to nonparasitic disorders than are ridge types. Badly-shaped fruits, premature yellowing of the foliage, and small leaves with short internodes, are some expressions of their discomfort when under stress. Fluctuating soil moisture and temperatures are often primary causal factors.

Harvesting. Cucumbers are usually ready for cutting 8-10 weeks after sowing during the most favourable growing period. The fruits should be removed with a sharp knife or secateurs about twice a week. The plants will lose vigour if mature fruits are left on them.

Pests. *Beetles* of several species appear wherever young cucumbers are growing. Some, often yellow and black in colour, feed on the leaf margins, where their feeding produces a scalloped effect. Others, like the ladybird beetle, feed on the underside of the leaves, where they skeletonize the foliage (although on this crop the damage is often not apparent on the upper leaf surface). Malathion is an effective weapon against beetles of all types if used at a strength of 1 teaspoonful to 5 ℓ of water. Dusting with BHC is also effective and practical when there are only a few plants.

Aphids, usually black in colour, often infest unthrifty plants and cause the leaves to curl and blacken. On more vigorous plants their presence is not so obvious and they can be found in small colonies on the undersides of the leaves. If only 1 or 2 young plants are severely affected they should be lifted carefully, roots and all, and burnt if possible or dunked in an insecticidal suspension for a few minutes. Systemic insecticides have revolutionized the control of aphids and other sucking insects on several crops and the cucumber is no exception. But systemics have a considerable residual effect and should only be used until the first flowers show; thereafter Malathion, which has a shorter safety period, should be used as a contact spray.

Red spider mite is often a problem on a wide range of vegetables, flowers and ornamentals, particularly during hot dry weather. The mites operate on the undersides of the leaves but the upper surfaces become silvery and yellow. Kelthane is a specific for most mites, but dimethoate and Malathion may also give a measure of control.

Fruit fly: refer to the entry on pumpkins for advice on control measures.

Diseases. *Powdery mildew* is a crippling disease that attacks cucumbers and related crops. Refer to the entry on pumpkins for further information.

Downy mildew is another fungal disease that is equally destructive on occasions. Refer to the entry on pumpkins.

Anthracnose is perhaps the most destructive of all diseases affecting cucurbits. Refer to the entry on pumpkins.

Mosaic is a viral disease affecting cucumbers and related crops. Aphids play a big part in its spread, while a high standard of garden hygiene will do much to control it. Refer to the entry on pumpkins.

Non-parasitic diseases. Fruits suffering from sun scorch display white areas that are sunken but firm. These are usually elliptical in shape and appear on the upper side, particularly from midsummer onwards as the foliage deteriorates. The regular removal of mature or near-mature fruits is the only practical remedy.

EGG PLANTS

Solanum melongena
Optimum pH 5,5-6,5

India and Southern Asia

The egg plant, often called the brinjal in Southern Africa and the aubergine in Europe, is related to tomatoes, potatoes and peppers. Like tomatoes and peppers it is sensitive to cold weather and is easily damaged by frost. For several centuries it was grown purely for decorative purposes because of its relationship to poisonous plants such as deadly nightshade (*Atropa belladonna*) and moonflower.

Half a dozen well-grown plants should be quite adequate for the average household. Although young plants from annual sowings produce the heaviest yields, I have seen plants that have been cut back after the first flush and well fertilized give an extended harvest period in mild areas.

Recommended cultivars. There are many types of egg plant, both in colour and size. White, green and striped ones are cultivated, in addition to the dark purple cultivars of commerce.

Black Beauty: A popular cultivar bearing fruits that are less pear-shaped than Florida High Bush. It appears to be more prone to fruit deformities, though, and frequently has a stitched effect along the base.

Florida High Bush: To my mind this is the leading cultivar for shape, colour and quality. The pear-shaped fruits are borne profusely on well-developed plants.

Long Purple: A cultivar with a small following among gardeners, it often has an unattractive skin colour and is not a heavy bearer.

One or two hybrids are now becoming available and should be given a trial in the home garden.

Soil preparation. As only a few plants are necessary it is best to prepare a separate station for each plant. The stations should be 300-400 mm in diameter with 750 mm to 1 m, centre to centre, between them. This crop appreciates a fertile soil rich in organic matter, and any soils that appear to be lacking in this commodity should be treated generously. A forkful or two of mature compost or manure should be worked into each station, plus a handful of 2:3:2 prior to planting. The station should be finished off by treading it lightly and shaping it into a dish-like depression.

Propagation. Egg plants are propagated by seed, usually sown in seedbeds or seedboxes. Some seed samples contain a proportion of empty seed-coats that are usually darker in colour, and this should be taken into account when sowing is carried out.

Sowing. The seeds can be sown thinly in shallow drills and covered with up to 10 mm of soil from late August to early December in most areas. Earlier sowings under protection can be tried in warmer areas. The seeds germinate in 10-14 days and require a further 5 weeks before they are ready for transplanting. Seeds sown in seedboxes are best pricked out later into individual containers so that they can develop into strong plants before going to the open garden.

Transplanting. This is best carried out when the plants are 100-125 mm high, for if they are allowed to get much bigger than this they receive a severe check from the move. They should be set out (one to each prepared station) a little deeper than they stood in the seedbed, and given a thorough soaking. As so few plants are usually required, any weak and spindly specimens should be discarded.

Further treatment. At all stages of growth, weed control must be carried out and the plants must be watered well. Pinching out

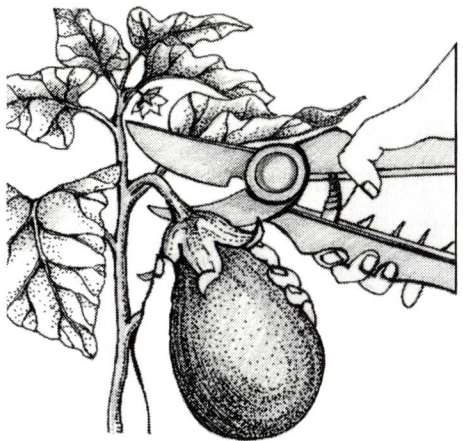

Because egg plants damage easily, harvest the fruits carefully with secateurs.

Tie endive loosely with raffia to blanch the inner leaves. To obtain more complete blanching, particularly of the curly-leaved type, cover the heads with flower pots or boxes, leaving a gap at the bottom for ventilation.

the growing point at 150-225 mm is often advocated, but I have never experienced any real benefit from this practice as most cultivars of commerce 'break' naturally and develop a desirable framework. Throughout growth the plants will respond to regular feeding, either by 3-weekly additions of 2:3:2 at 30 g per planting station or by applications of liquid manure. Mulching is a rewarding practice during really hot weather.

Harvesting. Fruits can be removed for use from the time they are 70-100 mm in diameter, which is usually about 3 months after transplanting. If they are removed regularly at this stage, there will be no need to limit the number of fruits per plant. A reasonable expectation, if good vegetative growth is developed, is 10-12 good-sized fruits per plant.

Egg plants are rather brittle and the fruits should be removed carefully with a sharp knife or, preferably, secateurs. Pulling off the fruits by twisting usually results either in damage to the plant or in the fruits pulling away from the calyx, both of which are undesirable. The fruits should be removed while they still have their lustre, and should be handled with care for they bruise and graze easily. Once removed from the plants, the fruits do not keep for any length of time.

Pests. *Leaf beetle* often feeds voraciously on egg plant foliage and on potato haulms. It is a close relative of the Mexican bean beetle (*Epilachna verivestis*), which is a big problem in the U.S.A. Both the adult beetle and the larvae feed rapidly, usually on the underside of the leaves, which eventually have a lace-like appearance. Dusting with BHC or spraying with mercaptothion should give good control.

Cutworms can be a problem at transplanting time. Water-in with a half-strength solution of mercaptothion and distribute a proprietary bait.

For information on measures to control *nematodes*, refer to Chapter 8.

Diseases. *Bacterial wilt*, which attacks egg plants, potatoes, tomatoes, peppers and a few related weeds, is often a problem on old soils that have carried these susceptible crops over a period. Long rotations between

these crops and the regular removal of possible weed hosts are the only practical methods of control in the home garden.

ENDIVE
Origin uncertain
Cichorium endivia
Optimum pH 5,5-7,0

Endive is a salad crop that is quite popular in Europe but not widely known or grown in South Africa, possibly because lettuce is almost always available. It is similar to lettuce in colour and habit and can be used in salad dishes or, like Chinese cabbage, can be cooked as a spinach substitute. For salad purposes it is necessary to blanch the heads otherwise the leaves will be bitter and tough.

Recommended cultivars. Endive cultivars are few the world over and can conveniently be split into two classes – the broad-leaved (often called 'escarolle') and the curly-leaved.

Broad-Leaved Batavian: The leaves of this cultivar are large, broad and thick, similar to lettuce, medium-green in colour and have white mid-ribs.

White Curled: This cultivar is more popular than Broad-leaved Batavian. It produces curly, light green leaves of good quality and is ideal for blanching.

Soil preparation. Like other salad crops, endive prefers to follow a well-manured crop such as cabbage in the rotation instead of being given a heavy dressing just prior to planting. A pre-planting dressing of 2:3:2 at the rate of 60 g per m² should ensure the rapid initial growth that is so essential.

Propagation. Propagation is by seed, preferably sown where the plants are to mature, although transplanting is also a recognized practice, particularly where larger areas are involved.

Sowing. The improved soil should be raked to a fine tilth and drills made 300-450 mm apart when only a few rows are needed. The seed should be sown thinly, covered with 8-12 mm of soil, firmed and watered with a

fine sprinkler. The periods August/September and February/March are the most favourable for sowing.

Further treatment. When the plants are 60-75 mm high, directly-sown rows should be thinned so that the plants are 300 mm apart. Transplants can be set out the same distance apart. After 5-6 weeks, a regular feed at intervals of 2-3 weeks with a liquid manure or LAN will be beneficial. In addition, weed growth should be controlled and regular watering should be carried out in dry weather to keep the plants growing.

Endive does not form a true heart but, instead, a full rosette of leaves that must be blanched to be palatable. Blanching can be carried out to a satisfactory degree by drawing up the outer leaves and tying the head loosely as with cauliflowers. After tying, all watering must be carried out by flooding or furrow irrigation, otherwise 'heart rot' may occur. The curly-leaved type can be more completely blanched by covering the heads, a few at a time as required, with large flower pots, boxes or cartons.

Harvesting. Blanching may be necessary for two weeks to get sweet, succulent heads. Too many plants should not be tied up at any one time, for they deteriorate very quickly once mature and, like lettuce, they run to seed in hot weather. Directly-sown endive should be ready for cutting 3-3½ months after sowing.

Pests and diseases. There are no pests or diseases of real consequence. *Leaf spots* caused by *Septoria* and *Cercospora* fungi appear occasionally but seldom warrant control measures. *Cutworms*, *slugs* and *snails* may require control during wet periods and in fertile soil. Proprietary bait broadcast between the rows should be sufficient.

KALE
Northern Europe
Brassica oleracea var. *acephala*
Optimum pH 6,0-7,0

Kale, also known as borecole, is a type of non-heading cabbage and is very similar to collards. The main difference between the two is that kale leaves are tightly or loosely curled while collard leaves are plain. Kale is an extremely hardy crop, even by European standards, and prefers cool, moist growing conditions.

Recommended cultivars. In Europe there are 5 or 6 distinct types and they range from tall to short and from slightly curled to tightly curled. In addition there are sprouting types. Several cultivars are really fodder crops for livestock and others have tinted foliage, often with green leaf margins, and are used for decorative bedding purposes. The short-growing, curled cultivars are most suited to the home garden, *Moss Curled Dwarf* being one of the few catalogued.

Soil preparation. Like other leaf brassicas kale will perform satisfactorily on most soils, even those on the heavy side, provided that they are improved with suitable organic matter or follow a crop that was treated generously. A fertilizer dressing of 60-90 g per m² incorporated prior to planting (2:3:2 being the most suitable) should be regarded as standard practice.

Propagation. By seed, sown in seedbeds or boxes.

Sowing. The seeds should be sown thinly in shallow drills, covered with 10-15 mm of fine soil, firmed and watered. The rows can be covered with a light mulch in hot weather until emergence, which should take place after 7-10 days.

Transplanting. After 4-5 weeks the seedlings should be about 100 mm tall and ready for setting out. The plants should be spaced 450-500 mm apart in rows 600 mm apart.

Further treatment. Weed control, regular watering and the control of pests are the only chores involved, though an effective mulch once the plants are growing away will greatly reduce the amount of water needed.

A side-dressing of LAN 3-6 weeks after transplanting, and drawing up the soil to the stems, are additional practices that will improve growth.

Harvesting. In the home garden kale is usually harvested by removing 2 or 3 leaves at a time from each plant. This can usually be started 2-2½ months after transplanting. Some growers recommend that the growing point be taken out to encourage side growths.

Pests and diseases. Pests and diseases are as described in the entries on broccoli and cabbage. However, if clean seed is sown *aphids* are likely to be the most troublesome pests. Kale appears to have some resistance to club root.

KOHLRABI
Europe

Brassica oleracea var. *coulorapa*
Optimum pH 6,0-7,0

Kohlrabi, sometimes called knolkohl, is one of the newer vegetables although it was first described over 400 years ago. Its name, of German origin, literally means 'cabbage-turnip', which is as good a description as any of its appearance and flavour. It is sometimes found classified as a root crop, though the edible portion is the swollen, fleshy stem, which develops above the ground. Its culture is extremely easy, and a row or two will handsomely repay any effort involved. It is more tolerant of hotter weather than any turnip cultivar.

Recommended cultivars. Only two are commonly catalogued here:

Purple Vienna: This is a less popular cultivar than White Vienna but not far behind in quality.

White Vienna: This is by far the most popular cultivar and almost all the strains are excellent.

Soil preparation. Kohlrabi will grow on most soils, except those that are particularly sandy and hot, and is less demanding than its more esteemed relatives. It will follow tomatoes, potatoes or beans in the rotation if a dressing of 60-90 g of 2:3:2 per m² is incorporated before sowing takes place.

Propagation. Although kohlrabi can be raised in a similar way to cabbage, it is usual, when there are only a few rows, to sow the seed where the plants are to mature. The best-shaped produce is obtained in this way.

Sowing. The seeds should be sown thinly in shallow drills 225-350 mm apart and covered with up to 10 mm of soil. Germination should take place in 7-10 days. Seedlings raised in seedbeds can be set out about 4 weeks after sowing, allowing 100-125 mm between plants in the row.

Further treatment. Thinning of directly-sown rows is usually necessary. Provided that the stand is not too thick, thinning can be carried out in one operation 4 weeks after sowing, leaving the plants 100-125 mm apart to mature.

If lifted carefully, the thinnings can be used to plant out another row or two, which will mature about 2 weeks later than the rest. Hand-weeding between the plants and hoeing shallowly between the rows should be carried out when necessary, but hoeing should be discontinued as the plants approach maturity. At this stage the plants usually lie over on both sides of the row and the swollen stems are easily damaged with a sharp cultivating tool such as a Dutch hoe. To obtain tender produce never let the plants be short of water during the growing period.

Harvesting. Unless kohlrabi are harvested when young (i.e. when the stems are 50-75 mm across), they become woody and coarse.

Pests and diseases. While kohlrabi is susceptible to most of the diseases that beset its relatives in the cabbage family, it is rarely troubled by them to any extent. *Cutworms* in the seedling stage and *aphids* throughout growth need to be controlled.

LEEKS
Eastern Mediterranean

Allium porrum
Optimum pH 6,0-7,0

Leeks are a milder member of the extensive onion family and are not only useful for flavouring soups and stews but also form the main ingredient of several dishes. They will tolerate a wide range of soil types and climatic conditions, provided that a steady supply of moisture is available, and are relatively untroubled by pests and diseases. It is therefore rather surprising that one rarely encounters leeks in home gardens, though their rather long growing season may be considered by some as a major disadvantage. January to April is the best period for

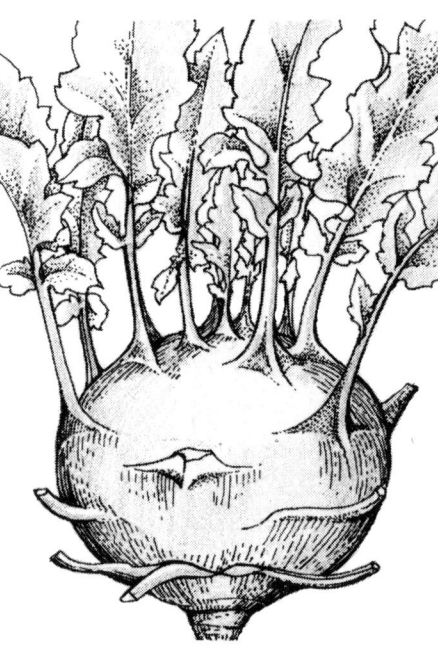

Harvest kale by removing 2 or 3 leaves at a time from each plant.

The edible portion of kohlrabi is the swollen, fleshy stem.

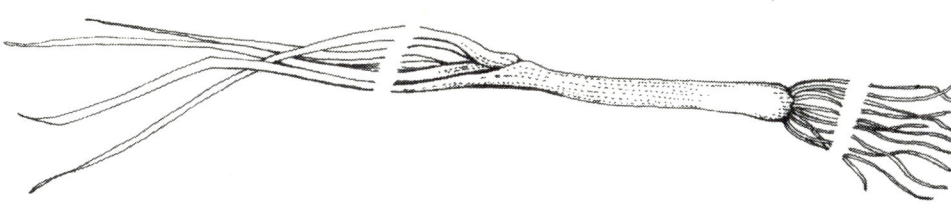

Trim the tops and roots of leeks before transplanting.

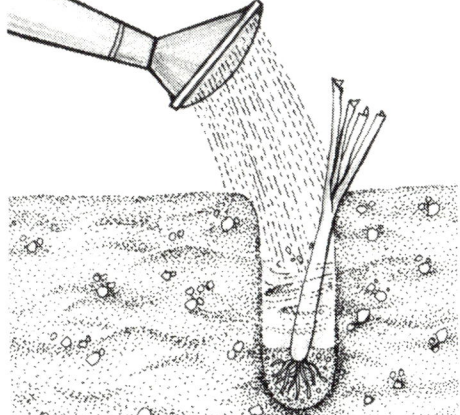

Water-in leek transplants without *closing the dibber hole.*

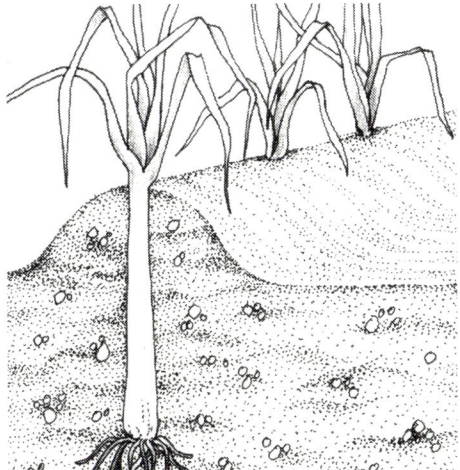

Gradually earth-up leeks to obtain a good length of stem.

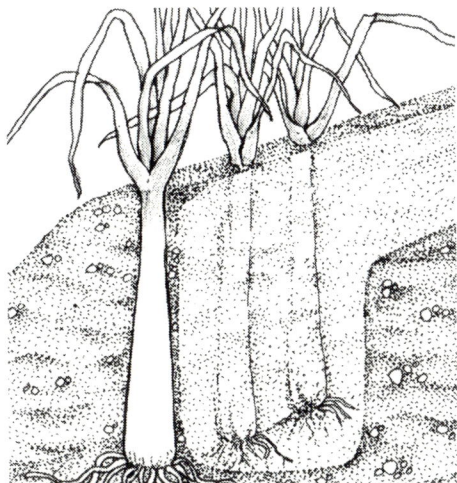

To harvest leeks, dig a trench parallel to the row.

sowing, but August/September can also give satisfactory results. The finest stems are grown during a cool, moist season.

Recommended cultivars. *Carentan, Giant Italian* and *London Flag* are all reliable cultivars of long standing.

Soil preparation. Deep digging is essential for leeks because, apart from the length of the blanched stem, the plants develop extensive root systems. As much compost or manure as can be spared should be incorporated during digging, and a dressing of 2:3:2 at the rate of 90-120 g per m² should be given.

Propagation. Propagation is by seed, sown in seedbeds or seedboxes.

Sowing. The seeds should be sown in shallow drills and covered to a depth of 8-10 mm. Germination is somewhat slow but can be assisted by covering the bed with a light mulch to retain moisture and prevent the soil surface from crusting. At around 8 weeks the seedlings should be approaching pencil thickness and can be set out into prepared ground.

Transplanting. If the tops of the plants are longer than 150 mm when the 'pencil' stage is reached, they should be trimmed back to this length, while the roots should be cut back to 10-15 mm to facilitate transplanting. The most common method of setting out leeks for normal use is to make holes, 150-200 mm deep, with a dibber that has a diameter of 30-40 mm. The trimmed plants are then simply dropped in the hole *without firming.* The initial watering, which should be done with a sprinkler or with a can and rose, should settle sufficient soil around the roots, and subsequent watering and cultivation will gradually close up the holes with loose uncompacted soil. This will enable the plants to develop and swell without difficulty, provided that the soil is kept moist. The plants can be set out 150 mm apart in single rows 350 mm apart, or they can be planted in double rows 225 mm apart allowing at least 600 mm between each set of rows to facilitate ridging.

Large exhibition leeks can be obtained if the cultural directions for celery are followed closely, particularly with regard to blanching.

Further treatment. When the plants are 150-250 mm above ground level they will respond to fortnightly feeding with LAN at the rate of 30-45 g per metre of row or with a proprietary organic or inorganic liquid at the recommended strength. As with all side-dressings, 'little and often' should be the aim. As growth proceeds, the plants can gradually be earthed up to obtain a good length of stem, care being taken not to cover the leaf sheath. As with celery, a collar of cardboard or strong paper can be tied around the stems to protect them from the soil.

Harvesting. Leeks can be harvested at almost any time for flavouring purposes but, if allowed to develop fully should reach a diameter of 30-40 mm 4 months after transplanting. Blanched stems are brittle and should be lifted carefully, not pulled. Digging a trench parallel to the row is the best method of lifting (see illustration).

Pests and diseases. *Cutworms* may cause damage at any stage of growth.

Pink rot is a fungal disease that occurs in some areas on most onion species, although leeks are relatively resistant. Long rotations between related crops is the only practical method of control, while it has been observed that vigorous plants are rarely affected.

LETTUCE   Europe and Middle East
Lactuca sativa
Optimum pH 5,5-7,0

Lettuce, together with tomato and cucumber, is an indispensable salad vegetable. The lettuces usually available at the local greengrocer or supermarket can never compare with those grown in the home garden. It is not a difficult crop and can be grown during most months in most localities, provided that the ground is well prepared and well drained and that snails and slugs are controlled. However, lettuces prefer cool, moist conditions, and in very hot and dry weather the plants are inclined to run to flower quickly.

Recommended cultivars. There are four recognized classes of lettuce: loose-leaf, cos or romaine, butterhead and crisphead. The first group is the least grown and the last is by far the most popular.

Loose-leaf lettuces deserve more attention as they are ideally suited to the home garden and perform well in the hotter months. *Grand Rapids* is a cultivar known and grown world-wide.

Cos lettuces, also suited to the home garden, have somewhat coarser outer leaves than the others and a pronounced mid-rib. *London White Cos* and *Paris White Cos* are reliable cultivars.

Butterhead lettuce is the type found on most tables in Europe, and is being grown on an increasing scale in South Africa. Butterheads have smaller heads than crisphead cultivars, with leaves that are soft, soapy to the feel, and with less prominent mid-ribs than the other types and therefore less brittle when handled. *All The Year Round* and *White Boston* are leading cultivars of their class.

There are many crisphead cultivars, with the several strains of *Great Lakes* being the most commonly used, both commercially and in the home garden. Crispheads were initially developed to withstand summer conditions in California and other areas in the southern U.S.A. and are therefore an obvious choice for most parts of South Africa.

Soil preparation. Lettuces must grow rapidly if they are to be sweet and succulent, and this calls for a well-improved, fertile soil. They will grow well when they follow a crop that was treated generously with organic matter, provided that a dressing of 60 g per m² of 2:3:2 is incorporated before planting or sowing. Soils that are not up to this standard should be given a dressing of compost or manure, forked in prior to sowing, together with 60 g per m² of 2:3:2.

Propagation. In the home garden lettuces can be grown from seed sown where the crop is to mature or in seedbeds and seedboxes for later transplanting. Transplanted lettuces appear to produce, on average, larger heads than directly-sown ones. In weedy ground direct sowing is unsatisfactory. June and July are the worst months for sowing in all areas.

Sowing. Lettuce seed is light and fine and does not run easily between finger and thumb. Considerable care should therefore be taken when sowing it in order to obtain an even distribution and avoid wastage. The seeds should be sown in shallow drills, covered with 6-8 mm of fine soil, firmed and watered with a fine spray or rose. A light mulching of the rows with fine grass or short mowings will assist germination and the emergence of the tender seedlings, which should appear 4-10 days after sowing. Direct sowings can be made in the open ground, allowing 300 mm between rows where only a few rows are involved or where the bed method is used. Allow 450 mm on larger plantings.

Sowing at intervals of 3-4 weeks will ensure that there is never a shortage.

Transplanting. Seedlings can be set out when they are 70-100 mm high, allowing 225-300 mm between plants in the row. The plants are extremely brittle and firming should be carried out with care. Watering-in should also be carried out with care, either by giving a fine overall sprinkling or by applying 250 mℓ of water to each plant with a can. Transplanting is best done late in the afternoon.

Further treatment. In directly-sown rows hand-weeding must begin as soon as the mulch is lifted and the rows can be clearly seen, for the seedlings are tender and get away rather slowly. Water should be applied carefully until the plants are 70-100 mm high, for damping-off is often troublesome on old garden soils. The rows should be thinned out 3-4 weeks after sowing, to leave the strongest plants 225-300 mm apart in the row. The thinnings, if handled carefully, can be used to fill up obvious blanks or to plant up another row or two. Three weeks after transplanting or sowing, the plants will respond to a dressing of 2:3:2 or LAN at the rate of 30 g per metre of row. Liquid manures and foliar feeding are equally beneficial. Lettuce is a brittle, shallow-rooted crop and any necessary hoeing should be as shallow and accurate as possible. It is also a crop where large heads should not be the primary aim. Extra-large heads, particularly of the crisphead group, are nutritionally inferior to heads that are small to medium in size and frequently have internal discoloration, particularly during hot weather.

Throughout growth, water should be plentiful; however, once the heads become full, watering should be reduced otherwise 'bottom rot' may cause losses. Shortage of water at any stage of the growth will give the plants an excuse to run to flower. In extremely hot weather, shading with 30% shade cloth will bring the plants some relief and improve quality and yields.

Harvesting. Lettuces are usually ready for cutting 11-12 weeks after sowing, although they can be cut earlier to get a longer season from one sowing. They can either be pulled up with their roots, which are trimmed off, or they can be cut with a sharp knife as close to the ground as possible. In hot weather the rows or beds should be gone over every 2-3 days to avoid losses by 'bolting'.

Pests. *Cutworms* are often troublesome in well-improved soils. A pre-emergence drench with Karbaspray is an effective deterrent where trouble is expected, while a weak solution of Malathion poured into the dibber hole after transplanting also gives good control. Baiting may also be carried out among seedlings and transplants.

Aphids occasionally give trouble during hot, dry weather and particularly on unthrifty plants. Malathion and Dedevap are suitable spray materials.

Caterpillars can also be controlled effectively with Malathion and Dedevap if these pesticides are used at an early stage.

Snails and *slugs* can be a problem during wet periods. Snail bait in pellet or flake form is usually effective.

Diseases. *Leaf spot* is a very common and damaging disease that can be caused by more than one fungus although the symptoms are similar. Leaves take on a scorched appearance as the disease spreads. Spraying with Dithane M45 or copper oxychloride is only effective if carried out at an early stage and when the weather is dry. Watering by sprinkler assists the development of the disease.

Bottom rot is occasionally a problem on maturing lettuces in contact with wet soil. It shows up as rust-coloured lesions on the lower mid-ribs touching the ground. Secondary soft-rots often take over and later spread into the head itself. Crop rotation is the only real answer.

MELONS, SWEET

Probably tropical *Cucumis melo* var. *reticulatus* and *C. melo* var. *inodorus* subtropical Africa
Optimum pH 6,0-7,0

Sweet melons, also called cantaloupes, musk melons or (in South Africa) spanspek, can conveniently be separated into two distinct groups. These are the netted melons (*Cucumis melo* var. *reticulatus*) and the winter mel-

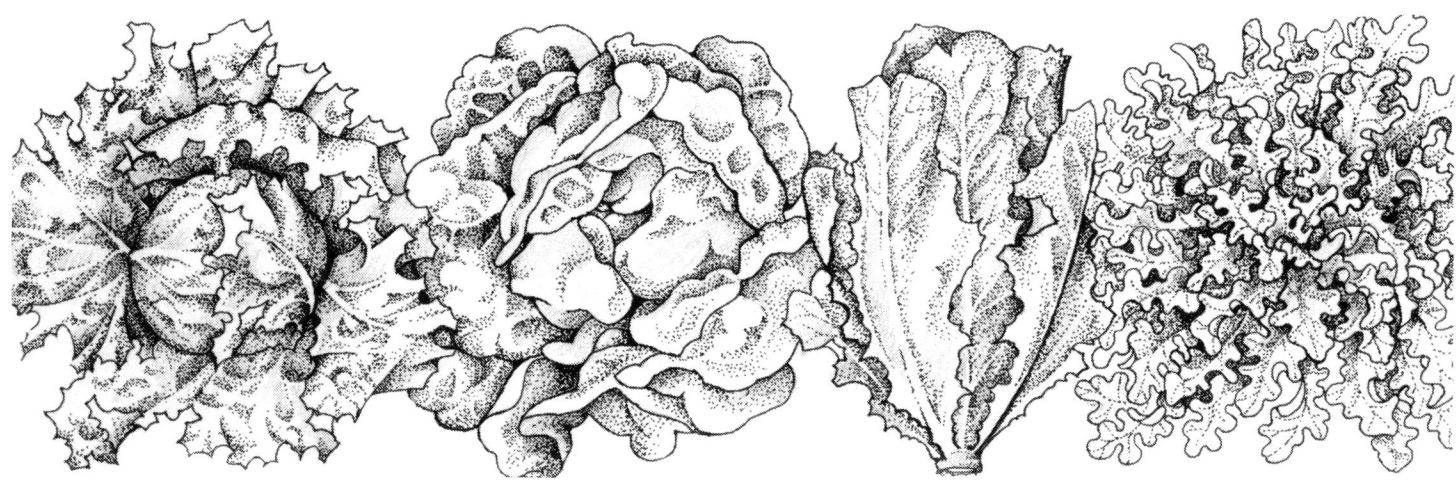

The four classes of lettuce: crisphead, butterhead, cos and loose-leaf.

ons (*C. melo* var. *inodorus*), of which the cultivar Honeydew is typical. That the two subspecies hybridize readily with each other is evidenced by the melons one buys at the supermarket. Melons are sometimes a little disappointing in the home garden because they do not get the attention they need. Although they are often thought of more as fruit, they require almost identical treatment to other cucurbits and are usually found in the vegetable garden.

Recommended cultivars. There are many cultivars available, particularly of the netted sort. They vary in fruit characteristics but most have the typical orange flesh. The flavour is more dependent upon soil and climatic conditions and on stage of ripeness than on cultivar.

Edisto: A newer cultivar with good-sized oval fruits that have a thickish rind.

Hale's Best: An older cultivar than Imperial 45. The fruits are slightly smaller on average and are rounder.

Honeydew: A winter melon bearing smooth roundish fruits light cream to ivory in colour depending upon the strain. It has some keeping qualities.

Imperial 45: A popular cultivar with oval fruits, which are densely netted in most strains.

Soil preparation. Melons fare best in light to medium soils that have been improved, very heavy soils rarely producing satisfactory yields. Planting stations at least 1 m apart and 300-450 mm in diameter should be prepared. If the bed method is used, an overall addition of compost or manure should be incorporated. Planting stations should be well dug and a good forkful of compost or well-decomposed manure plus a handful of 2:3:2 should be well worked in.

Propagation. Propagation is by seed sown under protection or directly in the open ground.

Sowing. Early sowings can be made in August in Jiffy Pots, Jiffy 7s, or any small pot or container from which they can be set out without disturbing the young root systems. Direct outdoor sowings can be made from September to early December, depending upon the area. Early outdoor sowings should be rather shallow (i.e. 15-20 mm) as should those in containers, while 20-25 mm is the usual depth when the soil has begun to warm up. The seeds should be sown 5 or 6 to a planting station, later leaving the 3 strongest plants to grow on if germination is good. Where bigger plantings are carried out, the plants should be at intervals of 200-300 mm in rows 1 m apart. Sowings from early November onwards may produce a better stand of plants if a thin mulch of mowings or straw is used, particularly in warmer areas.

Further treatment. Watering is extremely critical at all stages of growth. Too much water after sowing causes poor germination, while insufficient water after the fruits begin to set is equally undesirable. As the plants develop and the warmer weather comes along, watering should be increased to 2 soakings per week. Watering with a can or a hose lying on the soil is preferable to sprinkling.

Any feeding should be done at an early stage, for once the vines are growing away it is difficult to avoid causing damage by treading and leaf burn by spillage. Liquid manuring with any suitable material, using a watering can without a rose, is the ideal way of maintaining plant vigour.

Mulching is a rewarding practice with this crop, for it not only imparts all the benefits previously described but also provides a cushion for the maturing fruits and thereby reduces fruit rot. As with feeding, mulching is best carried out before vine growth begins to cover.

When the runners are 600-700 mm long they should be 'stopped' by pinching out the growing points to induce flower and fruit formation on the sub-laterals. From the time the first fruits set, baiting and spraying for fruit fly should be standard practice. This is particularly important with later sowings. Where mulching is not practised, it is advisable to put a handful of grass or a small wooden slat under each fruit as it begins to turn colour.

Harvesting. With cultivars such as Hale's Best and Imperial 45 it is not too difficult to determine the stage of ripeness as overall colour changes are usually visible, particularly on the 'ground spot'. The blossom ends of the fruit also yield to gentle pressure from the thumb.

Maturity is more difficult to determine with Honeydew and other cultivars of this type. However, slight colour changes do occur and the blossom-end of the fruit again becomes somewhat softer. In the long run experience is the only guide to harvesting.

Pests and diseases. In general the problems associated with melon culture are those described in the entry on pumpkins.

MUSTARD AND CRESS Mustard: Europe
Sinapis alba   Cress: Persia
Lepidium sativum
Optimum pH 6,0-7,0

These two plants are related botanically and are closely associated by usage. Although they do not constitute crops of commerce in this country as they do in Europe, they are ideal short-season salad crops for the home gardener and flat dweller. As their culture is basically identical they will be coupled together in this discussion. They simply require a light soil or other suitable medium, moisture and reasonable warmth, and will mature in 10-20 days.

Cultivars. Mustard and cress are found separately in most seed catalogues and are easy to obtain. Rape (*Brassica alba*) can be used as an alternative to mustard, apparently having a better flavour and usually being much cheaper.

Propagation. Propagation is by seed sown fairly thickly. Mustard and cress are best sown in separate containers as their rate of growth differs and the usual 'mix' for salad purposes is 4-6 parts mustard to 1 part cress.

Container preparation. Conventional seed-trays or boxes can be filled with sterilized potting soil, peat, vermiculite or a mix-

Place maturing melons on small wooden slats if the plants are not mulched.

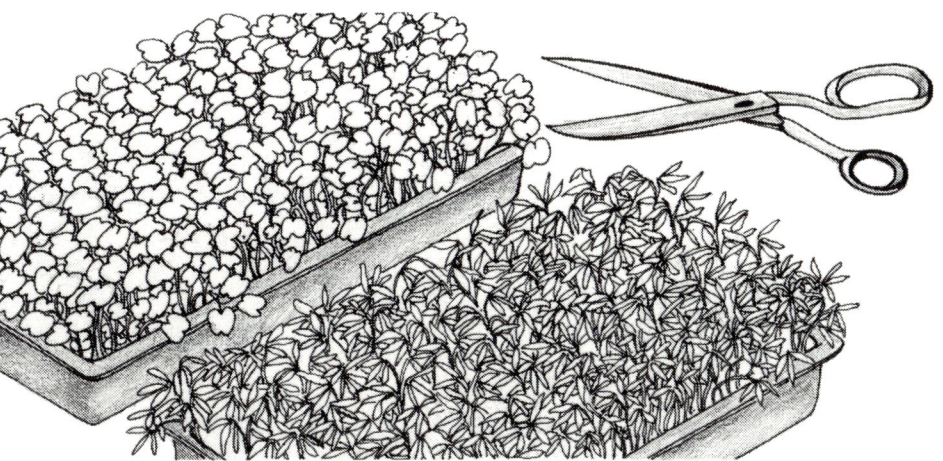

Cut mustard and cress with long scissors or a sharp knife.

ture of these. Sterility is important because it ensures that there are no weed seeds to germinate simultaneously with the crop and because it eliminates the possibility of damping-off, which would be disastrous.

Sowing. The seed should be broadcast on the thoroughly wetted medium, i.e. it should be sufficiently wet to carry the crop through to maturity. If the seed is sown on a standard medium it should be pressed firmly into the surface with a flat board. The seed-tray should then be covered with clean hessian or brown paper to cut out the light and prevent drying out. This cover must be removed when the seedlings are 20-25 mm high to allow 'greening' of the cotyledons before cutting commences. Mustard and rape germinate far more quickly than cress, which should be sown 3-4 days earlier to achieve a simultaneous harvest.

Harvesting. Cutting takes place when the seedlings are about 50 mm high and should be carried out with a very sharp knife or a pair of long scissors. A fairly deep seedbox (100 mm or more) filled with clean soil can support 2 or 3 successive crops provided that the top 10 mm or so of soil is removed each time and the surface loosened with a table fork or similar instrument. Sow every 2-2½ weeks to ensure continuity.

Pests and diseases. There should be no problems if a clean medium is used.

OKRA   Central America
Hibiscus esculentus
Optimum pH 6,0-7,5

Okra, also known as gumbo or lady's finger, is not an important vegetable because its use is rather limited. A summer annual that thrives on light to medium soils, it is a member of the mallow family and is a relative of the several species of ornamental hibiscus. Most cultivars are markedly upright in habit. As the plants are brittle they require a sheltered, warm, full-sun situation and will not tolerate wind. Okra is grown for the long light-green pods produced singly in the leaf axils. In Central Africa certain indigenous peoples use the young leaves as a spinach, just as they do with the garden hibiscus.

Harvest okra pods every 2-3 days.

Recommended cultivars. *Clemson Spineless:* This appears to be the only cultivar in local catalogues.

Soil preparation. Because okra requires a soil of moderate fertility, poor soils will have to be improved. Like green beans, okra matures quickly and will make excellent use of residues, both organic and inorganic, from a previous crop that was well manured and fertilized. A dressing of 60 g of 2:3:2 per metre of row can be incorporated shallowly before sowing takes place.

Propagation. Propagation is by seed, sown where the plants are to mature.

Sowing. The seeds resemble dark round-seeded peas and are best sown, 2 or 3 together, 300 mm apart in the row at a depth of 15-20 mm. Where only 2 rows are grown they can be 600 mm apart to give some support to each other, but larger plantings will require at least 900 mm so that cultural activities can be undertaken without damaging the plants.

Further treatment. If germination and emergence is good, the plants can be thinned out to allow the strongest specimens to grow to maturity 300 mm apart.

A side-dressing of LAN or a liquid manure feed when the first pods are picked will lengthen the picking season considerably.

Harvesting. The pods develop quickly after petal fall and should be removed while they are still young and tender. Picking should be possible 60 days after sowing in favourable weather and the pods should then be 50-75 mm in length. The plants should be examined every 2-3 days and all pods of edible size removed. They are usually chopped up to give a little body to soups and stews. Any surplus pods can be cut into strips or rings, dried out on muslin, and then stored in airtight jars for future use.

Pests. *Aphids* on this crop are usually green in colour. The habit of the plants facilitates control by spraying with Malathion or Thiodan.

Diseases. There are no diseases of consequence, although *mildew* has been reported in isolated cases.

ONIONS   Near East, Asia
Allium cepa
A. fistulosum
Optimum pH 5,5-7,0

The only two onions that are widely grown in South Africa are the bulbing onion and, to a lesser extent, the Welsh onion (also called the Japanese bunching onion or nebuka). Many home gardeners fight shy of the former, because it needs constant attention and has a fairly long growing season. The bulbing cultivars grow well on a wide variety of soils, provided that they are sown and planted shallowly. Heavy, clayey soils should be avoided if possible, for they crust and interfere with the emergence of the seedlings and with the swelling of the bulbs of such popular cultivars as Texas Grano,

Granex and Australian Brown. Sowing time is more critical with bulbing onions than with any other vegetable if good yields of firm bulbs with good keeping qualities are to be obtained. Welsh onions, often packeted as 'spring' onions, can be sown during most months of the year. However, as they are accommodating hosts to most of the pests and diseases that threaten bulbing onions, it is unwise to keep them growing throughout the year unless a regular spraying is given.

Onions require an abundance of moisture during their vegetative period and prefer cool growing conditions, especially for the first few months.

Recommended cultivars. The selection of suitable cultivars for the particular growing area is more important with bulbing onions than with any other vegetable crop, and to ignore this is to invite unsatisfactory results. All onion cultivars require a certain number of daylight hours (often termed a photoperiod) before they will begin to bulb, and unless this requirement is met they will continue to make vegetative growth and show little inclination to bulb.

Not all cultivars require the same number of daylight hours, and they are consequently classified as either 'long-day' cultivars or 'short-day' cultivars. In addition to day length, temperature is an important factor. Low temperatures can delay maturity, while temperatures greatly exceeding the optimum will hasten it.

Australian Brown: An excellent late, long-day cultivar with a distinctive reddish-brown skin. An excellent keeper.

Caledon Globe: A late, long-day cultivar, round in shape with strawy outer scales and pale yellow flesh. Popular in the Cape.

De Wildt: An early cultivar similar to early *Cape Flat.* It produces a fair-sized flat bulb and is a short-day type.

Hojem: A mid-season cultivar, round in shape and with darkish scales.

Texas Grano: An early mid-season cultivar, of which there are several strains – some distinctly top-shaped and others a little shallower. A very heavy yielder with soft scales.

Australian Brown and Caledon Globe should be grown only in the Cape and southern Free State, where Texas Grano also has a big following. De Wildt and Hojem are the best cultivars for the other areas, although Texas Grano is again widely grown, particularly for 'green' onions.

White Welsh: A 'green' bunching onion that can be raised from seed and propagated by division.

'Spring' onions are not a separate cultivar but are the seedling stage of any cultivar. However, white cultivars such as White Welsh and White Pearl are often preferred.

Soil preparation. Onions may occupy permanent quarters for 4-7 months, depending on cultivar and on whether the crop is directly-sown, grown from transplants or grown from 'sets'. To maintain a plant in vigorous growth for this relatively long

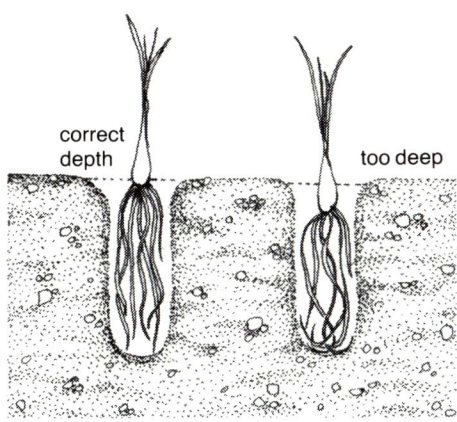

Do not plant onion seedlings too deeply.

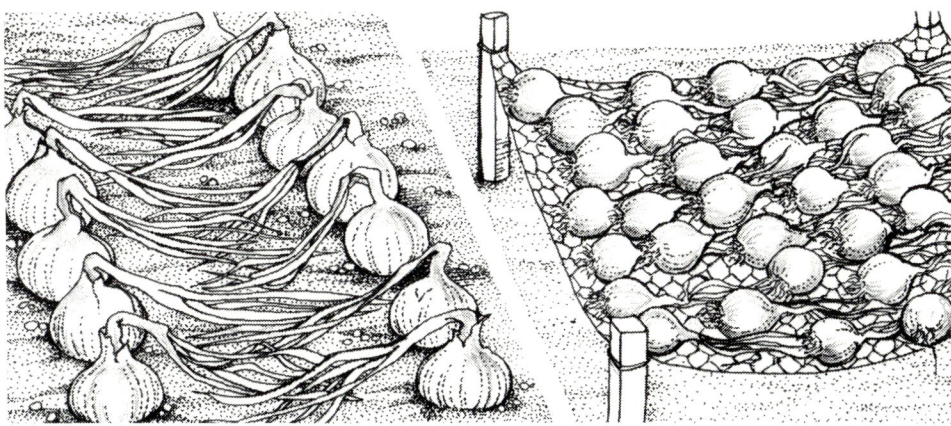

If necessary, bend over the tops of onions to assist ripening. After harvesting, store them in a dry, shady, and well-ventilated place – ideally on wire racks – to dry out thoroughly.

period demands thorough soil preparation. Onions are usually successful on well-worked friable soils that have been well improved for a preceding crop by liberal dressings of compost or manure, or by the incorporation of a bulky green-manure crop. Fresh manure dressings immediately before sowing or planting frequently promote rank, soft top-growth and produce bulbs with poor keeping qualities. A basic fertilizer dressing of 90-120 g per m² should be worked into the topsoil because rapid early growth is necessary and the plant population is usually high. Another requirement of an onion soil is that it be free of perennial weeds and invasive annuals such as purslane. This is even more important if direct sowing is practised. On commercial plantings several materials can be used under carefully controlled conditions to eliminate or reduce weed growth, but in the home garden the hand and the hoe are the only practical weedkillers.

Propagation. Propagation is by seed, which can be sown either in seedbeds or seed-trays for later transplanting or directly where the crop is to mature. In Europe and the U.S.A. a third method is quite widely used. This is by planting out 'sets', which are small onions (15-22 mm in diameter) produced the previous season by sowing thickly and late, and which have been stored over winter to get an early start the following spring. The sets are occasionally offered for sale in South Africa, although in this country they are of course stored during the summer months for autumn planting.

Sowing. It is advisable to obtain fresh seed every year for bulb crops, and to use any left-over seed for spring onions (where seed failure is not such a calamity). Its longevity, like that of all seed, depends almost entirely on the moisture content of the seed and on storage temperature. Modern packaging in sealed units has been a big step forward in this regard, but as soon as the packet is opened the seed deteriorates rapidly, particularly in hot, humid conditions.

The soil should be well dug over, trodden slightly to make it firm, and then raked to a fine tilth. The seed should be sown thinly in drills and covered with 10-12 mm of tamped-down soil. Germination can take up to 14 days. Sowing time is almost as important as the selection of suitable cultivars and is in fact complementary to it, for very early and very late sowings are often prone to splitting and 'bolting'. February/March is generally the best time for sowing, though March to May is more suitable in the Cape. Spring sowings are also worthwhile in most areas.

Pickling cultivars are best sown rather thickly in August/September, as are bulbing onions for sets. Because onions are relatively shallow rooted, it is important that the soil be kept moist for most of the first 5 or 6 weeks. This is particularly important if a good stand is to be obtained in directly-sown rows.

Transplanting. If the plants are raised in seedbeds or seedboxes they are usually big enough to set out 7-8 weeks after sowing, when they should be approaching pencil thickness. Any seedlings that show an appreciable swelling at the base should be discarded, for they are unlikely to make satisfactory vegetative growth when they are set out. To facilitate planting – and this is the only reason – the roots can be trimmed back to 10-15 mm and the tops to 100-125 mm. The plants should be set out 75-100 mm apart with a dibber, allowing 225 mm between rows when there are only a few rows and 300-450 mm when larger plantings are involved. Care should be taken to set out the seedlings shallowly so that they just stand up. The recommended spacing may seem rather close, but it does appear to encourage the development of medium-sized bulbs, which are most suitable for use in the average household and which ripen off and store better than large specimens.

Further treatment. Throughout growth weeds must be destroyed regularly, and water must never be in short supply until the ripening stage is reached. Any cultivating should be as shallow as possible, a Dutch hoe being the best tool for the job. I usually cut off the 'wings' of the blade with a hacksaw to leave a cutting edge of only 100 mm, which can easily be used in even the

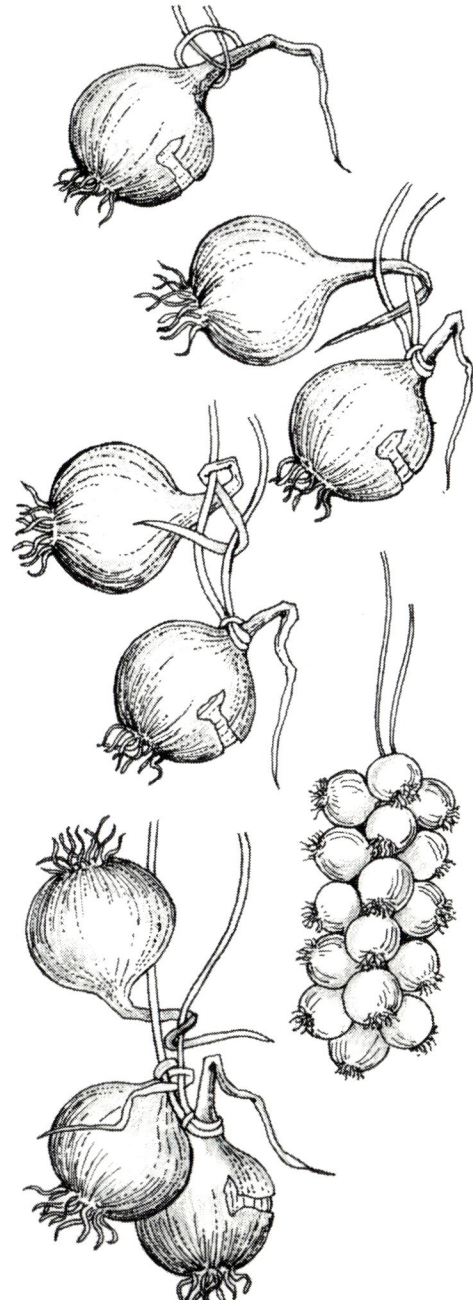

Plait onions into strings while the tops are still slightly moist.

most closely planted rows. A month or so after transplanting it will be necessary to give a side-dressing of nitrogenous fertilizer if the plants are making slow progress. Too generous an application may retard bulbing during critical photo-periods (i.e. when the day is sufficiently long to induce bulbing) and a deficiency of nitrogen at this time will hasten bulb formation.

Directly-sown rows should be thinned out after 5-6 weeks in one or two stages, to leave the plants 75-100 mm apart. The early thinnings can be used to set out further rows if space is available, while the final thinning should produce material suitable for use as spring onions or for flavouring soups and stews.

Once bulbing is well advanced, watering should be gradually reduced to encourage the bulbs to firm-up and dry off. Many of the plants dry off naturally and these are the best keepers. However, the tops of others may need to be bent backwards and forwards a few times and then laid over to encourage the plants to dry off. Bending over the tops *does not* encourage bulb development and should only be carried out when the bulbs are of good size. Bending over is a futile exercise with very thick necks, which often snap off.

Harvesting and storing. Onions can of course be used at any stage of their growth, but as the plants approach maturity any coarse and thick-necked ones should be used as should any that have been damaged. Onions dry off satisfactorily when laid out in a shady, dry, airy spot – either on the floor in a single layer or on racks made of wire or wooden slats. If they are to be plaited into strings this should be done while the tops are still *slightly* moist. Damaged bulbs should be used as soon as possible and should be kept well away from sound ones to prevent the occurrence of storage rot, which often starts on damaged bulbs.

Pests. *Thrips* appear whenever and wherever onions are grown, and are often quite a problem, particularly on late plantings. Attacks are most damaging when the plants are young. The adults are dark brown and the nymphs yellow, and they feed by rasping the foliage and sucking the plant sap released from the damaged tissue. They usually congregate in the sheath at the base of the foliage, where they feed on the emerging leaves and can be seen scurrying along if this sheath is opened. As the damaged leaves grow they take on a grey or silvery appearance. Early measures are necessary to control these pests, sprays being more effective than dusts in the home garden. Malathion and Thiodan are two effective chemicals for control, provided that they are used with a wetting agent. Thrips can be carried over on sets.

Diseases. *Downy mildew* is occasionally troublesome during wet periods, especially if these coincide with high temperatures, and it affects onions and most close relatives at all stages of growth. Its symptoms are a purplish mould on the leaves (very noticeable when the foliage is wet), which turns pale green, then yellow and finally dies off. Dithane M45 is one of the best chemicals for controlling this disease. It should be mixed with a wetting agent and used every 5-7 days for 2-3 weeks. Plantings of chives or Welsh onions should also be sprayed for they can easily carry over this disease from one main crop to another.

Pink rot: for information refer to the entry on leeks.

Storage rot is caused by several different fungi and is most prevalent during wet weather. The infection is usually initiated on damaged and incompletely dried bulbs. All stored bulbs should be inspected weekly, and those showing any sort of mould or discoloration should be removed.

PARSNIPS
Europe
Pastinaca sativa
Optimum pH 5,5-7,0

The rather strong and distinctive flavour of parsnips is not to everyone's liking, yet there are those who look forward very much to each season's crop. Parsnips are relatively easy to grow once a good stand of seedlings has been obtained, but even with fresh seed this is sometimes difficult to achieve. Whatever cultivar is used, a fairly deep soil is essential if long, smooth roots of good shape and quality are to be produced. It is quite useless to sow on shallow soils, which do not allow the long taproot to develop properly. Parsnips, like carrots, prefer a cool growing season and can take 4 months and longer to mature.

Recommended cultivars. Few cultivars are catalogued in this country and even fewer for those who grow from small packets of seed. The following are those usually offered:

Guernsey: A medium-length cultivar which, on a wide range of soils, produces thick, fleshy roots. Similar to the cultivar Offenham, which is not available here.

Hollow Crown: A long-rooted cultivar, which grows satisfactorily only on deep soils.

Soil preparation. Of all the important root vegetables, parsnips are perhaps the most demanding in terms of soil type and preparation. They require a rather loose and deep soil with, ideally, a fairly high sand content if they are to give of their best. Like most other roots, they prefer soil that was well dug and improved for the preceding crop. On such soils, 60-90 g of 2:3:2 per m² incorporated prior to sowing, should be an adequate basic dressing. On poorer soils, deep digging should be followed by the incorporation of a limited quantity of *well matured* compost or manure in addition to the fertilizer dressing recommended above. If possible this should be carried out a month or so before the sowing date. At every stage of soil preparation stones should be removed, hard clods broken up, and weed growth and residues taken out.

Propagation. Propagation is by seed, sown where the plants are to mature. Use only fresh seed!

Sowing. Prior to sowing, the soil should be raked to a fine tilth and shallow drills taken out 225-300 mm apart. Because of their shape, parsnip seeds do not 'run' easily, and to ensure an even stand they should be positioned carefully about 20 mm apart in the row. They can then be covered with fine soil, which should be well firmed and watered. Firming is extremely important with this crop if an even stand of seedlings is to be obtained. Watering should be done carefully in the early stages, for parsnip seed appears to rot easily in cold, wet soil, particularly if the seed is not fresh. On the other hand, hot soil conditions are also a problem, which can be eased considerably if a temporary mulch of grass or dry mowings is used. Spring sowings (August to October) and autumn sowings (March/April) are both worth a trial.

Further treatment. Parsnip seed is inclined to germinate rather slowly, and in my experience this is one of the few occasions where adding a few radish seeds to the drills is really justified. Not only do radishes germinate very quickly, thus indicating clearly the rows and thereby facilitating early cultivation but, by their vigorous emergence, they open up any surface crust that may form and so assist the rather weaker parsnip seedlings.

At around 6 weeks the rows should be thinned, if necessary, to leave the plants 100 mm apart. This spacing is quite adequate in the home garden although double the distance is often advocated. However, where

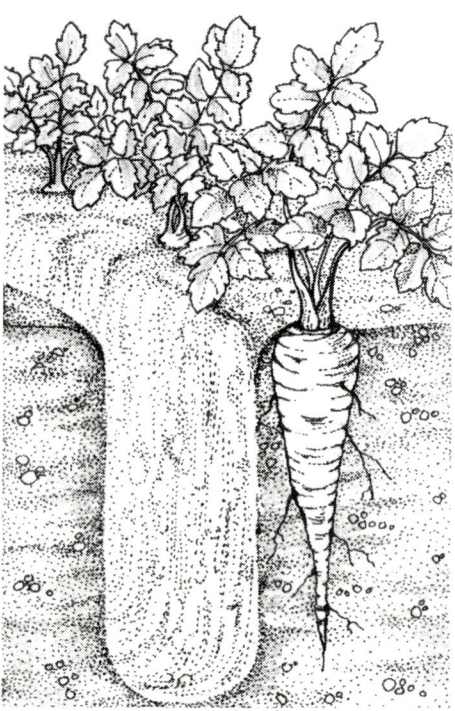

In heavy soils, harvest parsnips by digging a trench parallel to each row.

roots are being grown for exhibition 150 mm is the bare minimum. As with carrots, the plants can be earthed up slightly once the rows have been thinned. Side-dressing is rarely necessary in well-dug ground that is in good heart, but if the plants show any unthriftiness an application of 2:3:2 at the rate of 30 g per metre of row should bring a favourable response.

Harvesting. Parsnips are not the easiest of vegetables to harvest even in the most well-worked soils, for it is rarely possible to 'pull' them without damage occurring. In moist soil they can be removed without too much difficulty, however, by placing a garden fork in the soil 150-250 mm away from the row and levering it back so as to lift the roots without damaging them. In heavier soils it may be necessary to dig a trench parallel to the rows. Parsnips are best lifted row by row rather than at random.

Pests. *Cutworms* are the only likely problem, and damage can occur at any time between the emergence of seedlings and harvest. Cutworm bait can be distributed between the rows, while dusting with Bexadust and spraying with Karbaspray are also of value.

Diseases. *Angular leaf spots* may appear during wet weather, but they are seldom serious enough to require treatment.

PEAS
Probably Far East

Pisum sativum
Optimum pH 6,0-7,5

Garden peas are among the most nutritious of vegetables, particularly if eaten shortly after they are picked. Nowadays frozen or canned peas are easy to come by, but even the best of these does not compare with produce from the home garden – either in flavour or nutritional value. Because peas are essentially a cool-season crop they rarely grow vigorously in hot weather and consequently become hosts to damaging insects and diseases. Although they are able to perform satisfactorily on a wide range of soil types their preference is for a deep and well-drained soil with a fair organic content. Good drainage is of great importance throughout their growth as they are very susceptible to parasitic soil fungi.

Recommended cultivars. Most home gardeners and commercial growers use dwarf or semi-dwarf cultivars, principally because they can be grown satisfactorily without support. Nevertheless, even these cultivars give higher yields and have fewer damaged pods if they are supported by twiggy sticks. Peas are usually classified, apart from their habit and season, into smooth- and wrinkle-seeded cultivars.

Black-eyed Susan: A late cultivar and one of the better performers in hotter weather. It definitely requires support, for it can grow as high as 1,2-1,5 m in favourable soil.

Cape Freezer: A dual-purpose cultivar, a little earlier than Greenfeast.

Greenfeast: A standard cultivar of long standing, much used by home gardeners. It has a long growing and picking season.

Sugar Snap: This is an edible-podded cultivar that requires support.

Soil preparation. Peas respond well to good treatment, but the deep trenching advocated in more temperate climates is not at all necessary, provided that the ground is well dug over and drainage is not a problem. Deep soils that have been developed by intelligent gardening practices (i.e. the regular incorporation of manure, compost or green manures) are particularly suitable. On such soils a dressing of 2:3:2 at the rate of 60-90 g per metre of row is sufficient. Poorer soils should be improved by working in a dressing of mature compost or manure, together with the recommended fertilizer dressing, before sowing. The incorporation of fresh manures just before sowing is not recommended for it encourages rank top-growth at the expense of flowers and fruit. Like most legumes, peas appreciate a dressing of lime, worked in shallowly, 3-4 weeks before sowing.

Propagation. Propagation is by seed, sown where the plants are to mature.

Sowing. The seed can be sown either in single rows, or in double rows 150 mm apart with 750 mm to 1 m between each pair of rows. Shallow drills 30-40 mm deep can be made and the seeds sown 45-50 mm apart. Autumn and winter sowings (March to July) usually achieve the best results, though in some areas sowings made one month either side of this may be successful. Peas generally have a relatively short picking season and it will be necessary to make sowings every 3 weeks or so to ensure continuity.

Further treatment. Watering should be carried out with considerable care until the plants are growing away, for seed decay, pre-emergence damping-off and 'foot rots' often cause losses. In cold, wet soil, these organisms can be very damaging.

Hand-weeding and delicate hoeing is essential from an early stage if there is any weed growth. Once the plants are growing away a little soil can be drawn up to give them some support and make them less vulnerable to winds and heavy rain. A few twiggy sticks or small branches placed along the rows will give extra support. The following are additional benefits to be derived from supporting the plants: support allows inter-row cultivation to be carried out; it facilitates spraying; it makes harvesting much easier; it allows the plants to be fed and watered below the foliage, thereby reducing the chances of disease establishment; it ensures better quality produce by keeping the pods off the soil; and, finally, it lengthens the picking season by 10-14 days.

When flowering commences, and most cultivars are white-flowered, liquid manuring will assist the plants to maintain their vigour. Mulching is also most rewarding for it keeps the soil cool in warmer weather and suppresses weed growth.

Harvesting. Depending upon cultivar, season and degree of vegetative growth, peas mature 3-3½ months after sowing. During early picking the plants should be handled with extreme care for they are very brittle around the soil line, especially if they are unsupported. The pods should be removed

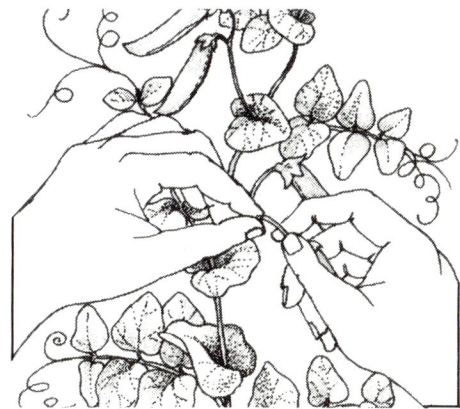

Use both hands when picking peas to avoid damaging the plants.

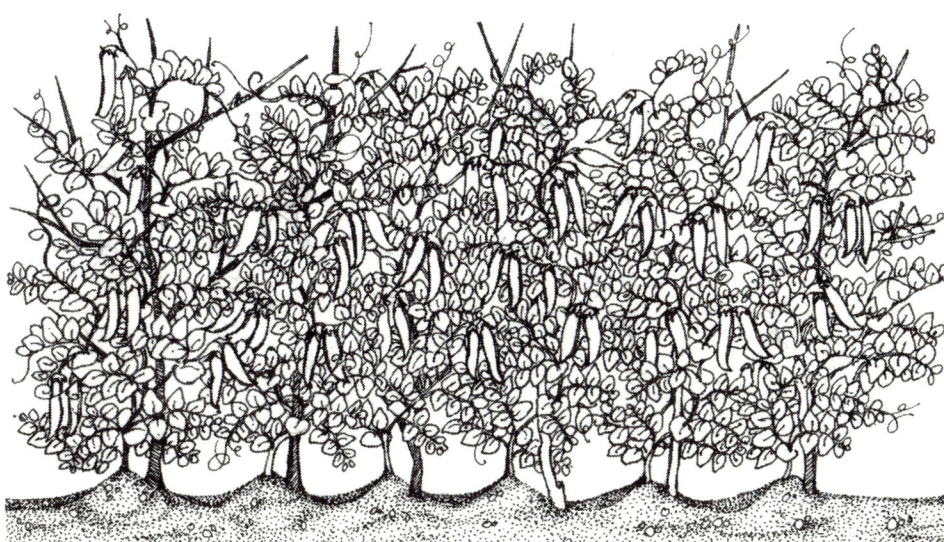

Support peas by drawing up the soil and placing twiggy sticks along the rows.

by holding the plant firmly with one hand and pulling them off with the other. Picking should be carried out at least twice a week, for the vigour of the plants declines and the picking season is shortened if a number of pods are allowed to remain.

Pests. Peas that are growing vigorously during the cooler months are seldom affected to any degree by pests, although unthrifty plants may attract attention. These are best removed completely and destroyed. Rogor and Malathion should effectively control any infestations of *aphids*, while also providing a measure of control for *thrips*, *leaf miners* and *red spider mites*. Kelthane is a more specific material for red spider mites.

Diseases. *Downy mildew* is occasionally very troublesome, especially in the Cape. It is dependent on wet conditions and high humidity to spread and often clears up spontaneously during dry spells. Control is somewhat difficult, however, and standard fungicides are not always really effective. Dithane M45 and Bayleton are perhaps the best materials for the home gardener.

Powdery mildew is a serious disease that usually appears first on the lower leaves and is able to spread rapidly. Dithane M45 or Bayleton sprayed at 7-10 day intervals give adequate control.

PEPPERS South America
Capsicum annuum var. *grossum*
C. annuum var. *longum*
Optimum pH 5,5-7,0

Peppers, often catalogued simply as capsicums, are not grown by the home gardener to the extent that they deserve. Neither the 'sweet' or bell peppers, nor the hotter types, or 'chillies', are related to the true pepper *Piper nigrum*, which is a perennial tropical vine indigenous to India and Malaysia.

Peppers are warm-weather vegetables related to tomatoes, egg plants and tobacco. Their culture is very similar to that of tomatoes.

Recommended cultivars. There is very little difference between most of the sweet pepper cultivars, although some have thicker fruit walls than others.
California Wonder: This is a reliable and vigorous cultivar. The fruits are large, thick-walled, have 3-4 lobes and are dark green in colour.
Chilli: A small-fruited, 'hot' cultivar with a strong flavour.
Keystone Resistant Giant: A mosaic-resistant cultivar with thick walls, which has performed outstandingly in many locations.
Long Red Cayenne: A 'hot' cultivar bearing intense red fruits 100-150 mm long.

There are many other cultivars – some hot, some sweet, some grown for the table, some for purely decorative purposes – but all require very similar culture.
Soil preparation. Peppers are not too fussy about soil type and can be grown without

difficulty in most gardens. The needs of the average family should be met by 4-6 well-grown plants of the 'sweet' type, while 1 or 2 plants of the 'hot' type should be quite adequate as they are most prolific bearers. A lightish soil that warms up quickly in spring is just about ideal, but it will be necessary to improve the level of organic matter by dressings of compost and manure to ensure that the moisture-holding capacity is adequate for the hot summer months. Flowers and young fruits are apt to drop off if there is any shortcoming in this direction.

As with egg plants, the best results are obtained if separate planting stations are prepared for each plant. A good forkful of compost plus a handful of 2:3:2 can be worked in with the topsoil at each station. A planting distance of 600 mm in rows 800 mm apart is not too generous, even where only a few rows are concerned. Up to 1 m between rows may be necessary on larger plantings.

Propagation. Propagation is by seed, usually sown early in seedbeds or seedboxes under protection. Direct sowing can also be practised by sowing 3-4 seeds 20-25 mm apart at each planting station, later thinning to leave the strongest seedling to grow on.

Sowing. Pepper seed should be sown thinly at a depth of 10-15 mm. The soil should be firmed and watered, and a thin mulch of grass added to assist germination and emergence during hot weather. August to November is the best sowing period, though this can be extended in mild areas.

Transplanting. Peppers, especially outdoor sowings, are a little slower than most crops to reach the transplanting stage, and around 6 weeks may be necessary for this growth. The plants should be set out somewhat deeper than they were growing in the seedbed. If they are transplanted in hot, dry weather, and this is often the case, shading with a handful of light grass or with 'shadycaps' may be warranted. A thorough watering-in should re-establish all but the weak-

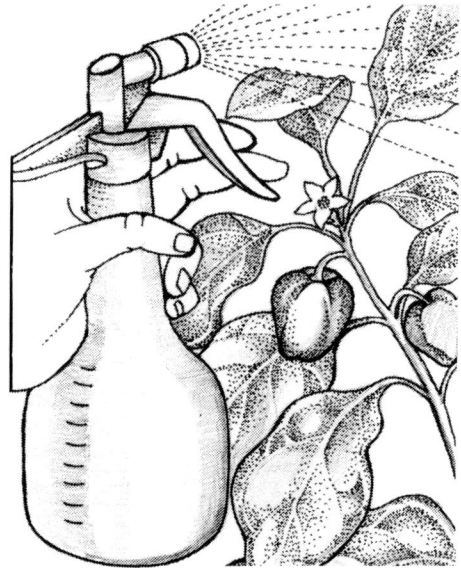

Spray pepper plants regularly to promote humidity and thereby increase the set of fruit.

est plants. Leggy seedlings and any transplants that show buds or flowers should be pinched back 10-12 mm.
Further treatment. Peppers require little attention if set out in improved soil, provided that adequate water is available (especially from the flowering period onwards). Syringing the plants down or watering with a fine spray should increase the set of fruit by stepping up the humidity. Any necessary work among the plants should be carried out with some care, for they are extremely brittle, especially when under the stress of a good set of fruit, and even large branches break easily. Late afternoon, when the plants are softer, is the best time for cultivating. In most cases it is quite unnecessary to pinch out the tops to encourage branching.
Harvesting. Although some plants may set a fruit or two at an early stage, it usually takes 60-75 days for fruiting to begin in earnest, and up to 90 days from transplanting for large fruits to be ready for picking. Harvesting should be done carefully, otherwise the plants may be damaged by pulling. The fruits of the sweet cultivars are removed when they are a good size, secateurs being the ideal tool for the job. The larger hotter cultivars are usually left until the fruits are quite red. Those with smaller fruits, such as Chilli, can easily be harvested by nipping the stalk with finger and thumb. All cultivars, but especially sweet peppers, need to be harvested regularly to maintain the vigour of the plant and extend the picking season.
Pests. Apart from *cutworms* in the early stages, when routine baiting should be effective, peppers rarely attract the attention of damaging pests.
Diseases. *Bacterial wilt*, described more fully in the entry on tomatoes, is often troublesome on old cultivated ground. Care should therefore be taken to use peppers wisely in the rotation to prevent a build-up of organisms that may jeopardize more profitable related crops.

Sun scald is a non-parasitic condition causing white to yellow-white sunken areas on the fruits, particularly in late summer. These areas are then subject to attack by several sorts of rot. Feeding the plant regularly to encourage growth, particularly leaf development, is the only practical step that one can take.

POTATOES Bolivia and Peru
Solanum tuberosum
Optimum pH 5,0-6,5

Potatoes, often referred to as Irish potatoes where sweet potatoes are also grown, are a vegetable crop of great commercial importance. They have adapted well to temperate climates, and the highest yields and finest 'seed' are in fact produced in these areas. With their relatively wide spacing, potatoes take up quite a lot of room and it is only in very large gardens that sufficient ground can be spared to meet the family's year-round requirements in full. Nevertheless, most gardeners can afford to devote a few square metres to the growing of a row or two of 'new' potatoes, the flavour of which surpasses most of the produce bought in a shop.

Potatoes are not roots, although they are often classified as such, nor are they formed on roots. They are tubers and form on the tips of stolons or modified stems, which spring from the scale leaves on the underground portion of the stem.

Recommended cultivars. Relatively few cultivars have found their way to South Africa, though in recent years much research has been carried out in this country to develop new cultivars, especially disease-resistant ones.

BP 1: A popular cultivar in many areas, producing medium to large tubers. It performs well on a variety of soils, often in less than ideal climatic conditions.

Up-To-Date: A high-yielding cultivar very popular in most areas except Natal. Unfortunately it is extremely susceptible to late blight and leaf roll.

Van der Plank: A relatively early cultivar producing large tubers and heavy yields. It prefers warmer conditions than most.

Soil preparation. Potatoes will handsomely repay generous treatment, and although they can be grown successfully on most soils, stiff clays should be avoided. Heavy soils of a clayey nature have several disadvantages: they interfere with the emergence of the shoots; they prevent the development of large, well-shaped tubers; and, when ridged up, they crack badly, exposing the tubers to 'greening' and to tubermoth infestation. Sandy to medium loams are ideal for this crop, but they must be improved with compost or decayed manure if satisfactory results are to be achieved. Initially the plot should be deeply dug, all clods broken up and all perennial weeds removed. If organic material is available, a 50 mm layer should then be spread on the ground and thoroughly incorporated, together with a dressing of 2:3:4 at the rate of 75-100 g per m². If compost is scarce, trenches can be dug. These should be 150 mm wide, of a similar

depth and at least 600 mm apart, centre to centre. A 50 mm layer of compost should be placed in the bottom of the trench and incorporated, together with a dressing of 2:3:4 at the rate of 50-75 g per metre of trench. This should then be covered with 50 mm of the removed topsoil to form the bed on which the tubers can be planted. It is most undesirable for the seed tubers to come into direct contact with concentrations of fertilizer granules or with fresh manure. When this happens the tuber is often damaged by burning, secondary rots set in, and the result is poor, spindly growth followed by low yields. Although potatoes are often described as a cleaning crop, this applies only to annual weeds, which are suppressed by the canopy of shade created by the foliage of the potatoes and destroyed by cultivation and ridging. Perennial weeds such as couch grass, nut grass and kikuyu are not so easily kept under control and where possible should be removed as completely as possible before planting.

Propagation. Potatoes are propagated by 'seed' tubers, which, for preference, should have a mass of 60-80 g, although considerably larger specimens are often sold as seed. Imported tubers come from favourable growing areas in Scotland, Ireland and elsewhere. Wherever possible it is best to purchase locally-grown seed tubers that are government-certified; they are usually dearer than uncertified tubers but well worth the investment.

However, it is not always possible for the home gardener to obtain small quantities of tubers of named cultivars, let alone certified seed tubers. The average gardener will therefore have to obtain his requirements by selecting from potatoes on offer at the greengrocer or supermarket. In doing so he must choose mature, firm-skinned specimens that are free from nematode pustules, tubermoth tunnels and skin blemishes.

The 'greening' of tubers in trays prior to planting – a standard procedure in the U.K. to encourage the development of strong shoots – is rarely practised here, although it does result in more even rows of plants. If the tubers are purchased well before the ground is ready or before they are suffi-

ciently sprouted they should be given a good dusting of BHC to prevent tubermoth damage.

When flabby potatoes are planted the results are usually disappointing, for such tubers produce weak growth and often rot off before the plants have developed an adequate root system. When this is the only sort of material available it is best to delay planting until the tubers have had an opportunity to firm up a little. This can be achieved by putting them in trays, or on a sack, and watering them regularly with a fine rose. If it is necessary to cut the tubers (only very large specimens need to be cut) the cut faces should be dusted with hydrated lime or a fungicidal dust to reduce the chances of decay. One should also ensure, when cutting, that there are strong sprouts or prominent eyes on each piece.

Planting. Seed tubers sprout mostly from the 'rose' or broad end of oval cultivars such as Up-To-Date, and from 3 or 4 sunken eyes on round cultivars. Before planting, it is a good idea to rub off all sprouts arising from lateral buds elsewhere on the tuber so as to encourage the development of strong sprouts in the correct area. Plants arising from well-sprouted tubers get away to a flying start and reach maturity more quickly than plants grown from unsprouted ones.

The tubers should be carefully pushed into the soil with their sprouts upwards and should then be covered with 70-100 mm of fine soil. If trenching is not practised, planting can be done with a standard garden trowel or a bulb trowel, again ensuring that the tubers have their sprouts upwards. If the tubers are not evenly sprouted, it is advisable to sort them out and plant them in batches as the shoots develop, otherwise uneven rows will result. Plant spacing in the row has a marked effect on tuber size at harvest: the closer the spacing the smaller the tubers and the yield. For the average garden, 225-250 mm between plants in the row is satisfactory.

Although potatoes can be grown for home consumption throughout the year in many areas where water is available during dry periods and no frost is experienced, spring and autumn plantings are usually the most

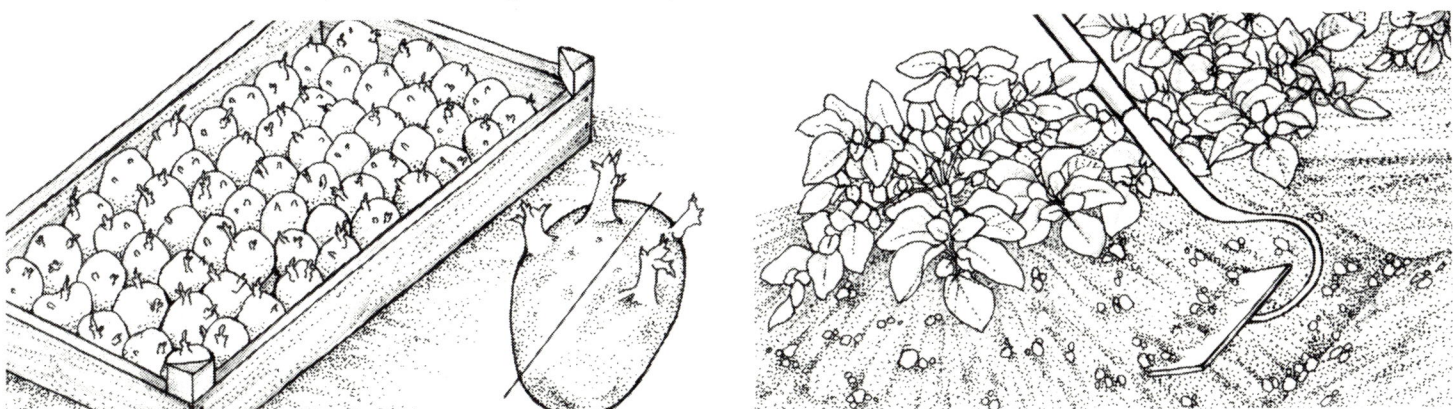

Allowing potatoes to sprout in trays prior to planting encourages strong shoots, which lead to more even rows of plants. If seed potatoes need to be cut, ensure that each portion has two strong shoots. Use a draw hoe to earth-up potatoes.

rewarding. In areas where frosts occur, planting can be carried out when most of this danger has passed, say in September/October.

Further treatment. Well-sprouted tubers should push through about 2 weeks after planting. Until then any cultivation should be carried out with extreme care to avoid severing or damaging the brittle shoots. If the shoots emerge during a late snap of cold weather, when frost could occur, a handful of grass thrown over each plant will give some protection, as will a little loose soil drawn over the shoots, and still allow growth to continue.

As the tops grow the soil can gradually be drawn up to the rows so that by the time maximum vegetative growth has been achieved a substantial ridge will be formed. Throughout growth weeds should regularly be removed and destroyed, for they compete with the crop for nutrients, moisture and light. Couch grass and nut grass are particularly difficult and can actually penetrate the soft tubers. From the time tuber formation begins – and this varies greatly according to factors such as day length, sunshine hours and nutrient availability – all serious weed growth should be tackled with extreme care and preferably by hand. A sharp cultivating tool used carelessly can sever the stolons and cut off the tubers from their food supply, and any direct damage it causes can lead to infection by fungi and other parasitic organisms.

Any cracks in the soil, especially when tuber formation is in progress, should be closed off regularly to reduce tubermoth damage, prevent 'greening' and guard against tuber infection if late blight is severe on the foliage.

Cultivars vary greatly in their capacity to flower, while climatic and weather conditions are also influencing factors. Up-To-Date is a cultivar which, under most conditions, produces flowers freely over an extended period. Fruiting is much rarer but it does occur.

Potatoes should be watered regularly throughout growth if rainfall is inadequate, but this should be carried out with some care on flabby seed tubers and on cut tubers until the plants are of good size. Owing to

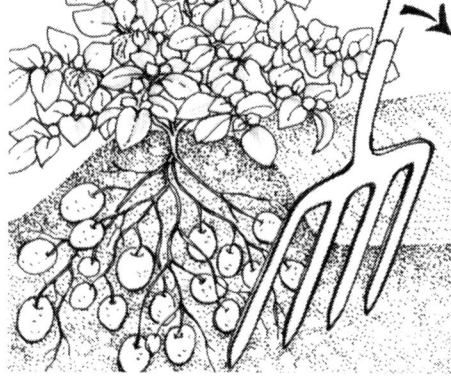

Lift potatoes with a flat-tined fork to avoid damaging the tubers.

the high incidence of fungal disease in this crop, wetting the foliage regularly is undesirable and the furrow method of irrigation is to be recommended once the shoots have emerged. As the crop approaches maturity the water supply should be gradually reduced to encourage ripening of the tubers and discourage deformities.

Harvesting. In the home garden the most suitable tool for lifting tubers is a 4-pronged garden fork. A spade and a hoe should not be used as they can easily cause damage. Where only a few potatoes are required for the table they can, in most soils, be removed by hand as they reach a suitable size. When lifting complete plants the fork should be pushed in vertically some distance away from the plant and levered backwards. The lifted plant can then be dropped back on top of the soil and the tubers removed. After this has been carried out, plant by plant, the whole row can be forked over to ensure that no tubers have been missed, especially very small tubers or 'chats', which will subsequently produce 'volunteer' growth.

In dry weather mature tubers can be left in the soil for some time without damage, provided that water is withheld and all soil cracks are closed. Should rain of any consequence occur, the crop should be lifted before the plants have had a chance to take up the moisture and before regrowth, which causes tuber deformities, takes place. In wet weather there should be no delay in lifting tubers as soon as they reach a suitable size, for second growth, glassiness, enlarged lenticels and other non-parasitic conditions may reduce the quality of the produce.

It is most important that potato residues be removed completely from the ground and not be left lying on the surface. This applies especially to 'chats', to rotten and damaged potatoes, and to the mother seed, which is frequently firm but glassy when the crop is lifted. These residues and any subsequent 'volunteer' growth can easily carry over diseases and pests, including nematodes.

Pests. *Cutworms* frequently cause considerable damage to the young shoots, which is apparent when they wilt suddenly or fall over. The tubers can also be damaged by these larvae and made unattractive and difficult to prepare for the table. Sometimes considerable damage is done before the inexperienced gardener realizes that he has a problem and identifies it. Handpicking around damaged plants is practicable where only a few rows are concerned. Dusting between the rows with Bexadust has proved effective, while spraying with chlorpyrifos and distributing cutworm bait are other useful methods of control.

Snails and *slugs* are sometimes troublesome during wet periods. Carbaryl/metaldehyde baits in both liquid and pellet form are the only real weapons the home gardener has. They are most effective if applied early in the evening.

The *leaf beetle*, a ladybird beetle that completes its life cycle on the plant itself, can

weaken the plant considerably and reduce the sugar-producing capacity of the leaves. For information on control measures refer to the entry on egg plants.

The *tubermoth* is a nocturnal insect that can cause considerable damage in its larval stage to maturing crops and stored tubers. The larvae grow from 2 mm to 18 mm in length and attack both the foliage and the tubers. They tunnel through the plant tissues between upper and lower leaf surfaces like leaf miners, and throughout the tuber, although favouring sub-surface tissue. During their feeding they leave behind quantities of mealy debris or 'frass' in the tunnels, making the tubers completely inedible and quite unsuitable for seed purposes. To prevent damage to a standing crop, the ridges should be well maintained to close off cracks. This cultural practice is by far the most effective method of protecting tubers. Malathion sprayed on the foliage in a regular spraying programme is also worth trying.

Diseases. *Late blight*, often called 'roes' in South Africa, is a serious disease caused by the fungus *Phytophthora infestans*. It was this disease that caused famine in Ireland in 1845/46 at a time when potatoes were the staple diet of the majority of the population.

The disease first appears as brown, water-soaked markings on the leaves, usually beginning at the leaf margins on the lower foliage. The brown lesions are usually surrounded by narrow (2-3 mm) haloes of pale green tissue. On the underside of this halo region will be found a white mould, similar in appearance to mildew, which is obvious in the early morning when the plants are full of dew. The disease spreads rapidly in warm, cloudy weather and can cause the tops to be destroyed completely in 7-10 days. If the tops become affected to a marked degree they should be removed and all soil cracks covered to prevent spores dropping through on to the skin of the tubers, where they cause exterior and interior browning. Spraying with Dithane M45, Antracol or Cupravit at 10-14 day intervals, stepped up to 7-10 day intervals should prevailing weather conditions favour the diseases's establishment or should it actually appear, is a recommended programme. Copper sprays occasionally cause damage to young, soft growth of tomatoes and potatoes but the plants usually shake if off and grow away satisfactorily. With any of the three spray materials mentioned, anything less than 100% coverage of all the foliage is not good enough and is a futile exercise. Avoid walking between affected plants if possible.

Early blight is caused by the fungus *Alternaria solani* and is also widely known as 'target spot' because of the typical concentric brown markings it causes on the foliage. It sometimes appears in wet weather although it is rarely as serious a problem as late blight. The spray programme outlined for the latter should also keep this disease in check.

Potatoes are subject to several serious viral diseases, which cause rolling, crinkling and mottling of the foliage. These diseases rarely kill the plants outright but distort them to such an extent that the leaves cannot function properly and yields are greatly reduced. Aphids and other insects that feed on the foliage should be controlled, for it is these agencies that are in most cases responsible for the spread of viral diseases. As most diseases of this group can be carried over in the tubers, the use of 'clean' (preferably certified) seed is of the utmost importance.

Non-parasitic diseases. Like tomatoes, potatoes are subject to several non-parasitic diseases. Cracking, second growth, waisting, glassiness, hollow heart, internal discoloration and flecking, and enlarged lenticels are all tuber defects resulting from physiological disturbances. These upsets, which can reduce the quality and palatability of the tubers markedly, are caused mainly by unfavourable soil and climatic conditions, poor drainage, and nutrient deficiency or toxicity. Very often large and extra-large tubers suffer the most from these internal disorders, and it would appear that quick growth makes the tubers particularly susceptible. The only practical remedies for these disorders are as follows: only grow potatoes when climatic conditions are most favourable; manure and fertilize adequately; and maintain a steady supply of moisture throughout growth. A mulch is also a useful weapon against tuber defects because it reduces moisture loss from the soil and helps to keep soil temperatures down.

Common scab is a very widespread tuber disease and has been reported from almost every corner of the globe. On potatoes the disease expresses itself as small brown specks at a breathing pore, and in favourable conditions these lesions coalesce into a continuous area of scabby, corking tissue. The disease is most troublesome on soils with a high pH. On no account should liming materials be added to the soil prior to planting potatoes, and scabby seed should never be used for planting. Keeping the soil cool and moist appears to reduce the amount of scab.

PUMPKINS

North and South America

Cucurbita maxima
C. pepo
C. moschata
Optimum pH 6,0-7,5

All pumpkins and squashes of commerce belong to one of the three species detailed above, and what are sometimes referred to as squashes are true pumpkins and vice versa. The three different species can readily be identified by the characteristics of the fruit stalks and leaves and to a lesser degree by the seeds.

Plants belonging to *Cucurbita maxima* have roundish leaves, free from markings and spines, and the fruit stalks are round and fleshy with no flaring where they attach to the fruit. Examples are Hubbard squashes and Queensland Blue pumpkins. Those belonging to *C. pepo* have deeply-lobed leaves, often covered on the underside with nasty spines, and the fruit stalks are hard and rough, distinctly grooved, but with no flaring at the points of attachment to the fruit. Examples are Small Sugar pumpkin and Table Queen squash. *C. moschata* is a relatively unimportant species, the Butternut squash, with its dry pumpkin-like flesh, being the only representative in most South African seed catalogues. Many pumpkins grown by the indigenous peoples of Central and Southern Africa belong to this species, while some may belong to *C. lundelliana*. They usually produce fruit of rather poor quality and are low yielders, but are generally most resistant to diseases such as powdery mildew and have exceptional storing qualities. Plants belonging to the last two species usually have silver or white markings on the leaves, while the fruit stalks are grooved and in some groups flared at the point of attachment to the fruits and in others slightly swollen. However, I propose to deal with pumpkins and squashes as they are usually catalogued to avoid unnecessary confusion. Several gourds, including the calabashes, belong to the species *Lagenaria siceraria*, sometimes known as the white-flowered gourd.

Pumpkins are warm-weather subjects, easily damaged by light frosts, and they demand a moderate level of soil fertility to grow well. They are not suited to the small garden because of their rampant habit, which swamps and suppresses less vigorous subjects. In addition, they occupy the ground for the whole summer and do not give as high a yield as most crops in relation to the area they cover.

Recommended cultivars. *Flat Boer:* There are several distinct strains of this popular cultivar, which, strange to say, is rarely catalogued outside South Africa. Its characteristics are too familiar to need description. *Ironbark:* This cultivar produces round, greyish fruits, which stand and store well. The fruits of some strains are prominently ribbed.

Queensland Blue: In my opinion this is the outstanding pumpkin cultivar. It has a slate-grey skin with solid orange flesh and stores exceptionally well. The toughness of its skin allows it to lie on wet soil longer than most other cultivars. It does suffer from sun scald in some areas but the affected tissue rarely spreads and the fruit remains sound.

Soil preparation. Pumpkins require wider spacing than any other crop, and as so few are planted, even in larger home gardens, it is better to treat a few planting stations generously than to undertake an overall distribution of organic matter and fertilizer. No crop is more responsive to liberal dressings of manure and compost, which also help to ensure moisture retention – an essential requirement of any soil on which pumpkins are grown (the plants lose considerable amounts of moisture because of their large leaf area). Adequate drainage, however, is equally important.

A planting station can be prepared by digging a round hole at least 450 mm in diameter and 250-300 mm deep. The bottom of the hole should be opened up, and a forkful or two of mature compost or manure, together with a handful of 2:3:2, should be thoroughly mixed with the removed soil. This material should then be replaced in the hole, trodden lightly and the surface fashioned into a dish-like depression. When sowings are made during wet seasons, the planting stations can be in the form of 'hills' of a similar diameter to ensure adequate drainage.

Propagation. Propagation is by seed, usually sown where the plants are to mature. Seeds can also be sown early, under protection, in Jiffy 7s, Jiffy Pots, or similar containers, and set out when the weather and the soil have warmed up a little.

Sowing. The planting stations should be at least 2 m apart each way. In each station 5 or 6 seeds can be sown 100 mm apart at a depth of 20-30 mm, depending upon soil and weather conditions, using a dibber or

Harvest pumpkins together with 50 mm of stalk to prevent destructive fungi from penetrating the fruit.

pointed stick. If germination is satisfactory the plants can be thinned after about 3 weeks to leave the 3 sturdiest specimens to grow on to maturity. To assist germination in hot, dry weather, a thin mulch of grass or mowings can be laid over each station and the seedlings can be allowed to grow through this covering. However, in early spring and in cool, wet weather this practice can cause the seed to rot and will result in a poor stand, possibly necessitating resowing. Sowings can begin outdoors in August in mild areas, although September to November is the most favourable period country-wide except for the Lowveld, where autumn and winter sowing is the recognized practice.

Further treatment. Pumpkins grow away very vigorously and rapidly in favourable conditions once the first 2 or 3 true leaves have been produced, and from then on watering, in the absence of good rainfall, should be carried out generously. However, wilting of the leaves at midday does not always indicate the need for water. Nematodes can cause this symptom, while frequently the early growth is in cloudy to partly cloudy weather and when this is replaced by warmer, clearer conditions the soft growth takes some time to adjust. In addition, plants that are well mulched tend to make softer and more luxuriant growth than unmulched plants and wilt easily.

Any check in growth will cause stunting and premature flowering and will result in low yields. Like several other vegetables, pumpkins prefer their water to be supplied beneath the foliage. A can without a rose or a gently running hose are suitable methods of application. The regular wetting of the foliage assists in the premature establishment of mildew in some cases and also removes bait deposits once the fruits have set.

Pumpkins appreciate generous treatment throughout growth, a good diet being liquid manure applications at intervals of 2-3 weeks, starting when the first flower buds open. About 5 ℓ per planting station following a good watering is just about ideal. If watering is confined to the stations, weed growth will be minimal because the foliage of pumpkins will suppress and weaken all but tough perennial weeds. If the runners encroach on adjacent vegetables they can be lifted gently and placed in a clearer area, and can also be 'stopped' by nipping off the growing point.

Harvesting. Most pumpkin cultivars reach maturity 3-4½ months after sowing, depending upon the season. The fruits are picked when the skins become hard and lose their shiny appearance. Most cultivars, if well ripened, can be stored for several months. The fruits are best removed together with 50 mm of stalk, using secateurs or a sharp knife. Breaking them off at the point of attachment creates an entry spot for several destructive fungi, particularly in humid conditions. Pumpkins should not be left on the ground too long after the foliage has

died down, for wet soil and sun scald can cause damage and certainly reduce storing qualities. Although one often sees mature fruits stored on the roofs of sheds, cool and airy conditions are preferable.

Pests. *Pumpkin flies* in larval form are a problem on most cucurbits, particularly in the home garden where the gardener does not anticipate attack and where neighbours may not maintain a reasonable standard of garden hygiene. The adult flies lay their eggs in the soft tissue of the newly-set fruits, which are invaded by the larvae when they hatch. As the adult flies neither chew nor suck on the foliage, and are in fact seldom seen, a rather unusual method of control is necessary. This consists of mixing an attractive but poisonous sugar-based bait and splashing it in coarse droplets on the leaf surfaces. A suitable bait mixture is described in Chapter 8. To obtain satisfactory control, it is most important to begin the baiting programme when the very first flowers appear. A rather different and more recent approach to the problem resulted in the formulation of Lebaycid, an organo-phosphate used as a foliar spray. Late-maturing cucurbits are frequently troubled by the progeny of pumpkin fly that infested early and very susceptible crops such as marrows.

Aphids in large numbers are normally not as common on pumpkins as they are on cucumbers and squashes. Although their direct feeding is of little consequence (except on very young plants) they are the main agents for the transmission of mosaic, and for this reason alone they should be controlled. Aphicide, Rogor and Metasystox are effective systemic materials that will also keep *red spider mite* in check.

Leaf beetles of several species can cause damage, which is more serious on young plants. For recommended control measures refer to the entry on cucumbers.

Diseases. *Mosaic*, once established in any locality, appears at some stage of growth, season after season, and is rather difficult to keep in complete check. It is a viral disease that causes mottled, puckered and distorted leaves, stunted plants and lumpy, irregular and discoloured fruits. It is transmitted by aphids and possibly by leaf-chewing beetles, and if suitable host plants, including several weeds, are around for most of the year, it can be perpetuated indefinitely. If young seedlings are affected, normal foliage and fruit will not be produced. Frequently the disease attacks the plants later in growth, affecting only the new runners and growing points. Late sowings, as with fruit fly, are usually most affected.

Powdery mildew can be very destructive, particularly during hot, humid periods and when heavy dew is experienced. When all the foliage is affected the plants become stunted and the fruits small and worthless. Benlate and Bayleton are effective to a degree if spraying is carried out early and regularly.

Downy mildew produces light-coloured

angular spots on upper leaf-surfaces, and often a purplish fungus on the undersides. Treatment with a product such as Cupravit or Dithane M45 should commence when the disease is first noticed.

Anthracnose may attack the leaves, stems and fruit. On the leaves small yellowish or water spots appear, and these rapidly enlarge and turn brown. Oblong lesions may occur on the stems, and black sunken areas on the fruit. Weekly applications of Dithane M45 will control the disease if the spraying is started in good time.

RADISHES Europe and Asia
Raphanus sativus
Optimum pH 6,0-7,0

Radishes are not a very important vegetable but are found in most home gardens, probably because they are easy to grow, quick-maturing and can be grown throughout the year. They prefer cool weather, however, and when very high temperatures prevail the roots are inclined to be 'hot' and pithy.

Recommended cultivars. There are radishes of all shapes and sizes: turnip-shaped, oval, half-long and long. As all require similar culture, the choice of cultivar is purely a personal one.
Cherry Belle: A fine, cherry-red cultivar that has the ability to stay firm longer than most.
French Breakfast: Half-long cultivar, scarlet with white tip.
Saxa: A roundish, scarlet cultivar.
Sparkler: A popular turnip-rooted cultivar, deep scarlet with a white base and taproot.
White Icicle: A long-rooted sort, not grown to the same extent as the others.

Soil preparation. Gardeners rarely prepare the soil to any degree before sowing radishes, which is an indication that successful results can be achieved quite easily on a wide range of soils. Nevertheless, they will handsomely repay better treatment than this. They fare well on soils improved with organic material for a main crop, making good use of any residual nutrients. On poor soils 30-60 g per m² of 2:3:2 raked in should encourage the rapid growth that is so necessary.

Propagation. Propagation is by seed, sown where the crop is to mature.

Sowing. Although the seed can simply be broadcast and raked in, better results will be achieved if it is sown thinly in shallow drills, covered with 10-15 mm of fine soil and firmed. The surface of the bed should be brought to a fine tilth before sowing, and all clods broken up to allow the roots to develop properly. A distance of 125-150 mm between rows is ample when there are only a few rows. To ensure a continuity of crisp and succulent roots it will be necessary to sow every 2-3 weeks.

Radishes do very well in window boxes and other containers if they receive a fair share of direct sunlight.

Further treatment. Because of their quick emergence and rapid growth, radishes fare better than most crops where annual weeds are a problem. If the rows are too thick they can be thinned out a little, 22 mm between plants being adequate for most cultivars. In dry weather watering should be done regularly, as rapid growth is essential for crisp roots.

Harvesting. Most cultivars mature 3-5 weeks after sowing. Radishes must be pulled before they become large and puffy, and the rows should therefore be gone through regularly. Roots that are not up to scratch should be removed and put on the compost heap or used as a mulch, for if they are left standing they become a haven for pests of all sorts.

Pests and diseases. Although the radish is a member of the large cabbage family, it is rarely troubled to any extent by pests and diseases during its short growing period. *Leaf hoppers* and small *caterpillars* may attack the foliage, but a light dusting of BHC may clear up such trouble. *Downy mildew* may attack thick stands in the 7 days after emergence, particularly during warm, wet weather. Dithane M45 should control any outbreaks effectively.

RHUBARB
China and Tibet

Rheum rhaponticum
Optimum pH 5,5-7,0

Although by its use rhubarb can hardly be classed as a vegetable, it is usually found in the vegetable garden. Unfortunately the plants are rarely as vigorous, productive or long-lived in our climate as they are in Europe and other temperate regions. This is possibly because they do not get as distinct a resting period as they require, but I suspect it is also because they do not get a fair deal in terms of ground preparation and crop maintenance. Crown rot also takes its toll, and plants are lost and stands become gradually thinner. Nevertheless, half a dozen well selected and well treated plants will provide a regular supply of succulent sticks for the table for many months of the year. The petiole or leaf stalk is the edible portion of the plant. The leaves themselves contain oxalic acid and are poisonous.

Cultivars. Several outstanding cultivars are grown throughout the world, but they can only be perpetuated by vegetative propagation, for the seeds that are produced rather freely do not result in plants that are true to type. From a single packet of seeds one may obtain plants with greatly varying characteristics of vigour and colour. *Victoria* or, more correctly, *Myatt's Victoria*, is one of the older cultivars and is the only one normally encountered in local catalogues. The true strains are vigorous and productive with large green stalks heavily streaked with red.

Soil preparation. Rhubarb can be grown successfully on most soils provided that they are extremely well drained and improved with generous amendments of organic material. The planting station method of culture is particularly suitable for rhubarb, but it can also be grown using the improved bed method. Stations can be prepared as described for pumpkins but to a slightly greater depth and with a heavier fertilizer dressing (say 100-125 g per station) thoroughly incorporated into the improved soil. A distance of 750 mm each way between plants is not over-generous.

Propagation. Whenever possible, rhubarb plantings should be established by the division of vigorous crowns producing stalks of good size and colour and free from any obvious signs of disease. From time to time such material is offered for sale in national and local newspapers and magazines, but frequently the home gardener has to fall back on seed. The seeds are best sown 5 or 6 to a planting station, or thinly in rows that can be thinned out further if necessary. If sown in rows the plants can be moved to prepared permanent quarters when they are a good size. In the small seedling stage rhubarb does not transplant easily and many losses usually occur.

Sowing. Only fresh seed should be sown. As the winged seeds are quite easy to handle they should be placed individually 50-75 mm apart in shallow drills and covered with 20 mm of fine soil. If a satisfactory stand of seedlings is obtained, and germination is not always uniform, they can be thinned out finally to stand 150-200 mm apart, care being taken to retain those having predominantly red leaf stalks. Very often, however, the green-stalked ones are the most vigorous! Spring sowings are usually the most successful.

Planting and transplanting. Three- and four-year-old crowns can be divided in June/July, ensuring that each root portion has a strong bud. They should be set out in prepared stations, covered with about 50 mm of soil, firmed by treading and watered in if the soil is at all dry. Well grown seedlings from nursery rows can be set out in similar fashion. Where sowing was carried out *in situ*, the seedlings can be thinned out to leave one to mature at each station or even two if they are about 200 mm apart. Once a bed of rhubarb is established, further plantings should only be made from plants that have desirable characteristics in terms of vigour and colour.

Further treatment. In hot, dry weather, established plantings should be generously watered. Rhubarb appreciates a deep mulch, particularly if manure or compost can be spared for the purpose. Even fresh manure can be used as a surface mulch to a depth of 25-40 mm. Rhubarb also responds to liquid manure applications when it is in full growth.

When growth recommences each year, a side-dressing of fertilizer at the rate of 60 g per plant or 120 g per m^2, kept well away from the buds of the plants, worked in shallowly and watered in, is standard practice. In areas where rhubarb does not die back completely, this feeding can be repeated after 2-3 months. Rhubarb appears to respond better to organic feeding than to inorganic dressings, and no opportunity should be lost to satisfy this tendency. Guano is a useful material for the purpose.

Harvesting. 'Pulling' (and this is literally the way to harvest) should on no account begin until the plants are of good size (i.e. in their second year) and even then it should be done with considerable judgement, as with asparagus, if the plants are not to lose vigour and decline. Rhubarb is harvested by grasping the stalk as far down as possible and pulling and twisting it off with one action. The stalks must be pulled carefully otherwise young shoots will also be removed, to the detriment of the plant. Only stalks of good size (20-25 mm in diameter) should be harvested; smaller material should be left to die down and replenish the root reserves. All flower stalks should be removed as soon as they are identified for they drain away the strength of the plant.

Pests. Rhubarb seems to have little attraction for pests, though aphids and the odd caterpillar may appear, but not in sufficient numbers to necessitate control measures.

Diseases. *Crown rot* is by far the most serious disease affecting rhubarb and it is quite common in most areas, especially when warm, humid conditions are experienced. The disease is caused by the same fungus that causes buckeye-rot on tomatoes and several other diseases among vegeta-

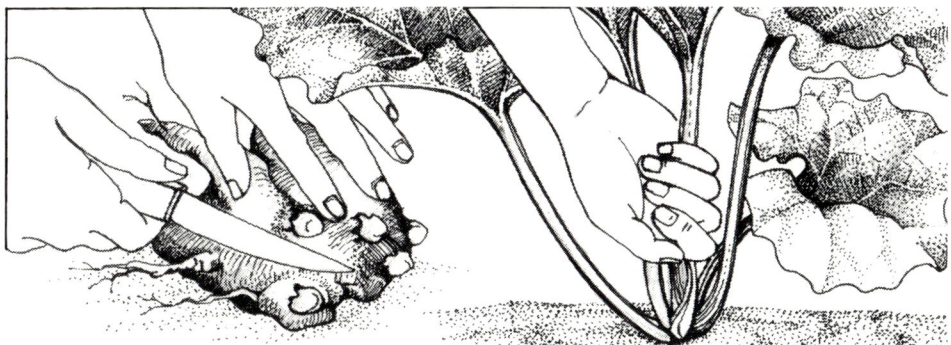

When dividing rhubarb crowns ensure that each root portion has a strong bud. The leaves are harvested by pulling and twisting them upwards.

bles. The symptoms of the disease on rhubarb are a rather rapid wilting of the foliage followed by a rotting and disintegration of the crown and root system. Once these symptoms are obvious the disease cannot be checked and the affected material should be lifted and, if possible, burnt. Ensuring that the ground is well drained before planting is one of the few practical steps that can be taken to keep this disease in check.

Leaf spot is sometimes encountered. All the proprietary fungicides are only partly effective against it. Keeping the plants in a vigorous condition by regular feeding, coupled with a high standard of garden hygiene, appear to be the easiest methods of reducing damage to the foliage.

SALSIFY   Europe
Tragopogon porrifolius
Optimum pH 6,0-6,5

Salsify, sometimes called the 'oyster plant' because of its rather distinctive flavour, is of minor importance among garden vegetables. The edible portion is the cream-coloured root, although in Europe, where the plants are often left in the ground over winter (salsify being a true biennial), fresh young growths or 'chards' are produced in spring and these are used as a spinach.

Recommended cultivars. *Mammoth Sandwich Island:* This is the only cultivar occasionally offered.

Soil preparation. As the roots are often 200-250 mm in length, deep digging is essential, as is the removal of any stones and the breaking up of any clods. Salsify grows well if it follows a well-manured crop such as cabbages or potatoes. As with carrots and parsnips, sandy to medium loams are the most suitable soil types. Before sowing takes place, 2:3:2 at the rate of 60 g per m² should be broadcast and raked in, bringing the surface to a fine tilth.

Propagation. Propagation is by seed, sown where the plants are to mature.

Sowing. Salsify prefers cool growing conditions, and early spring and autumn sowings are usually the most successful. In hot dry weather the roots produced are often of poor quality and flavour. The seeds are rather long and do not rub easily between finger and thumb. They are best sown singly 30-40 mm apart and can later be thinned to 125-150 mm apart if necessary. The seeds should be covered to a depth of 15-20 mm. In dry weather covering the drills with a light grass mulch will assist germination. In the home garden, 300-350 mm between rows is adequate.

Further treatment. Apart from weeding and watering in the rather long growing season, salsify needs little attention. Thinning out the plants as described above may be necessary if a high percentage stand is obtained. During hot periods a mulch of fine material will keep the soil temperature

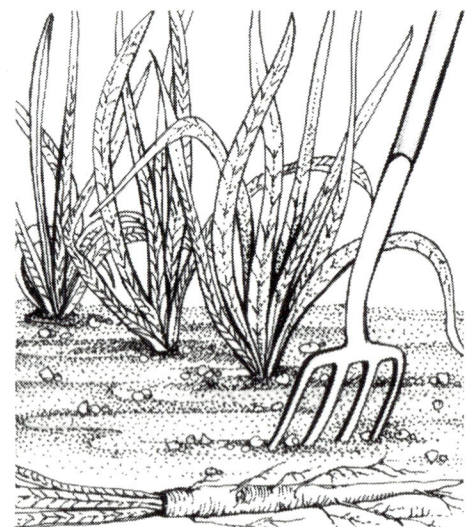

Salsify roots do not pull easily and must be harvested with a fork.

down and improve the flavour of the roots. It will also suppress weed growth and obviate the need to hoe, thus avoiding possible damage to the tender roots.

Harvesting. Because the roots are difficult to 'pull' and bleed easily, like beetroot, lifting with a fork is the most satisfactory method of harvesting. They are prepared for the table by scraping gently so as to remove only a thin layer of peel.

Pests and diseases. Salsify is rarely troubled to any degree by any sort of pest or disease. From time to time, however, cutworms, aphids, snails and caterpillars may do a little damage, but control measures are rarely necessary.

SCORZONERA   Europe
Scorzonera hispanica
Optimum pH 6,0-6,5

All aspects of culture are similar to those of salsify, the main exception being that if the rows need to be thinned, a distance of 75-100 mm between plants in the row is quite adequate.

Scorzonera is a true perennial, with black-skinned roots that have sweet-flavoured white flesh. It is quite hardy and in temperate climates is often lifted only the second year, when the roots are appreciably larger. Even at this stage the roots are thinner than well-grown salsify.

SPINACH   Probably Persia
Spinacia oleracea
Optimum pH 6,0-7,0

True spinach is not as widely grown as the more familiar Swiss chard, probably because it is not as productive and also because it has a fairly short picking season. It is also less tolerant of heat than Swiss chard and can only be grown with success in cooler weather.

Recommended cultivars. In Europe spinach is divided into two classes: summer spinach, which is smooth-seeded, and winter spinach, which is prickly-seeded. The cultivars usually offered in South Africa – *Bloomsdale* and *Viroflay* – both belong to the former group. Viroflay has leaves that are medium green in colour, while Bloomsdale is somewhat darker and rather puckered.

Soil preparation. A fertile, weed-free soil is almost a necessity for this crop. On poor soil the plants often run to seed before a good crop of leaves has been harvested. Spinach will grow satisfactorily on a wide range of soils and is very much at home when it follows a crop for which the soil was well improved. On such soils, a dressing of 60-75 g per m² of 2:3:2, incorporated thoroughly prior to sowing, should yield good initial growth. On poorer soils, particularly if they are on the light side, a liberal dressing of well-made compost or aged manure should be forked into the soil after the ground has been dug over. Such soils also require the fertilizer dressing specified above.

Propagation. True spinach does not give good results when transplanted and is therefore best sown where the crop is to mature.

Sowing. The seeds should be sown thinly in drills 250-300 mm apart, covered with 20 mm of fine soil, firmed and watered. The seed can be sown from spring to late autumn in most areas, provided that watering can be carried out if necessary. Sowing every 3-4 weeks will ensure a continuity of fresh leaves.

Further treatment. Most sowings will need thinning, which should be carried out at 3-4 weeks (the larger thinnings can be used for the table). To mature satisfactorily, 175-200 mm should be allowed between plants in the row. A month after sowing, a side-dressing of LAN at the rate of 30 g per metre of row will give the plants a welcome boost, as will an application of liquid manure. During dry weather water should be given generously, for any check will encourage the plants to produce seed stalks and curtail vegetative growth. A mulch is essential to help conserve moisture.

Harvesting. True spinach is usually ready 7-9 weeks after sowing. It is common practice to harvest a few leaves at a time, allow-

Harvest only a few spinach leaves at a time until the flower stalks appear.

ing a few to remain and grow on, but as soon as flower stalks appear all leaves should be picked and the plants removed completely. Alternatively, the plant can be cut off completely when it reaches maximum growth.

Pests. *Aphids* often colonize the undersides of the leaves, especially those that are heavily puckered. Aphicide and Malathion are suitable materials for use, provided that the safety period is rigidly observed.

Diseases. *Leaf spot* is common on Swiss chard and beetroot, and is sometimes also a problem on spinach. Dithane M45 or copper oxychloride may effect control if sprayed in good time.

SPINACH, NEW ZEALAND   Australasia
Tetragonia expansa
Optimum pH 6,0-7,5

Although New Zealand spinach is not a true spinach botanically, it is a very fine substitute and grows well, even in hot weather when other types would run to flower and seed very quickly. It has small, rather fleshy leaves, is of spreading habit, and 5 or 6 plants will produce a steady supply of greens over a period of several months.

Cultivars. No named cultivars or strains are catalogued.

Soil preparation. Although it will tolerate considerable neglect, well-improved soil is a basic requirement if the plants are to develop fully and remain productive over an extended period. Any available compost or manure worked into the rows or bed will not only improve the nutrient content of the soil but will also increase its moisture-holding capacity – a most important factor if the crop is to be a success. In addition, a dressing of 60-120 g per m² of 2:3:2 will assist in getting the plants into vigorous growth. If bulky improving materials are scarce, it is better to improve planting stations only. These should be at least 600-750 mm apart each way. A handful of 2:3:2 worked into each station is an adequate basic dressing.

Propagation. Propagation is by seed, sown either where the crop is to mature or in seed-boxes for later transplanting. The large seeds have extremely hard seed-coats and require abundant moisture until germination has taken place. This is one of the few cases where soaking the seeds overnight in tepid water is really justified and of proven value.

Sowing. Because the plants are prostrate, apart from the growing points, and spreading in habit, the seeds should be sown 100-150 mm apart in rows 750 mm to 1 m apart. Alternatively, 3 or 4 seeds can be sown at each planting station, allowing 750 mm centre to centre between stations. The seeds should be covered with 25-30 mm of soil, followed by a thin mulch of grass if the weather is very hot. August to November is the most favourable period for sowing.

Further treatment. If a good stand of

Soak the seeds of New Zealand spinach overnight in tepid water.

plants is obtained, the rows should be thinned out to leave the plants 300-450 mm apart in the row or 2 to a planting station. New Zealand spinach will show a marked response to fortnightly applications of liquid manure, commencing when the plants begin to cover and continuing throughout the picking period. Nitrogenous side-dressings every month at the rate of 30 g per plant of either LAN or sulphate of ammonia will also improve growth very considerably. These materials are best broadcast around each plant and then followed *immediately* with a watering, by hand spray or sprinkler, to remove any granules or crystals that may have lodged on the foliage. Once the plants begin to cover, any necessary weeding will have to be carried out by hand-pulling to avoid damage to the fleshy stems and tips. The plants are relatively drought-resistant, but the leaves produced in such conditions are sometimes poor in quality, while the plants themselves may suffer from pests that have little else to feed upon.

Harvesting. This crop is usually harvested by picking or cutting off the shoot tips together with 100-150 mm of stem. If picked in this way and fed regularly the plants will remain productive for 4 months or more.

Pests and diseases. Strong-growing plants are fairly trouble free, although occasional *leaf spots* can appear. *Cutworms, slugs* and *snails* may also take their toll of seedlings in the early stages, and may necessitate control measures.

SPINACH, OTHER

Several other plants are used as spinach, of which the following are the ones most often encountered under cultivation: Ceylon or Malabar spinach (*Basella alba*); Tampala or Chinese spinach (*Amaranthus gangeticus* and *A. oleraeceus*).

The former is an attractive, fleshy plant, somewhat twining in habit, and can be propagated by seed or by tip cuttings. As with all leaf crops, a soil containing an abundance of decomposed organic matter will ensure that the plants produce the desirable succulent growth.

Tampala or Chinese spinach is the name

given to several closely related plants of the amaranthus or celosia family. The two named above are sometimes catalogued in South Africa, and their relationship to the decorative plants of the flower garden is evident from the shiny black seeds that are produced in abundance by mature plants. They are harvested by nipping out the growing tips with 4 or 5 young leaves. Because of their relationship to several common weeds of our gardens, they have the ability to survive and grow away in soils that would never support more demanding crops.

SQUASHES   North, South and
Optimum pH 6,0-7,5   Central America

The botanical classification was dealt with at some length in the discussion on pumpkins and there is no need for further elaboration. Although squashes can belong to any of three distinct species and vary greatly in plant characteristics, they all require similar soil and climatic conditions, especially a full-sun situation. The bush and smaller trailing cultivars should find a place in any home garden, but the more vigorous plants, such as Hubbards, are suitable only for larger plots.

Recommended cultivars. This group of plants has received more attention than most from the hybridizers, particularly since 'baby marrows' or 'courgettes', long a feature of European dishes, became more popular. Only a few of the available cultivars and hybrids are detailed here, several of which are relatively old favourites while others still have to prove themselves. A good way out of the dilemma of deciding which cultivar to choose is to concentrate one's sowings on proven types, but each spring to try one or two of the newer kinds.

Ambassador and *Blackjack:* These two F1 hybrids have come to the fore in the past few years and are similar in type to Zucchini although they are more prolific and more uniform. They are of bush habit and are usually used very young as courgettes.

Butternut: A very fine, trailing, open-pollinated cultivar, which is approaching its 50th anniversary. The fruits vary slightly in shape depending upon the strain, but they are usually pear- or calabash-shaped and are cream in colour. The flesh is dry and orange in colour, and the fruit cavity is rather small.

Custard: Both white and yellow cultivars of this scalloped or 'patty pan' squash are usually obtainable. The flattened fruits have a similar texture and flavour to marrows.

Hubbard: Both green and golden types of this popular vigorous grower are available. Of the green there are both smooth-skinned and warted strains. All types have fine flesh characteristics, the warted sorts being superior but losing out in popularity because they are very large and their keeping qualities, on wet soil and in storage, are poor.

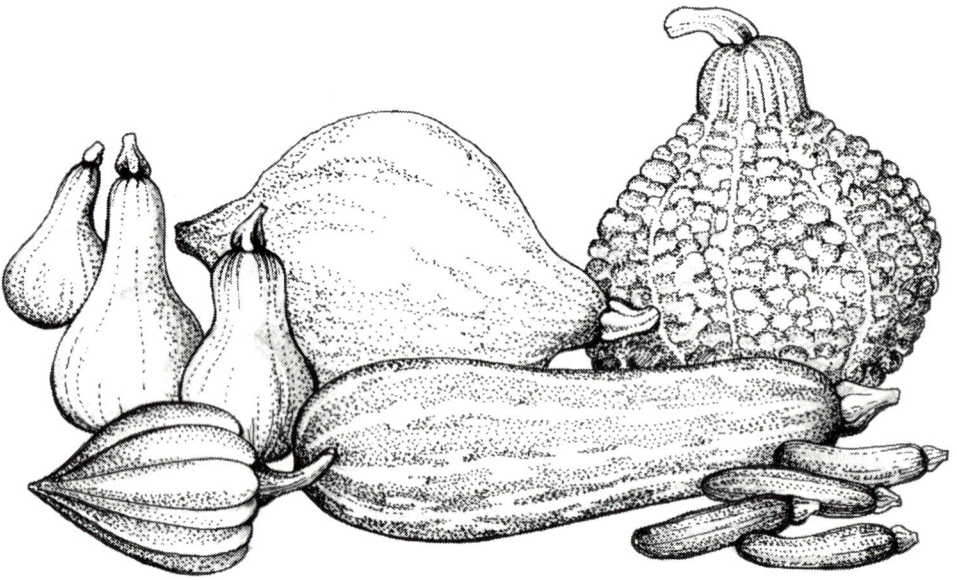

Squashes vary greatly in size and shape.

Little Gem: No South African book on vegetables would be complete without mention of this consistent performer, whose fruit characteristics are so well known. Botanically it is of the same species as Table Queen, and its growth habit and fruiting pattern are similar. Although it has fair storage qualities when mature, nothing can surpass the flavour and texture of freshly cut, young fruits.

Long White Bush: This is a large white marrow of bush habit. It is very early and prolific and appears to be a little less attractive to pumpkin fly than its green counterpart.

Table Queen: A cultivar also catalogued as Acorn or Des Moines, the fruits of which are small and fluted, medium to dark green in colour, with a yellow splash on the underside. It is of trailing habit. More recently a golden cultivar has been catalogued.

Zucchini: The name of this distinct cultivar, first introduced to vegetable growers in the U.S.A. over 50 years ago, has more recently been loosely used to describe any fruits that are used as courgettes. The fruits are very dark green in colour and will assume a considerable size if allowed to grow on.

Soil preparation. Planting stations, as described for pumpkins, are equally satisfactory for the above cultivars. However, because of varying growth characteristics, the distance between planting stations must be flexible. While the bush and small-fruited vining cultivars will grow very comfortably at a spacing of 1 m each way, up to 2 m each way is not being too generous for Hubbards.

Propagation. Propagation is by seed, usually sown in the prepared planting stations. Early sowings made under protection in Jiffy 7s, Jiffy pots or similar containers are often successful, but in most cases protected sowings a month before outdoor sowings will result in a maturity gap of only 1½-2 weeks. September to November is the most favourable period for sowing squashes outdoors, although earlier and later sowings are

successful in some seasons. With squashes of the type of Little Gem, and with bush marrows, it is wise to sow as early as the weather permits, because late sowings (as with cucumbers) frequently become hosts early in their growth to pests and diseases. Sowings made in sustained hot weather emerge and get away better if the rows or stations are covered with a grass mulch.

Further treatment. If germination is good the trailing cultivars should be reduced to 3 per station, and the bush cultivars to 2 (the 2 furthest apart if all are equally strong). As growth progresses and the weather warms up, watering should be increased if the weather is dry. This should be by irrigation, not by spraying or sprinkling. Bush squashes, in particular, are susceptible to both types of mildew, and the incidence of these diseases appears to increase very considerably when the foliage is continually wetted. Mulching the planting stations with rotted manure, compost or any short material will benefit the plants greatly, as will a feeding of liquid manure commencing when the first flowers appear. With this crop mulching appears to encourage soft, succulent growth, which rapidly wilts in hot weather. However, this is only a temporary condition and by late afternoon the plants will have regained their turgidity.

From fruit set onwards, a watch should be kept for any 'stung' fruits, which should be removed and destroyed by burning, if possible. Failure to carry out this measure of garden hygiene could result in major damage to late sowings of cucumbers, squashes and pumpkins.

Harvesting. Bush marrows and squashes should be cut with 20-40 mm of stalk, using a sharp knife or secateurs. Twisting is also a simple method of removing certain types of squash, but any attempt at a straight pull will only result in damage to the plants. Most bush cultivars mature about 60 days after sowing, but the small, trailing types

usually need another 2 or 3 weeks. Courgettes are picked when they have attained a length of 120-150 mm. With all types, cutting the fruits when they are of a size suitable for the table will lengthen the picking season and increase the overall yield.

Green Hubbard squashes do not stand well on wet soil, particularly the heavy warted strains, and in wet weather should be cut as soon as they mature. This cultivar is also very susceptible to sun scald once the foliage has dried off.

Pests and diseases. Squashes are susceptible to all the troubles described in the entry on pumpkins, with the bush types being particularly susceptible to *aphids, fruit fly* and both types of *mildew.*

SWEETCORN   Central America
Zea mays var. *saccharata*
Z. mays var. *rugosa*
Optimum pH 6,0-7,0

Sweetcorn is the home garden counterpart of field maize, and a place should be found for a row or two in even the smallest garden. Cobs freshly picked and cooked are far superior both in quality and nutritional value to the finest offered by the greengrocer. Like potatoes and sweet potatoes, sweetcorn does require rather wide spacing between rows, but some of the smaller-growing cultivars and hybrids can be spaced quite closely in the row with satisfactory results. Sweetcorn is essentially a warm-season crop and should not be sown until the weather and soil take a distinct turn for the warmer. Like pumpkins and squashes, sweetcorn is dioecious, the male flower or 'tassel' being produced at the very top of the plant and the female flowers or 'silks' lower down on the stalk. Sweetcorn is wind-pollinated and in sustained wet weather unfilled cobs often result from incomplete pollination.

Recommended cultivars. *Golden Bantam:* This is an early cultivar that has been in service for many years and is well suited to the home garden. The plants reach a height of 1,2-1,7 m and bear smallish cobs with yellow kernels.

Stowell's Evergreen: A leading white-seeded cultivar, which grows to a height of 2 m or more in fertile soil. Seeds of this cultivar have a characteristic shrivelled appearance.

Wondergold, Jubilee, and *Commander* are hybrids that are well worth the attention of the home gardener. All are medium to tall in habit and yellow seeded.

Soil preparation. To grow to perfection sweetcorn requires a clean, fertile soil of good depth. It is particularly successful on well-drained soils rich in organic matter. If it follows a crop that has been well treated organically, a dressing of 2:3:2 at the rate of 60-75 g per metre of row should be an adequate pre-planting dressing. On poorer soils this rate can be increased by 50% and a forkful of compost per metre of row can be added. A full-sun situation is essential for this crop.

Propagation. Propagation is by seed, sown where the crop is to mature.

Sowing. September to December is the usual period for sowing, with October and November being the very best months in most areas. The seeds should be sown in twos, 250-300 mm apart in the case of Golden Bantam, or 300-350 mm apart for other cultivars and hybrids, allowing 600-750 mm between rows. Sweetcorn is best sown in blocks, i.e. several short rows together, rather than 1 or 2 long rows. Such a planting pattern ensures more satisfactory pollination and also provides some protection from wind and heavy rain. Ideally the rows should run north-south to minimize the shading effect the plants might have on adjacent low-growing vegetables. The garden trowel or draw hoe can be used to open up the holes and the seeds should be covered with 40-50 mm of soil. A longer picking season from a single sowing can be had by simultaneously putting in a couple of rows each of an early cultivar and a main-crop cultivar or hybrid.

Further treatment. As with all directly-sown crops, early weed control is very necessary if the plants are to have any chance at all. Any weeds that spring up close to the seedlings should be carefully removed by hand, and hoeing should be carried out carefully between the rows. All cultivation should be as shallow as possible, for sweetcorn develops a root system fairly close to the surface. Nitrogen plays a key role in the production of high yields of sweetcorn, and few stands will fail to respond to a side-dressing (30 g per metre of row) when the plants are knee high and again 2 weeks later. Sulphate of ammonia and LAN are suitable side-dressing materials. After each of these side-dressings soil can be drawn up to the plants, for they are susceptible to wind damage, especially when wet.

The plants usually produce 1 or 2 cobs

each. Certain cultivars are inclined to throw out sucker growths from the base but there is no evidence to show that removing them has a favourable effect on yield. Mulching is a beneficial practice with this crop and once the cobs have been removed the sweetcorn plants can themselves be used as a mulch for later crops. I find a cane knife an ideal tool for chopping the stalks into shorter lengths for this purpose.

Harvesting. Few gardeners are unable to judge correctly when a corn cob is at its best. They should be picked when the kernels are plump and well filled but still 'milky' when pierced with the thumb nail. At this stage the silks are usually withered and dry. The cobs are removed with a sharp downward twisting pull, and because they deteriorate rapidly once removed from the plant they are best picked just before they are required for the pot. Most sorts need 2½-3 months from sowing to reach this stage.

Pests. *Cutworms* find sweetcorn seedlings most attractive and will even tackle them and cause damage when they are 250 mm or more in height. Late attacks do not completely sever the plants but weaken the stalks so that they become particularly susceptible to wind and rain damage. Drenching the rows with Karbaspray before or just after the seedlings emerge appears to effect some control, as does the distribution of a proprietary bait at regular intervals until the plants are well away.

Corn earworm larvae hatch from the eggs laid by adult moths on the young silks and enter the sheath of the cobs. Here they cause damage that is frequently undetected until harvest, though sometimes discoloration of the wrapper husks indicates their presence. They are particularly troublesome on late sowings. Dusting or spraying with BHC or carbaryl as soon as the silks appear often gives satisfactory control. This should be repeated 2 or 3 times at intervals of 5-7 days.

Diseases. *Streak* is a rather serious viral dis-

ease of field maize and occasionally appears on sweetcorn plantings in the home garden, especially on late sowings. It is transmitted from plant to plant by leaf hoppers, but because of its rather spasmodic appearance it is difficult to suggest any effective control measures, except to sow early.

SWEET POTATOES South America
Ipomoea batatas
Optimum pH 5,5-6,5

Sweet potatoes are related to the well-known garden creeper, Morning Glory, and are essentially a warm-season crop. They are more of a field crop than a subject for the home garden, but a row or two can be accommodated in larger gardens. The plants, which are spreading in habit, are of course grown mainly for their swollen roots, but some indigenous peoples relish the young shoots as a spinach substitute, while the mature tops make excellent stockfeed. Roots having a dry, floury texture when cooked are more popular than the earlier, moist cultivars.

Recommended cultivars. It is only in recent years that the breeding of sweet potato cultivars has really leaped ahead, and now every year or two new cultivars are released, some of them adapted to a special geographical area. However, obtaining the relatively few runners the average home gardener requires is sometimes extremely difficult, as they are usually only advertised for sale by the thousand.
Borrie: An old, but most reliable cultivar, popular in the Cape. It has reddish to copper skin and dry, light cream flesh.
Impala: This, like several other cultivars, was bred locally. It is red skinned with orange flesh.
Three Month White: A large, quick-maturing cultivar of rather low quality.
Soil preparation. Sweet potatoes will grow on a fairly wide range of soil types, with a well-drained, moderately deep sandy loam being about ideal. Heavy clays prevent the development of well-shaped roots, while very deep loose-textured organic soils tend to promote the formation of lush top-growth coupled with a profusion of long, stringy roots. When following a well-manured winter crop, such as cabbage or cauliflower, a dressing of 60 g of 2:3:2 per metre of row should be an adequate base dressing. On poorer soils the plants will respond to the incorporation of a dressing of well-matured compost or manure plus a similar dressing of 2:3:2. Fresh manure should never be added before planting this crop for it very often causes the plants to produce lush top-growth at the expense of root production. The plants can be grown on the flat or on ridges. In areas of high summer rainfall substantial ridges can be made, each carrying 2 rows of plants.
Propagation. Sweet potatoes are propa-

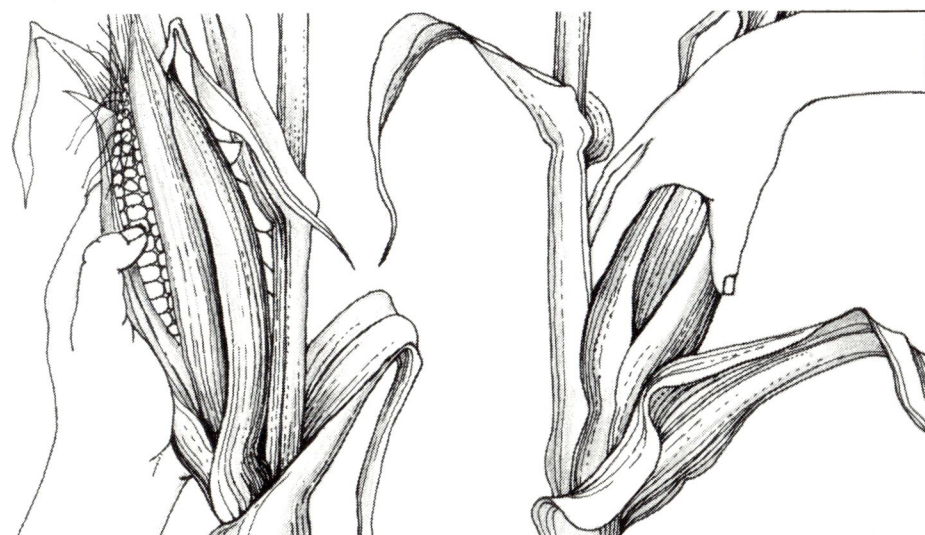

Pierce one kernel of each corn cob to test for ripeness. Harvest the cobs with a downward twisting movement away from the stem.

gated commercially either by rooted shoots or vine cuttings. The home gardener can produce such material either by selecting a few well-shaped 'clean' roots from a previous crop and storing them or by purchasing edible roots from the supermarket or greengrocer. These roots can then be closely planted, both ways, in beds of light soil in July/August, and covered with 50 mm of soil. Watering, if necessary, should be increased as the shoots appear and begin to run. Depending upon weather, material should be available for planting in 7-8 weeks. In colder areas the soil should be kept only slightly moist and given the protection of a thin mulch of loose grass or straw. If the gardener has a glass- or plastic-covered frame to spare this is ideal for inducing early sprout growth. If planting material is obtained from outside sources, it is advisable to remove any rooted portions in case nematodes are present.

Planting. If lengths of runners are used, and this is the more common practice, they should be cut into 300 mm lengths with a sharp knife and planted by covering them, for at least half their length, with moist soil. Firming after planting is extremely important in obtaining a good 'take' of cuttings. The holes for planting can be made with a trowel, a hoe or a spade, but in well-formed ridges I have often planted by hand. Rooted cuttings can be planted in a similar way. The plants can be spaced 350-500 mm apart in the row, 650-800 mm between rows being adequate when there are only a few rows. October to December is the most favourable planting period. Unrooted cuttings in my experience appear to yield more heavily than rooted ones.

Further treatment. Apart from weed control, and this is a relatively easy task once the vines cover the soil, sweet potatoes need little attention. As the cuttings take and begin to grow away, soil can be drawn up to the plants. In areas where the sweet potato weevil is troublesome, soil cracks should be closed off regularly to prevent infestation of the roots.

Harvesting. The roots can be lifted, preferably with a fork, as soon as they are of a good size, which should be 3-5 months after planting, depending upon cultivar. The flavour is said to be best if the soil is allowed to dry out before the roots are lifted. Sweet potatoes are not the easiest subjects to store for any length of time and the home grower would be well advised to lift them only as required.

Pests. The adult *sweet potato weevil* is reddish-black in colour and the damage it causes is very similar to that of the tuber-moth in Irish potatoes. The adult females enter soil cracks and lay their eggs on the root surfaces. Within a week the eggs hatch out and the larvae burrow into the roots, leaving behind a mass of excrement and other debris, which makes the roots unpalatable. The damage can easily be seen if the roots are snapped in half. Sometimes

all three stages (adults, larvae and pupae) can be seen. Closing off soil cracks regularly as the roots swell is a practical and effective method of control, while dusting the crop rows with BHC is a useful deterrent.

For a discussion of measures to control *nematodes* refer to Chapter 8.

Diseases. *Leaf mottle* appears to be a viral disease, which expresses itself in a similar way to mosaic, and odd plants are affected in some plantings. These should be removed and none of the roots should be used for propagation purposes.

Leaf spot occasionally appears on some plantings, particularly during wet periods, but it is usually not serious enough to necessitate control measures.

Storage rot caused by several fungi is a problem with sweet potatoes. They do not store well and it is therefore essential that any roots intended for storage should be 'clean' and free from cuts and other wounds caused by harvesting tools. It is also important that such roots are not bruised, grazed or chafed during subsequent handling.

Non-parasitic diseases. As with potatoes, unfavourable soil and climatic conditions can cause several disorders, both internally and externally, which lower the quality of the roots. Employing sensible cultural practices is the only way of reducing such losses.

SWISS CHARD   Europe
Beta vulgaris var. *cicla*
Optimum pH 6,0-7,0

Swiss chard is also known and catalogued as spinach beet, silver beet and seakale beet, though I think the last two names are used only to describe the Fordhook Giant type of plant, which has dark green leaves and wide, white, flat petioles or mid-ribs, which are often cooked separately. It has also been described as 'perpetual' spinach, though the picking season rarely extends over more than about 4 months, particularly if nematodes are a problem. Swiss chard, garden beets, sugar beets and mangelwurzels all belong to the same species, as is evident from their seeds, and they will 'cross' readily if seed crops are grown on adjacent plots, which explains why red-tinged plants sometimes show up in sowings.

Swiss chard is loosely called 'spinach' by most people in this country, the cultivars of true spinach being somewhat more difficult subjects as well as much lower yielding. The plants are grown mainly for their leaves, but the leaf stalks are used extensively overseas for certain dishes.

Recommended cultivars. *Fordhook Giant:* An upright cultivar with dark green leaves, sometimes heavily crumpled, while the leaf stalks are broad, flat and white. As the picking season progresses the stalks often appear to be a little out of proportion to the leaf area.

Lucullus: This is the most popular cultivar in

South Africa. The leaves are long, light green in colour, and sometimes distinctly arched in fertile soil. The stalks are relatively thin and similar to rhubarb in section.

Soil preparation. Swiss chard can be successfully grown on a wide range of soils, but the plants are heavy feeders over a long period and although regular side-dressings will stimulate growth, thorough soil preparation, before sowing or planting, is the foundation of success. Any manure or compost that can be spared should be incorporated thoroughly, but it must be in a fairly advanced state of decomposition otherwise it will continue to break down in the soil and this will have a deleterious effect on crop growth. A dressing of 60-90 g of 2:3:2 or 3:2:1 incorporated shallowly prior to sowing will encourage rapid growth. Swiss chard will not tolerate soil acidity of any consequence and a dressing of dolomitic limestone should be applied on suspect soils.

Propagation. Propagation is by seed, sown where the plants are to mature, though the seedlings transplant quite easily if necessary. As with beetroot and other close relatives, the rough cork-like seeds are actually fruit clusters containing several true seeds and careful sowing is necessary if excessive thinning out is to be avoided.

Sowing. If the crop is sown *in situ*, which is the easiest method when only a few rows are required, the prepared soil should be raked to a fine tilth, and shallow drills, 350-450 mm apart, taken out. As the large seeds are easily handled, an even stand is assured if they are sown singly 60-75 mm apart, covered with 15-20 mm of fine soil, firmed and watered with a fine spray. They can be sown during most months of the year, with May to July being the most unfavourable period. During hot weather the sowing can be covered with a light grass mulch.

If seedbed sowing is practised, the seeds can be sown a little thicker, say 25-40 mm apart in the drills, and the seedlings set out at about 4 weeks into rows, allowing 250 mm between plants.

Further treatment. The seeds germinate quickly in favourable conditions, 5-8 days being the usual time taken. If a good stand

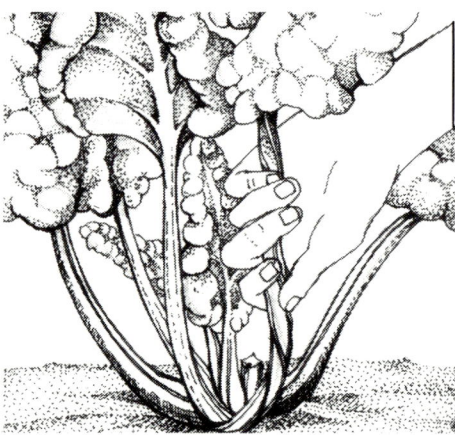

Swiss chard leaves are removed by pulling and twisting.

of plants is obtained in directly-sown rows, it will be necessary to thin the plants to give them ample room for development. This can be carried out at any stage from about 2 weeks, but if it is carried out a week or two later the thinned plants, if lifted carefully, can be used to fill up any gaps or plant out additional rows. Or they can be popped into the pot. The plants should finally stand 200-250 mm apart in the row to mature. From the time picking commences, monthly side-dressings of 3:2:1 or straight nitrogen will maintain the plants in vigorous growth, as will liquid manure applications at intervals of 2-3 weeks. Mulching with short material will prove beneficial, especially if compost or manure can be spared for the purpose.

Harvesting. The first leaves can usually be picked about 8 weeks after sowing, and once they are of good size they should not be left on the plant too long otherwise they will lose their fresh colour and become tough. The leaves are best harvested by moving along the rows and systematically removing 2 or 3 of the largest leaves from each plant. They are removed, as is rhubarb, by pulling with a twisting action. Cutting cannot be recommended, for inevitably the knife damages other leaf stalks and causes losses. Some gardeners cut or twist off the whole tuft of leaves from each plant at one time, but after such treatment I find that the plants take a long time to recover and seldom regain their former vigour and leaf size.

When vigorous upright growth ceases and the leaves spread out to form a loose rosette it is an indication that the picking season is coming to an end. At this stage the plants are best lifted with a fork, the leaves cut off and the root systems, if 'clean', added to the compost heap. It is far better to sow a few rows every few weeks to achieve succession, than to try to prolong the life of a single planting.

Pests. *Caterpillars* occasionally cause trouble, although Swiss chard does not have quite the same attraction for them as the Brassicas have. Malathion, Thiodan, Karbaspray or BHC powder are effective materials.

Diseases. *Leaf spot* (*Cercospora beticola*) can be quite a problem at certain seasons. Warm weather and high humidity are conducive to its establishment and spread. The spots are brown initially, later turning grey, 3-4 mm in diameter and have reddish-purple borders. In several cases the spots coalesce so that the major portion of the leaf is affected. Dithane M45 and copper oxychloride are effective if used early and if the weather dries out for a week or more. A second spray 5-10 days later may be necessary.

TOMATOES   South America
Lycopersicon esculentum
Optimum pH 5,5-7,0

The tomato is without doubt the most popular and useful of all vegetables. In the home garden, obtaining high yields of well-shaped fruits from well-tended plants is a source of great satisfaction. Botanically the tomato is a fruit, in fact a true berry, but by virtue of its use it is usually classified as a vegetable. It is a native of South America, with Peru/Bolivia/Equador being its possible home. Botanists still scour this area in an effort to find wild species of *Lycopersicon* that may have some resistance to certain diseases and pests and which can be used in developing resistant commercial cultivars.

The tomato is very much a warm-season crop and cannot tolerate more than a few degrees of frost. Growth is also extremely slow and laboured during cold, unfavourable weather. It is therefore essentially a summer crop except in the Lowveld, where late summer and autumn sowings are made and where excellent crops are produced under irrigation during the winter months.

Recommended cultivars. Throughout the world there are several hundred cultivars and strains of tomatoes, and in recent years much research has been done in breeding new cultivars and hybrids for specific purposes. Disease and nematode resistance have, quite rightly, received most attention, but producing types especially for processing has long been a primary consideration, particularly in the U.S.A. More recently the development of small-fruited cultivars of compact or cascading habit has also received considerable attention.

Red-, pink- and yellow-skinned cultivars are available and the shape and size of the fruits vary greatly. The red cultivars are by far the most popular, although Oxheart and Ponderosa are pink cultivars that often attract the attention of the home grower because of their large size and 'meatiness'. However, the plants are not very heavy yielders and the fruits are often of poor shape because of their susceptibility to several physiological disorders. The flesh of the pink cultivars is the same colour as that of the red ones, and it is only because the skin tissue of the former lacks yellow pigment that the fruits appear pink.

Apart from fruit characteristics, the plant habit of tomatoes separates them into two distinct groups, those that are 'determinate' in habit and those that are 'indeterminate'. Determinate cultivars reach a height of 1,0-1,2 m, at which stage the lead growth develops into a flower truss and a similar thing happens to all lateral branches. Indeterminate plants produce 1 or 2 stems, which grow on and on (as do laterals that are not removed) until they are 'stopped' by removing the growing point. Plants in the latter group usually have smaller fruit and reach maturity a little later. However, they bear fruit over a longer period and are ideally suited to staking and pruning, both in open ground and in tunnels. They also have much smaller pedicel scars than larger-fruited sorts.

The selection of a cultivar is therefore very much a personal one as such a wide choice is available. I believe it is a wise policy each season to grow a row or two of a new introduction and compare its performance in a particular area with that of a proven, standard cultivar.

The following are reliable cultivars that adapt themselves to a wide range of conditions and are available in small packets:
Flora Dade: Determinate. An American introduction, somewhat taller than similar cultivars. The plant foliage covers well but does show a particular susceptibility to late blight. The fruit stalks are not jointed, as is usual, and stay on the plants when the fruits are picked.
Heinz 1370: Determinate. A cultivar bred for processing but which also performs well under home garden culture over a wide range of soil and climatic conditions.
Homestead: Determinate. This is a splendid cultivar of American origin. There are several selections and strains, some of which are catalogued separately. It is a vigorous grower and a heavy yielder, although catface can be a problem on larger fruits.
Manapal: Indeterminate. A medium to large fruited, green-shouldered cultivar, which has become a great favourite because of its vigorous growth and high yields.

Determinate (left) and indeterminate tomato plants.

Moneymaker: Indeterminate. A relatively small-fruited cultivar. The fruits are uniform in colour and size, almost white when unripe and without the green shoulders typical of Ailsa Craig, one of the old standards.

Rodade: A new locally-bred cultivar having as one parent the reputable Flora Dade. It is not yet available in small packets but is mentioned here because it has a built-in resistance to at least one strain of bacterial wilt. Those of us who have had severe losses from this dreaded and persistent disease on tomatoes and egg plants will watch its performance with great interest. The plant habit and fruit characteristics are similar to those of Flora Dade.

All determinate cultivars are suitable for container culture.

Certain cultivars and hybrids have an inbred resistance to one or more diseases, and in seed catalogues these desirable characteristics are denoted with the following symbols:

V – resistance to verticillium wilt
F – resistance to fusarium wilt
N – resistance to certain species of *Meloidogyne* nematodes

Soil preparation. Tomatoes can be grown successfully on most soil types but to achieve high yields the ground must be well prepared and as much organic matter as possible must be incorporated. If nematodes are a problem (and this is increasingly common as most species of this microscopic pest find the tomato a most accommodating host), soil preparation should be completed 2-3 weeks before transplanting. This will allow the soil to settle and fumigation to take place. The rows should not be closer than 1 m apart, and so it is better to concentrate on the preparation of the planting rows than to carry out overall improvement. However, with a bed accommodating only 2 or 3 rows, overall treatment is more practicable and the returns will fully justify the generosity. The suggested 1 m spacing between rows is suitable only where indeterminate cultivars are staked and pruned; 1,2-1,5 m between rows should be regarded as the minimum for vigorous unpruned and unstaked determinates. This may appear to be rather wide spacing when the small plants are first set out, but less than this often results in low yields, undersized fruits and the creation of a humid micro-climate within the stand, which is conducive to the establishment of certain fungal diseases. In addition, the detection of damage from pests and diseases is difficult, as is spraying and harvesting.

Well decomposed compost or manure, or proprietary compost materials, should be worked into the rows generously together with a dressing of 2:3:2 at the rate of 100 g per metre of row. On organic soils in good heart, or following the incorporation of a green manure crop or a substantial decomposed mulch, the fertilizer dressing alone should get the plants off to a flying start.

Crop rotation is also important with tomatoes, and however well the soil is improved annually it is wise not to grow them on the same ground continually. Apart from the problems of wilt diseases and nematodes, evidence now suggests that tomatoes do not thrive on soils containing any residues of previous tomato crops.

Propagation. Propagation is by seed, usually sown in seedbeds or seedboxes for transplanting later. Direct seeding can also be practised by sowing groups of 2 or 3 seeds 600 mm apart in the row and then thinning out the seedlings later. However, weed competition and the difficulty of detecting and controlling pest damage at such widely-spaced stations are severe disadvantages of this system. In addition, well-used garden soil is often 'dirtier' than the often soil-less media used in seedboxes and seedbeds, while the plants occupy the ground for the best part of 6 months, which is undesirable for several reasons. Jiffy 7s, Jiffy Pots and compartmentalized seed-trays are ideal for raising strong, healthy plants, especially where early sowings are concerned.

Sowing. The seed-trays or seedboxes should be sterilized if soil is contained in the mix. A kettle of boiling water can be poured over the filled boxes, but Basamid and Jeyes Fluid are useful chemical sterilants for small quantities of soil. If seedbed sterilization is impracticable, choose a new piece of ground or at least one that has not carried tomatoes or a closely related crop for several years.

Tomato seeds do not 'run' well and are best sown 20-25 mm apart in drills covered with 10-12 mm of fine soil, sand or vermiculite, which should be firmed and watered. Sowing the seed in this way does take a little more time but it ensures that the young seedlings have room to develop and can be hardened-off satisfactorily. Tomato seed germinates quickly, particularly that of English cultivars and hybrids, and any temporary mulching material on the beds should be removed as soon as 50% of the seedlings have emerged, otherwise damping-off may occur. Mid-September to the end of November is the main sowing period in most areas, although earlier sowings from July onwards can be made under the protection of a frame or greenhouse. In the Transvaal Lowveld a winter crop is produced from sowings made from January to March. Sowings made under protection in seedboxes can be pricked out into individual containers or Jiffy Pots for later transplanting.

Transplanting. At 3-5 weeks, depending upon season and cultivar, tomato plants are usually 100-125 mm high, which is the most suitable size for setting out in open ground. If the stand of seedlings is thick, transplanting should be carried out early. Seedlings that are allowed to remain in the seed-rows too long will quickly become leggy and soft, with the result that they will keel over when transplanted and take a long time to re-establish themselves and grow away. For a few days before the move, water should be withheld from the seedlings to toughen up their tissues. Plants in containers should be thoroughly hardened-off a week or more before the intended move by increasing their exposure to the sun and the elements generally.

When plants have to be purchased, select those that have dark green foliage and sturdy stems, blue-green in colour, and roots that are free from nematode nodules.

The plants should be set out firmly, a little deeper than they stood in the seed-rows and up to the base of the lowest true leaves if necessary. If bare-root planting is carried out, the dibber is the best tool for the job. But where well-spaced, pricked-out plants are moved from a seedbox, or where seedlings have been raised in individual or segmented containers, a trowel should be used to set out the plants. Watering-in should follow and can be carried out either with water or with a starter solution at the rate of 250-500 ml per plant. In a small planting, 450 mm between plants in the row is quite adequate, but 600 mm is better when there are several hundred plants.

Shading is not really essential at any time of the year, provided that sturdy plants are set out firmly and watered-in thoroughly. If softer planting material is used, shading with 'shady-caps', grass or any other suitable protector for 4-5 days may be advantageous.

Further treatment. Before high yields of quality fruit can be achieved, there are several essential cultural operations that require attention, more so with tomatoes than with any other vegetable crop.

Watering. The most satisfactory results with tomatoes are obtained if a steady moisture level is maintained in the soil throughout growth. This is perhaps most important from the time the first fruits set. Several serious fruit disorders can directly or indirectly be attributed to an erratic water sup-

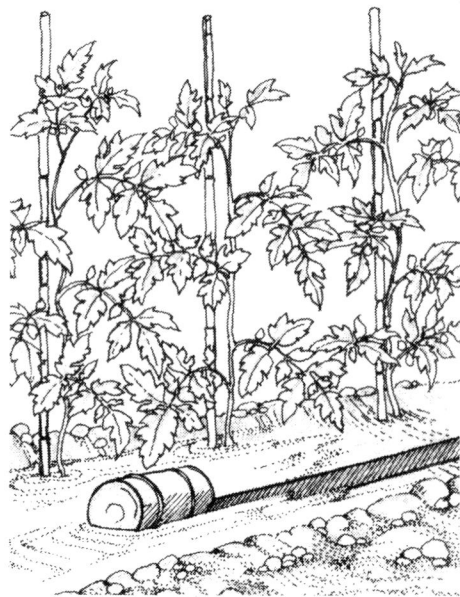

To avoid wetting the foliage, water tomatoes by flooding.

ply. Once the plants are established in their permanent quarters, which should be within a week of transplanting, a good soaking should be given every 7-10 days in cool to warm weather and every 4-5 days during the hotter months, assuming, of course, that there is no rain.

The method of supplying water to the plants is rather important with tomatoes if the plants are to remain 'clean' and the fruits free from damage. Perhaps more than any other crop, tomatoes detest being sprayed and sprinkled and are most content when the flood or furrow method is used. Wetting the foliage day after day with a hose or sprinkler is conducive to the establishment and spread of certain serious fungal diseases affecting foliage and fruits. In addition, this method of watering makes the maintenance of an effective spray deposit on the foliage a difficult task, and it encourages a shallow root system.

Cultivation. When the plants are established, the Dutch or Paxton hoe should be used whenever weed growth warrants it. However, once the plants are growing away any cultivation must be extremely shallow if damage to the roots is to be avoided. With untrained plants, hand-weeding only must be resorted to once the plants begin to spread, for hoeing may cause damage to both plants and fruit and open the way for diseases to enter the plant system.

Feeding and mulching. When the first fruits are well set, say 4-5 weeks after transplanting, a side-dressing, hoed in shallowly, of 2:3:2, 3:2:1 or LAN at the rate of 30 g per metre of row, will benefit the plants enormously. Organic or inorganic liquid manure applications, either with a home-made mixture or a proprietary material, carried out at fortnightly intervals, will be equally effective.

Mulching is also a beneficial practice, for it maintains the moisture in the topsoil and thereby lessens the chances of cracking and discoloration. During wet weather it is advisable to put a fistful of loose grass under any fruit truss that is in direct contact with the soil.

Staking and pruning. This is quite a controversial subject among commercial growers because of the labour and expense involved. In the home garden, however, where only a few rows are planted and where space is sometimes limited, staking is recommended for determinate as well as indeterminate cultivars. Unstaked, unpruned plantings are only a success in really dry weather and on relatively 'clean' soil. During wet weather the tangle of vegetative growth creates a very humid micro-climate, which is very favourable for the establishment and spread of serious fungal diseases. In such circumstances spraying with hand equipment is of doubtful value. In addition, staking the plants or supporting them in some other way keeps the lower fruit trusses off the soil. Sun scald can also cause heavy losses on unstaked plantings once the foliage begins to deteriorate.

Staking but not pruning is the most common method, particularly with determinate cultivars, and is the most suitable for the home garden in all but very wet seasons. The plants can be trellised along galvanized wire or up individual stakes, or lifted on to a rough frame 450 mm above the soil. No lateral growths are removed, but once the plants have been tied in it is good practice regularly to remove any new shoots that may arise from the base of the plants. Supporting them in this way keeps the fruits off the ground, protects them from sun scald, and facilitates feeding, side-dressing, mulching, weeding, spraying and harvesting. It is the method that gives the highest yields of top quality fruit.

Staking and pruning is the final method of handling tomatoes and consists of confining growth to one or possibly two main stems and regularly removing all side growths or laterals, which spring up in the axils between the main stem and the leaf petioles. This is a common practice overseas on glasshouse and outdoor crops and, with the cultivars and hybrids used, it results in very high yields of top quality fruit, over 100 tons per acre having been achieved by some commercial growers under glass. In South Africa, however, where most outdoor cultivars are multi-celled ones of American origin, this method has little to commend it. This system only pays dividends on such plants during wet periods, when a reduction of the foliage allows the plants to dry out more quickly and also facilitates an effective coverage of spraying material. When practised at other times it leads to reduced yields, despite the higher plant population it allows, and often to the appearance of certain functional disorders caused by the imbalance between top growth and root development.

However, on Alicante, Moneymaker and other small- to medium-fruited imported cultivars and hybrids it is to be recommended. Allowing these types to go unpruned results in the production of a large number of laterals and in very small fruits. The laterals should be removed when they are about 30-50 mm long and this should begin when the plants are about 300 mm high. They should be removed by gently bending them a couple of times from side to side and not by using a knife or nipping them off between finger and thumb, for such methods can transmit viral diseases.

These cultivars usually set the first truss of fruit after 5 or 6 true leaves, the second after another 4 and thereafter flowers are produced after every 3 leaves until the plants are 'stopped' by removing the growing point. If a side shoot is allowed to develop into a second main stem, it will produce fruit trusses after every third leaf.

The easiest way of supporting tomatoes is to tie each plant to a separate cane. Remove all lateral shoots from certain cultivars (see text). Pick tomatoes by breaking the joint in the stalk just above the calyx.

It is inadvisable to work among tomato plants when the foliage is wet, for certain fungal diseases are easily spread in this way. It is also most inadvisable to work among these plants wearing good clothes, for the foliage brushing against the body will stain them yellow.

There are several hormonal materials available to assist in obtaining a good set of fruits. They are sprayed on to the flowers to induce the fruits to start swelling without pollination having occurred. Such fruits are usually seedless, but they are also often puffy, hollow and misshapen. These materials were developed to improve the fruit set in unfavourable climatic conditions when insect activity is low. However, they are of little value in this country, where the climate during the growing season is favourable on the whole.

This much-prized crop is unfortunately vulnerable to attack by a host of damaging pests and diseases. It is therefore very necessary to spray, at 7-14 day intervals and after heavy rainfall, with a fungicidal/pesticidal 'cocktail', including a wetter.

Harvesting. It usually takes 6-8 weeks for fertilized flowers to become ripe fruits, and the flavour and nutrient content of the fruits is best when they are allowed to ripen on the plant. Tomatoes should be removed by breaking the joint in the stalk just above the calyx with the thumb. This is of course impossible with the new South African cultivars. Leaving the fresh calyx intact makes the single-layer tray most attractive, but where a large number of fruits are to be picked and placed in a lug box or similar container the calyxes should be removed otherwise many fruits may be damaged by them.

After the final picking, which should include all good-sized fruits regardless of degree of ripeness, the plants should be removed together with their roots by lifting with a garden fork. Those showing any sign of nematode infestation should not be incorporated into the compost heap, but burnt if possible.

Pests. *Cutworms* are often troublesome in the seedbed and when the plants are set out in heavily-manured ground. Use bait as required or a Malathion drench when the plants are set out.

White fly has become an extremely serious pest, which appears to have developed considerable resistance to most of the hitherto effective chemical controls. The insects gather in large numbers on the undersides of the foliage, often undetected until the leaves are disturbed, and their feeding causes the upper leaf surfaces to appear pale, mottled and spotted. In addition, the scale-like nymphs secrete large quantities of honeydew, the sweet sticky substance that leads to the growth of 'sooty mould'. Malathion, Metasystox, Dazzel and Thiodan are all materials that have given me reasonable control, especially when alternated.

Erinose is a condition caused by microscopic mites, which, by their feeding, irritate the tissues of the stem and leaves. This irritation causes the plants to put out a very large number of small white hairs, with the result that they take on a 'furry' look and appear to be affected by a type of mildew. This causes some of the leaves to dry up and fall off. Dusting the plants with sulphur-based preparations appears to keep these mites in check, while Kelthane, Malathion and Thiodan are also useful materials.

Caterpillars of the American bollworm and the tomato looper can both play havoc with young tomatoes if uncontrolled. The latter is particularly troublesome. In most cases the eggs are laid on the leaves and the young larvae quickly migrate to the fruits, frequently entering them under the calyx. Their feeding creates tunnels throughout the young fruits and eventually causes them to drop off prematurely. Malathion, Karbaspray and Thiodan are useful control materials.

Tomato russet mites frequently lower yields and yet their presence often goes unnoticed. They usually begin their activities at the base of the plants and, as they migrate upwards, the lower foliage turns bronze on the upper surfaces with a very characteristic silvering on the undersides. In severe infestations the fruit also becomes disfigured. Kelthane gives excellent control of this pest, while sulphur dusts and wettable powders are also effective. All spraying and dusting operations should be directed at the undersides of the leaves.

Nematodes: refer to Chapter 8.

Diseases. The tomato, like its relative the potato, is susceptible to many diseases, both parasitic and non-parasitic, with several of the former being common to both crops. Most of the foliage diseases are likely to occur in wet, overcast weather, and it is advisable to spray regularly at short intervals, starting at an early stage.

Late blight was described fully in the discussion on potatoes. The leaf and stem symptoms are the same as on potatoes, but on the tomato fruits the disease shows up as a dark grey, rather marbled discoloration, which may extend over the whole fruit. A characteristic is that although they are discoloured, the fruits are firm and not soft until the very final stages.

Early blight is sometimes called target spot. Apart from causing typical target spotting on the leaves and petioles, this fungus attacks the fruits, producing black depressions, which often split open, and concentric rings around the calyx scar. The same disease also frequently attacks young seedlings, which develop 'black-leg', causing the stems to become brittle and the plants to fall over. Copper oxychloride and Dithane M45 are effective materials provided that the programme commences when the first 2-3 true leaves appear and continues at 7-14 day intervals thereafter.

Septoria leaf spot is another fairly common and extremely destructive disease. Warm and moist conditions favour its establishment and spread. The spots are small, usually 3-5 mm in diameter, but their sheer numbers in severe cases cause the leaves to yellow prematurely and drop off, thereby making the fruits vulnerable to sun scald. Control measures as recommended for late blight should also keep this condition in check. Seedlings can be damaged by the careless use of copper sprays and care should be taken when young plants are treated.

Fusarium wilt is a common disease in the warmer areas and can cause severe losses. It begins as a yellowing and wilting of the lower leaves, or of one stem only on unpruned plants, but eventually, over a period of perhaps some weeks, the whole plant wilts and dries up. Plants approaching maturity appear more susceptible than younger plants. The removal and destruction of affected plants, long rotations between related crops, and the use of resistant cultivars, are the only practical methods of control, with the last-mentioned being essential in diseased soil. Heinz 1370, Manapal, and Homestead are cultivars with some resistance to this disease.

Bacterial wilt is also very destructive in the warmer areas and affects egg plants, peppers, potatoes and several common weeds. The gardener will have little difficulty with the symptoms on tomatoes, for it causes seemingly healthy plants to collapse overnight as though they had been severed by a knife or a cutworm. The collapse of the entire plant is so rapid that there is initially no accompanying yellowing of the leaves. At first occasional plants are affected, then adjacent ones, until eventually less than a 25% stand of healthy plants remains. The bacteria, of which there are several strains, persist in the soil for several years, and a long rotation is the only answer where complete soil sterilization is impracticable. Rodade, as mentioned earlier, is the only cultivar displaying resistance to certain strains of this wilt.

Bacterial canker is a fairly widespead disease that does not always display every symptom of the disease on affected plants. Wilting is the most common symptom and sometimes the only one, with subsequent loss of foliage on plantings in which diseased seed initiated the damage. The stalks of the plants show yellowish-brown streaks, which may or may not open into stem cracks or cankers. The fruits are not always affected, but those that are show slightly raised white spots with a tiny red or brown spot in the centre (hence the description 'bird's eye spot'). Long rotations and the use of 'clean' and (if possible) certified seed are the only answers to this disease at present.

Non-parasitic diseases. *Sun scald* sometimes affects unstaked and severely pruned plants in very hot weather. The fruits on plants that have defoliated for one reason or another are also affected. The condition causes grey or whitish sunken patches on the fruits, usually in the region of the fruit shoulders and on the side of the plant exposed to full sun.

Leaf roll, a condition in which the leaflets keep their colour but roll inwards, usually starting at the bottom of the plants, appears to be caused by severe pruning and is rarely a problem on untrained and unpruned plants. It does not affect the yield to any degree but it does render the fruits more liable to damage from sun scald.

Growth cracks are common when a very wet period follows a relatively dry one, and can also be brought about by heavy watering when the fruits on the lower trusses reach full size. On large-fruited cultivars the cracking is usually deep and radial, extending from the pedicel scar. On small-fruited English-type cultivars and hybrids, the cracks are shallower, sometimes concentric, and extend around the shoulders of the fruits. Careful watering is essential to prevent damage of this nature, while an effective mulch will keep the moisture content steady and ensure optimum growth. In areas with well-defined wet and dry seasons I have controlled cracking by getting the young seedlings and transplants used to wet soil conditions by watering rather copiously before the arrival of the rains.

Catface shows up as an extreme malformation of the fruits, which sometimes have a stitched appearance at the blossom end. The cause of it is not fully understood, but it is thought to be connected with the abnormal development of the pistil, imperfect pollination and unfavourable climatic conditions during the flowering period. There is no effective control, but some cultivars are affected less severely than others. It is most common on the flat, large-fruited cultivars, particularly those that are pink in colour.

Blossom-end rot is a disorder that causes dark, flat, sunken patches on the bottom or blossom end of the fruit. For many years it was attributed solely to haphazard or irregular watering practices, but more recently research workers in America and the U.K. have observed that calcium deficiency may be a primary cause, although fluctuating soil moisture conditions and an excess of nitrogen salts in the soil may be important secondary factors. I find it most troublesome on the first truss or two of severely pruned plants, particularly on early plantings. Corrective measures for calcium deficiency were described in Chapter 2. Careful watering, mulching and reduced pruning of the plants are additional measures that should be applied. There is also an internal expression of blossom-end rot, and affected fruits show no outward discoloration.

Flower drop. Occasionally flowers on the lower trusses do not set fruit and sometimes they drop off at the stalk joint. This is usually the result of unfavourable weather conditions and can occur when night temperatures drop below about 13°C and also when day temperatures are consistently around 38°C for a few successive days.

'Berg' winds are also responsible for fruit and flower drop and for leaf scorch on a wide variety of plants in coastal areas.

TURNIPS   Europe
Brassica campestris var. *rapa*
Optimum pH 6,0-7,0

Turnips are grown primarily for their swollen roots, but many gardeners also use the tender leaves as a spinach. The final thinnings are particularly good for this purpose.

Turnips prefer cool conditions: in hot weather growth is often unsatisfactory and the roots are frequently discoloured internally or hollow. Aphid populations also appear and increase alarmingly in such weather, while flea beetles are frequently a menace and destroy the foliage.

The swede turnip (*Brassica napus* var. *rutabaga*), which is hardier than the ordinary turnip, is not grown to any extent in this country, despite the fact that it is considerably sweeter and more tasty (though the roots rarely attain the size or quality of those grown in more temperate regions).

Recommended cultivars. The range of cultivars has been somewhat static for many years, but the following are proven sorts that can hardly be improved upon.
American Purple Top: Almost the only swede cultivar available locally. The flesh is cream to light yellow in colour.
Purple Top White Globe: The rather unwieldy name of this cultivar is fully descriptive.
Snowball: A popular cultivar with white skin and flesh, usually picked when young.
Soil preparation. The turnip cannot be classified as a demanding vegetable, but unless the soil is fairly fertile and able to retain moisture the roots will be of low quality. It should be grown in soil that was well manured for a previous crop, and is therefore an ideal vegetable to follow tomatoes, cauliflowers or broccoli in the rotation. Cauliflowers and broccoli are of course also brassicas, but apart from club root they have few diseases in common. On such improved soils 45-60 g of 2:3:4 or 2:3:2 per m² should be an adequate fertilizer dressing, but this rate can be doubled on lower-grade soils. With turnips rapid growth is one of the secrets of success, as is a firm bed. Soils that have been well dug over and loosened up should be lightly trodden to meet the latter requirement. All clods should be broken up and all couch grass, water grass and other weeds removed.
Propagation. Propagation is by seed, sown where the roots are to mature.
Sowing. Turnip seeds are rather small and run through the fingers so easily that sowing should be carried out with considerable care. The ground should be well raked over and the seeds sown in shallow drills, 250-300 mm apart, covered with 10-12 mm of soil, which should be firmed and watered with a fine spray. Swedes require 450-600

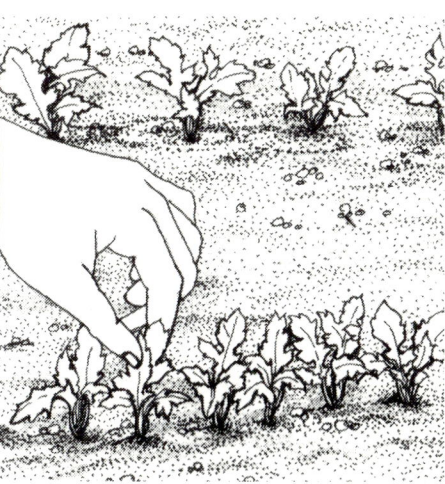

Thin out turnip seedlings in stages.

mm between rows. Turnips, like radishes, germinate very quickly once moisture is supplied, and the seedlings frequently appear within 3 or 4 days. Sowings can be made during most months of the year, with May and June being the most unfavourable in most areas.
Further treatment. However carefully sowing is carried out, thinning is always necessary if well-shaped roots are to be harvested. The first stage of this operation should be carried out 2 weeks after emergence. The final thinning, at 4-5 weeks, should leave the plants 60-75 mm apart. Following this final thinning a little soil drawn up to the rows will give the plants support. When thinning any vegetables I water well beforehand to facilitate their removal and again the following morning when the remaining plants are standing up again. Watering should be done carefully in the initial stages, for damping-off can be a problem in warm weather, but once the rows have been finally thinned the plants will welcome generous treatment.
Harvesting. This operation is particularly easy with turnips. Most cultivars should be ready for pulling 8-10 weeks after sowing, at which stage they should be 50-60 mm in diameter. Swedes mature much more slowly, but can usually be pulled from 12-14 weeks onwards.
Pests. *Aphids* may be troublesome during hot weather. Aphicide and Malathion are useful materials, the latter also controlling *flea beetles.*
Diseases. Although in theory turnips are susceptible to several diseases, few are ever troublesome – except *club root* in certain localities. The control of this disease is described in the entry on cabbages. *Leaf spots* of one sort or another appear from time to time during wet periods but rarely necessitate control measures.
Non-parasitic diseases. Like most root and tuber crops, turnips are occasionally subject to disorders of one sort or another, internal and external, which lower quality. Some of these are caused by unfavourable soil conditions such as extreme wetness or dryness, while others can be the result of a

deficiency of a specific trace element, such as boron. Unfortunately these disorders are only apparent when it is too late, i.e. when the roots are lifted. Glassiness, internal discoloration and hollowness are typical defects. Where a deficiency of boron has been indicated, possibly by sensitive crops such as beets, cauliflowers or celery, the rows of young plants can be lightly watered with a suspension of 20 g of borax per 5 ℓ of water.

WATERCRESS   Europe
Nasturtium officinale
Optimum pH 6,0-7,0

This is a relatively minor crop in South Africa, but deserves more popularity because it is rich in certain minerals and vitamins, has a pleasant tangy flavour and makes a welcome addition to any salad bowl.

Cultivars. In Europe, where watercress is a crop of economic importance, there are two main types – 'green' and 'brown' – and many different strains, selected because of their suitability for a particular growing area. Our local catalogues usually confine themselves to one unnamed cultivar, usually of the 'green' type.

Soil preparation. Watercress is aquatic in origin and requires soil that is fertile, reasonably deep, and retentive of moisture. The soil should be improved with liberal dressings of compost and manure or, if it is highly organic in nature, with a dressing of manure only. All these materials should be thoroughly incorporated into the top 200-250 mm of the well-dug soil. A broadcast dressing of 2:3:2 at the rate of 60-90 g per m², well raked in, will provide an additional nutrient supply. A semi-shady spot is acceptable to this crop, particularly during the summer months.

Propagation. Propagation is by seed or rooted cuttings. As planting material is seldom available, the former method is most common in this country. Subsequent plantings may be established from cuttings with white adventitious roots at the base.
Sowing. The seeds should be sown thinly in the prepared beds and covered with about 6 mm of fine soil, which should be firmed and kept moist. A thin mulch of fine grass will keep the soil moist and ensure a good stand of plants.
Transplanting. If too thick a stand is obtained from seed, the plants can be set out 150 mm each way into well-prepared soil. Rooted cuttings can be set out the same distance apart. The plants are somewhat straggling in habit and easily root when in contact with wet soil. Indeed, large plantings are established by simply laying the prepared cuttings on the wet soil or gravel bed.
Further treatment. Directly-sown beds can be thinned out, if necessary, to leave the plants 150 mm apart each way. In containers 100 mm is quite sufficient. Like several other subjects that are true perennials, in garden practice the profitable season of a watercress planting rarely extends beyond 3 or 4 months. This can be lengthened to the very maximum by regular and thorough watering, by applications of liquid manure every 3-4 weeks (ideally one that is organic in origin), by strict hand-weeding, and by the removal of flower heads as soon as they appear.
Harvesting. This is best carried out by cutting with a sharp knife or by nipping off 'sprigs' 100-150 mm long, ensuring that the plant itself is not removed from its bed during the operation. Care should always be taken to leave a short length of stem with several eyes to provide new growth and further pickings.
Pests and diseases. For *slugs* and *snails* the

standard baiting materials should be used. Small *beetles* sometimes cause damage in hot dry weather; Malathion should control these, provided that a 10-14 day safety period is observed.

WATERMELONS   Africa
Citrullus vulgaris
Optimum pH 6,0-7,0

Watermelons are not really suitable for the average home garden, as the small returns of edible fruits usually obtained do not justify the space that the crop occupies for much of the summer season.

The culture of watermelons is similar in all respects to that of other cucurbits, especially pumpkins and squashes. The recommended soil preparation and the sowing and planting procedures described for these crops also apply in this case.

Cultivars. There is an increasing number of cultivars and hybrids offered for sale. If it is available in small quantities, hybrid seed should be chosen, especially that of the small-fruited sorts.
Harvesting. The home gardener frequently has some difficulty in deciding just when the fruit is ripe, and although experience is the only real guide to this, the following points are valid for most cultivars: 1. The fruits emit a dull sound when rapped hard with the knuckles. 2. A colour change from pale green or white to yellow occurs on the 'ground spot', i.e. the part of the fruit that rests on the soil. 3. The tendril nearest to the fruit withers and dies off.
Pests and diseases. This crop is usually less troubled than other cucurbits, although *powdery mildew*, *downy mildew* and *anthracnose* are troublesome during some seasons, as are *fruit fly* and *red spider mite*.

12 HERBS

Few home gardeners worry about herbs, apart from parsley and mint, and most housewives find their requirements among the ever-increasing range of products on the supermarket shelf. Nevertheless, most gardeners have space for a small bed containing 4 or 5 herbs, which will provide a steady supply of fresh flavouring for many months of the year as well as material to be dried and stored. In addition to their flavouring qualities, some herbs have an attractive scent, are quite decorative, and can be included to advantage in mixed borders and rockeries.

In this book only a few of the most widely-used plants are dealt with, as well as some that are perhaps not true herbs but which are used fairly extensively for flavouring and garnishing. An extensive range of literature is now available for those gardeners who wish to make a formal or informal feature garden of herbs.

Most herbs can be grown successfully on a wide range of soils, but they are particularly at home on garden soils that have been built up with manure and compost over a number of years. In the absence of such suitable ground, a small bed or portion of the garden can be dug over and given a generous overall dressing of well-decomposed compost or leaf mould. A handful or two of 2:3:2 fertilizer per m^2 raked in well before sowing or transplanting will give the plants an added boost.

Several herbs are annuals or are treated as such and grow away slowly, while others are true perennials. It is therefore important that in all pre-planting soil cultivations every opportunity should be taken to remove the roots of perennial weeds. Good drainage is as essential for most herbs as it is for vegetable crops, with one notable exception – mint. Mint thrives in moist situations and on heavier soils, and some of the most vigorous and healthy clumps can be found beside leaking garden taps.

Most herbs grow extremely well in containers. If fed regularly, and this is rather important with such a small root run, the plants will provide a constant supply of fresh, valuable material. The containers can be filled with a proprietary fortified potting compost or with a mixture of 2 parts good garden soil, 1 part sharp sand and 1 part rather coarse compost with a complete fertilizer added at the rate of one handful for each 20 ℓ container. One part vermiculite (horticultural grade) may also be incorporated.

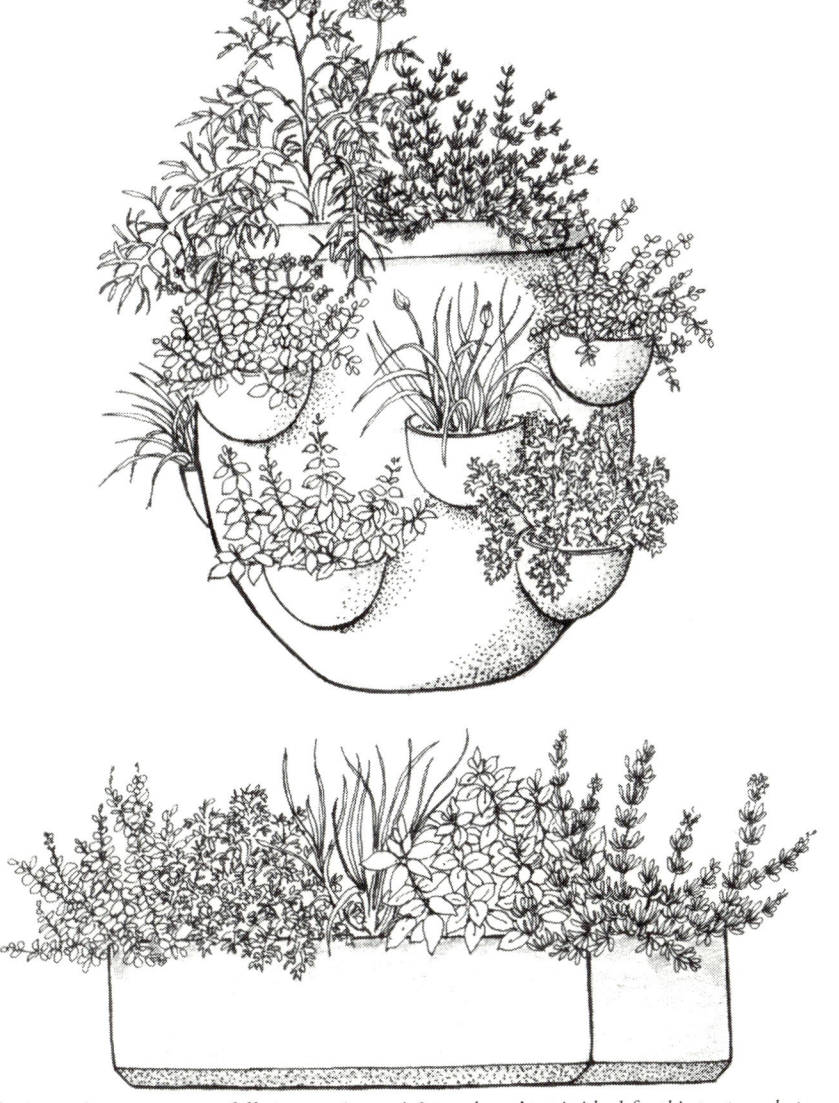

Many herbs can be grown successfully in containers. A 'strawberry' pot is ideal for this purpose, but even an ordinary asbestos trough is an adequate container for a miniature herb garden.

BASIL
Ocimum basilicum

Sweet basil is an annual that can be grown successfully for most months of the year if started in early spring. It is extremely tender and is easily raised from seed. Although it transplants easily, direct sowing saves much time and trouble where only the customary few plants are required. The soil surface should be raked to a fine tilth and the seeds sown thinly in rows 250-300 mm apart covered with 10 mm of fine soil, which should be firmed and watered. Germination is usually quick and thinning should begin early, the final thinning leaving the plants 200-250 mm apart in the row to mature.

Basil is a strong-flavoured, spicy herb, similar to cloves, and the fresh or dried leaves are used for flavouring soups, stuffings, salads and meat dishes. In autumn it can easily be dried by cutting the plants off completely when they are in 50% flower and hanging them in a dry, airy shed or garage, or on a stoep.

BAY
Laurus nobilis

Bay can be used in a wide range of meat dishes, sauces and soups, and it is said that its flavour is better when the leaves are dried off. It is an evergreen tree or shrub with considerable decorative value and prefers a full-sun situation but will tolerate partial shade. Planting material is not always easy to obtain as few nurserymen carry it and the rooting of cuttings is somewhat difficult. Leaves for flavouring can be removed throughout the year and can either be used fresh or dried off and stored. A dressing of 2:3:2 at the rate of 60-120 g per tree in early spring will promote new growth and can be repeated in January/February. Bay can be established in a large container but this will restrict its growth considerably.

BORAGE
Borago officinalis

This strong-growing plant is not too fussy about soil type and is relatively drought-resistant. It needs plenty of room to develop to its full height of around 750 mm with a spread of 450 mm or more. Borage is best sown thinly *in situ* and covered with 10 mm of soil. If broadcast it should be well raked in, firmed and watered. The stems are succulent, and the juice, which runs freely when the stems are broken, is often unexpectedly cold to the touch. The leaves when crushed are thought by some to smell like cucumber and they are often used with water and ice to make a refreshing drink. The small leaves can be chopped up and added to salads. The plants branch freely and on the tips of each are produced azure blue, saucer-shaped flowers, followed by seeds that self-sow easily.

CHIVES
Allium schoenoprasum

Chives are a very useful perennial of the onion family. Apart from their use as a flavouring for soups, stews and other meat dishes, and as a component in salads, the plants have considerable decorative value. The tufts of bluey-green grass-like leaves topped with globular, pale mauve flowers make, if planted in small groups, a feature at the front of the perennial border.

Chives grow readily from seed but once a few plants are established an easier and quicker method of propagation is by division of the clumps. If sown *in situ*, the seeds should be sown thinly and covered with 6-10 mm of fine soil, allowing 225-300 mm between rows if more than one row is required. The seeds can also of course be sown in seedboxes for later transplanting to permanent quarters. The seedlings grow away somewhat slowly and weakly and hand-weeding is usually necessary for some weeks after emergence. In fertile soils the plants will, by the end of the first season, have grown into clumps 30-40 mm across. It is best to lift, divide and replant them every 2 years to maintain vigorous growth and a regular supply of leaves.

Watering should be adequate, although once established the plants will stand without damage during hot weather. An occasional side-dressing, a light mulch of manure, or monthly applications of liquid manure will benefit the plants greatly.

Chives are usually harvested by cutting off the tops when they are 150 mm or more in height, but the small bulbs can also be used.

FENNEL
Foeniculum vulgare

A popular herb used for flavouring soups, omelettes, stews and a wide range of interesting dishes. Like most perennial vegetables and herbs the second and third years are the most rewarding, after which the plants begin to decline.

Fennel is not too particular about soil and will attain a height of 1,5 m or more with very little care and attention. The seeds should be sown thinly in rows 600 mm apart, and the seedlings should be thinned out to leave the plants 400-450 mm apart to mature. In less sheltered spots the plants may need to be staked loosely to avoid wind damage, and if the seeds are not to be used the flower stems should be cut off as soon as they become evident, particularly early in the season. The leaves can be removed and used as required. Regular weeding and a mulch with manure or compost in July/August should ensure satisfactory regrowth.

GARLIC
Allium sativum

Garlic is yet another member of the onion family and is certainly the most strongly flavoured, a characteristic that sharply attracts or repels people.

Some remarkable claims have been made for this plant, which has been in cultivation for thousands of years. These include its alleged ability to prevent baldness and cure impotence!

Garlic forms a bulb similar to the onion, and for this reason it is most profitable when grown on light to medium sandy loams, which allow the bulbs to develop fully.

Garlic is propagated by the sections, or cloves, that make up the bulb, and the larger, outer ones should be selected for a new planting, care being taken to see that they are plump and not shrivelled.

February to April is the most favourable planting period and the cloves should be set out singly at a depth of 40-50 mm, allowing 75-100 mm between plants in the row, and 300-450 mm between rows. If at any stage the plants appear to be standing still (or as a routine measure every 3 weeks) a light nitrogenous side-dressing, 20-30 g per metre of row, or a proprietary liquid manure, will stimulate growth.

As the leaves begin to dry off, any supplementary water should be discontinued. Garlic can be harvested by pulling, in loose soil, or by carefully lifting with a spade or fork. It should be left in the sun for a day and then hung up or laid shallowly on racks in a shady, airy spot. Two or three well-ripened bulbs of good size and shape should be saved to provide planting material for the following season.

MARJORAM (Oregano)
Origanum onites (Pot Marjoram)
O. majorana (Sweet Marjoram)
O. vulgare (Wild Marjoram)

Pot Marjoram is the one usually encountered although Sweet Marjoram is also popular. They are true perennials, somewhat woody in nature and untidy in habit. They can be propagated by division but are often grown from seed and treated as annuals. Marjoram prefers a well-improved, light-textured soil with good drainage. The seedlings can be set out 300-450 mm apart each way as soon as they are 75-100 mm high. Divided portions of established plants can be set out in early spring, again allowing 300-450 mm between plants. The leaves can be used fresh or dried, as a flavouring for meat dishes, egg dishes and pizzas.

MINT
Mentha rotundifolia
M. spicata

There are many species of mint but most of them possess similar characteristics in terms of smell and flavour, and their cultural requirements are identical. As most gardeners know, mint can be propagated very easily indeed at almost any time of the year by cutting off roots or runners. It spreads rapidly once established, however, and can become a problem where space is limited. The pieces of runner can be planted end to end in drills 50 mm deep, and covered with fine soil. An alternative method is to cut the roots or runners into 50-75 mm lengths, broadcast them on the prepared soil, and cover the bed with 25 mm of mature compost or good garden soil, which should then be firmed with the back of a spade and watered well with a fine spray.

Owing to the spreading habit of mint, hand-weeding must be carried out regularly, at least until the stand is thick enough to choke out all but the most vigorous perennial weeds. Harvesting should initially be carried out judiciously by nipping off a few sprigs at a time as required. Matted beds soon lose their vigour and become less productive, and for this reason it is best to replant the beds every 2 years.

When growth appears to be on the decline, or early in August/September, the planting can be chopped back to remove most of the runners and stimulate rooting. The bed can then be lightly raked over and covered with a dressing of mature 'clean' compost plus a handful of 2:3:2 at the rate of 30-60 g per m². Moisture is important at all times.

PARSLEY
Petroselinum crispum

Parsley is among the most useful and decorative of herbs, and 5 or 6 well-grown plants in open ground or container will provide a wealth of material for garnishing and flavouring. Although it is a true biennial, annual sowings are normal practice. Even more regular sowing may be necessary if nematodes are a problem, for an infestation will gradually sap the vigour of the plants and result in small leaves of poor colour. The curly-leaved cultivars are generally preferred to the plain, particularly for garnishing, with Moss Curled and Champion Moss Curled being the ones usually available in small packs.

Parsley will thrive in full sun or light shade and appreciates a well-improved soil, with nitrogen being particularly necessary for vigorous growth and high yields. Although it can be transplanted without too much difficulty it is far easier to sow it *in situ*, when only a few plants are required, and to thin it out later if necessary. The seeds are small and should be sown carefully in shallow drills, covered with 8-10 mm of fine soil, firmed and watered. During hot weather in full-sun situations a light mulch will ensure an even stand as the seed tends to germinate rather slowly, like celery. It is important that fresh seed be used each year, for once a packet of parsley seed is opened it will deteriorate rather quickly. Parsley seed has responded favourably to being soaked overnight in lukewarm water before sowing.

If a good stand of seedlings is obtained, thinning will be necessary. This can be done in 2 or 3 stages with the final thinnings being utilized in one way or another. The final thinnings should leave the plants 200-250 mm apart each way, which will allow for maximum development. Once the plants are growing away they should be watered generously in dry weather. After picking has begun, side-dressings with 2:3:2 or LAN, liquid manuring and mulching will keep the plants in a vigorous and productive condition.

Parsley leaves are usually harvested a few at a time from each plant, as required. However, on occasions when I have needed basketfuls of material for garnishing and decorating the show bench, I have cut off all the leaves with a sharp knife just above soil level. If this drastic cutting is followed by a thin manure mulch, a generous nitrogenous dressing or a series of liquid manure feeds the planting will take on a new lease of life.

Flowering stems should be removed by pinching as soon as they appear, for they will suppress vegetative growth and cause the leaves to deteriorate in flavour.

ROSEMARY
Rosmarinus officinalis

This is an evergreen perennial shrub with an attractive appearance. It usually reaches a height of around 1,2 m with a spread of 600-900 mm in favourable circumstances. The leaves are narrow, dark green in colour, with a somewhat furry underside. Rosemary prefers a full-sun situation. The plants can be started from seed sown in spring but once a few plants are established propagation can be from cuttings, which root without difficulty in late summer.

In late summer the plants can be cut back and the removed sprigs bunched and hung up to dry in a protected, airy situation. A handful of 2:3:2 and a mulch with compost or manure in spring will maintain the plants in a vigorous condition.

The leaves can be used fresh or dried to flavour a variety of meat dishes.

SAGE
Salvia officinalis

This relative of the popular garden salvia is a true perennial, but in practice new plants should be raised every 2-3 years. Wild claims have again been made over the years regarding the medicinal properties of this herb, but in the kitchen it is rather more limited in use than most of the aforementioned herbs. The flavouring of stuffings, meat dishes and cheeses are its more common uses.

Sage can easily be propagated by cuttings, rooted or unrooted, but when no material of this sort is available it will be necessary to raise plants from seed. The seeds can be sown thinly in shallow drills 350-450 mm apart when more than one row is required, and covered with 8-10 mm of fine soil, which should be firmed and watered. Sage is not too particular about soil, but a full-sun situation is preferred. The seeds are best sown in August/September and the plants thinned to stand 300 mm apart in the row. Cuttings should ideally be taken in the period October to February, using vermiculite, perlite or river sand as a growing medium.

Plants tend to become woody in sub-tropical areas, and are best cut back at least twice during the growing period. The removed material can be laid out on a newspaper in a dry, well-ventilated and shady spot to dry out.

SHALLOTS
Allium ascalonicum

Shallots are easy to grow and a place should be found for them even in the smallest home garden. They are useful for flavouring (being milder than garlic and most onion cultivars) or for adding to salad, when young, as 'spring onions'. They thrive on most soils except heavy clays and are nothing like as demanding as bulbing onions. They perform well if they follow a crop such as cabbage, cauliflower or tomatoes for which the ground was well improved. Although the plants flower and set seed in certain conditions and seasons, seeding is not the normal method of propagation and the seeds are not catalogued by leading South African seed houses. Shallots are almost always propagated, like chives and Welsh onions, by division of the clumps, which may consist of 10-12 bulbs. Alternatively, the clumps can be dried, like onions and garlic, and the bulbs or cloves replanted. Suggested planting distances are 100-150 mm apart in rows 300 mm apart, and dried bulbs should be set out with the tips at ground level.

Once established, this crop requires little attention apart from weeding and watering, although an application of liquid manure or a side-dressing of nitrogenous fertilizer at the rate of 30 g per metre of row when the plants are 150-200 mm high and again a month later will not go unrewarded. Shallots multiply in a similar way to Welsh onions and can be used green or can be dried off, when well ripened, for later use.

SORREL
Rumex scutatus

This is not a popular herb, possibly because of the sharp taste of the leaves and because its uses are somewhat limited. The young leaves are usually incorporated into fresh salads or are used in soup, being added when the soup is almost ready for the table. It is a subject that will tolerate a fair amount of shade for an hour or two each day.

The plants are not too particular about soil, but like most other herbs they respond well if they follow a well-improved crop. Sorrel can be propagated by seed sown in August/September or by division of the plants. A suitable planting distance is 225-300 mm each way. For a steady supply of leaves the flowering stems should be cut off, low down, as soon as they appear.

TARRAGON
Artemisia dracunculus

True 'French' tarragon, a perennial that is completely hardy in South Africa, is much sought after as its leaves add their unique flavour to a wide range of dishes and sauces. True tarragon does not set viable seed easily and is usually propagated from cuttings or by division of the underground runners or rhizomes. The plants can be set out 450-600

Propagating Herbs

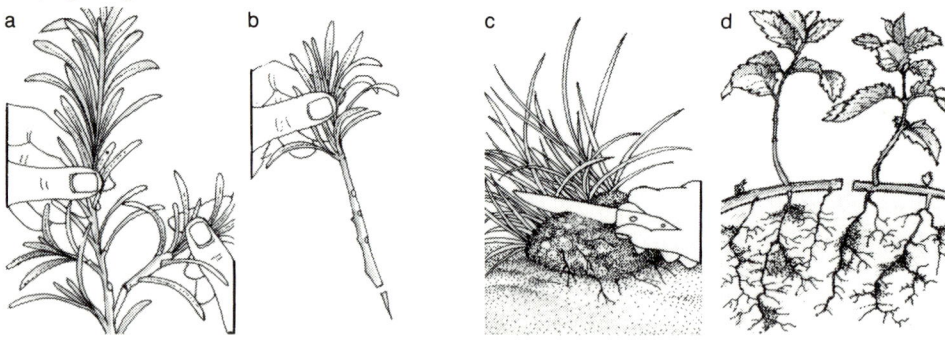

Most herbs can be propagated easily by means of cuttings or root division. For example: (a)-(b) A cutting of rosemary is obtained by stripping away a side-shoot together with a 'heel' or sliver of bark and wood. Trim the heel and remove the leaves adjacent to it before planting the cutting. (c) Lift chives every two years and divide the root clumps to maintain vigorous growth and obtain new planting material. (d) Mint is easily propagated by dividing and replanting the underground runners.

mm apart each way and grow to a similar height. The fresh leaves are harvested as required. It is a wise policy to make completely fresh plantings every 3 years or so, although it is often quite difficult to obtain material for establishing the initial bed.

The tarragon seed that is sometimes catalogued is not the above cultivar and is somewhat coarser and lacks the flavour of 'French' tarragon. It is commonly known as Russian tarragon and can be grown if planting material of the former is difficult to obtain.

THYME
Thymus vulgaris

Although specialist herb growers cultivate several species of thyme, the above is the one usually encountered in the catalogues of every reputable seed house. It is a small (200-250 mm high) bushy perennial with green or bluey-green foliage and is an ideal container plant. It can be propagated by division, by cuttings taken with a heel from the old stem, or by seed. Cuttings give the quickest and best results. Divided plants, I find, often become woody early in life, while seedlings tend to be slow in 'getting away'. The cuttings should be taken just before flowering occurs. Seed can be sown in spring, early summer and autumn. Cuttings should be 50-75 mm long and can be rooted in vermiculite, coarse sand, or a perlite/peat mix. They should later be transplanted to stand 225 mm apart in rows 300 mm apart. Seed can be sown in drills 300 mm apart, covered with 6-8 mm of fine soil, and the seedlings thinned out to 200-225 mm apart. They prefer a light soil and appreciate an annual spring side-dressing of 2:3:2, hoed in shallowly. They should also be given an annual mulch of compost or manure.

Each autumn or winter the plants can be cut back by half and this material can be bunched and dried out for use until fresh early summer growth is ready for harvesting. The plants often lose their vigour after 3 years and new plants should be raised in anticipation of this decline.

PESTS AND DISEASES

Pests and diseases are rarely a problem. If pests are evident (e.g. aphids or red spider) a strong soap solution is often sufficient to effect control. If this is unsuccessful Malathion at the rate of one teaspoonful to 5 ℓ of water can be used, taking care strictly to observe the recommended safety period.

APPENDIX 1 INSTANT VEGETABLES: SPROUTING

For many years mustard and cress were the quickest fresh foods to grow, but they are now being rivalled in nutritional value and speed by the increasingly popular salad sprouts. It is claimed that half a cupful of lucerne (alfalfa) seed, when sprouted, contains as much vitamin C as 6 glasses of fresh orange juice, as well as vitamin B_2 and other vitamins, proteins and minerals. Unlike other vegetables, sprouts are still growing when eaten, and have lost none of their nutritional value. While many seeds have been used for sprouting, it would appear that legumes are by far the most palatable and nutritious.

Methods of sprouting. Overseas seed catalogues regularly advertise several different seed mixtures for sprouting, as well as special sprouting containers. Some sophisticated ones make provision for the simultaneous sprouting of three different sorts of sprouts in separate trays. However, sprouting is just as effective using standard Consul jars, which should be cleaned and rinsed thoroughly before use. One or two slightly heaped tablespoonfuls of seed should be placed in the clean, empty jar and the mouth covered with wet muslin or mutton-cloth secured with a strong rubber band. The jar can then be filled with water and left overnight. The following morning the water should be poured off and thereafter the seeds should be thoroughly wetted at least twice a day. Each time the water should be poured off and the jar placed on its side for growth to take place. Depending upon the type of seed and the prevailing temperature, 3-6 days should be adequate to bring the sprouts to the eating stage. The cleanliness of the container is extremely important at all times and if any rotting seed is evident it should be removed at once.

(a) Place seed in clean jar.

(b) Cover mouth of jar, fill with water and leave overnight.

(c) Pour off water and repeat wetting process at least twice a day.

(d) Between wettings, place jar on its side to allow maximum room for growth.

APPENDIX 2 EXHIBITING VEGETABLES

As both a judge and an exhibitor of vegetables and flowers for over 30 years, I feel that information on the preparation and presentation of vegetable exhibits will be of value not only to the exhibitor but also to judges and those who compile show schedules, especially in the smaller centres. Showing is an interesting exercise that provides a useful stimulus to keen gardeners to strive for better quality in their produce. It also provides an agreeable forum for discussion with other gardeners on the many aspects of vegetable growing and on the particular problems encountered. In addition, the show bench is an ideal place for introducing new cultivars and hybrids.

There is a widespread belief that vegetables for exhibition must be enormous to justify a place on the show bench. Nothing could be further from the truth, and grossly oversized specimens should earn no more points than undersized ones, for in many cases extra-large vegetables are coarse in texture, have serious internal defects, are of poor colour and are quite tasteless. Vegetables for exhibition should be true to type, of average size or *slightly* larger for the particular cultivar, and of top quality in terms of freshness and condition. Freedom from insects, diseases, nematodes and mechanical damage is, of course, a basic requirement if the exhibit is to warrant serious consideration. Large vegetables do create some interest, however, especially leeks, cabbages, marrows and pumpkins, and 1 or 2 classes may be set aside provided that the object is *clearly* stated in the schedule.

SHOW SCHEDULES

Most organizing committees put out a schedule of the various classes, prizes and trophies to be awarded and of the rules to be observed. The intending exhibitor should obtain a copy in good time and study it carefully. In many cases, unfortunately, the show date is made known too late (4 months being the very minimum) and quite often the schedules themselves are only available a month or so before the day of the show. In addition, these publications do not always state clearly enough what is required in the various classes and this sometimes leads to confusion and disappointment, especially among novice exhibitors. Ambiguities in describing classes are also disconcerting to the judge or judges, and it is therefore most desirable that the description of classes should be absolutely clear. The words 'of any one cultivar' are the ones that I have found

missing from schedules most often. The result of this omission is that in a class asking for 'two cabbages', for example, an inexperienced exhibitor may place one head of Copenhagen Market and one of Early Jersey Wakefield side by side. When judging a cabbage exhibit in this class, the judge mentally allocates points to freshness, firmness, trueness to type, size and uniformity, and therefore on the last-mentioned point alone this exhibit loses much ground.

Point-judging is rarely justified and in my experience frequently causes more confusion and trouble than it is worth. Very often the schedule compilers allocate points for relatively unimportant characteristics and none or fewer points for more important ones. It is only very occasionally, when competition is keen (say 8 or 10 exhibits of the same cultivar in the same class) that pointing need be resorted to. Then the judges (if there are more than one) can decide amongst themselves on a simple pointing system based on some of the desirable characteristics mentioned above.

The show schedule should always stipulate clearly how many pods, roots, fruits, stems or heads of a particular subject are required, and the exhibitor should show only the number called for. Exhibits with fewer than the required number should have their exhibit cards endorsed 'Not according to schedule' and should not be considered *however high the quality may be!* Where too many are tabled the same rule should, technically speaking, disqualify the exhibit. However, this is rarely done by experienced judges. A far more satisfactory way out when there are too many specimens is to ask the attending steward to call the Show Secretary and then to ask him or her to remove surplus specimens before the judging of that class is seriously undertaken.

At most shows trophies are awarded for the highest points in a particular section, e.g. the vegetable section. The usual method of awarding points towards such a trophy is 3 for first, 2 for second and 1 for third in each class. At first glance this may appear quite fair, but it does not take into account the degree of difficulty in growing a crop to maturity. It means that an exhibitor who throws in a packet of radish seeds a month or so before the show has a far greater chance of obtaining 3 points than the grower who has battled for several months, in both seedbed and open ground, to get a couple of heads of cauliflower or celery on the show bench. Depending upon the season to some extent, vegetables that are allocated points towards a trophy should, I feel, be grouped

into three classes based upon the degree of difficulty in growing them through to maturity. As a guide I would suggest:

Group 1: (first 9 points, second 6 points, third 3 points) Cauliflowers, Brussels sprouts, tomatoes, blanched celery

Group 2: (first 6 points, second 4 points, third 2 points) Beetroot, beans, broccoli, cabbages, carrots, cucumbers, egg plants, kohlrabi, leeks, lettuce, onions, parsnips, pumpkins and squashes, potatoes, spinach, Swiss chard, peas, turnips, sweet potatoes.

Group 3: (first 3 points, second 2 points, third 1 point) Radishes, shallots, spring onions, Welsh onions.

This suggested scale of pointing can be modified easily by the show committee, who can take into account the local climate, the season and similar factors, but it is a system that recognizes skill and effort. In addition (and this is very important), in points towards a trophy only *one* prize in each class should count for each exhibitor. If this is not applied an exhibitor can collect the trophy with points derived from firsts, seconds and thirds in poorly-supported minor classes such as radishes, turnips, spring onions and Swiss chard. This is especially important if the 3-2-1 pointing system is used, for it prevents shrewd exhibitors from cramming the easier classes with several entries and promotes support for the more difficult ones.

Most schedules feature a class for a 'collection' or 'display' of vegetables. Producing the vegetables for such an exhibit and staging them properly demands considerable skill and effort, and show committees should see to it that a good exhibit in this class is suitably rewarded and not just treated as any other single-dish class. In some centres local seedsmen, nurserymen and garden shops sponsor such a class and award vouchers or nursery stock as prizes. In this class the schedule should state quite clearly, especially where commercial exhibits are solicited, how much bench or table area is to be allowed for each exhibit. The usual sizes are 1,0 x 0,5 m, 1,2 x 0,5 m, 1,2 x 1,0 m and 2,0 x 1,0 m, with the first figure being the frontage allowed. As larger collections require a backdrop to be staged attractively, they should be allocated space against a wall rather than be set out on centre tables.

PREPARATION AND PRESENTATION OF EXHIBITS

This aspect of exhibiting is extremely important and even first-class produce will not win a prize unless it is prepared and presented carefully.

Remember, first of all, that produce for exhibiting should be ready to be eaten. Immaturity, under-ripeness and over-ripeness are serious defects, and many points are forfeited as a result. Provided that they are handled carefully, it is not at all necessary, nor desirable in many instances, to harvest the exhibits on the day of the show. Indeed, if some distance has to be travelled to the show, preparation and harvesting should begin several days beforehand. Mature specimens of dry onions, potatoes and sweet potatoes can be prepared well in advance, while lettuces, spinach, sweetcorn and similar subjects can be harvested the previous day.

Labelling is not always called for by the schedule, but if it is done neatly on a plain card it will be of interest to the judges, other exhibitors, and the general public. It enables interested persons to weigh up and compare the characteristics and relative merits of the different cultivars and thereby assists in future planning. Labelling should, however, be restricted to the single-dish classes, for it is impracticable on collections and is apt to lower the impact and attractiveness of such exhibits.

Below are detailed a few hints on the preparation and presentation of the more important vegetables (unless of course the schedule calls for something quite different):

Beans, Broad: Pick the straightest pods, avoiding any that are oversize and too puffy. Uniformity is important.

Beans, Dwarf: Choose pods that are fresh, of good colour and free from spots, and which show no swelling of the seeds. Remove them from the plant with scissors or secateurs, together with 10 mm of stem. They should be as straight as possible, and should be picked the day before the show and wrapped fairly tightly in damp mutton cloth or something similar. Uniformity, and the ability to snap cleanly, are factors that are concentrated on by judges.

Beans, Lima: Pick fresh, well-filled pods with 10 mm of stalk. As with all peas and beans in the pod, succulence and uniformity are the most desirable characteristics.

Beetroot: Trim the tops back with a sharp knife to around 50 mm from the root shoulder. Completely remove any dead or damaged leaves and any fibrous roots, taking care not to nick the root itself, and leave a taproot of 50-70 mm. Wash the roots thoroughly with a sponge or soft cloth, not a brush.

Broccoli: Carefully cut the central head together with 150 mm of stalk, taking care not to remove the 'bloom', particularly on the buds that make up the head. Choose close, compact heads, mushroom in shape. If only side shoots are available at show day, select 5 or 6, preferably from the same plant, as colour varies slightly from plant to plant, and tie them together as inconspicuously as

possible. Broccoli yellows very quickly when cut, at normal temperatures, and so it should be one of the last subjects to be harvested.

Brussels Sprouts: Choose firm, uniform, medium-sized sprouts and remove as few as possible of the outer leaves. Trim the heel carefully with a sharp knife.

Cabbages: Choose well-shaped heads of good size, true to type and free from splitting and pest or disease damage. Cut off the plant at soil level, wash it carefully and remove the outer leaves, allowing 4 or 5 to remain. Trim back the stalks further if necessary. Where more than one specimen is called for, uniformity of size and form will receive consideration from the judges. Cape Spitzkool and other conical types are perhaps the most attractive on the show bench.

Carrots: Pull carefully or lift with a fork if the soil is dry or heavy. Soak in cold water to loosen adhering soil and sponge off. Trim the foliage back to 50-75 mm and retain 25-50 mm of fine taproot. Avoid roots that are forked or which have nematode damage at the root tip or at the base of fine lateral roots. Roots with green shoulders or with insect damage of any sort should be discarded. Never use a brush to prepare carrots for the show bench.

Cauliflowers: Tie or cover up heads that are to be exhibited a week or two before the show. A medium-sized head, close-grained and white in colour, will always have the edge on much larger but discoloured heads or heads that have started to 'blow' or are 'ricey' in texture. Cut the plant just above soil level, trim off any larger outer leaves, and wash thoroughly with a spray. Just prior to staging, trim back the 6 or 8 inner wrapper leaves to just behind the head to emphasize its depth. Care should be taken not to nick the curd, which is extremely brittle, whilst trimming. Keep the head covered and out of strong sunlight until it is placed on the show bench.

Celery: Blanch prospective exhibition heads for at least 2-3 weeks before the show. Lift them carefully with a fork, wash off excessive soil and then remove the root system with a sharp knife, leaving a 15 mm wedge, which can be trimmed to a point when the head has been washed. Remove any cracked or discoloured outer sticks and any basal side-shoots. Open the head, wash thoroughly and re-tie neatly with raffia just below the leaves, which should be discreetly trimmed if necessary with scissors to remove discoloured and spotted leaves.

Cucumbers: Choose young, straight fruits of good colour and without blemish. Remove them from the plant with secateurs together with about 10 mm of stalk attached to the fruit. Any necessary washing should be done carefully with a sponge and any spines that may be present should be retained. Marketer and Ashley are good exhibition cultivars. Frame cultivars are usually left unwashed with the blossom intact if possible.

Egg Plants: Select medium-sized fruits that have a good bright colour and sheen. Remove them carefully from the plant with secateurs, together with 25-35 mm of stalk. Pack carefully in tissue paper, or similar, as bruising and rough handling show up within a few hours. Florida High Bush has fruits that are of good colour and shape and well suited to the show table.

Kohlrabi: Choose specimens that have a flat base and slender taproot. Wash thoroughly, especially around the base, and cut off the taproot *carefully* with a *sharp* knife. Remove all the leaves carefully at their base with a knife, leaving a tuft of 2 or 3 new leaves, which are usually 40-50 mm high. Throughout preparation endeavour to retain the 'bloom' on the swollen stem, especially when purple cultivars are used.

Leeks: Show leeks of standard cultivars should have a minimum of 150-200 mm of blanched stem. Any that are flabby or bulbous should be discarded. They should be lifted carefully with a fork, and then washed and sponged. Any *odd* discoloured outer leaves or leaves with soil beneath them may be removed, but this should not be overdone. The roots should be cut back cleanly and squarely to within 15-20 mm of the base plate. This 'stubble' should be cleaned thoroughly so that no soil particles remain. The leaves can be trimmed back a little, squarely or in a fan fashion, to within 150 mm of the blanched portion. However, in a collection a bunch of leeks can be shown with the full length of leaves, and I usually conceal a wooden dowel or cane inside to give the exhibit some rigidity.

Lettuce: Choose good-sized heads that are fairly firm, yet fresh in colour with attractive outer leaves. Heads that are obviously about to run to seed and which have no outer leaves are unlikely to collect any prizes. Lettuces for exhibition should be handled with extreme care at all times for the succulent outer leaves are extremely brittle and prone to damage and even one broken leaf is likely to spoil the appearance of the head. I usually lift the heads with a fork and wash them thoroughly, leaving the relatively weak root system intact and only removing it with a sharp knife when mounting the exhibit. The heads should be washed carefully and any diseased and damaged lower leaves removed. If cut the day before the show, lettuces can be freshened up in cold water for an hour or so before the show. They should not be left completely immersed in water overnight, for the leaf tissue becomes water-soaked and useless for exhibiting.

Marrows: Choose straight fruits of good colour and size but avoid oversized, coarse ones that will inevitably have stringy flesh. The skin of a show marrow should pierce readily with the thumb nail. The fruits should be *cut* from the plant and the stalks trimmed back squarely to within 25 mm of the point of attachment to the fruit. These can be trimmed back neatly for another 6 mm when the exhibit is mounted.

Onions: Schedules often have classes for dry onions, green bulbing onions and spring onions. Green bulbing onions should be lifted carefully, washed thoroughly, the roots trimmed back to within 10 mm of the base plate, and the tops left intact or trimmed back to a length of 200-250 mm. The peeling off of outer leaves and skins should be avoided if at all possible, as the inner scales do not have the 'finish' of the outer ones. Dried onions should also be handled with care so that they do not lose too many skins, and should not be washed. Any remaining roots can be removed and the base plate can be finished off with an old toothbrush, used dry. The tops can be twisted off and then trimmed square with a pair of scissors. This is especially effective with the Australian Brown cultivar. With larger sorts the tops can be cut back squarely to 20-25 mm or so, doubled over carefully and tied neatly with a single strand of clean raffia. Spring onions are usually called for in bunches, which should be tied neatly, again with clean raffia. The roots should be trimmed back to 10 mm and washed thoroughly. The foliage should be left intact. Stems that have commenced to bulb, however slightly, are not really suitable for showing.

Parsnips: As for carrots. Lifting the roots with a fork or a spade is essential in most soils. The roots of long cultivars are extremely brittle and care is necessary when cleaning. All lateral roots should be carefully removed. As with carrots, any forking of the roots is regarded as a major defect.

Peas: Select well-filled, unscarred and green pods of good length. *Cut* the pods from the plant together with 10 mm of stem without handling them. Lay them in single layers in tissue paper or similar, ensuring that they do not rub against each other. With both peas and beans it is advisable always to take at least 25% more pods than the schedule calls for and to remove the surplus ones when staging the exhibit. Pea pods should never be touched by hand at any stage, or else the 'bloom' will be removed. This is not too difficult, and on many occasions I have mounted multi-tiered arrangements of peas by threading hundreds of pods with a needle and thread or thin wire without removing the bloom from a single pod.

Peppers: A straightforward subject: Choose good-sized fruits that have thick walls, a shiny, unblemished skin and which are true to type as far as colour and shape are concerned. Cut with secateurs, leaving 10-15 mm of stem.

Potatoes: Show tubers should be mature and should be lifted carefully a week or so before the show. Washing should be done carefully with a sponge and plenty of water. If the tubers are slightly immature and the skins slip, washing should be delayed until a day or two before the show to allow the skins to firm up a little. Tubers (6-10 are usually called for) should be of good size, uniform in shape and should be characteristic of the cultivar. Enlarged skin lenticels, evidence of second growth, scab, nematode damage, internal discoloration and hollowness are defects that devalue the exhibit enormously.

Pumpkins and Hubbard Squashes: Choose good-sized fruits of good shape and colour, rather than coarse, outsize specimens. Cut from the plant if the stalks are green and wash thoroughly.

Radishes: Roots should be young, firm and crisp, bright in colour and of good shape. They should be pulled and washed carefully. The foliage, which should be fresh and free from damage, should be kept intact. The fine taproot of round and olive-shaped cultivars can be 40-50 mm in length. Sparkler, Saxa and Scarlet Turnip are excellent cultivars for showing.

Squashes, Small: Little Gem, Butternut, Rolet and Table Queen are all admirable show subjects. With Butternut, choose short, stocky fruits rather than those having a long handle that is usually curved like a calabash. With the others, choose fruits that are of good size, green and with a good skin sheen. Cut from the plant and trim the stalks to around 10 mm from the point of attachment.

Sweetcorn: Choose good-sized, well-filled cobs. Trim off carefully all but 1 or 2 wrapper leaves around the cob and remove a narrow strip of this 20 mm or so in width to display the placement and fullness of the kernels. The kernels should easily pierce with the thumb nail (but *do not* try this out on exhibits – leave it to the judges!).

Sweet Potatoes: Roots should be of good colour and shape, free from weevils and cracks, whatever the cause. They should be washed thoroughly using plenty of water and a sponge and care should be taken not to scratch or otherwise damage the skin in any way.

Swiss Chard: The schedule usually calls for 12 leaves or so of this subject. Select bright leaves of good colour, well puckered and free from leaf spots or pest damage and with a good length of trimmed stem. Pull the leaves from the plants and trim the butts neatly with a sharp knife. Wash and sponge if necessary. I prefer the Lucullus cultivar for exhibition.

Tomatoes: As the show schedule usually calls for 6 or 8 fruits, uniformity of colour and size is of extreme importance. Ideally, twice as many fruits as are required should be collected *with the calyx intact* 4-7 days before the show date, depending upon weather conditions. They should then be placed in a cupboard or drawer in single layers to complete ripening; any dirty fruits can be wiped clean with a damp cloth. The fruits should be inspected daily to ensure that caterpillars have not emerged to cause damage. On the day of the show, those of an even colour should be displayed the right way up with the calyx still intact, as per the schedule. If there is an abundance of fruit, picking can be delayed until a day or two before the show as this will ensure that the calyxes are fresh and green, a vital factor if competition is keen. Like other subjects, some cultivars are more attractive and more suitable for exhibition than others. Generally the small- to medium-fruited cultivars are better than the larger-fruited ones. They are less susceptible to radial cracking, are more symmetrical and have smaller calyxes and scars than the bigger ones. Moneymaker, Manapal, Alicante and hybrids of the Eurocross series are excellent exhibition sorts.

Turnips: Roots for exhibition should be clean, of good shape and skin texture, with the swollen portion ending abruptly at the base and terminating in a slender taproot, 50-75 mm long and free from defects such as nematode nodules. The roots should have clean, smooth shoulders and the foliage scar should be small and should not extend across the whole top of the root. The foliage, if it is in fresh condition and free from insects and insect damage, can be left intact, particularly if the schedule calls for a bunch; or it can be trimmed back to 75-100 mm if exhibited in a dish.

STAGING A COLLECTION

As with all classes *quality* counts the most, but the staging and appearance of the exhibit is also important and most show societies award points for this. Establish in good time how much space is allowed for the exhibit and the exact dimensions. A week or so before the show lay out the same area on a table with the exact number of plates, dishes, trays, baskets or any special stands that are to be used, and get a good idea of the number of onions, tomatoes, carrots, beets, or whatever, that will be needed on the day of the show. It is imperative that each vegetable should be seen clearly when a collection is viewed from *any* angle, and that none are hidden or partly hidden. To achieve this with 8-12 different subjects, perhaps more, it will be necessary to lift some subjects above table level. This can be done with bricks or boxes or, ideally, with a collection of wooden blocks 150 x 150 mm or 228 x 228 mm in section and of several lengths, in increments of 75 mm or so. They can be spaced in step fashion, depending upon the height of the subject, and should balance on both sides of centre, viewed from the front. In addition, tall subjects should be placed at the back and smaller subjects in front. The exhibit must balance and must not have a one-sided appearance. When staging a large exhibit I prepare a list, in good time, of all the vegetables to be included and make a sketch, to scale, a day or two beforehand of the proposed layout of the exhibit. Celery and leeks, peas and beans, carrots and parsnips, beets and turnips, onions and kohlrabi, lettuces and cabbages, and so on, are pairs of vegetables of similar size and general shape. They balance each other admirably if placed opposite each other on either side of centre. Tomatoes and cauliflowers of top quality make an attractive focal point and are usually placed in the centre of the exhibit – cauliflowers at the back in a triangular or pyramidal arrangement and tomatoes more to the front with radishes, if used, adding a touch of colour right in the front.

Schedules in this country do not always call for a specific number of vegetables to be included but some specify a minimum to be used in a 'collection'. Consequently many exhibitors believe that the more they can muster and cram in, irrespective of quality, the better their chances of success. This is not so, and a well-balanced collection of 6 or 8 vegetables of *top quality* is superior to the conglomerations one sometimes encounters.

Most show societies provide a basic covering of paper or material for the table but I always take my own along. Vegetables show up particularly well against a dark background, either dark green or black, and a metre or two of material, satin if available, is very suitable for the purpose. It should be draped carefully once the staging blocks have been placed and before the vegetables are mounted. An apron of similar material pinned on the front of the table is also very effective. Garnishing the individual vegetable classes is not always permitted so read the schedule carefully. But curled parsley, fresh and of good colour, can be used to advantage when staging a collection. It contrasts well with the dark background and also shows off good quality vegetables to perfection.

APPENDIX 3 HOME GARDEN METRICATION GUIDE

In some cases the figures are approximate and in others they have been rounded off.

Abbreviations

cc	= cubic centimetre
ft	= foot
ft^2	= square foot
gal	= gallon
g	= gram
ha	= hectare
in	= inch
ℓ	= litre
lb	= pound
m	= metre
m^2	= square metre
mℓ	= millilitre (= cc)
mm	= millimetre
oz	= ounce
yd	= yard
yd^2	= square yard

Mass

1 oz	=	30 g
4 oz	=	125 g
1 lb	=	500 g
1 moderately-heaped teaspoon of wettable powder	=	5 g
1 moderately-heaped dessertspoon of wettable powder	=	10 g
1 moderately-heaped tablespoon of wettable powder	=	16 g
1 handful of granular fertilizer	=	50-60 g
1 teacupful of granular fertilizer	=	200 g

Area

1,2 yd^2 or 10,76 ft^2	= 1 m^2
2,47 acres	= 1 ha
1 acre	= 4 050 m^2

Length

0,394 in	= 10 mm
1 in	= 25,4 mm
3,28 ft or 39,37 in	= 1 m
1,094 yd	= 1 m

Capacity

1 cc	= 1 mℓ
1,76 pints	= 1 ℓ
1 gal	= 4,55 ℓ
1 teaspoon	= 4-5 mℓ
1 dessertspoon	= 9-10 mℓ
1 tablespoon	= 16 mℓ
⅓ cup	= 80 mℓ
½ cup	= 125 mℓ
1 cup	= 250 mℓ

Temperature

To convert degrees Celsius (C) to degrees Fahrenheit (F), multiply by 1,8 and add 32 degrees.

Standard packs of pesticides

Liquids: 100 mℓ, 200 mℓ, 500 mℓ, as well as a range of 5 mℓ mini-packs.

Wettable powders: 200 g, 500 g.

JANUARY

- As summer temperatures soar, all vegetable crops will benefit from a mulch of organic material. If such material is scarce it should be used on tomatoes and leaf crops, which will show a more marked response than beets, carrots, leeks and onions.
- Tomatoes, egg plants and peppers will also respond to side-dressings or to applications of liquid manure.
- Sowings of Brussels sprouts and cauliflowers can be made for winter cropping, using hybrid seed if possible.
- Successional sowings of short-season crops such as beans, beets, lettuce, radishes and turnips can be continued.
- Weeds should be removed as soon as they can be handled. Do not cultivate unnecessarily between plant rows during dry weather.

FEBRUARY

- Watering will be necessary if growth is to continue unchecked. Watering by sprinkler should be completed before late afternoon to enable the plants to dry off rapidly. This will help to control several serious diseases.
- The regular spraying of tomatoes with a fungicide/pesticide/wetter cocktail should be continued, as problems often build up at this time.
- When perennial herbs approach full flower they can be cut back by half and the removed material dried off by loosely bunching it and hanging it up out of the sun in a dry, well-ventilated place.

MARCH

- Clean residues from early crops can be incorporated into the compost heap or chopped up and used as a mulch. Lawn mowings can also be utilized in this way.
- Pumpkins and squashes to be stored or kept for seed should be allowed to ripen off thoroughly on the vine. If seeds are to be kept they should be dried off, cleaned, and dusted with a pinch of Dithane M45 or vine sulphur.
- Sowings of onions and peas can now be made, while cauliflowers, broccoli, cabbages and Brussels sprouts can be set out in well-prepared and improved ground.

APRIL

- Spent organic mulches used on summer crops can be dug in, together with a dressing of LAN at the rate of 1-2 handfuls per m², when the crop residues are removed.
- Weeds on empty plots should be destroyed as should any 'volunteer' tomato seedlings arising from dropped fruits. This is most important.
- Brassicas that are growing away will respond favourably to a side-dressing of 3:2:1 or 2:3:2 at the rate of 1 handful per metre of row.
- Main-crop sowings of broad beans can be made this month, double rows being better than singles.

MAY

- Onions can be set out *shallowly* in well-prepared ground as soon as they are of pencil thickness.
- Brassicas should be kept free of loopers, aphids and other pests when they approach maturity. Carefully observe the recommended safety periods if pesticides have to be resorted to, particularly when cauliflowers and broccoli begin to head up.
- Successional sowings of beetroots, carrots, lettuce, radishes and turnips can be made in milder areas.
- Peas can be given a light side-dressing or an application of liquid fertilizer and the rows can be supported by drawing up a little soil and by using twigs and small branches if these are available.

JUNE

- This is largely a maintenance month with winter crops maturing and few, if any, sowings to be made.
- It is a good time to clean, sharpen and repair garden tools.
- It is also a good time to construct additional permanent cropping beds or to make a cold frame or two. The latter modify the climate in a favourable way during colder weather and allow early sowings and plantings to be made under protection.

JULY

- The planning of the summer garden should receive top priority early in the month so as to allow sufficient time to purchase or order seed for early sowings.
- It is a good time to carry out soil tests, particularly on plots where growth for one or more seasons has been unsatisfactory.
- When winter crops are removed the ground should be well dug over and dressings of organic material incorporated, together with a dressing of lime if this is required.
- Broad beans can be side-dressed, earthed-up and given support, if necessary, with string or wire.
- In mild areas early sowings of tomatoes can be made in seedboxes or Jiffys.

AUGUST

- This is a busy sowing month for early summer crops, both under protection in seedboxes and outdoors. Sow outdoors as shallowly as possible, particularly with cucurbits, and carefully control the soil's moisture content because the ground is still cold. Use seed that is as fresh as possible for early sowings if conditions are less than ideal.
- Cucumbers, squashes and marrows can be sown under protection or, towards the end of the month, directly outdoors. Sowings of main-crop tomatoes can be made, with the seed sown thinly to obtain strong plants.
- Slugs and snails will be active and should be controlled with a proprietary bait. Bait should also be distributed on the perimeter of the plot from whence these troublesome pests come.

SEPTEMBER

- If watering is necessary, give only moderate amounts to directly-sown crops, particularly in heavier soils. If they are over-watered, large seeds will rot before germination occurs, while in thickly-sown rows damping-off may occur.
- Perennial crops such as globe artichokes, asparagus, rhubarb and pole lima beans will benefit from having the soil around them *carefully* loosened, followed by a dressing of 2:3:2 at the rate of 1-2 handfuls per m². If compost or manure can be spared, a generous dressing will stand the plants in good stead for the summer cropping period.
- Sweet melons can be sown outdoors, as can peppers and egg plants when the weather warms up.

OCTOBER

- A regular programme for the control of pumpkin fly on cucurbits should be initiated as soon as the first flowers appear. Any plants showing leaf symptoms of mosaic should be removed and destroyed.
- Aphids also become a problem when the weather warms up. Regular spraying with a systemic material on young plants or with Malathion or Carbaryl on more mature plants should clear up any infestations.
- Main-crop sowings of pumpkins, sweetcorn, dwarf beans and runner beans should be made during the month, while sowings of beets, carrots, lettuce, radishes and spring onions should continue.

NOVEMBER

- Crops such as beans, marrows, cucumbers and squashes should be harvested as soon as they reach edible size. Allowing them to mature more fully results in a lowering of quality and is also an unnecessary drain on plant vigour.
- Tomatoes and cucumbers will now be producing new foliage at a considerable rate and this will need to be sprayed regularly to prevent disease establishment. Fungicidal materials are, in the main, protective rather than curative and an effective deposit must be maintained on all plant surfaces.
- Successional sowings of most vegetables can be continued throughout the month, while early sowings of cauliflowers can be made during the final week.

DECEMBER

- Because of their high rate of growth all leaf crops will benefit from side-dressings or from applications of liquid manure.
- Crop residues and unthrifty plants should be removed regularly. Such material frequently harbours pests and diseases and can jeopardize adjacent plantings.
- When plots become empty they should be dug over, improved if necessary, and planted with short-season crops such as beans, lettuce, beetroots, radishes, etc. Main-crop sowings of cauliflowers can begin towards the end of the month, care being taken to control aphids and downy mildew in the seed rows.

APPENDIX 5 GENERAL SOWING AND PLANTING GUIDE

	Jan	Feb	Mar	Apr	May	Jun	Jul	Aug	Sep	Oct	Nov	Dec
Artichokes, Chinese								●	●	●	●	
Artichokes, Globe	●										●	●
Artichokes, Jerusalem								●	●	●	●	
Asparagus (crowns)								●				
Asparagus (seed)									●	●	●	●
Beans, Broad			●	●	●							
Beans, Dwarf	●	●						●	●	●	●	●
Beans, Lima	●								●	●	●	●
Beans, Runner	●							●	●	●	●	
Beetroot	●	●	●	●				●	●	●	●	●
Broccoli	●	●									●	●
Brussels Sprouts	●	●	●									
Cabbages	●	●	●	●				●	●	●	●	●
Cabbages, Chinese	●	●	●	●								
Carrots	●	●	●	●				●	●	●	●	
Cauliflowers	●	●									●	●
Celeriac		●	●					●	●	●		
Celery		●	●					●	●	●		
Chayote									●	●	●	
Chicory								●	●	●		
Cucumbers								●	●	●	●	●
Egg Plants								●	●	●	●	
Endive	●	●	●					●	●			
Kale		●	●					●	●	●	●	
Kohlrabi	●	●	●	●								
Leeks	●	●	●	●								

	Jan	Feb	Mar	Apr	May	Jun	Jul	Aug	Sep	Oct	Nov	Dec
Lettuce	●	●	●	●				●	●	●	●	●
Marrows	●							●	●	●	●	●
Melons, Sweet								●	●	●	●	
Mustard/Cress (indoors)	●	●	●	●	●	●	●	●	●	●	●	●
Okra								●	●	●	●	
Onions		●	●	●	●							
Parsley	●	●	●					●	●	●	●	●
Parsnips		●	●	●				●	●	●		
Peas		●	●	●	●	●	●	●	●			
Peppers								●	●	●		
Potatoes	●							●	●	●	●	●
Pumpkins								●	●	●	●	●
Radishes		●	●	●	●	●	●	●	●	●		
Rhubarb								●	●	●	●	
Salsify		●	●					●	●	●		
Scorzonera		●	●					●	●	●		
Spinach	●	●	●	●				●	●	●	●	●
Spinach, New Zealand								●	●	●		
Squashes	●							●	●	●	●	●
Sweetcorn								●	●	●	●	●
Sweet Potatoes									●	●	●	
Swiss Chard		●	●	●				●	●	●		
Tomatoes								●	●	●	●	
Turnips		●	●	●				●	●	●	●	
Watercress	●							●	●	●	●	●
Watermelon								●	●	●	●	

This chart should serve as a general guide to sowing and planting. However, with the aid of well-kept records each gardener will be able to determine the optimum period for his or her particular area.

APPENDIX 6 GARDENING DIARY

VEGETABLE AND CULTIVAR	SOWING/PLANTING DATES													NOTES ON SEED/SEEDLING SOURCE, SOIL PREPARATION, NUTRIENTS, PLANT GROWTH, YIELD, PESTS, DISEASES, ETC.
	Jan.	Feb.	March	April	May	June	July	Aug.	Sept.	Oct.	Nov.	Dec.		

YEAR: 19......

YEAR: 19......		SOWING/PLANTING DATES												NOTES ON SEED/SEEDLING SOURCE, SOIL PREPARATION, NUTRIENTS, PLANT GROWTH, YIELD, PESTS, DISEASES, ETC.
VEGETABLE AND CULTIVAR	Jan.	Feb.	March	April	May	June	July	Aug.	Sept.	Oct.	Nov.	Dec.		

| YEAR: 19...... | SOWING/PLANTING DATES | | | | | | | | | | | | | NOTES ON SEED/SEEDLING SOURCE, SOIL PREPARATION, NUTRIENTS, PLANT GROWTH, YIELD, PESTS, DISEASES, ETC. |
VEGETABLE AND CULTIVAR	Jan.	Feb.	March	April	May	June	July	Aug.	Sept.	Oct.	Nov.	Dec.		

| YEAR: 19...... | | SOWING/PLANTING DATES | | | | | | | | | | | | NOTES ON SEED/SEEDLING SOURCE, SOIL PREPARATION, NUTRIENTS, PLANT GROWTH, YIELD, PESTS, DISEASES, ETC. |
VEGETABLE AND CULTIVAR	Jan.	Feb.	March	April	May	June	July	Aug.	Sept.	Oct.	Nov.	Dec.	

YEAR: 19......	SOWING/PLANTING DATES												NOTES ON SEED/SEEDLING SOURCE, SOIL PREPARATION, NUTRIENTS, PLANT GROWTH, YIELD, PESTS, DISEASES, ETC.
VEGETABLE AND CULTIVAR	Jan.	Feb.	March	April	May	June	July	Aug.	Sept.	Oct.	Nov.	Dec.	

BIBLIOGRAPHY

Annecke, D.P. and Moran, V.C. *Insects and Mites of Cultivated Plants in South Africa*, Butterworths, Durban, 1982.

Bayer South Africa *Spray Programme for Vegetables*, Bayer South Africa, Isando.

Biggs, Tony *Vegetables* (a title in the Royal Horticultural Society's Encyclopaedia of Practical Gardening), Mitchell Beazley, London, 1980.

Billitt, A. *Growing Vegetables and Fruit*, Hamlyn, London, 1980.

Crockett, J.U. *Vegetables and Fruits*, Time-Life International, 1972.

Efekto *Green Fingers* Vol. 1, Efekto, Silverton.

Gilbert, Z. *Gardening in South Africa*, C. Struik, Cape Town, 1983.

Hall, M.T. (ed.) *Growing Fruit and Vegetables*, Orbis, London, 1980.

Hemy, Capel *Growing Vegetables in South Africa*, Macmillan South Africa, Johannesburg, 1984.

Hessayon, D.G. *Be Your Own Vegetable Doctor*, Pan Britannica Industries, Waltham Cross, 1978. *Vegetable Plotter*, Pan Britannica Industries, Waltham Cross, 1977.

Mossman, Keith *Growing Your Own Food*, Macdonald Educational, London, 1978.

Radecka, H. and Seddon, G. *Your Kitchen Garden*, Mitchell Beazley, London, 1975.

Reader's Digest Association *Illustrated Encyclopaedia of Gardening in South Africa*, The Reader's Digest Association, Cape Town, 1984. *Complete Guide to Gardening in South Africa* (2 vols), The Reader's Digest Association, Cape Town, 1971.

Sheat, W.A. *The A-Z of Gardening in South Africa*, C. Struik, Cape Town, 1982.

Wager, V.A. *Plant Pests and Diseases*, Jonathan Ball, Johannesburg, 1984.

GLOSSARY

Annual: A plant that is grown from seed and completes its life cycle in 1 year. In the vegetable garden, several biennials are treated as annuals.

Bare-root planting: Lifting and transplanting a seedling or older plant with little or no soil adhering to the roots.

Biennial: A plant that, especially in temperate climates, completes its life cycle in 2 years, bearing flowers and seed in the second year.

Blanching: The practice of excluding light from the stems or leaves of a plant (e.g. celery, leeks, chicons and endive) to reduce bitterness and increase succulence.

Blind: A condition in which a plant has no 'eye' or growing point. This usually occurs at the seedling stage, with brassicas commonly affected.

Bloom: The whitish, waxy substance on the leaves of crops such as cabbages, cauliflowers and kohlrabi.

Bolting: The premature production of a seed stalk on crops such as lettuce, carrots and beetroot.

Broadcasting: The scattering of seed and fertilizer over the soil surface as opposed to distributing it in drills or rows.

Calyx: The outer protective cover of a flower, usually divided into individual segments called sepals.

Chlorosis: The loss or poor production of chlorophyll in plant foliage, causing the leaves to be pale or yellow. Often caused by nutrient deficiencies and faulty watering practices.

Cloche: A small glass- or plastic-covered structure used outdoors to protect young seedlings and promote early growth.

Crocks: Pieces of broken earthenware pots used to improve drainage in containers. Nowadays the term is loosely used to describe any similar drainage material.

Crown: Strictly speaking the point at or just below the soil surface where stem and root join. Also used to describe planting material of asparagus and rhubarb.

Cultivar: A distinct variant of a species, bred in cultivation.

Curd: The mass of immature flower buds that forms the head of a cauliflower.

Drill: A shallow trench, usually V-shaped, in which seeds are sown.

Frame: A box-like construction of timber or brick, usually having no bottom and covered with plastic or glass.

Friable soil: Well-worked, crumbly soil that is easily raked.

Fungicide: A substance used to prevent or retard the development of fungal diseases.

Habit: Manner of growth of a plant.

Hardening-off: The process of gradually preparing plants, especially seedlings that have been raised under some degree of protection, for the open garden.

Haulm: The stems and leaves of beans, peas and potatoes.

Herbicide: A material used to kill weeds and other undesirable vegetation.

Hybrid: A plant produced by crossing two distinct cultivars, species or, very occasionally, genera.

Insecticide: A toxic material used to control insects on plants.

In situ sowing: Sowing seeds where the plants are to mature.

Lateral: A side-shoot or branch of a plant.

Micro-climate: Special conditions, differing from the prevailing conditions, that exist in a garden or portion of a garden, and in structures such as shade-houses, tunnels and cloches.

Mulch: A layer of material laid on the soil surface, primarily to conserve moisture but with many other benefits.

Nematodes: Minute roundworms, many species of which are plant parasitic.

Nymph: An immature stage in the growth of certain insects.

Parasite: A pest or plant that lives on or in another organism and obtains its nutrient requirements from its host.

Peat: Partially decayed organic matter obtained from ancient bogs and swamps.

Perennial: A plant that usually lives for several years and does not die after flowering and seeding.

Perlite: A volcanic substance, white in colour, that has been heat-treated and is usually used in soil-less container mixes.

Pesticide: A toxic material used to control insects and other pests on plants.

Photo-period: The hours of light required each day by a plant to reach maturity.

Pricking out: The first transplanting of young seedlings from the container in which they were raised into other containers to allow more room for development.

Propagate: To increase plants by seed, cuttings, division or other means.

Saprophyte: A plant that gains its nourishment from dead organic matter.

Side-dressing: An application of fertilizing material to a growing crop to maintain and improve plant vigour.

Stopping: Pinching out the growing point of a plant.

Strain: A group of plants of any cultivar that display special characteristics, e.g. improved size, colour and disease resistance.

Sucker: A shoot that arises at or below ground level, usually from the rootstock.

Systemics: Materials that are applied to plants and are absorbed and translocated through the plant system, causing the juice or sap to be toxic to certain pests and diseases.

Tamping: The practice of lightly firming the soil surface, particularly after sowing seeds, using a flat hand, a rake head or the back of a spade.

Tilth: The fine, crumbly surface after raking.

Toxic: Poisonous.

Truss: A cluster of flowers or fruits.

Tuber: A thickened, fleshy underground stem, the purpose of which is to store starch as a reserve of food material for the plant.

Turgidity: The condition in which plant cells have sufficient moisture to cause them to expand fully.

INDEX